AF574465

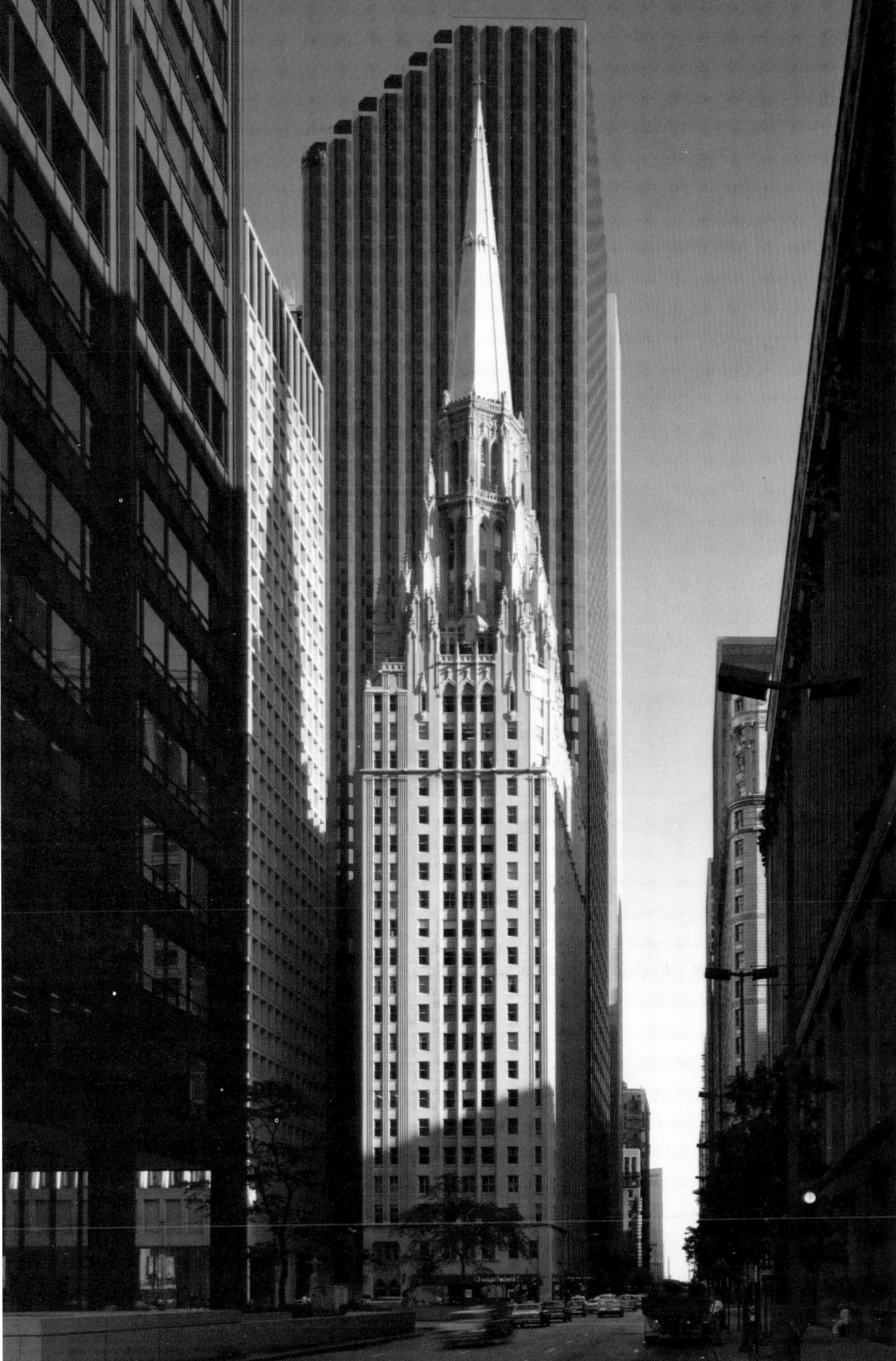

THE PHOTOGRAPHY OF ARCHITECTURE

TWELVE VIEWS

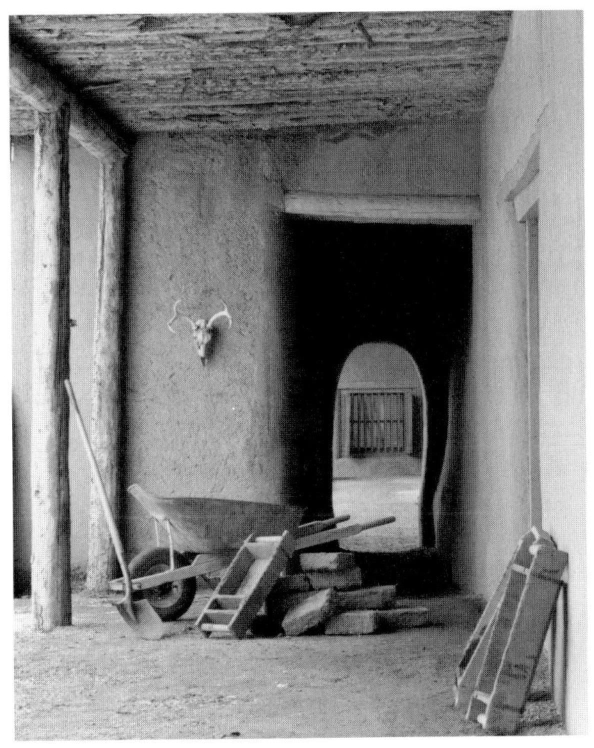

AKIKO BUSCH

VNR VAN NOSTRAND REINHOLD COMPANY
New York

Frontispiece: Three First National Plaza. Chicago, Illinois.
Photo by Nick Merrick. Courtesy of Nick Merrick, Hedrich-Blessing.

Library of Congress Catalog Card Number 86–5627
ISBN 0-442-21109-0

Printed in the United States of America

Designed by Ann Gold

Van Nostrand Reinhold Company Inc.
115 Fifth Avenue
New York, New York 10003

Van Nostrand Reinhold Company Limited
Molly Millars Lane
Wokingham, Berkshire RG11 2PY, England

Van Nostrand Reinhold
480 La Trobe Street
Melbourne, Victoria 3000, Australia

Macmillan of Canada
Division of Canada Publishing Corporation
164 Commander Boulevard
Agincourt, Ontario M1S 3C7, Canada

2 - 4 - 6 - 8 - 10 - 12 - 14 - 16   15 - 13 - 11 - 9 - 7 - 5 - 3

Library of Congress Cataloging-in-Publication Data

Busch, Akiko.
The photography of architecture.

Bibliography: p. 227
Includes index.
1. Photography, Architectural. I. Title.
TR659.B87 1986 778.9′4 86–5627
ISBN 0–442–21109–0

C O N T E N T S

INTRODUCTION

That ours has been a century of architectural achievements is not news. From the drama of early International Style architecture, to the more restrained modernist buildings following the Second World War, to the current colorful and lively visual debates between modern and postmodern esthetics, the architectural styles of the twentieth century have been provocative, inventive, aspiring. "The people with money to build today are corporations—they are our popes and our Medicis," says architect Philip Johnson. "The sense of pride is why they build. Nietzsche would call it the will to power, the French would call it *la folie des pierres,* and developers call it good business." [1] And good business it continues to be. The restraints are few. Johnson's own pink granite Chippendale addition to Manhattan's skyline designed for AT&T, Michael Graves's landmark postmodern Portland Public Service Building, Richard Meier's more modernist and restrained design of the High Museum in Atlanta—all of these are testimony to the inventive spirit of contemporary architecture, corporate and otherwise.

Yet it is not only on the urban or rural landscape that these buildings abound. With the interest they provoke and the controversies they arouse, they are as evident on the printed page. Often, it is through the printed page that critics and the public alike become familiar with these structures. Our ideas, reactions, that is, often come not from the actual building, but from a photograph of it. Sometimes, the photograph will reinforce, negate, or otherwise shape images we have constructed from our own direct impressions of architecture. At other times, the photograph is the sole perpetrator of the image; all we know is what the photograph tells us.

The architectural photographer, then, is in a position of undeniable responsibility, for it is often through his eyes that we see the built world. His focus is ours and his frame is ours, and frequently, the images we remember most clearly are images he has built with great deliberation. Yet it is a role of importance that is rarely acknowledged. We prefer to think of the photograph as a mirror, with little identity of its own.

It is the premise of this book to concede the role of the photographer, to look at architecture through the photographer's eye, and to examine the ways in which photographs are constructed, for it is often through these photographs that our own ideas are constructed.

When the daguerreotype was introduced in 1839, it was most valued for its precision and reliability. For the first time, the graphic image was trustworthy representation. As Phyllis Lambert, director of the Canadian Centre for Architecture, points out, "From the beginning, photographers, critics, historians, and architects were aware of two special attributes of photography: rapidity of notation and accuracy of representation." [2] Indeed, the photographed image offered to the nineteenth century both speed and accuracy heretofore unknown.

The efficiency of the camera in the documentation of architecture served several purposes in the nineteenth century. With industrialism had arrived a new class of poor, and with that, the desire to escape. That unknown and unfamiliar landscapes lured many was made evident by the large numbers of emigrants who fled to the New World. While travel was the most obvious means by which to escape to distant locales, for many the thirst for it could be quenched only visually —by representations of remote geographies rather than the real thing.

But as much to the point as nineteenth-century man's desire to travel was his compulsion to diminish the horizons that so confined him. As much a part of his psychological makeup as escapism was the spirit of investigation; he was distinguished by his efforts to make of the unknown a coherent system, to understand the world at large, to bring it within his intellectual confines. And in an effort to make the great monuments of the world visible, if not accessible, to all, the camera spanned geographical distances that until then had been reached more effectively by steam. Witness then the enduring appeal of photographs of the Great Buddha of Kamakura, the Parthenon, and the Pyramids, and the temples, tombs, and fortresses that represented foreign cultures. Considering, moreover, the length of time required to make a plate, these stationary monuments, in all their grand immobility, made for ideal subject matter.

Indeed, the work of English photographer Francis Frith clearly demonstrates the unrestrained appetite for travel photography. Usually disguised as a Middle Easterner, Frith, between 1856 and 1860, documented the great archaeological monuments of Egypt—the minarets of Cairo, Pyramids and Sphinx of Giza, and colossi at Thebes and at Abu Simbel. Noteworthy is that, almost as painstakingly, he omitted visual evidence of the less majestic present. "Egypt's own hectic present was of no interest to Frith," one account observes. "He never photographed talkative customs officials or begging Arabs, leprous Bedouins or fellahin tilling the fields with stone ploughs." [3] Finding the natives "useful only as extras in his composition," Frith created photographs with a grandeur and solemnity to them, as well as a noticeable disregard for topical detail; they also set a certain tone for architectural photography as it was later to be established.

Francis Frith was only one of many who saw in the camera the opportunity to reach more exotic climes and who was undeterred by the sometimes monumental technical challenges required in reaching them. Rudimentary equipment coupled with the difficulties of working outdoors demanded of the photographer skill, patience, and endurance and discouraged all but the most stalwart. A heavy view camera, its tripod, barrels of distilled water, and a darkroom tent, all made for a cumbersome load that became all the more formidable when carried long distances.

Nevertheless, the rewards gained from meeting these challenges were substantial. Consider these remarks from the *Edinburgh Review,* printed in January 1843:

> How limited is our knowledge of the architectural ornaments of other nations—of the ruined grandeur of former ages—of the gigantic ranges of the Himalayas and the Andes—and of the enchanting scenery of lakes, and rivers and valleys, and cataracts, and volcanoes, which occur throughout the world! Excepting by the labours of some travelling artists, we know them only through the sketches of hurried visitors, tricked up with false and ridiculous illustrations, which are equal mockeries of nature and art. But when the photographer has prepared his truthful tablet, and "held his mirror up to nature," she is taken captive in all her sublimity and beauty; and faithful images of her grandest, her loveliest, and her minutest features are transferred to her most distant worshippers, and become the objects of a new and pleasing idolatry. [4]

Not only did the "truthful tablet" document the unknown, but it did so with unfailing precision, and herein was the second great service architectural photography provided the nineteenth century. The matchless efficiency of the camera was appreciated as well in the visual transcription of more local architecture. Whether the subject was a minute ornamental detail or the structural organization of the entire building, the camera was a far more efficient means for documentation than the human hand; what had been possible to convey before only after hours of laborious drawings could now be reproduced more quickly and more accurately. Edward Bradley, an Oxford scholar of theology, wrote in 1855 that:

> It will be obvious that Photography can be made most serviceable to Engineers and Architects, in illustrating—either for themselves or their employers—the progress of the works on which they may be engaged. Accurate ideas may thus be obtained of newly built mansions, churches, or public edifices. Indeed, estate agents are already awake to the advantages of the art; and, in place of the gaudily coloured idealities which they were in the habit of exhibiting as the correct representations of the villas and mansions of which they had the disposal, many of them now set forth before you the less attractive, but more faithful Calotypes. May such truth-telling prosper as it deserves! [5]

Such truth telling did indeed prosper as is made beautifully clear in the work of Edouard-Denis Baldus and Henri Le Secq, to name only two of its skilled practitioners. Like numerous others of his colleagues, Baldus had a background in painting. In 1851, however, he was selected by the Commission des Monuments Historiques for the immense task of photographically documenting "the architectural heritage of France, region by region." His subsequent records of Parisian monuments, railroad lines, and the Louvre, to name only some of his subjects, are both precise and evocative historical records. The time of day during which light might best reveal his subject, careful visual indication of a building's scale, details of its constructions—all of these are considered in Baldus's documents. [6]

Le Secq's greatest contributions were his photographs of the cathedrals of France, most notably the cathedral of Chartres. The twenty-five plates work as a group; their effect is sequential. Le Secq had grasped the cumulative effect a photographic series might make; each of his deliberate compositions represents a greater whole. He exploited the use of the architectural detail, recognizing its capacity to represent what lay outside of the frame. It is a process of selection, an approach to framing in which the part is made to stand for the whole, that is intrinsic to much architectural photography as it is practiced today. [7]

With the advance of industrialization throughout Europe, the photograph was one way by which traditional culture—and architecture—was salvaged. But photographic documentation visually preserving the past was only half of the medium's contribution. The photography of architecture addresses itself as strongly to the present; and equally important were the photographs that acted as chronicles of the present, that recorded the disruption of urban culture, the demolition and deterioration of preindustrial cities, and the new urbanization that followed. In his comprehensive study of photography and urbanization, *Silver Cities,* Peter Bacon Hales observes of photographers that "their vision of the city became the heritage of modern America. . . . Their influence has come under scrutiny only rarely, even though, like their predecessors, the mapmakers of the sixteenth, seventeenth, and eighteenth centuries, they served crucial functions for their time and culture. Offering not simply facts but information, they were cultural messengers, and their messages both reflected and defined how Americans saw their cities." [8]

There is accuracy in the analogy between mapmakers and photographers. Maps did not simply illustrate terrain and its borders, but suggested routes by which these might be explored and transversed. Likewise, photographs do not simply give us the facts, but suggest ways in which we might absorb and accommodate them. The frame, the composition, the angle at which the subject has been recorded—all of these give us a visual context for the information.

But as the art and craft of photography evolved to a simpler process by the end of the nineteenth century, it also demanded less of the photographer. The dedication and talent of those who took up the profession had noticeably diminished in comparison with that of their predecessors, and the creativity and skill that had been so apparent in its early years declined and were rarely enjoyed again until the twentieth century. Hales notes that by the 1870s "nearly every American household had a collection of stereo photograph cards and a magnifying stereoscope through which to view them, [and] photography had become the visual vehicle of American democratic experience." [9] While this development was surely a bellwether to the visual excesses that so mark contemporary culture, it also attests to the popularization of the craft and the diminishment of talent and discipline that inevitably accompanied it.

A notable exception to this in the United States was Joseph Byron, professionally established in New York City in the early 1890s. The clients of the architectural photographer at the turn of the century varied, from the architect to the architect or designer's clients, and Byron counted among his many theatrical and society clients Cornelius Vanderbilt II, Mrs. William B. Astor, and William Collins Whitney. His documentation of their homes, their parlors, conservatories, and drawing rooms affords us a rare glimpse of the eclectic period of American interior design.

While Byron's photographic documentation of society was a sizable contribution to the archives of design history, he made another contribution of a more questionable nature. He was perhaps the first architectural photographer whose work bestowed a sense of glamor on its subject. Once Byron had photographed one of these great rooms or houses, it received a final accolade or seal of approval. Not unlike some eighteenth- and nineteenth-century portrait painters whose canvases seemed to endow their subjects with a new grace and stature, Byron's photographs lent a new prestige to their subjects. It is an accolade that has since become a convention of the profession, but it was with Byron that the tradition was established. Its premise is that the documentation or interpretation of architecture by certain select photographers might elevate its status from architecture to higher art. For better or worse, in later years, the photographs of Ezra Stoller and, later, Judith Turner often bestowed upon their subjects a more celebrated and revered position in the art world than a building might achieve so readily on its own. Buildings are places in which we live, work, carry out our lives. They are inhabited by the mundane, and for this reason, we are not always prone to seeing architecture as art unless so instructed—which is just what the photographs often do. While this is not to say that it remains to photographers to bestow legitimacy upon architecture, it does point out the curious ease with which the public will accept the esthetic value of the representation more readily than the original.

While this was a practice that clearly could elevate the value of both photograph and building, it was not one that originated with the photographer (though it may have benefited his business). To the contrary, most architectural photographers work with such a profound respect for the buildings they photograph and the architects who designed them, that the idea that their photographs might confer their own legitimacy is almost laughable.

By the early twentieth century, photographic sensibilities had subtly shifted. Author and curator Richard Pare notes that "for the pioneers of photography [working in the mid-nineteenth century], the obsession with clarity of rendition drove them to great lengths of extraordinary feats of endurance. . . . Their overriding concerns were clarity, directness, and rationality. In a great photograph, artistry of the photographer is never out of balance with subject, and what is sought is the maximum of information conveyed in an objective way." [10]

By a half century later, however, the obsession with clarity had paled somewhat. The esthetic sensibilities of the early twentieth century valued not the realities of the subject at hand so much as the artists' perception of them. The purpose of the photograph was no longer simply to preserve images of past and present. Rather, the photographic image tended to become more expressive, recording not simply the building, but the photographer's impression of it. How these impressions entered the frame, subtly or more dramatically, marked new generations of work. The issue of whether it entered the frame at all, and if so, to what degree, was first argued in the early days of the present century, and is one that remains lively in the profession of architectural photography as it is practiced today.

In introducing an exhibition of Eugene Atget's photographs, John Szarkowski, director of the Museum of Modern Art's photography department, noted, "Like most artists of consequence, Atget is remarkable not because he started with a new idea, but because through his work he constructed one. He began by trying to describe clearly his knowledge of the ordinary, important facts of his world and he brought to this ancient problem independence of mind, seriousness of character, an original sensibility, energy, and talent." [11] Atget's photographs taken at the turn of the century not only record the avenues and streets, the shops and cafés, the gardens and bridges of Paris, but give them a serenity of their own. Their realism is imbued with a sense of quietude. Through the photographs evolved not only a sense of place, but a sense of time. While they make for a visual encyclopedia of Parisian culture, that they are the work of a singular vision is also clear.

Similarly, Frederick Evans's photographs of the interiors of cathedrals record not so much their material structures, but how light strikes their surfaces. Lux Feininger's photographs of Bauhaus architecture transcribe a weightlessness with a weightlessness all their own. By declining to recognize the base ground to his architectural photographs, Feininger recorded buildings that seemed, somewhat miraculously, to float. [12] This was not necessarily at odds with the architecture; these traditions in photography were being broken at just a time in history when the International Style was beginning to shatter traditions of architecture.

In discussing the work of photographer Alvin Langdon Coburn, John Szarkowski notes that "for those around the turn of the century who were seriously committed to the potential of photography as a creative art, the fundamental stumbling block seemed to be the medium's uncompromising specificity. If allowed to follow its natural bent, the camera described not Man but men, not Nature but countless precise biological and geological facts. This tendency was not in harmony with the artistic spirit of the time, which preferred an idealized view." [13]

While this may have been true for Man and for Nature, it was less true for Architecture. Architecture of that period was itself idealized. With the translation of Bauhaus canon to the International Style, architecture and photography enjoyed a new fusion. Their coalescence was pure. The camera had little problem recording architecture as abstraction, simply because much International Style architecture was itself abstract. Its empathy with architecture was innate.

The abstractions of the International Style seemed almost made for photographic expression. Windows and doors were no longer so concisely framed; rather, they hovered, floated, and worked to extend space. Interior spaces opened up with sheets of glass acting as walls that flowed and wrapped, and whose movement was defined as much by light as by more material substances. Spatial relationships, light and shadow, surface texture, the plasticity of materials—all of these became architectural elements just as surely as steel, concrete, masonry, wood. Just how these could best be recorded by light and its absence on a piece of film made for provocative visual investigations.

The fact that architecture and architects were enjoying such an intellectually and esthetically productive period had a dual effect on architectural photographers. On one hand, their subject matter had become more compelling, more stimulating, more affecting; on the other hand, the commercial ends to which their work was often applied frequently prevented it from being considered a fine art. Not until recently, in fact, has that demarcation been obscured. Fortunately, most photographers who chose architecture as their subject matter did so paying scant attention to the esthetic pigeonholing that so limited the number, and interest, of critics.

Surely the photographs shown in these pages will demonstrate that distinctions of art and commerce have little bearing on the esthetic value of the photograph.

The 1930s was a time of change for the profession. Ezra Stoller, widely recognized as the dean of the profession, points out that before the Depression, a portfolio of photographs was generally thought to be part of the architect's commission. That is to say, the client paid for the photographs, commissioned by the architect, and these photographs were then submitted to architectural reviews and magazines. After the Depression, Stoller recalls, "Nobody was building houses, and if they did build one, it was ridiculous to suggest that they pay for photographs. And so it came to be the magazines who were really responsible for the reporting." In more recent years, the commissioning of the architectural photograph has again become a part of the architect's domain. Because the cost of photography so often exceeds the magazine's design budget, the magazine frequently publishes photographs commissioned and submitted by the architect rather than those it has itself commissioned. How such issues direct the photograph is discussed by some of the photographers whose work is shown here. For some, shooting for editorial purposes gives the photographer a wider latitude. Stoller, on the other hand, states that who the client is makes little difference to the photograph in the end: "In a sense, you always work for the architect. Even if someone else is paying for the job, it's the architecture that counts."

Architectural photography after the Second World War served a purpose somewhat different from that of its earlier days. Architecture of the modern movement had been launched into the corporate-built world with a postwar restraint and efficiency. As Stoller himself points out, much of the great architecture of that period was generated as monuments to great chief executives who "had built these companies up, and the same qualities and instincts that made them great businessmen made them choose great architects. And where a great man chose a great architect, you got a great building."

The purpose in photographing these buildings, then, was not simply to record the built world; rather, the visual document acted almost as a treatise, clarifying and elucidating not only the physical facts of the architecture, but its less material truths as well. The photograph no longer simply documented, but it also frequently instructed, and what it instructed, more often than not, was the art of seeing. While photographs by nature suggest a context for the facts they provide, it was a context all the more in demand for much modern architecture. To many, the arrival of modernist buildings in the urban landscape was taken almost as a move of aggression. Despite its intent, the architecture was often seen as inhospitable, inaccessible, cold. Often, the photographs softened this image and presented an alternate view. Without reducing the solemnity or the grandeur of much of this new corporate architecture, it also pointed out where, exactly, its beauty might be found. By highlighting a detail, or deliberately framing an entrance or a plaza, the photographs singled out the significant facts in an unimposing and accessible way.

This fusion between architecture and photography raises another important question, that is, the effect of the photography on architecture. Exactly how photography has influenced architecture cannot be qualified in precise terms. Nevertheless, by putting a frame around the building, the camera suggests ways in which it might be perceived. The photograph gives us the building in a precise composition—with or without occupants, viewed in remote splendor or in closer, more accessible range. It chooses the salient details, and the angle at which these are photographed leads the viewer's eye in the most revealing, informative, and persuasive route. It does not merely document the building, but by visually cataloging what is important, it suggests ways in which we might see and remember it.

And this being the case, the images and perceptions we have of the built world are often derived from photographs. How buildings are planned and used often has to do with information found in photographs. While it is almost impossible to qualify how this occurs and to what degree, that it *does* occur is perhaps worth keeping in mind when determining the purpose and effect of architectural photographs.

Despite the short history of photography, it has seen significant changes since the mid-nineteenth century, going, as Richard Pare points out, "from a rudimentary and intransigent process into a highly refined and consistent technical procedure." [14] Most outstanding of these refinements, surely, is in the equipment that is used. Most contemporary architectural photographers use a four-by-five camera whose "view box classicism," as it has sometimes been called, establishes a rigorous and controlled composition. The photograph acts as a portrait of architectural space; exposures are long; composition is studied, controlled. While this approach continues a basic photographic tradition, other photographers today choose to document buildings with the smaller 35mm camera, which permits a faster shooting. Composition tends to be a more ephemeral affair. The sudden gesture of a bystander, an unexpected shaft of light, the shape of a cloud—faster films and smaller cameras can accommodate these more readily.

Clearly, these are choices in documentary approach as well as in equipment, but once the choice has been made, it can be executed more effectively by the wide range of equipment available to the contemporary photographer. And this again points out the vast ground the profession has covered in its brief history.

In selecting the photographers whose work was to appear in this collection, it was necessary to establish a working definition of the term *architectural photographer*. Certainly "any photographer who uses a building as his predominant subject matter" was inaccurate, as well as far too broad to serve any useful purpose. The term, then, in this book, refers to photographers who use the camera to record architecture. Many photographers use architecture as their subject matter. But once the subject matter has been chosen, the photograph is usually about something else altogether. It is not about light and surface and space so much as a metaphor for something far from any architectural realm. This work, then, though it may be provocative and illuminating in other ways, has not been included here. The photographers whose work has been shown here use photography as a means to convey information about buildings. Often, the beauty of the record itself may equal or surpass the beauty of the building. Nevertheless, it remains the intent of the photograph to reveal the building. And while it may often end up having its own presence, it remains informative.

How it informs, though, is often a matter of debate among photographers. For many, it is the purpose of the architectural photograph to reveal the intent of the architect. But as critic Paul Goldberger observes, "The architect is not necessarily the best judge of his work." Goldberger states that rather than photographs that depict the building "pristine, in its own reality," he prefers photographs that reveal the full potential of the building, "the building as part of a larger world, including people who see and use the building, and whose sense of it may not match the architect's." [15] This, then, is one of the choices implicit in the profession as it is practiced today—whether to accept and represent the architect's vision of the building or to represent a broader vision. Naturally, the tone of the question shifts somewhat from building to building, from architect to architect, as it takes into account the latitude of the architect's concerns.

Goldberger observes that "the photographer's responsibility is to give the building the fairest chance to speak for itself." [16] The photographers whose work is shown in these pages have assumed this responsibility, and indeed, the buildings shown in their photographs speak concisely, eloquently, sometimes more lyrically, sometimes more epically, for themselves.

This said, however, it must also be pointed out that most of the photographs shown here have been removed from their original context. It was the purpose of most of these photographs to document and clarify specific points of specific buildings; they set out to elucidate materials, lighting, site, the flow of interior space, surface texture, structural design, or any number of the other precise and imprecise qualities of architecture. A purpose many of them may serve in the future is to account for buildings that are no longer standing. In the following pages, however, they have been removed from these purposes. They are less about specific buildings and surpass the specific narrative for which they were originally intended.

Besides the intent to reveal the building, these photographers share another quality. Ours is a culture in which visual literacy is at a high. We have been visually force-fed information from an early age. Sophisticated graphics in packaging, aggressive advertising, on-the-spot television coverage of news events, New Wave film—all of these and more have given us a visual literacy that frequently borders on overload. Unless we have been informed in aggressive visual terms, we tend not to believe. This said, it is with an almost surprising modesty that most of these photographers work. While it is by habit that many of us tend to think we can judge a product or understand an event from seeing its reproduced image, these photographers are quick to point out that the photograph is not a surrogate for the building. Perhaps it is because they have a clear understanding both of their subject and of their medium. The photograph may direct our attention to a detail that might otherwise have been missed; it can also offer a view not easily obtained by the casual pedestrian; and sometimes, it can interpret. But it is never a stand-in for the building.

Architecture is experiential; buildings employ all our senses. They have sounds and smells; each has its own feel. Photography is, by nature, visual. It is not the simultaneous experience of the senses that architecture can be. It does not presume to be, nor should we expect it to be. As architect Hugh Hardy succinctly observes, "The camera has one eye; you have blind authors and one-eyed musicians, but you have very few one-eyed architects. An architect depends on his spatial perceptions." [17] And it is perhaps appropriate, then, in this age of visual aggressiveness and excess to recognize that there are limits to the photographic medium. They are limits, certainly, that are recognized and appreciated by the photographers whose work is shown here, and therein lies a large part of their skill and talent.

What these photographs are evidence of is the power and creativity demanded *to represent* with precision and truth. And this perhaps is one of the more provocative and ironic points of architectural photography. While the notion that one needs imagination to grasp reality is perhaps subtle for a culture that puts such a high value on personal expression, it is indeed the premise to architectural photography. The creative skills used to comprehend and convey fact are often a good deal more than those used to produce more original work grafted from the personal imagination. To observe accurately facts that are outside of the self and to express them clearly can demand patience, insight, imagination, and the none-too-small ability and inclination to dismiss ego. Photographer Berenice Abbott mentions this in response to her critics who suggested that the documentary nature of her work prevented it from achieving greater or more universal truths: "There is no such thing as being too objective. Goethe said it—'Few people have the imagination for reality.' " [18]

That the photographers whose work is shown in these pages have the imagination for reality is indisputable.

---

1. *New York Times,* 20 January 1985, section 3, p. 1
2. Richard Pare, *Photography and Architecture 1839–1939* (Montreal: Canadian Centre for Architecture, with Callaway Editions, 1982), p. 7
3. Rainer Fabian and Hans-Christian Adam, *Masters of Early Travel Photography* (New York: The Vendome Press, 1983), p. 59
4. *Edinburgh Review,* January 1843, quoted in *Photography in Print: Writings from 1816 to the Present,* ed. Vicki Goldberg (New York: Simon and Schuster, 1981), p. 64
5. Cuthbert Bede, "Photographic Pleasures," in *Photography in Print,* ed. Goldberg, p.84
6. Pare, *Photography and Architecture,* p. 17
7. Ibid.
8. Peter Bacon Hales, *Silver Cities: The Photography of American Urbanization, 1839–1915* (Philadelphia: Temple University Press, 1984), p. 3
9. Ibid., p. 5
10. Pare, *Photography and Architecture,* p. 16.
11. John Szarkowski, "The Work of Atget, The Ancien Regime" (Notes for exhibition at the Museum of Modern Art, New York, N.Y., 14 March–14 May 1985).
12. Pare, *Photography and Architecture,* p. 26.
13. John Szarkowski, *Looking at Photographs: 100 Pictures from the Collection of the Museum of Modern Art* (New York: The Museum of Modern Art, 1973), p. 62.
14. Pare, *Photography and Architecture,* p. 12.
15. Conversation with author, 30 January 1985.
16. Ibid.
17. Conversation with author, 9 April 1985.
18. Avis Berman, "The Unflinching Eye of Berenice Abbott," *ARTnews* (January 1981), pp. 87–88.

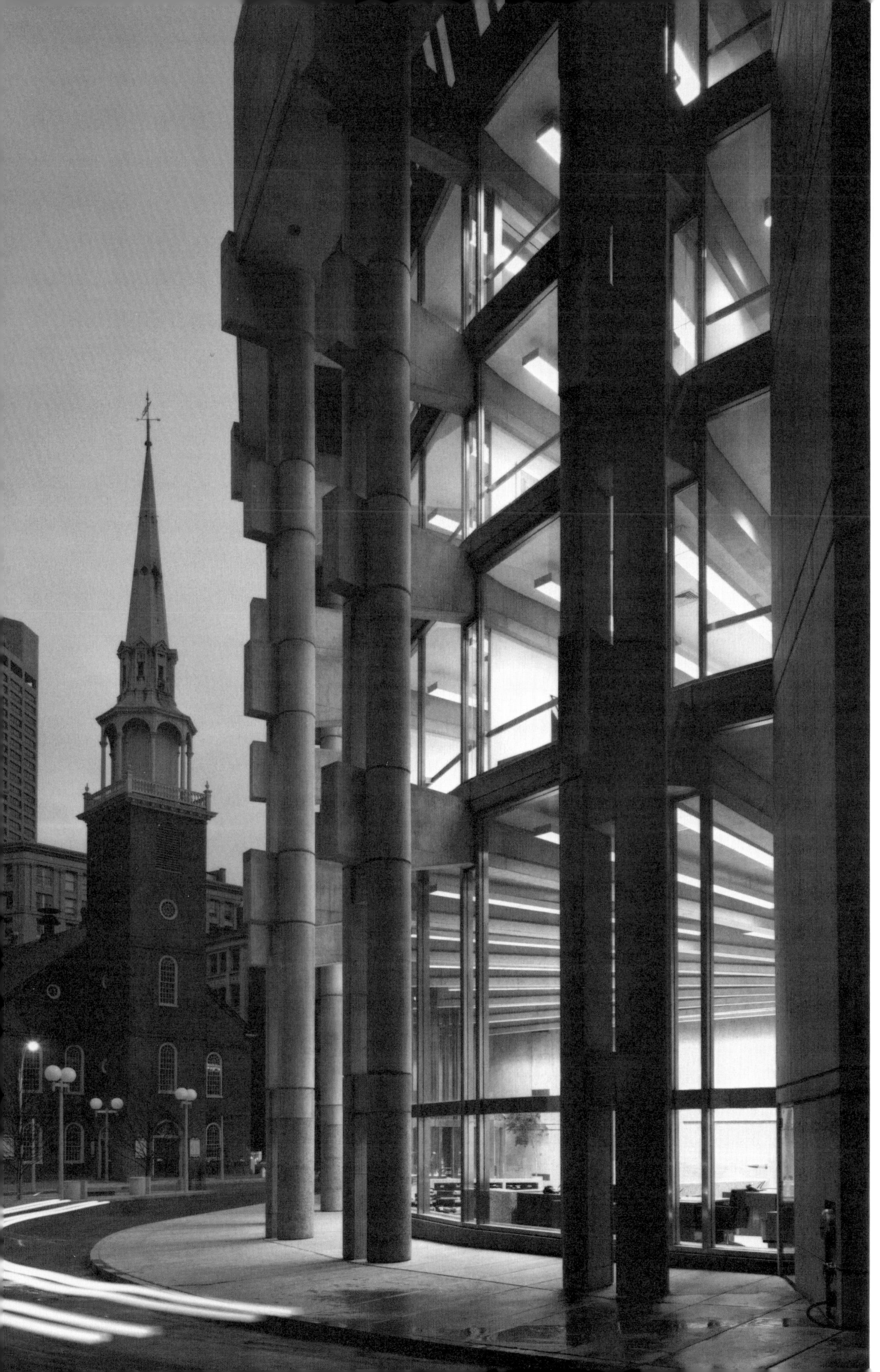

EZRA STOLLER

The path taken by architecture of the modern movement has followed a soaring trajectory, literally and figuratively. Documenting its course has been a question not only of relaying the material information, but of clarifying its less obvious tenets, evoking its subtle philosophies, and observing its often grand aspirations. The undisputed dean of contemporary architectural photography, Ezra Stoller has perhaps earned that title for doing all these with precision, wit, and clarity. And in so doing, he has established the ground rules of the profession as it is practiced today.

Modest in regard to his achievements, Stoller operates with a premise that observes the limitations of the craft: "An architectural photograph can never do more than suggest a part of that space in a segment of time. . . . As interpreters with cameras we are called upon to resolve a myriad of conflicting conditions in terms of an extremely limited medium and to communicate a four-dimensional experience (yes, time is one of the elements involved) with a flat piece of paper and restricted tonal palette." [1]

Nevertheless, what Stoller has managed to achieve with the flat piece of paper and restricted palette makes up an archive of documents that not only represents the facts of the architecture, but reveals the more subtle intent of the architect. Great architects, he points out, always try to teach people how to live. The obvious correlative, of course, is that a great photographer will try to teach people a new way to see, and Stoller's collection of work spanning the last fifty years is explicit visual evidence of this lesson. As one critic has noted, "Public resistance to the stark modern buildings was considerably softened by Stoller's widely published pictures." [2] His images not only made the public familiar with the architecture, but they suggested ways in which these buildings might be observed and appreciated.

Indeed, Stoller's early work of the thirties and forties was done at a time when the modern movement introduced a vigor and creativity that has rarely been matched in the history of architecture. International Style architecture spoke an entirely new building language based on modern science, engineering, and technology. Le Corbusier had redefined the house as "a machine to live in," suggesting that its construction observe "the same rational manner in which automobiles and airplanes are conceived, designed, and produced." Dense mass was to be replaced

FACING PAGE: Kallman and McKinnell. Boston Five Cents Savings Bank. Boston, Massachusetts, 1972 (courtesy of Ezra Stoller, copyright © ESTO).

by the open box; structure was left exposed. Material determined esthetic; glass and steel were the skin and bones of these new structures.

Stoller's photographs not only record this language, but transcribe it with an eloquence and literacy of their own. They document not only the radical changes in the architectural landscape, but the often less conspicuous polemics on the landscape of ideas. That esthetics are determined by function was a cornerstone of modernism, and it is a principle that attends Stoller's photographs as well as the buildings that are their subject. His photographs too express their function; they are composed to inform, to reveal the important facts about the building, rather than to be appealing pictures. Which is to say, the beauty of the photographs lies in their documentary purity.

"People come out of their experience with a great architect altogether different," Stoller has stated. "A photographer can do the same things by helping, as sort of a handmaiden for the architect, by accentuating those meaningful things. He can only do it visually, which is one aspect of the experience." By seeing the building through the photographer's eyes, the observer then may absorb or acquire some of the same visual acuity.

Stoller attributes his own visual acuity to his "architectural approach," by which is meant a complete immersion and involvement in the job. Architecture is a language, he says, and if you understand it, you can photograph it sympathetically. His own conversance in the language of architecture stems from his profound respect for the subject, acquired initially as a student of architecture. "I'm interested in the statement the architect has made, whatever progress he can show, and whatever originality there is, whatever new thing he has to say that is important in the field. I'm more interested in the message than in the architect."

Stoller is also less preoccupied with creating visual documents that stand on their own artistic merit; but they almost always do in spite of his intentions. The precision and accuracy of his documents are distinguished by their utter lack of embellishment or photographic flattery of any sort. "Architecture, as any art, should be interpreted with a minimum of intrusion," he says. Implicit in the discipline of photographing architecture is a choice: what matters is either in front of the camera or behind it. Is the building merely source material, or is it everything?

In Stoller's photographs it is clearly everything. The honesty toward subject is what determines its success, and it is an honesty determined in large part by the reticence of the photographer's ego. Ego is deferred to architecture, and what emerges through the deference is the splendor of fact. Stoller's photographs are visual evidence of the rigorous discipline and prolific imagination that are demanded in the reconstruction of fact; they suggest that observing, absorbing, and recording those facts that exist outside of the self demand an imagination that is no less than that applied to more personal, private expression.

While it may be Stoller's objective to represent the intent of the architect, this is not to say that the photographer's own experience and background do not come into play, or that his own intuitive skills are not put into practice. Stoller's premise is that subject dictates all, and it is a premise that extracts from the photographer a knowledge and understanding of his subject. "If I take a photograph of Angkor Wat, I'm not doing it in the same state of mind that I would photograph a house.

It might be a little closer to Le Corbusier's chapel; they're both religious, ceremonial buildings, so you look at them in those terms. Everything comes out of the subject." Likewise, architecture of, or derived from, the modern movement might demand an intuitive grasp of spatial relationships, while Georgian architecture might ask for an understanding of the elegance that can be a result of visual symmetries and proportion. Stoller's objective to represent the intent of the architect also considers the users of the architecture. Who the building was designed for and how it is used is as basic to the architecture as its more material structures.

It is not Stoller's practice to defer to the architect on the site. He discovers the building on his own terms. "A work of architecture is a spatial experience and one must wander through it and about it until its organization becomes clear. I'll go in advance so that I can quietly spend some time walking around without any pressure, studying the thing and deciding what it says to me and what the best angles and light would be. No two buildings are the same." While such a process may be arduous and time consuming and at the expense of spontaneity, Stoller points out that the visual documentation of architecture is an intellectual discipline above all rather than an exercise in spontaneity. It is a system of seeing, a visual organization of space, that the photographer alone makes. "Architects don't have a photographic vision," he observes. "A really good architect is almost automatically a bad photographer. They're trained to see things in space and depth; and we're trained to reduce all those things in depth down to a flat sheet of paper."

To do so effectively may nevertheless demand visual manipulation. The point, however, is that such manipulations work to reinforce the specifications of the architect rather than to shape them with private interpretations for the sake of enhancing composition. Objects in the foreground are arranged in such a way so as not to obscure one another. There is a clarity in the relationships between architectural elements and furnishings. Each is presented on its own terms, rather than as visual props that together might make for an artificially dramatic effect. "Each thing is where it belongs in pictorial truth," says Arthur Drexler, director of the Department of Architecture and Design at the Museum of Modern Art. [3] While the bough of a tree or railing of a staircase might appear in the foreground of a photograph as a compositional element that frames the subject, such devices are used with a feeling for what the architect had in mind. They support the image of the architect. Indeed, a pictorial truth is conveyed, and it is one that locates and expresses the often less obvious architectural truths.

It is a pictorial honesty that is also in part due to Stoller's sense of economy in materials and format. If his work translates the language of architecture, it suggests that the most effective vocabulary is the one most simple. "The name of the game," he says, "from beginning to end, is control." The camera is a large-format view camera that is capable of this authority; while he prefers to use the longest lens possible, a medium wide-angle lens is the one he uses most frequently, rarely ever resorting to an extreme wide angle. And although everything is shot in black-and-white and in color, he has found that black-and-white photographs convey spatial information most clearly.

"We are not shooting at space," Stoller says, "but as a part of it, a sense which is rather subtle and easily distorted by resorting to queer angles, exaggerated composition, forced perspective, and overdramatic lighting." The viewer is not so much observing the space as entering it. Architecture is a spatial experience; it is about junctures of form and space, how they connect with one another, and how they depart from one another. Likewise, photography is a spatial enterprise in that it must annotate these movements to a two-dimensional surface. Stoller's work skillfully exploits their coincidence.

Stoller's wide influence on the succeeding generations of architectural photographers has not been limited to issues of esthetics and technique. His establishment of ESTO Photographics has helped to confirm the rights of photographers. "We were the ones who really set up the business of stock photos," he explains. "The idea existed for a long time, but we were working for people who had very limited budgets, and because it's an exacting and demanding kind of work, early on we had to devise a way of spreading costs." ESTO has since come to represent an association of architectural photographers for whom it serves as a business office, handling assignments and working in postproduction. Its archives help to ensure the repeated use of photographs from a single job, as a way of spreading costs, as well as the consistent crediting to the photographer. Both services are often overlooked, and by underscoring their practice, ESTO has made a significant contribution to the profession.

Arthur Drexler succinctly observes that, "for better or worse, [Stoller's] photographs have been more real to architectural students, and more intensely experienced, than most of the buildings they memorialize. Their instrumental value in spreading the good word may now yield to their more durable value as art." [4] Stoller's photographs do not pretend to be surrogates for the buildings they represent. But by drawing our attention to specific spatial characteristics, they suggest ways in which our own observations of architecture might be more informed and further refined. And it is perhaps on this account that they have been so instrumental in the past fifty years in giving a shape to our perceptions of architecture. It is also on this account that they have become powerful esthetic statements in themselves. Stoller's work has indeed exceeded its intentions, for in spite of them, it is valued not only for the great buildings it sets out to document, but for its own enduring esthetic value.

---

1. Ezra Stoller, from lecture notes written and copyrighted in Rye, New York, August 1984.
2. Herbert Muschamp, "The Portable Room," *Art & Antiques* (June 1984), p. 81.
3. Arthur Drexler, "Photographs of Architecture 1939–1980" (Introduction to exhibition catalog, Max Protetch Gallery, 4 December–12 January 1981).
4. Ibid.

FACING PAGE: Le Corbusier. Notre Dame du Haut. Ronchamp, France, 1955 (courtesy of Ezra Stoller, copyright © ESTO).

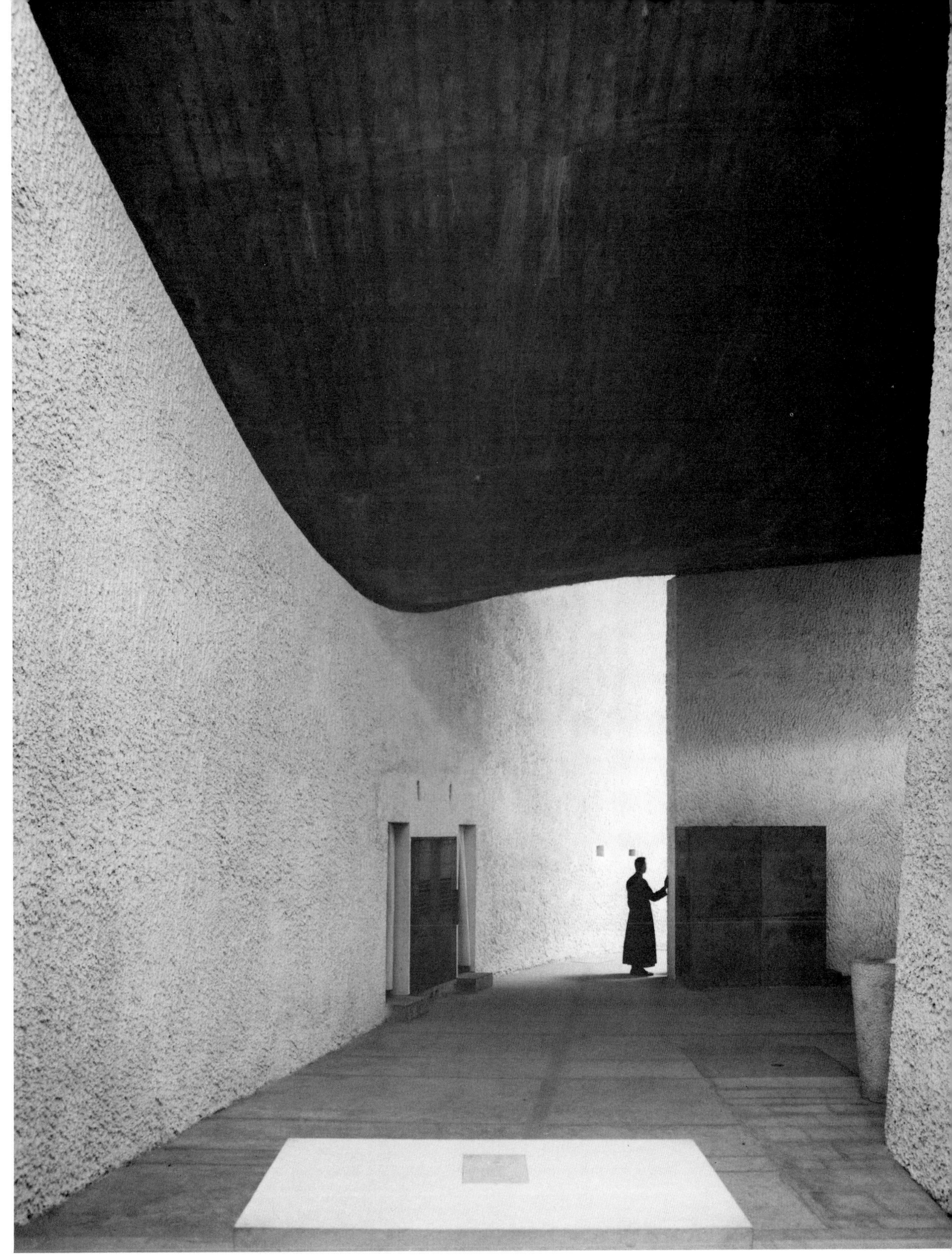

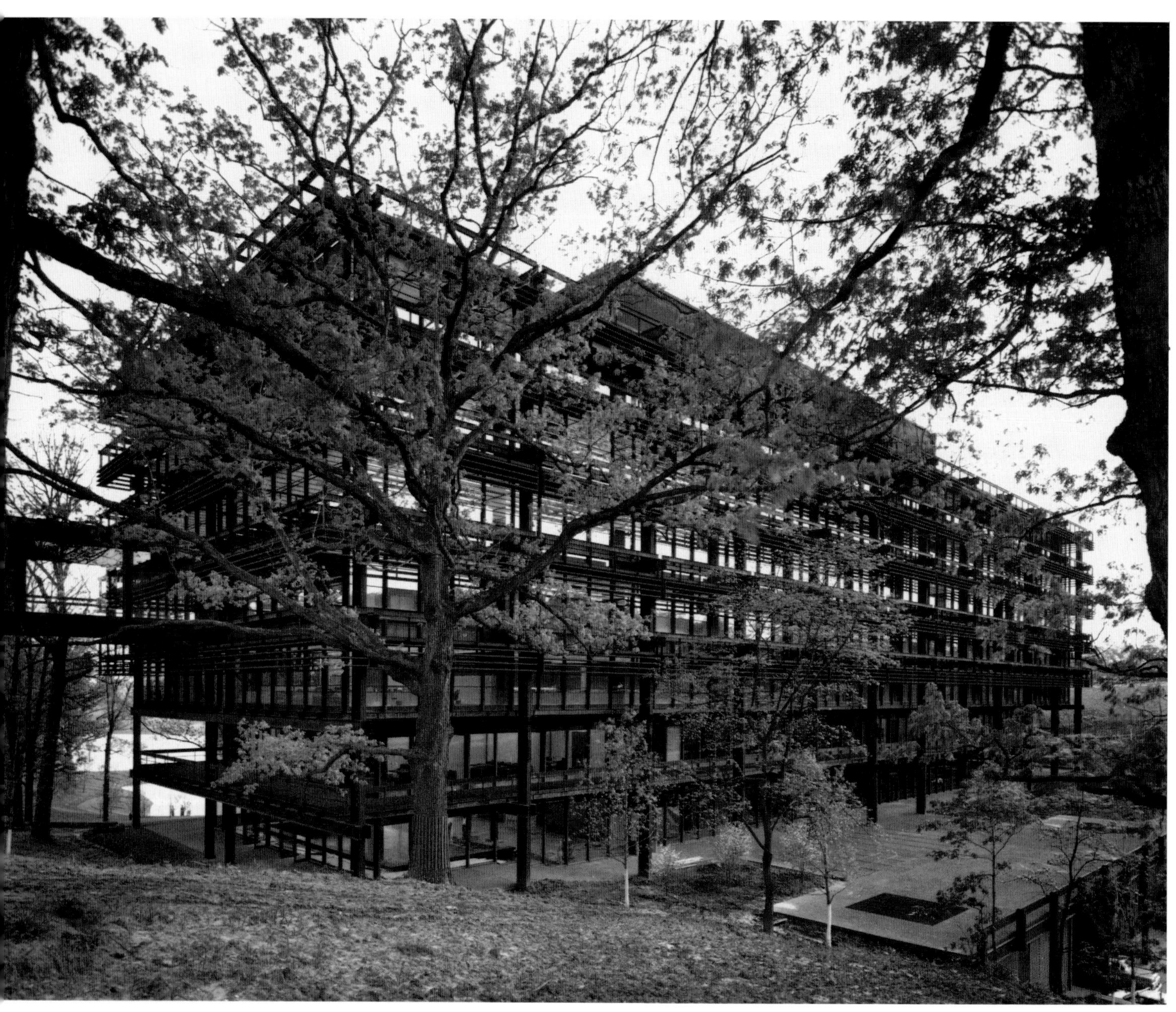

ABOVE: Eero Saarinen. John Deere Office. Moline, Illinois, 1964 (courtesy of Ezra Stoller, copyright © ESTO).

FACING PAGE: Richard Meier. The High Museum. Atlanta, Georgia, 1983 (courtesy of Ezra Stoller, copyright © ESTO).

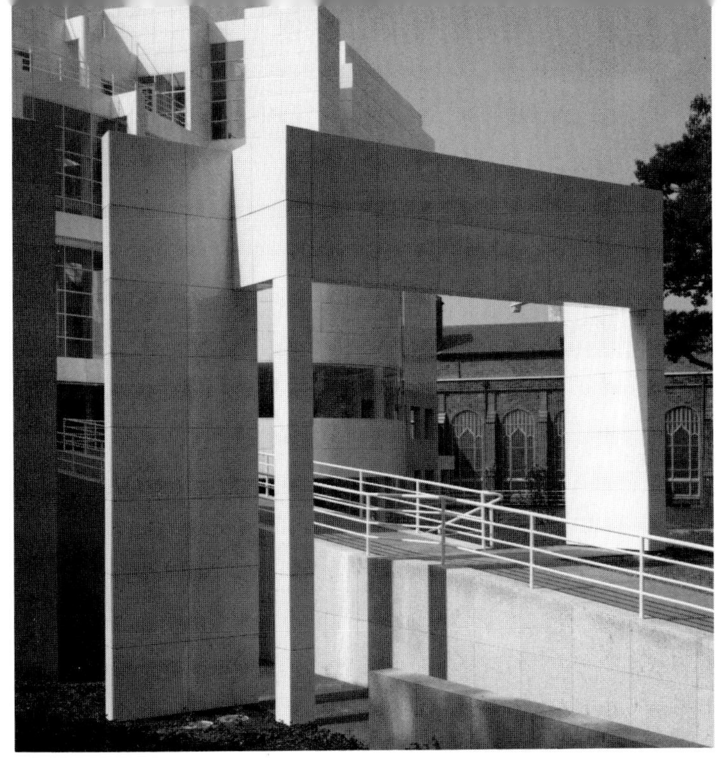

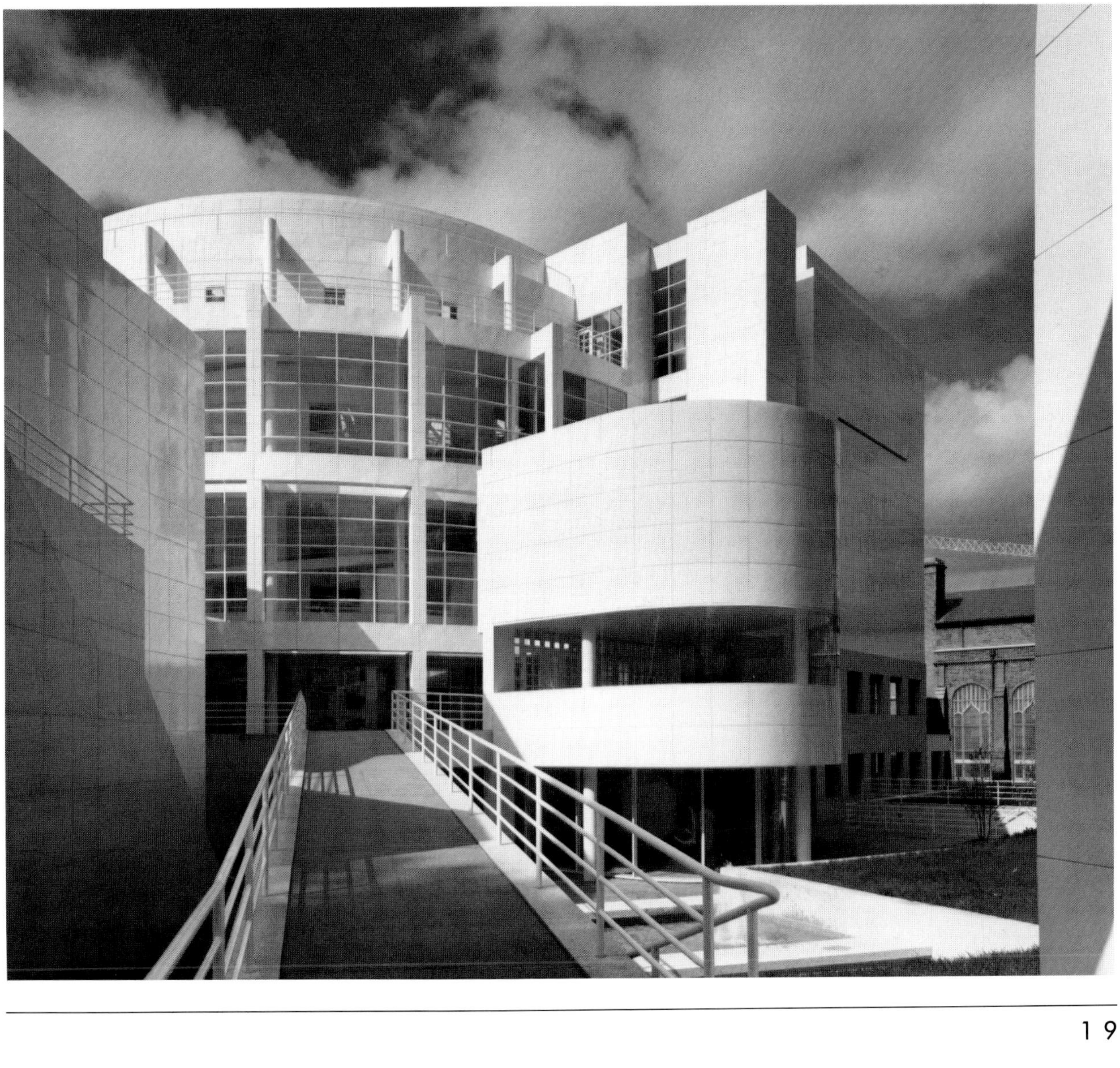

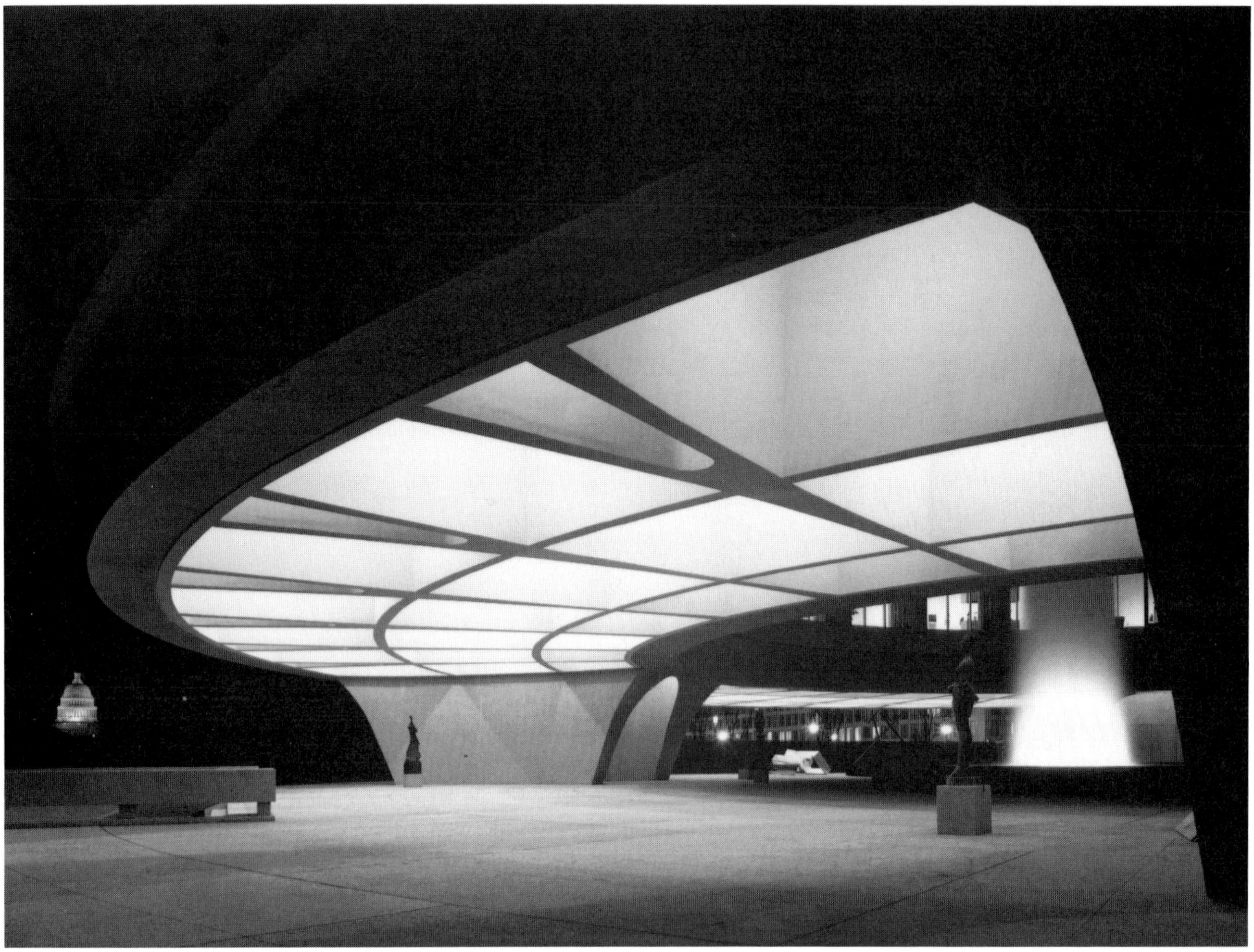

ABOVE: Skidmore, Owings & Merrill. Hirschhorn Museum. Washington, D.C., 1974 (courtesy of Ezra Stoller, copyright © ESTO).

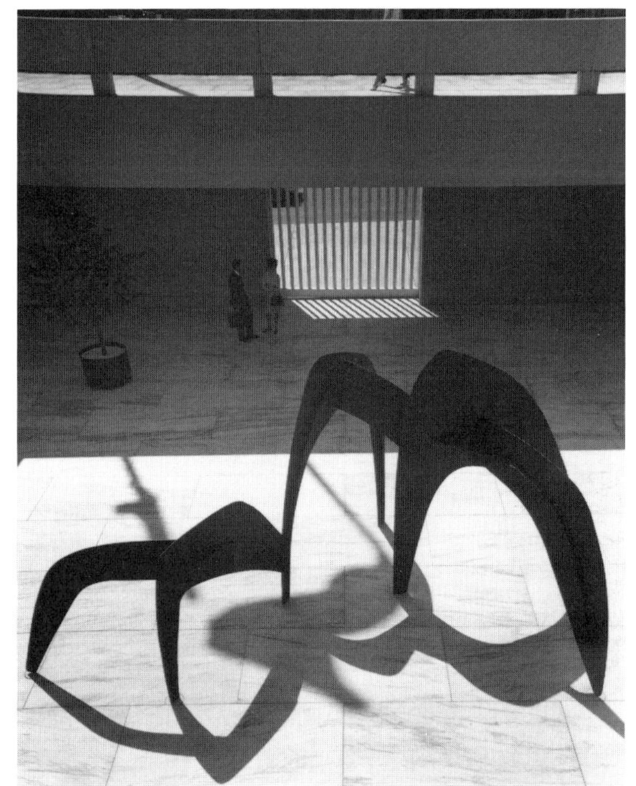

RIGHT: Skidmore, Owings & Merrill. American Republic Insurance Company. Des Moines, Iowa, 1965 (courtesy of Ezra Stoller, copyright © ESTO).

FACING PAGE: Eero Saarinen. Dulles International Airport. Chantilly, Virginia, 1964 (courtesy of Ezra Stoller, copyright © ESTO).

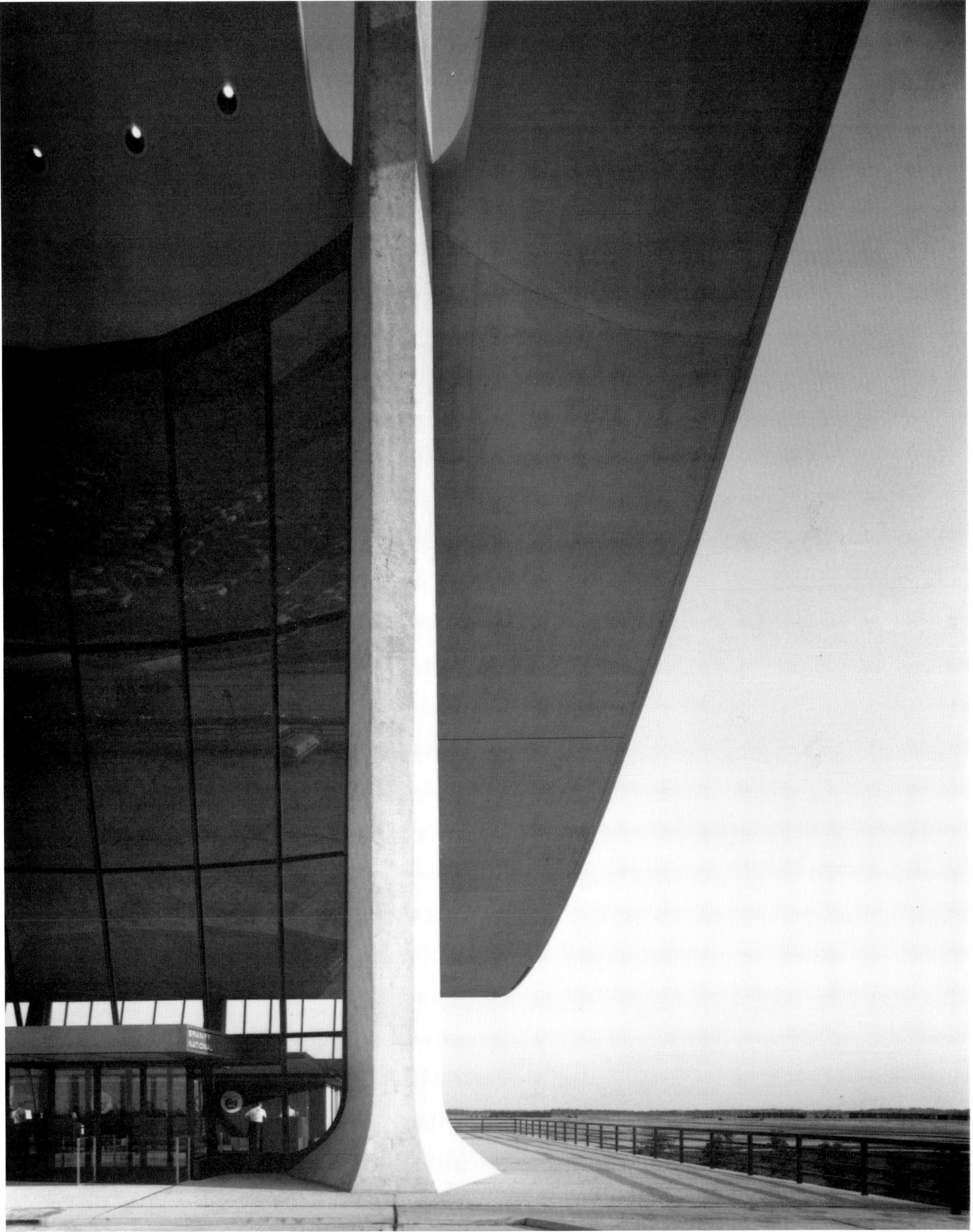

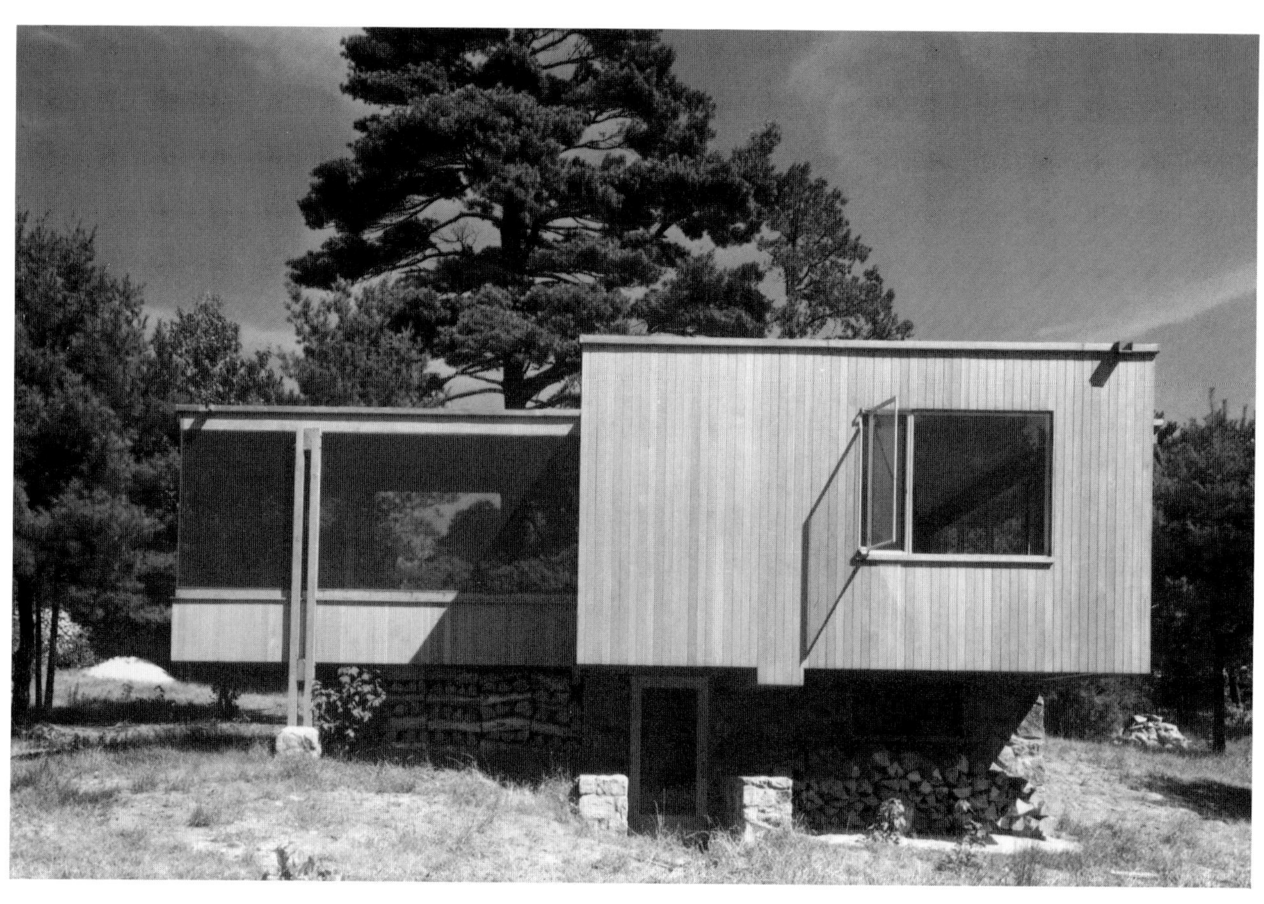

Walter Gropius and Marcel Breuer. Chamberlain Cottage. Wayland, Massachusetts, 1940 (courtesy of Ezra Stoller, copyright © ESTO).

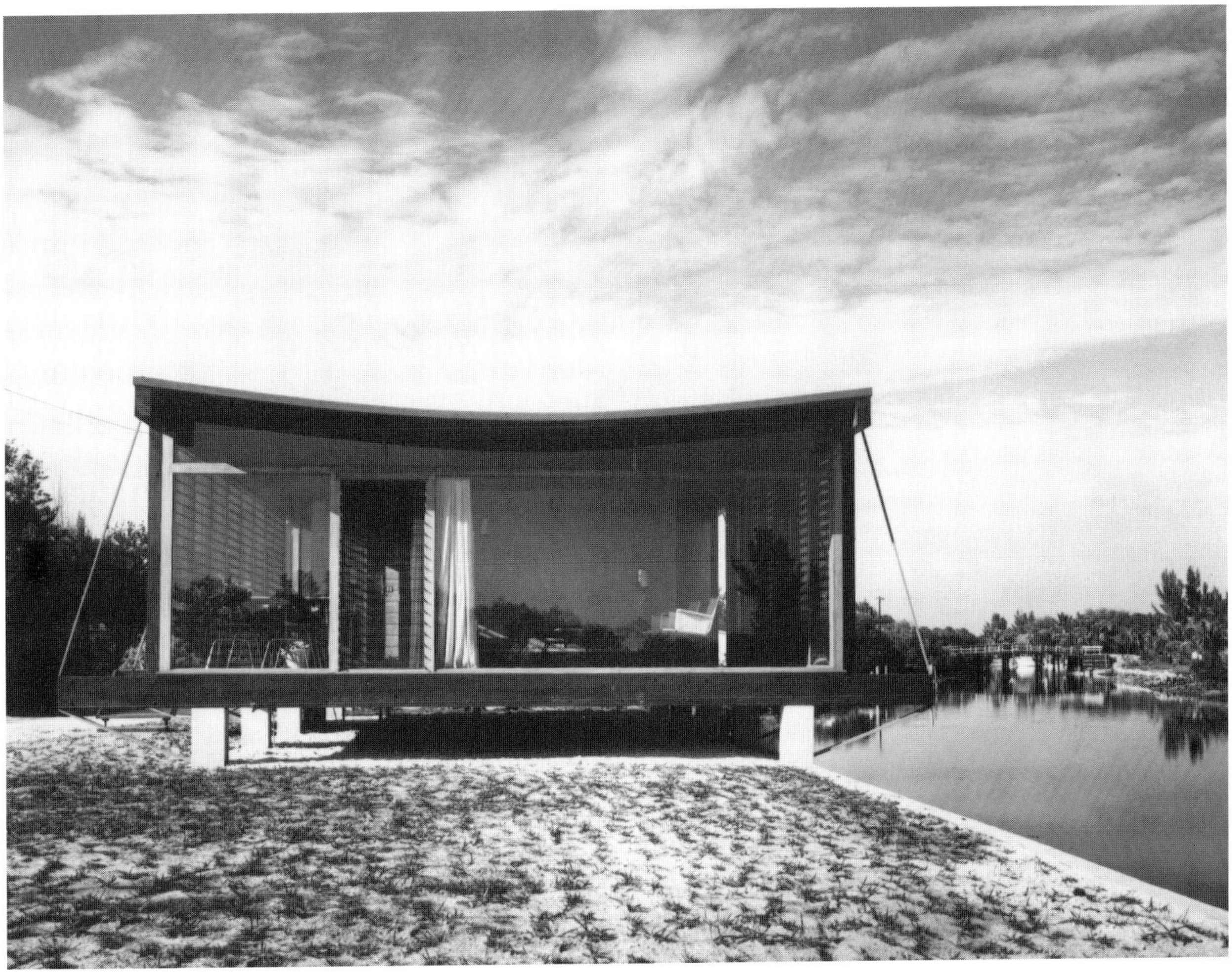

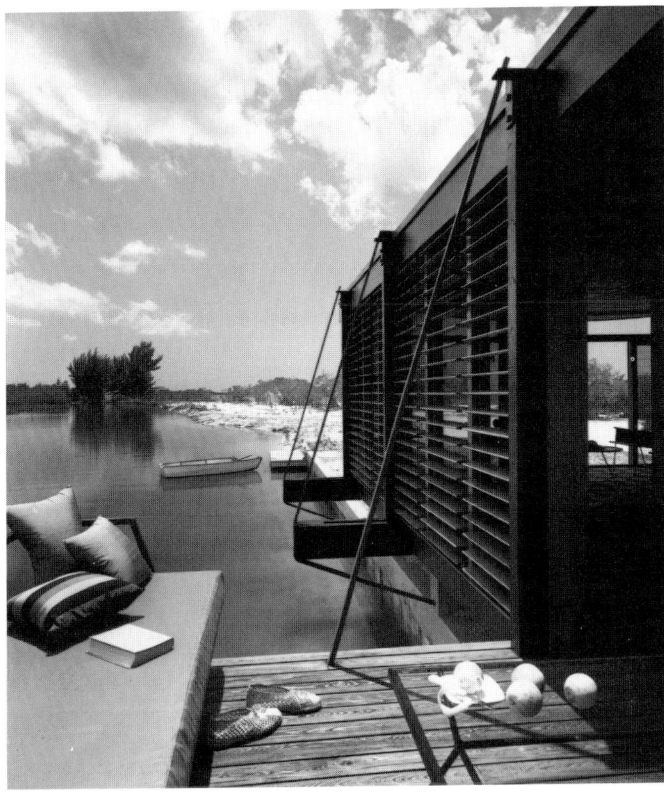

Paul Rudolph. Healey House.
Sarasota, Florida, 1950
(courtesy of Ezra Stoller,
copyright © ESTO).

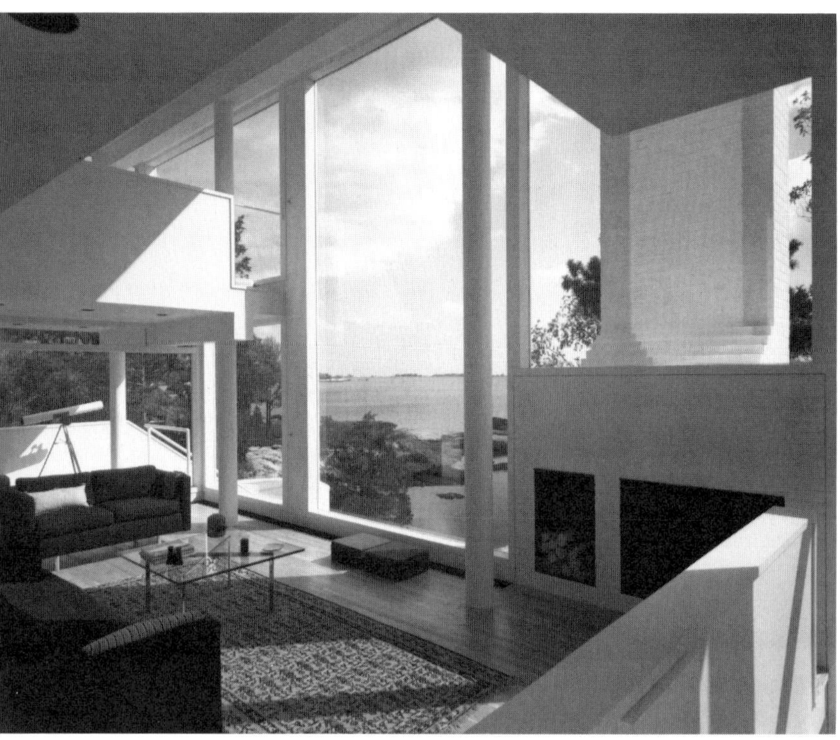

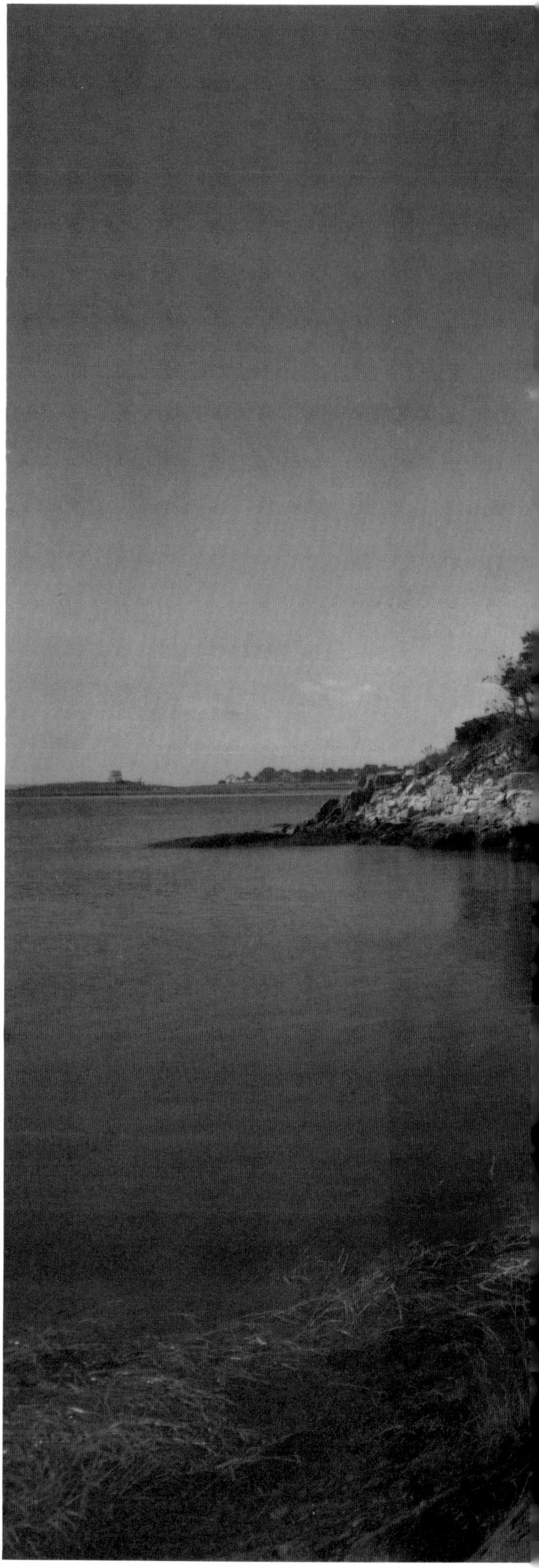

Richard Meier. Smith House. Rowayton, Connecticut, 1967 (courtesy of Ezra Stoller, copyright © ESTO).

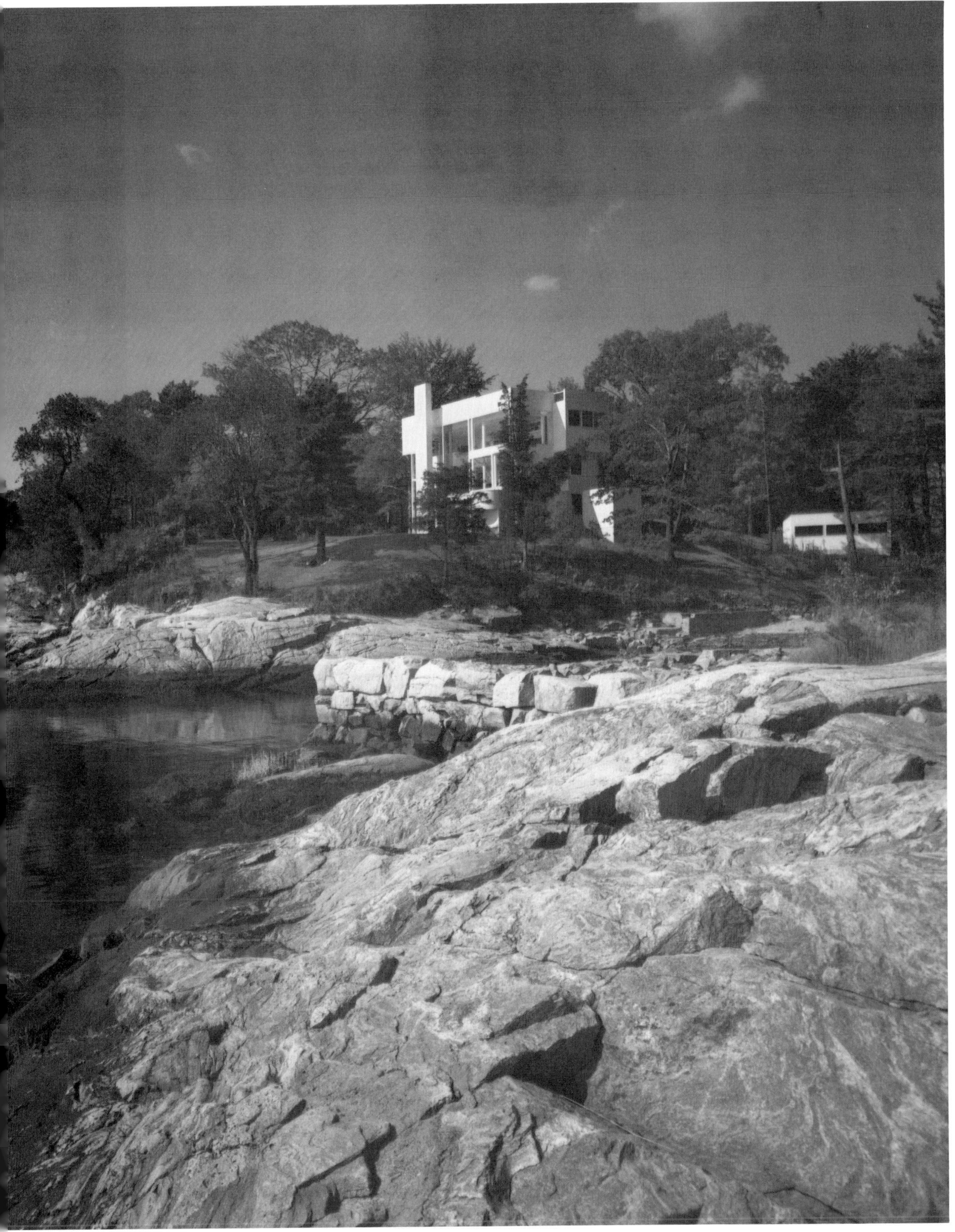

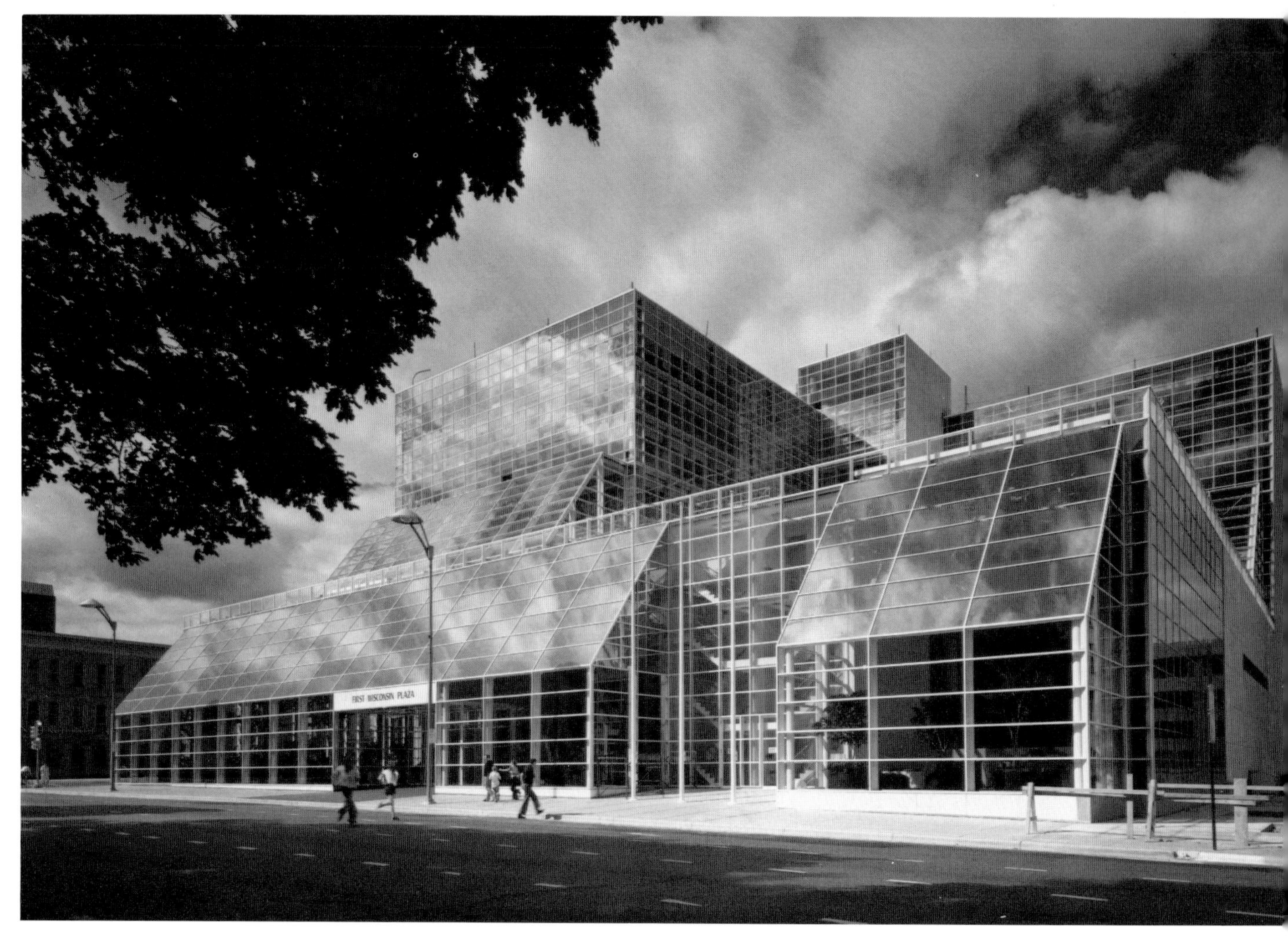

ABOVE: Skidmore, Owings & Merrill. First National Bank of Wisconsin. Madison, Wisconsin, 1974 (courtesy of Ezra Stoller, copyright © ESTO).

FACING PAGE: Richard Meier. New Harmony Atheneum. New Harmony, Indiana, 1979 (courtesy of Ezra Stoller, copyright © ESTO).

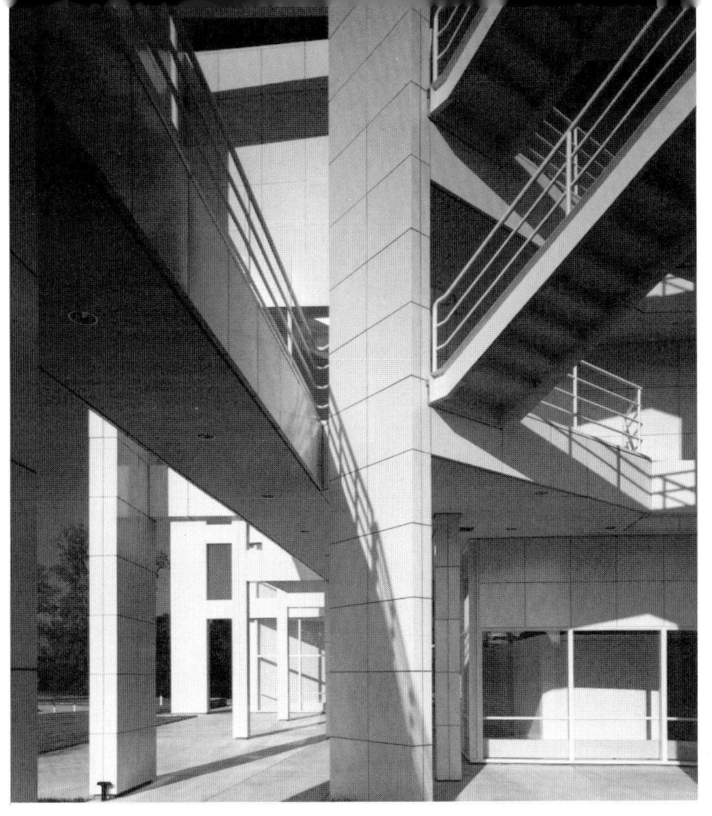

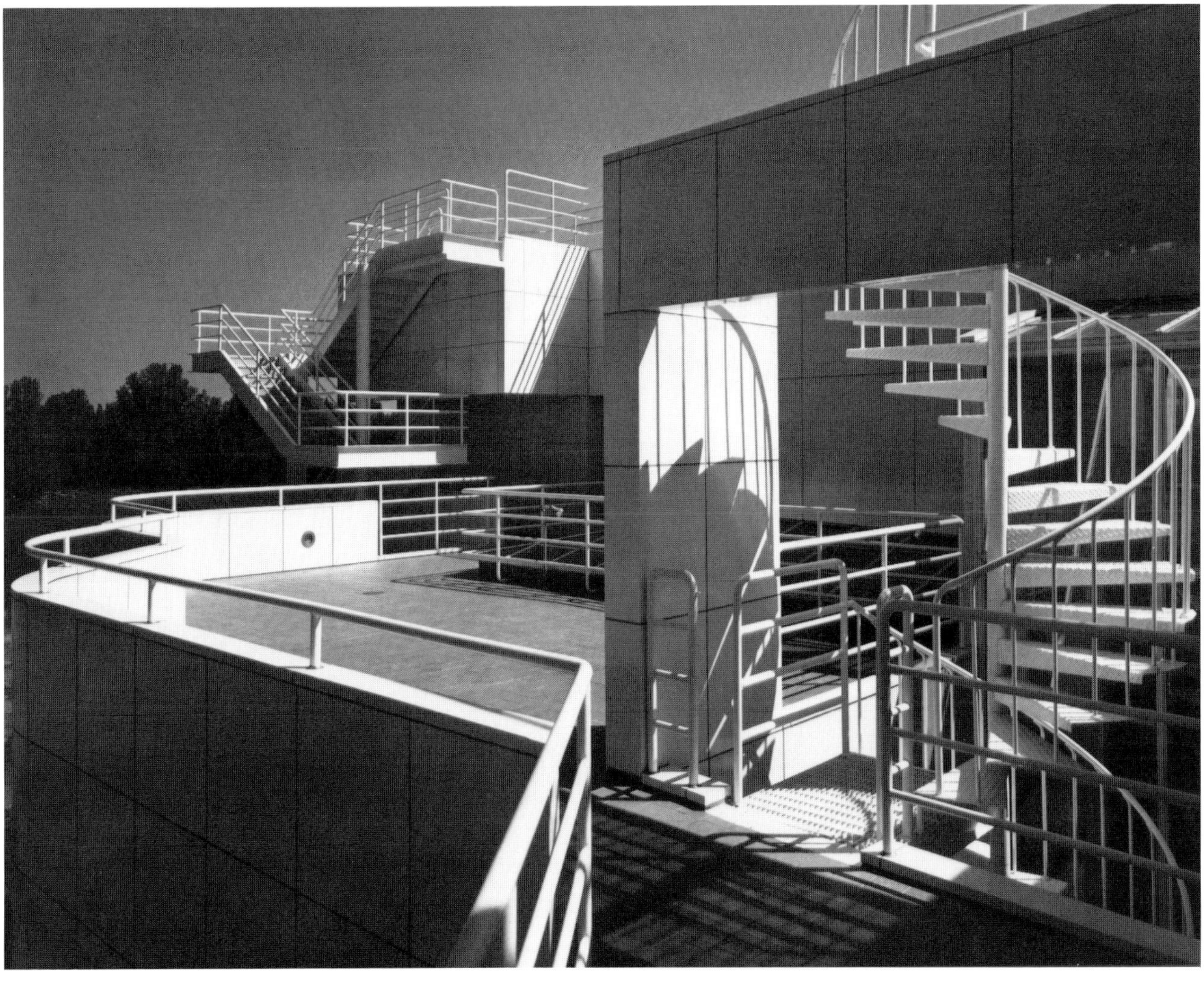

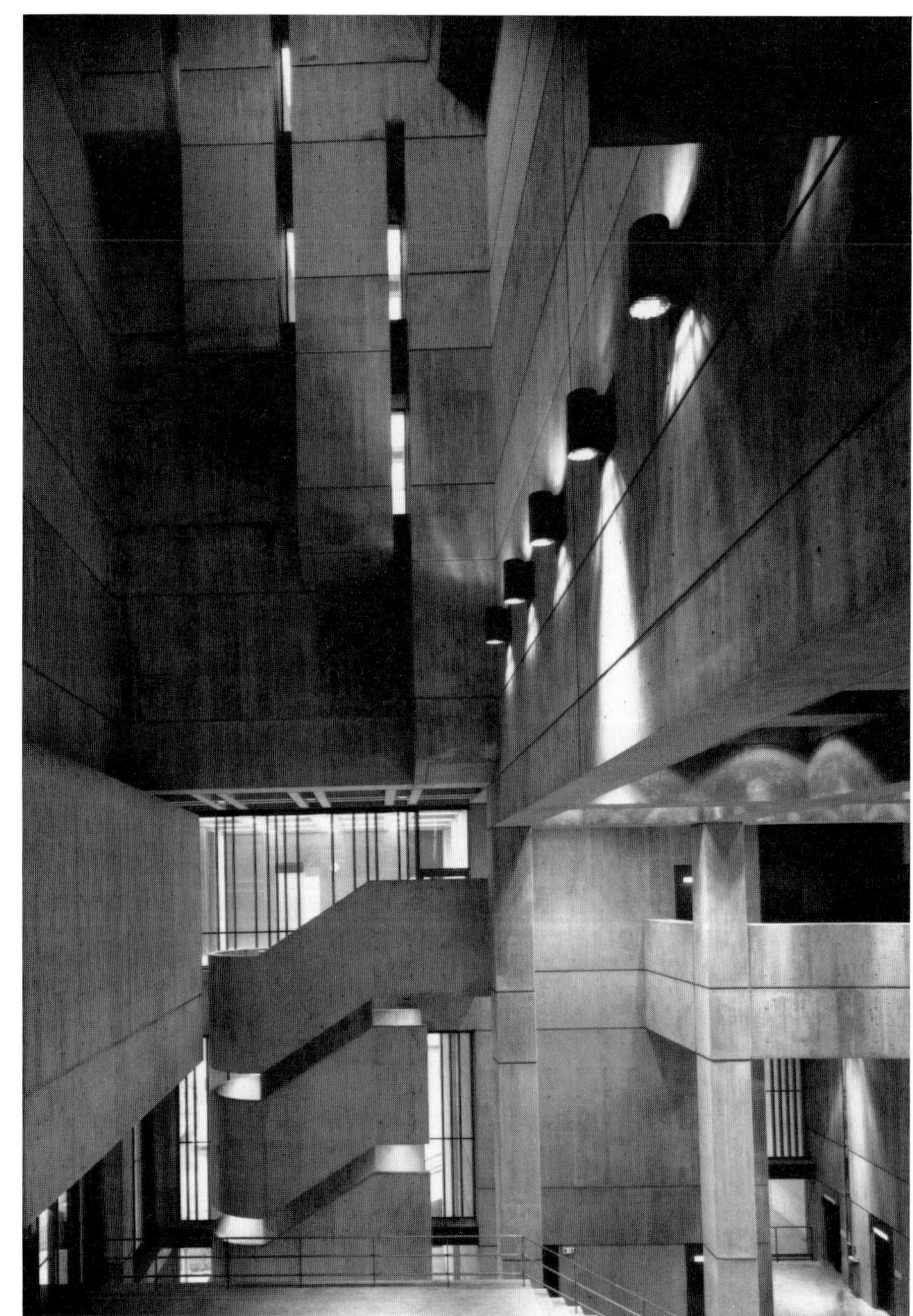

RIGHT: Kallman and McKinnell. Boston City Hall. Boston, Massachusetts, 1968 (courtesy of Ezra Stoller, copyright © ESTO).

FACING PAGE: Skidmore, Owings & Merrill. Oakland Coliseum. Oakland, California, 1968 (courtesy of Ezra Stoller, copyright © ESTO).

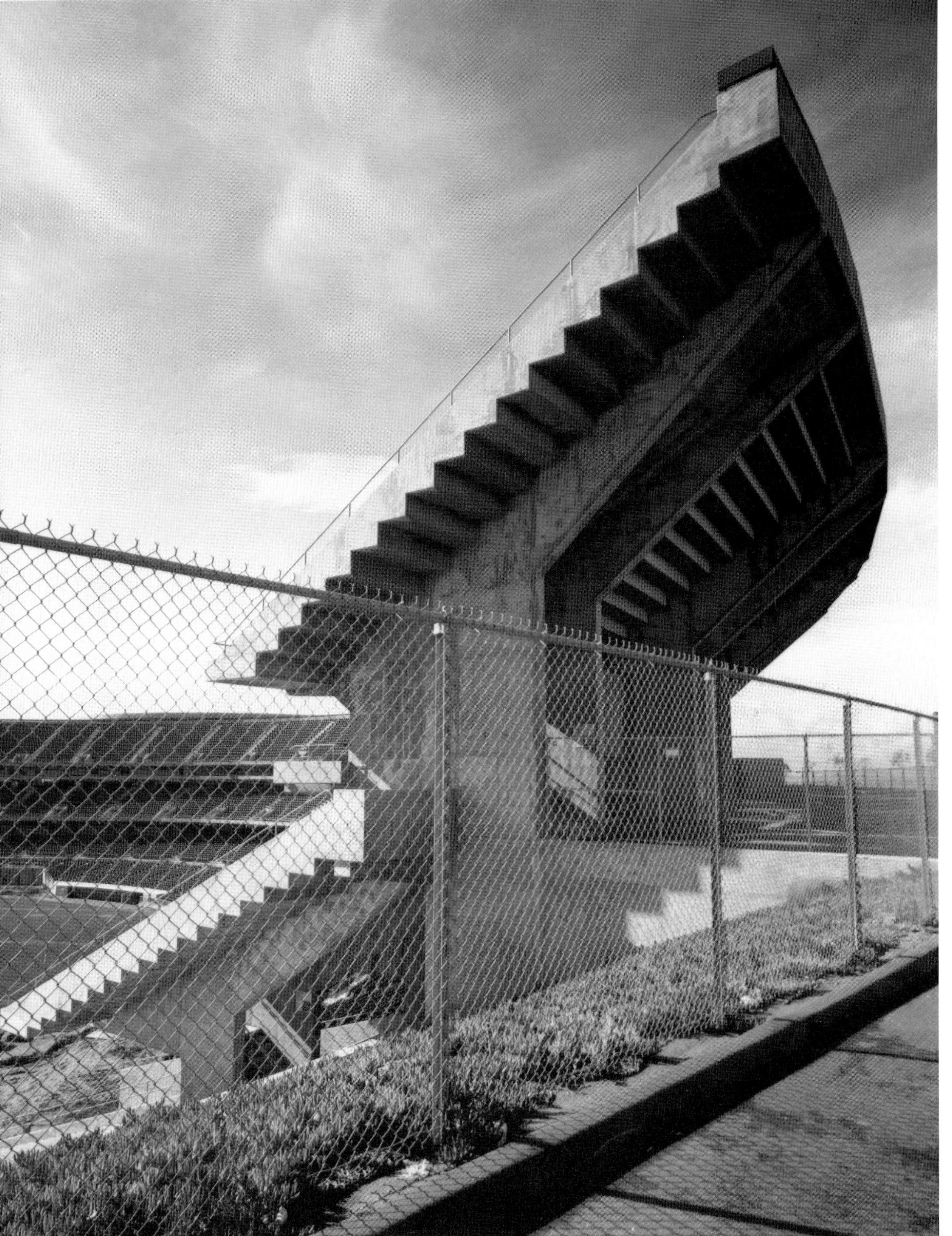

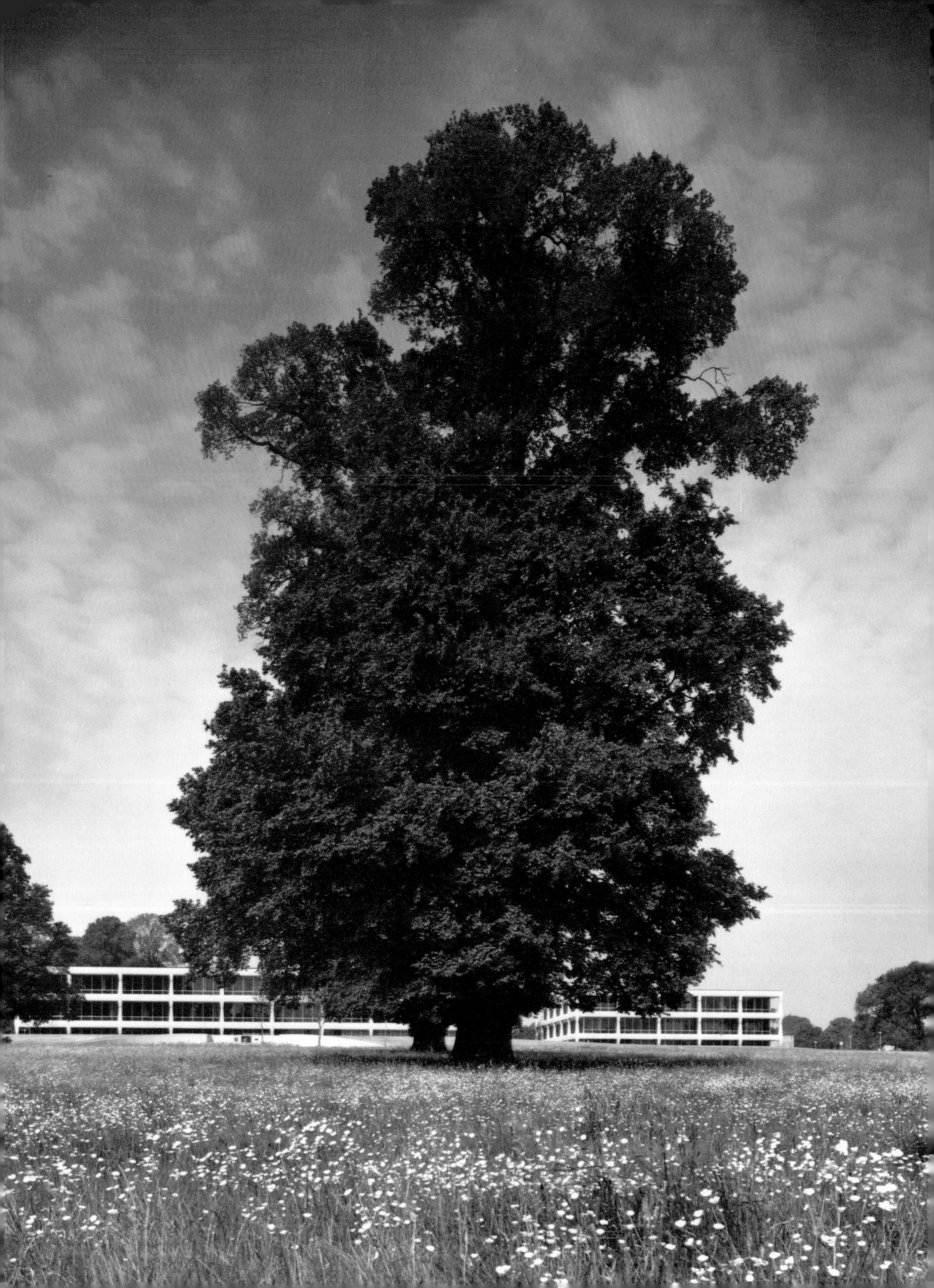

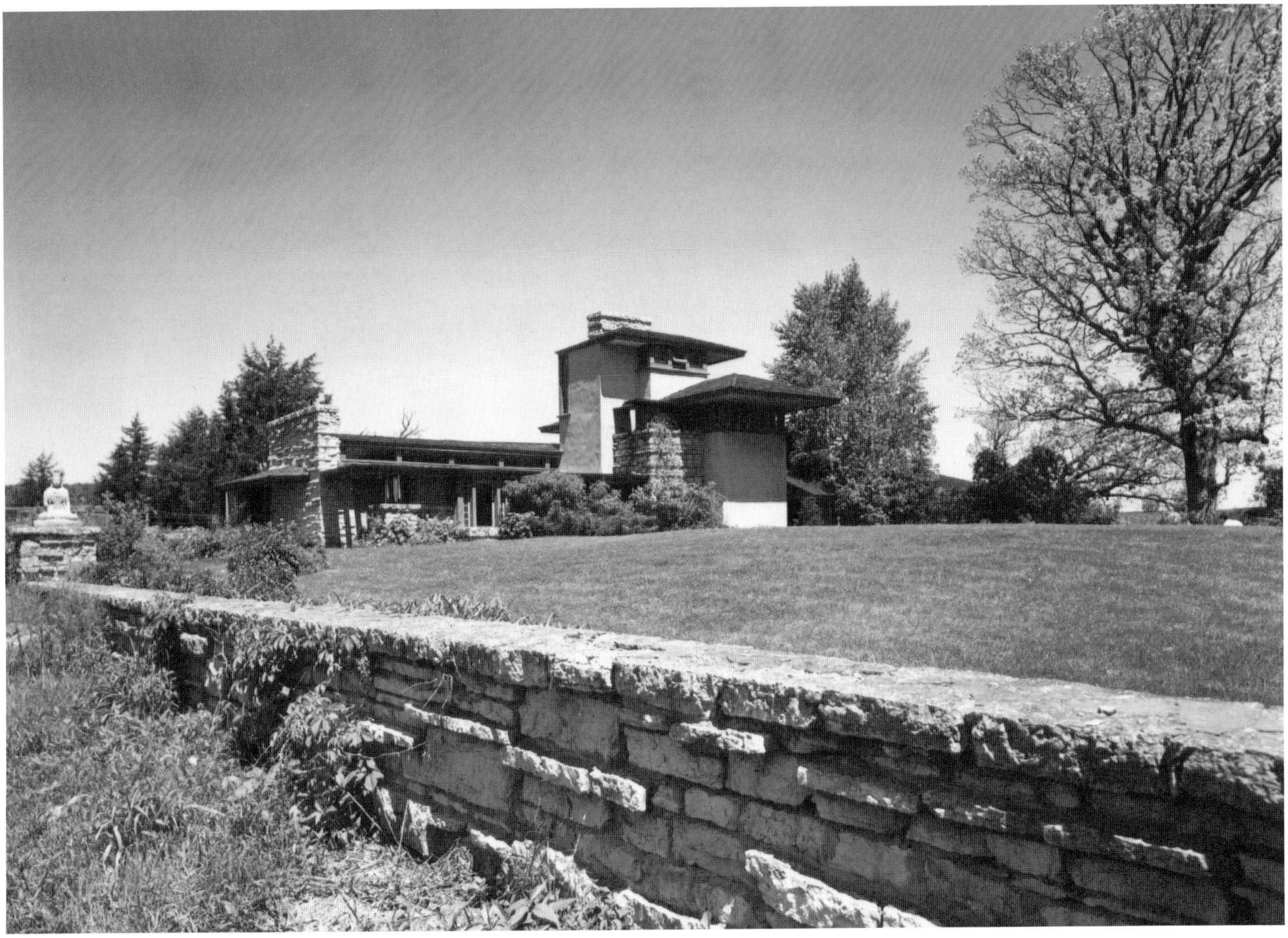

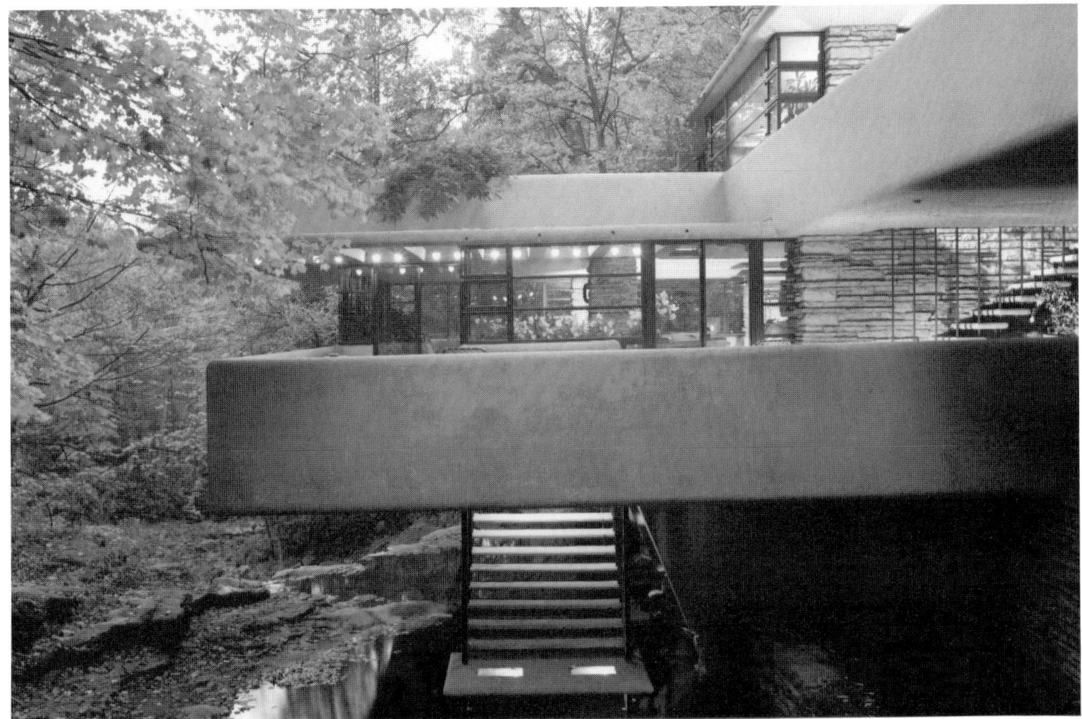

ABOVE: Frank Lloyd Wright. Taliesin East. Spring Green, Wisconsin, 1945 (courtesy of Ezra Stoller, copyright © ESTO).

LEFT: Frank Lloyd Wright. Fallingwater. Bear Run, Pennsylvania, 1963 (courtesy of Ezra Stoller, copyright © ESTO).

FACING PAGE: Skidmore, Owings & Merrill. H. J. Heinz Research Center and Office. England, 1965 (courtesy of Ezra Stoller, copyright © ESTO).

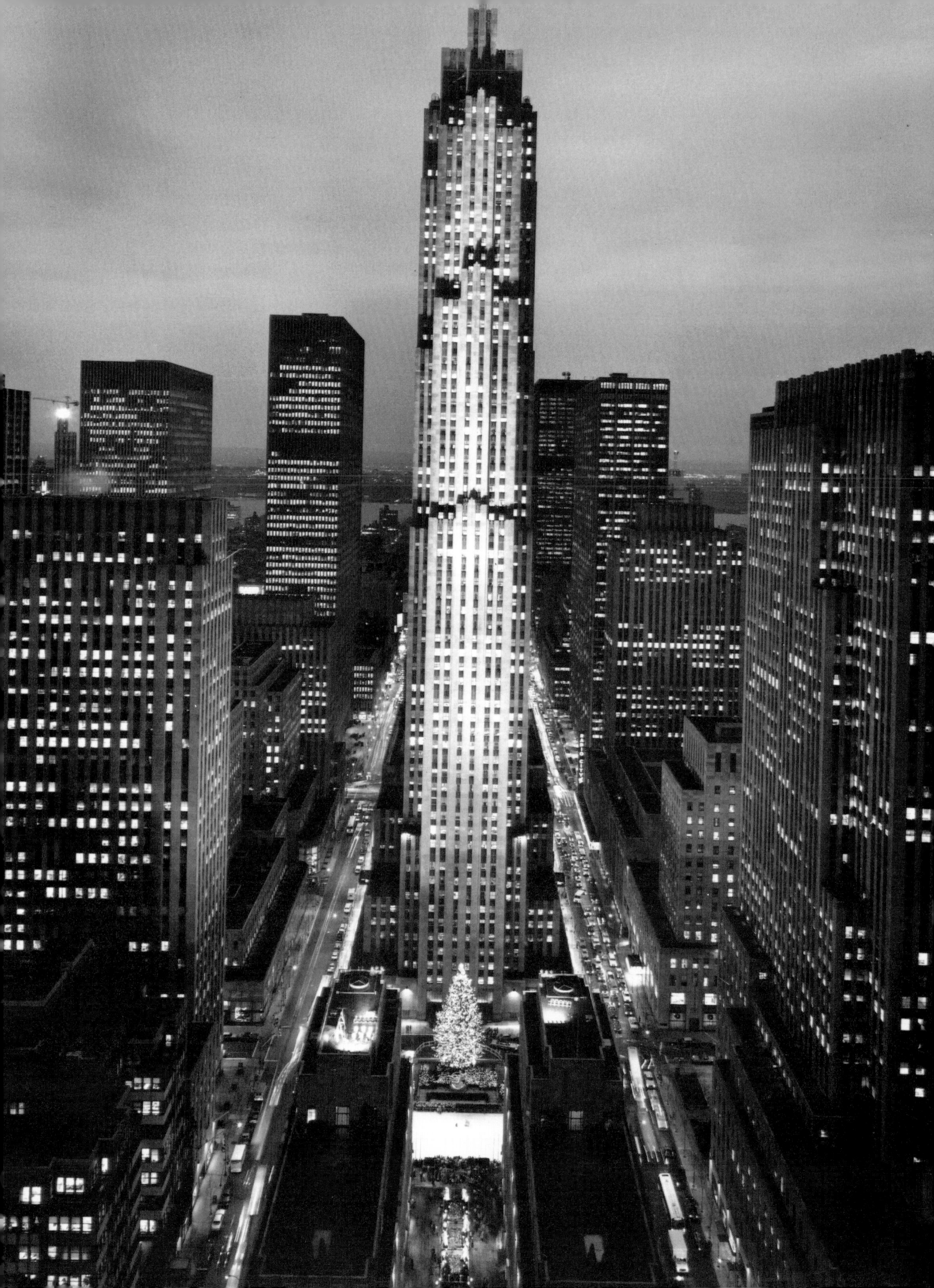

WOLFGANG HOYT

That ours is an image-conscious society is not news; more in this age than ever, how we learn, discover, and absorb facts has to do as much with our grasp of visual images as with more cognitive exercises. The downside to this visual sophistication, of course, is that it is often had only at the expense of our verbal literacy. We must see to believe; and if we are not to see the actual object, its image or icon will do. At least as important as the actual building is the image of the building, in the sense that it will be more publicized and seen by a far wider public.

"Unfortunately, though, a building is more than an image," says Wolfgang Hoyt. "An image is really only a two-dimensional piece of paper. I think it's important for people to walk the space, to see the building, to really feel it." This recognition or sensitivity to the fact that visual literacy can be costly is especially welcome from a photographer, himself an image maker. Hoyt's photographs are informed by the same sensitivity. Insofar as an image or photograph can help the viewer in the effort to know the space, rather than deter him from it, Hoyt's photographs do; they work to draw the viewer in, and through them, the viewer enters the space. Hoyt's photographs ask the viewer to feel the space rather than simply to observe it.

That Hoyt's photographs are spatial observations is not surprising, considering that his mentor and teacher, whom he still frequently works with, is Ezra Stoller. And like Stoller, Hoyt is drawn to architecture that is composed of space, volume, light. The flat, graphic quality of much postmodern architecture—"the light is only used to illuminate it, rather than define it"—leaves him with less provocative subject matter.

As important to Hoyt's work, however, is its record of context, and this is perhaps what distinguishes it. "Stoller, for the most part, photographed modern architecture," explains Hoyt. "And I think one of the great problems with modern architecture was that much of it was designed in a vacuum and didn't really pay attention to its context. So in a sense, it had to be photographed in a vacuum too. But in the last five or ten years, architects have been much more concerned with context, especially in cities."

Just as styles of architecture have evolved, so too have the approaches to photographing it. Modern architecture was more often than not a case of the pure object representing the pure vision. It asked to be taken for its forthright ideals

FACING PAGE: Reinhard & Hofmeister; Corbett, Harrison & MacMurray; Hood & Foulihoux, Architects. Rockefeller Center. New York, New York, 1984 (copyright © Wolfgang Hoyt/ESTO).

and, often, to accept it as such, the viewer removed it from its environment. The architecture that followed, however, has taken note of the oversights made by the International Style. Its lack of context was also, all too often, a lack of humanity. That these elements have been reinstalled in contemporary architecture demands that they also be documented in the photograph.

It is Hoyt's objective to convey the building in its entirety, and almost without exception, he has found that the photographic series rather than the single image does so most effectively. Especially if a building is forty or fifty stories high, he asks, how can you, from pedestrian level, possibly get any sense of it? The story is told, then, by a series of images that address: base level, middle, and top; its access and interior; architectural detail and overview; its relationship to its site, the skyline, and the other buildings surrounding it.

John Szarkowski, director of the department of photography at the Museum of Modern Art in New York City, has observed that it is frequently "a series of photographs [that] can convey a meaning greater than the sum of the individual images. The individual pictures of a photographic essay can be considered as sentences. Each should have clarity and precision of form, but their functions will vary profoundly. Some will define the problem and state the photographer's approach, some will be narrative, some fundamentally illustrative, some parenthetical and suggestive, some declamatory, and some will state conclusions. Some will stand as independent statements; others will be relatively meaningless out of context. The sequence in which these photographs appear is obviously important." [1]

Szarkowski's point is that unlike painting, in which the single image makes a complete statement, photography has more to do with the series of images and the effect made by their total. Images are seen in a sequence; one affects the other, and that one affects the next. The effect can be subtle and imperceptible, or it can be more dramatic. Nevertheless, the point is that images tend to work as a narrative to reveal the building sequentially. Hoyt clearly recognizes the value of this sequence. "I believe that one picture *can* become symbolic of a job," he says, "but it's difficult. It's hard to hit the nail on the head."

As well as being the most difficult photographs to take, symbolic images are also more difficult to judge. That is, unless the architecture is so clearly about one idea, and one idea only, representing it with a symbol is a subjective act that may lie closer to interpretation than documentation. The image or images may be powerful as formal abstractions but less so as notations of the actual architecture. "To do any kind of justice to the job," Hoyt observes, "you have to keep your objectivity. To keep from being bored, you approach each job with fresh eyes."

Because it is Hoyt's intent to locate architecture in its environment, it is not surprising that a substantial part of his work—20 percent—is model photography. Again, because its height and limited viewpoints can make urban architecture especially difficult to perceive as a whole, architectural models offer an alternative full view. A model permits perspectives, angles, and distances that the finished building, especially in an urban area, rarely allows. "You can walk around the model," says Hoyt, an option rarely open to viewers of the urban landscape. Through models, then, one can sense a totality of the building that may be less apparent in the finished product.

"Models are about the most difficult thing to photograph," he continues. "You use one light as the source, but then to highlight all the little facets, you use ten or fifteen smaller lights." And because a strong model photograph may be what sells the project to the developer, owner, board, and tenants, its role is often more important than finish photography.

As is often the case, Hoyt photographs both model and finished building, and the balance of model and exterior photography is a nurturing one. Photographing the model allows the photographer to become familiar with the angles, the lighting, the location of the building in its site. "Most buildings are built true to the model, so photographing it gives you a huge headstart." Likewise, exterior photography is likely to give the photographer a sense of how light and shadow will subtly alter the contours of the building, a valuable lesson in model photography, the lighting of which can all too often appear theatrical and contrived.

Hoyt shoots models, interiors, and exteriors in four-by-five, in color, and in black-and-white. Like many of his colleagues, he finds the 35mm camera "a snapshot camera." "A four-by-five," he explains, "makes you take the subject more seriously. The simple process of setting up the shot takes more time, and it's time that makes you observe more closely." Add to this its perspective control capabilities and larger format, and the photographs that emerge are likely to be studied portraits. Such scrutiny is apparent in the photographs, which themselves imply a sense of persistence. Hoyt's architectural observations have a certain tenacity to them; the lighting and, very often, the angle from which a building is recorded suggest that the photographer waited long hours for light and shadow to compose themselves or searched far for the appropriate window or ledge from which to shoot.

Nevertheless, the photographer's efforts are not in the picture; his ego and stamina remain well out of the frame. These are portraits, rather, that let the presence of the building speak for itself. As architect Jim Bodner at Skidmore, Owings and Merrill says, "Hoyt works from a modern point of view. His images are abstract and geometric rather than painterly." And indeed there is nothing romantic or sentimental in the work. It is controlled, precise, communicating clearly the facts of the architecture. "Hoyt shoots a tight photograph," says Bodner. "The edges are sharply defined; the composition is complete. You get a complete image. What's in the frame is balanced." [2]

Architecture has surely become more accessible in recent years. It invites a greater public. International Style architecture has undeniably left an imprint of elitism. While Le Corbusier's idea of the house as a "machine for living" certainly had a democratic ring to it, the polemics behind it were not necessarily understood, nor meant to be understood, by any greater public. While postmodern architecture has been often denounced for its banalities, lack of substance, and surface flash, its recognition of human interest and appeal cannot be denied. Whatever else its color, ornamentation, and decorative surfaces have brought to the built world, they have also brought a new warmth and human interest.

"I think it's true that Philip Johnson has done more for architecture than almost any other architect, in the sense that he brought it into people's living rooms," says Hoyt. "I like this idea of architecture being brought to the public." And while he continues to suggest that history may overlook much of postmodern architecture, he also suggests that it *will* take greater note of an approach to building that puts a higher value on accommodation, assimilation, context. "It's nice for me to see people having this contact with architecture," he concludes.

That Hoyt enjoys this sense of contact, and his not insignificant role in it, is clear in the photographs. "Hoyt has that rare quality to perceive what the architect perceives," says Bodner. "But he also has a strong, photographic eye, an intuitive eye for angles, framing, composition, for the geometry of a building. And it is the marriage of these two perceptions, the architectural and the photographic, that makes his work so valuable." [3] If architecture is accessible to a greater public, it is in large part due to the photographers who bring it to the public, to its carriers as it were. Hoyt's approach to documenting architecture balances his enjoyment in doing so with the responsibility that comes with it.

While Wolfgang Hoyt's work is surely the synthesis of photographic and architectural perceptions, it is also a bridge between two different ways of recording architectural ideas. As a student of Stoller's, Hoyt is accomplished at finding the facts of the building and presenting them clearly, knowledgeably, gracefully. But as a member of a different generation, he has also suggested new ideas. He is likely to locate the building in its context; its site, occupancy, and literal and figurative climate are likely to be recorded as well. That Hoyt has acknowledged and synthesized both views is perhaps a mark of his skill and complexity.

---

1. John Szarkowski, "Photographing Architecture," *Archetype,* vol. 2, no. 2 (Spring 1981), p.10.
2. Conversation with author, April 1985.
3. Ibid.

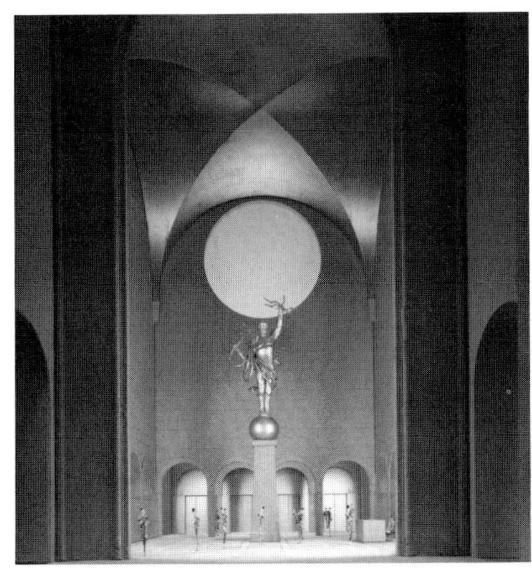

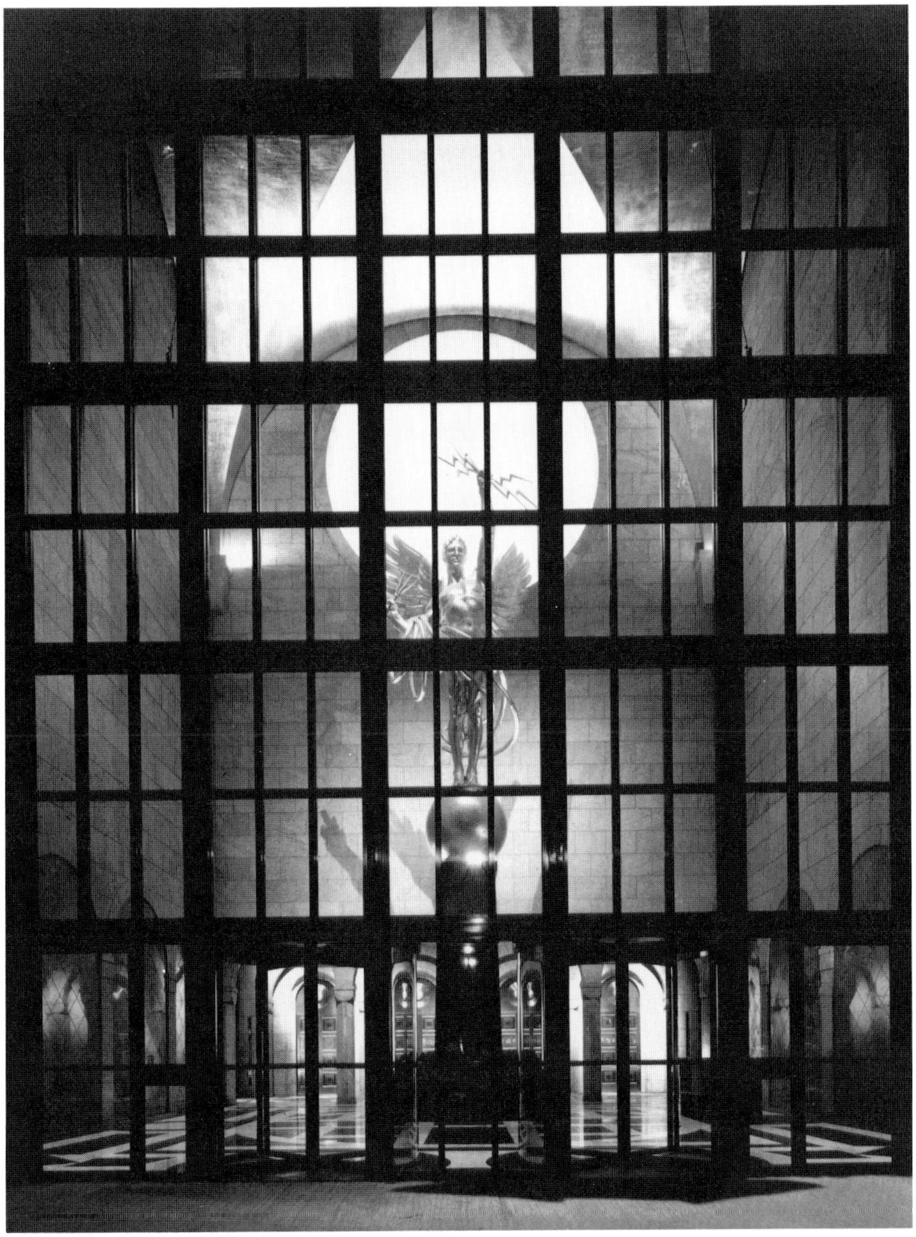

ABOVE: Johnson-Burgee Architects. AT&T Study Model. New York, New York, 1980 (copyright © Wolfgang Hoyt/ESTO).

LEFT: Johnson-Burgee Architects. AT&T Building. New York, New York, 1983 (copyright © Wolfgang Hoyt/ESTO).

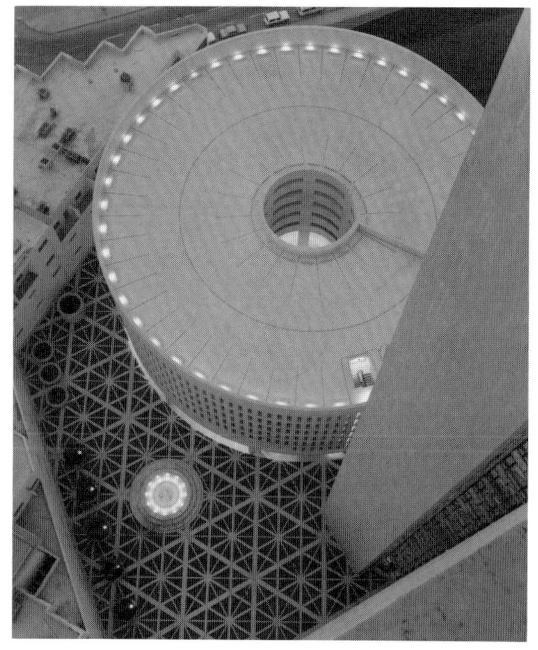

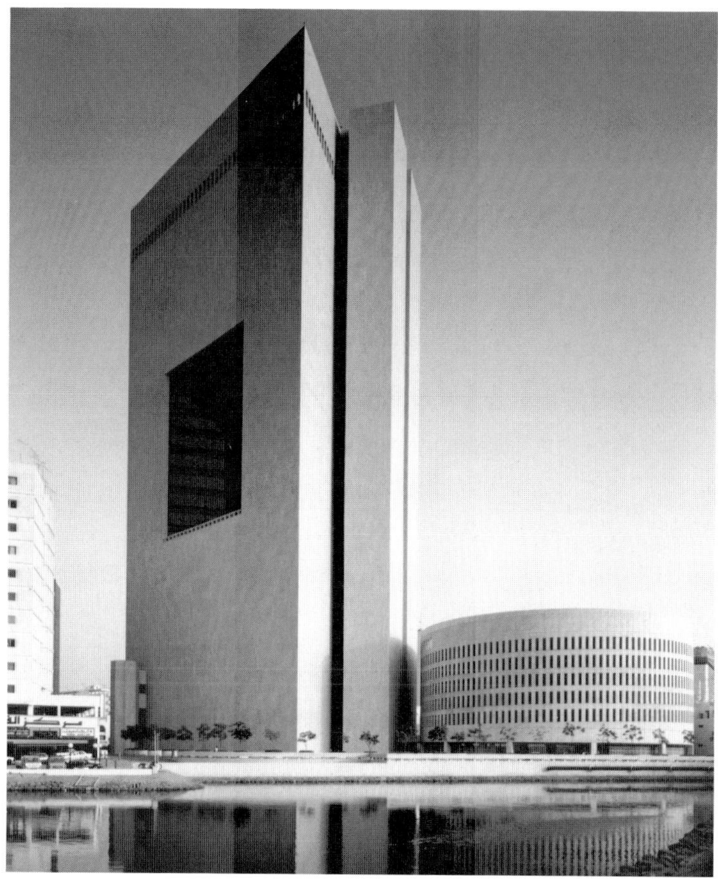

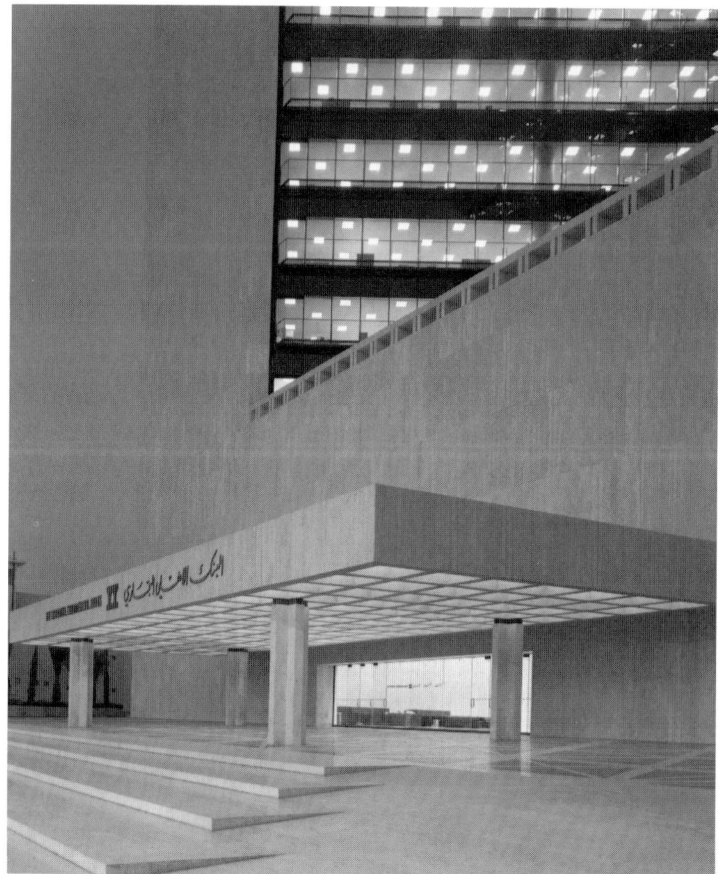

Skidmore, Owings & Merrill. National Commercial Bank. Jeddah, Saudi Arabia, 1984 (copyright © Wolfgang Hoyt/ESTO).

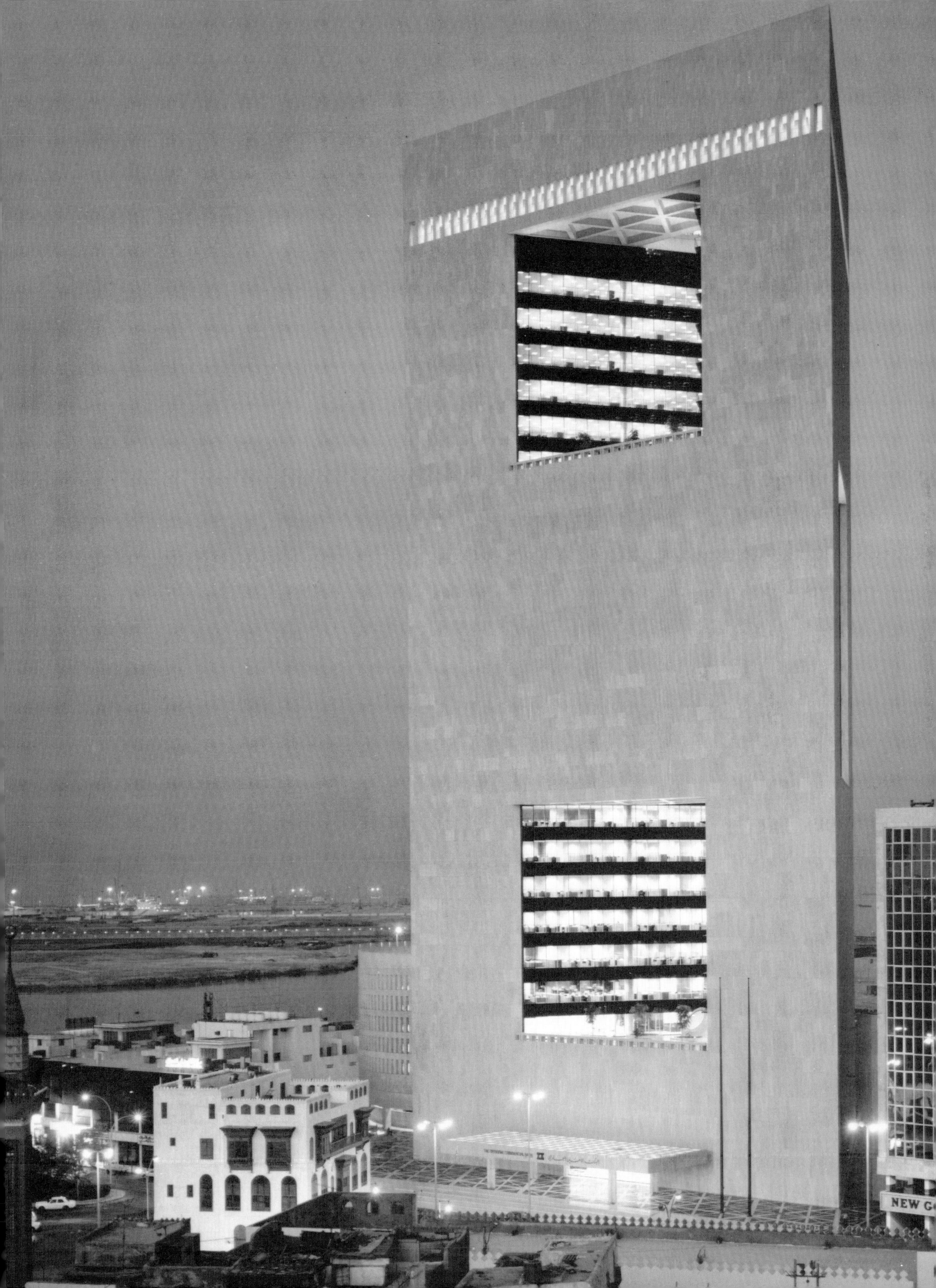
NEW G

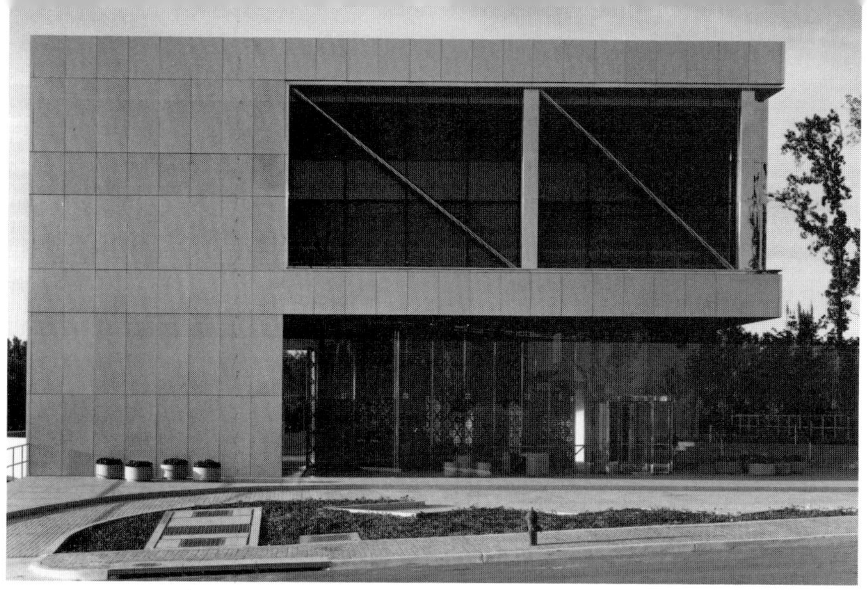

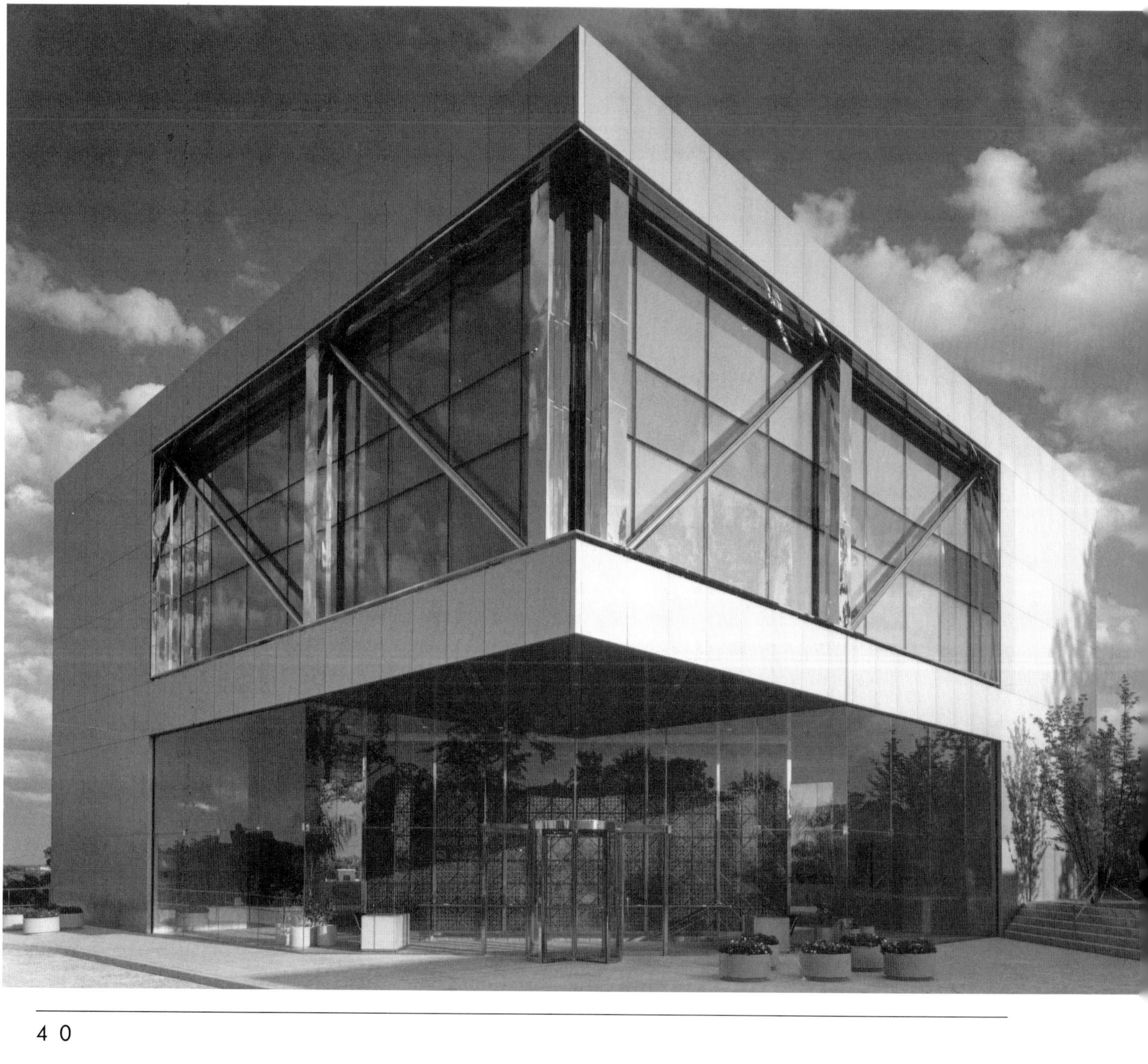

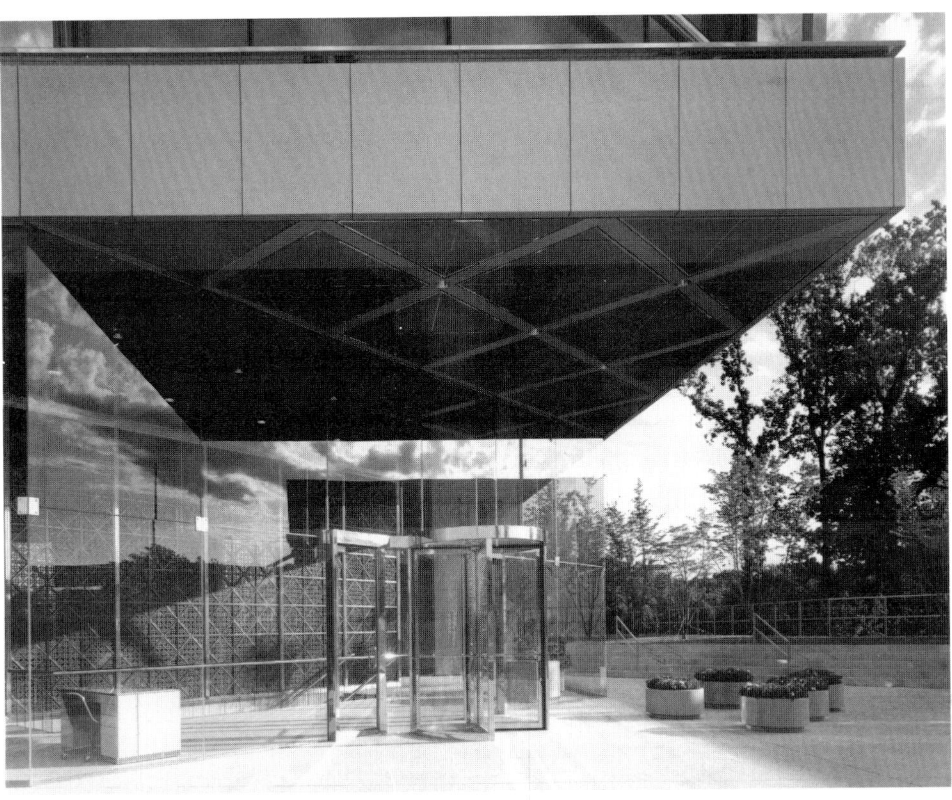

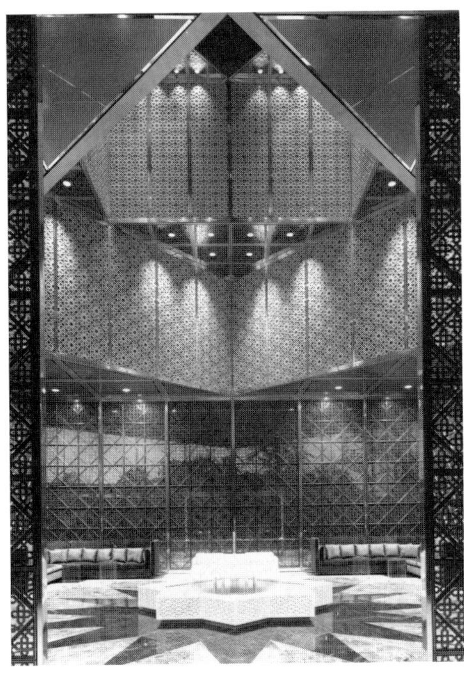

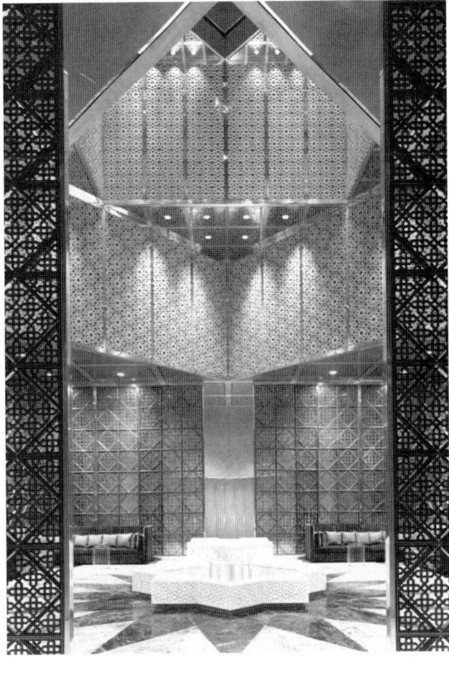

Skidmore, Owings & Merrill. Kuwait Chancery. Washington, D.C., 1982 (copyright © Wolfgang Hoyt/ESTO).

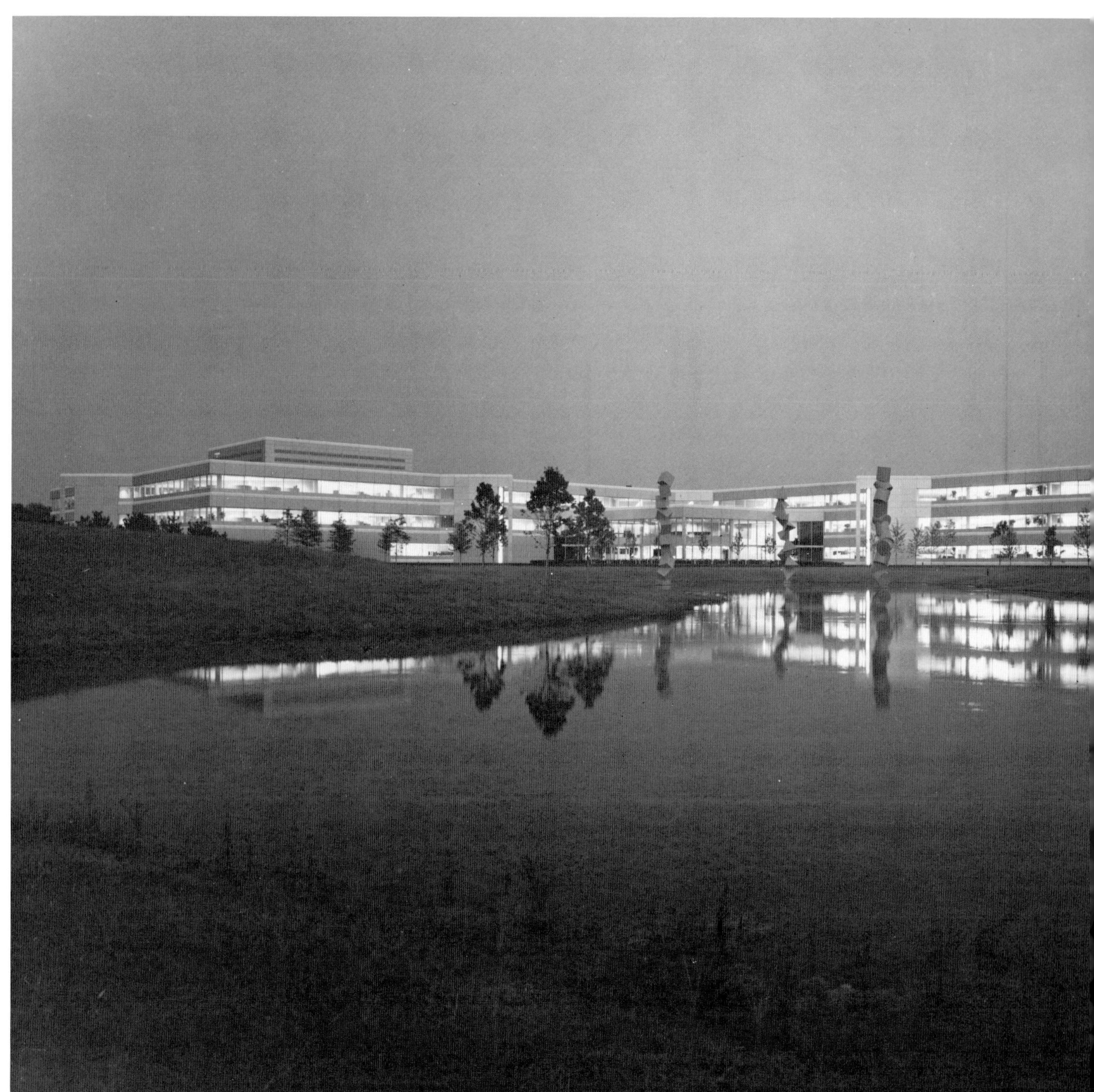

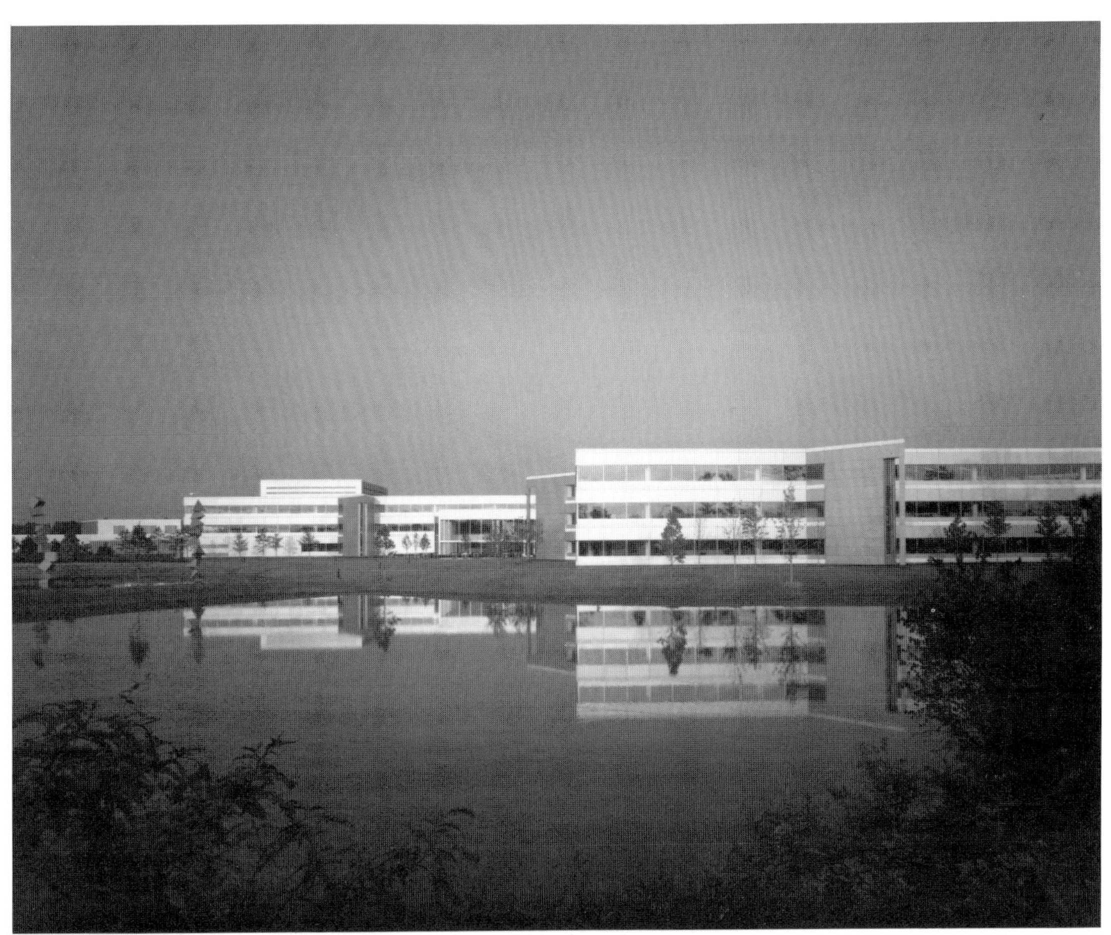

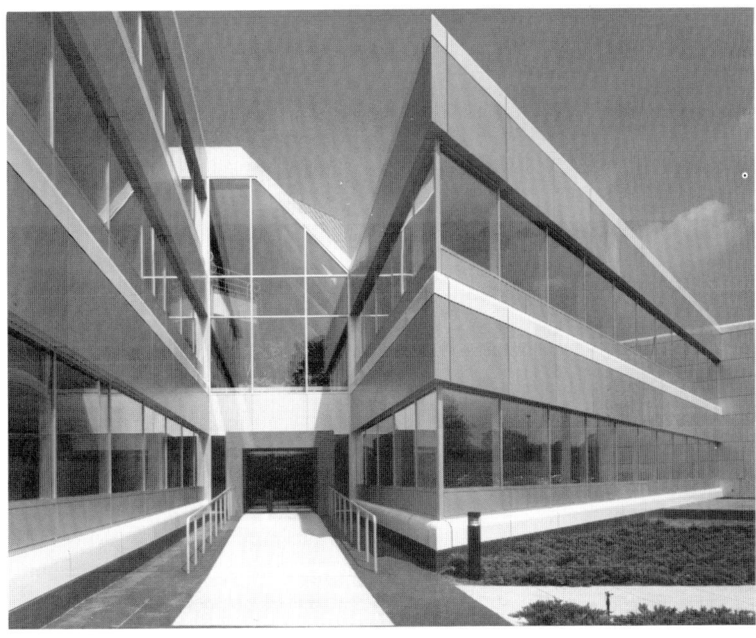

Davis, Brody and Associates. Philip Morris U.S.A. Operations Center. Richmond, Virginia, 1982 (copyright © Wolfgang Hoyt/ESTO).

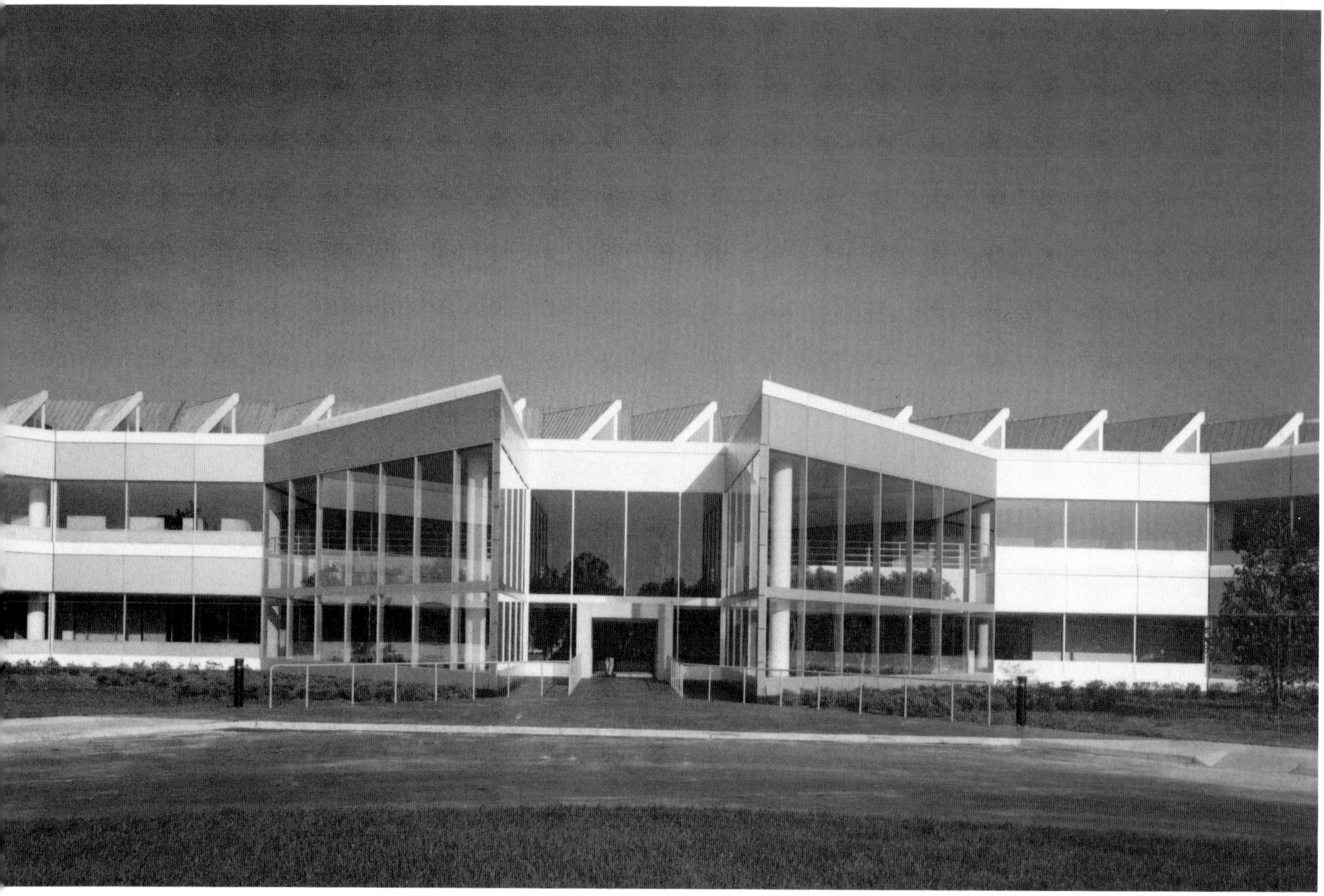

Davis, Brody and Associates. Philip Morris U.S.A. Operations Center. Richmond, Virginia, 1982 (copyright © Wolfgang Hoyt/ESTO).

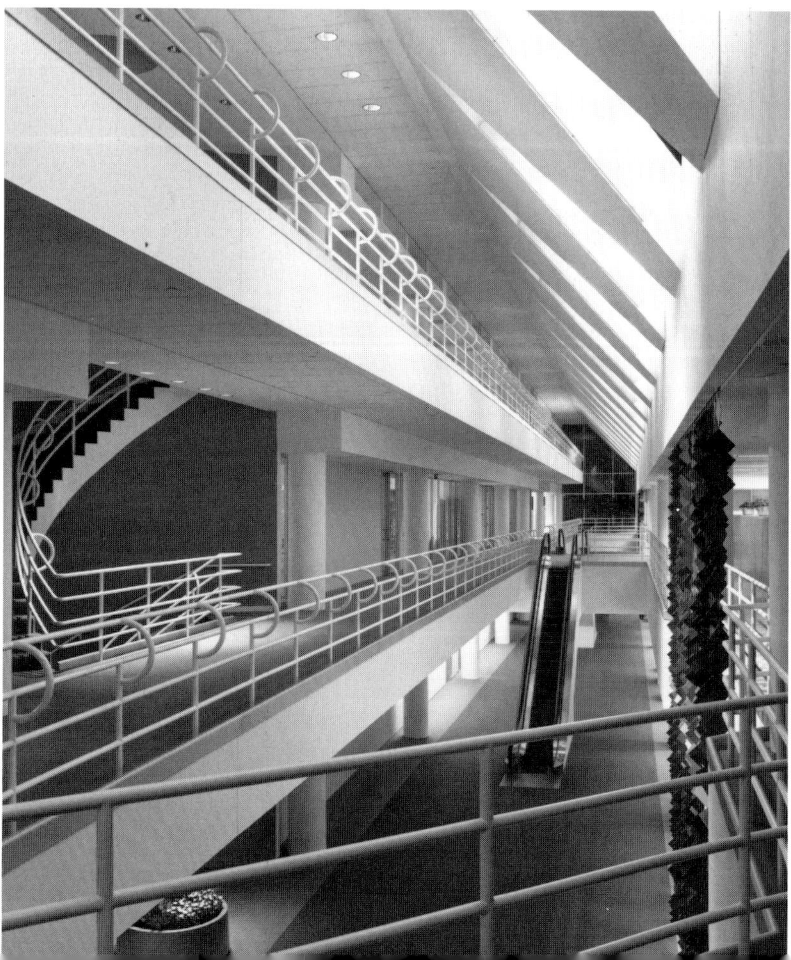

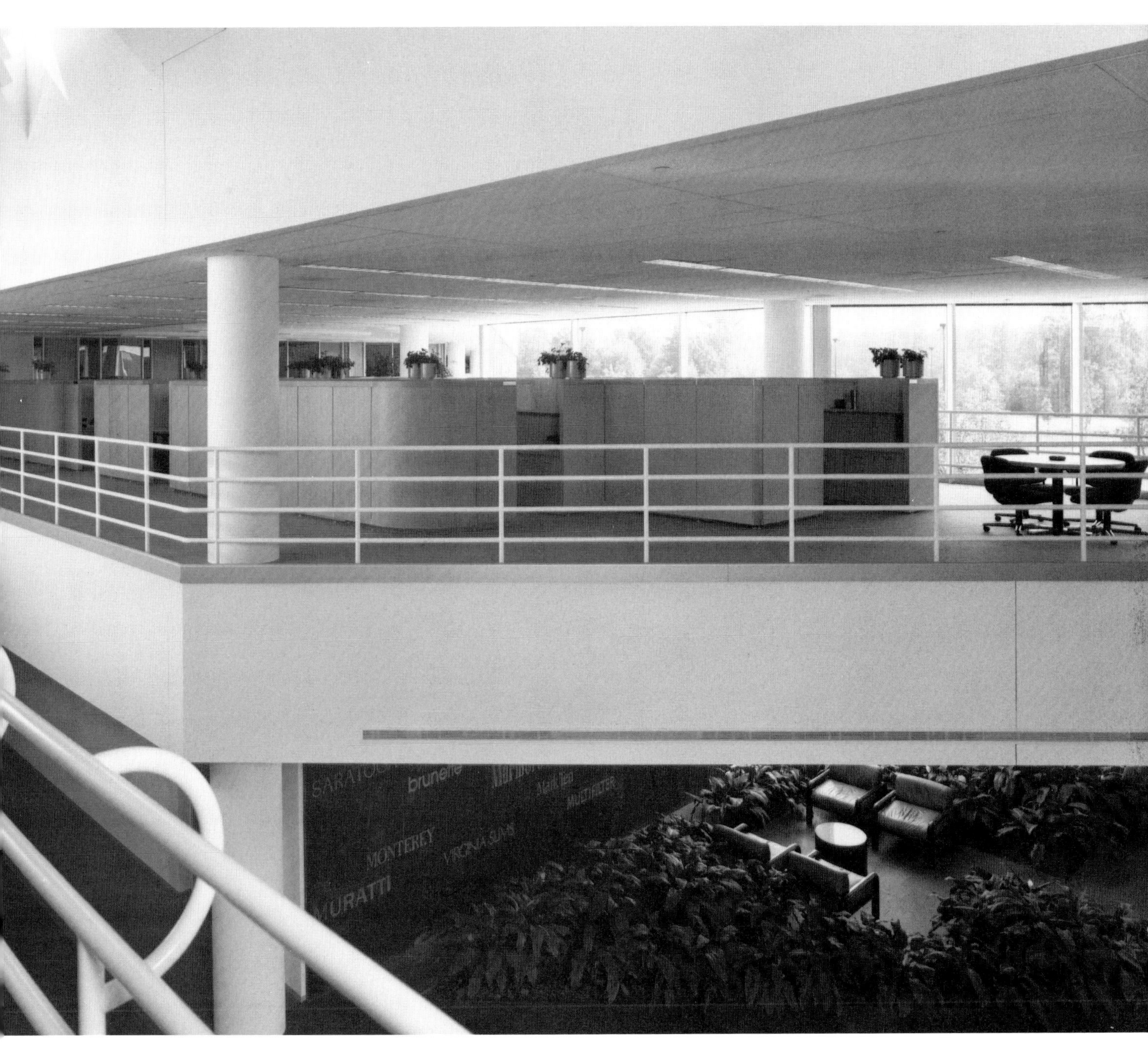
MONTEREY
VIRGINIA SLIMS
MURATTI

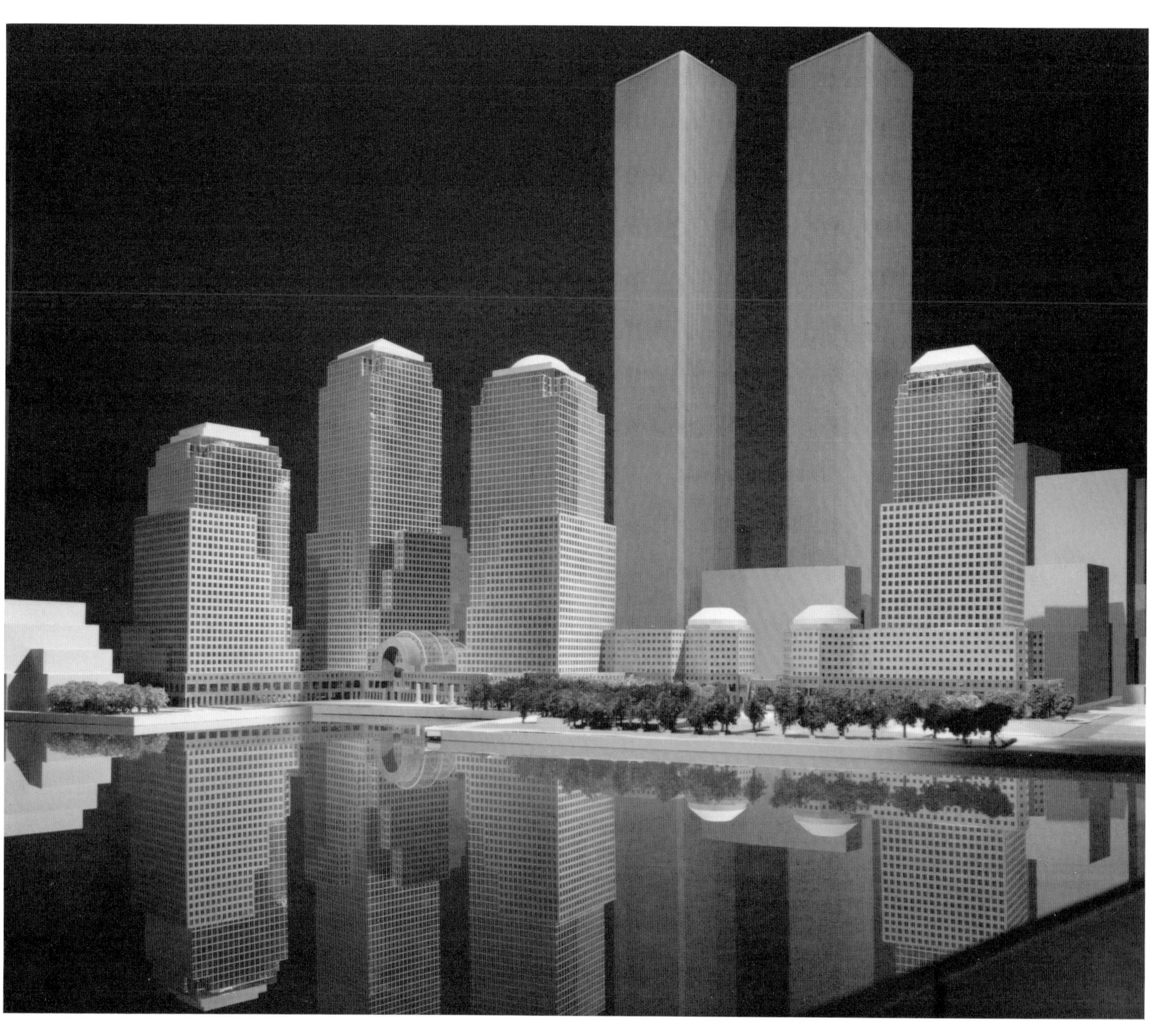

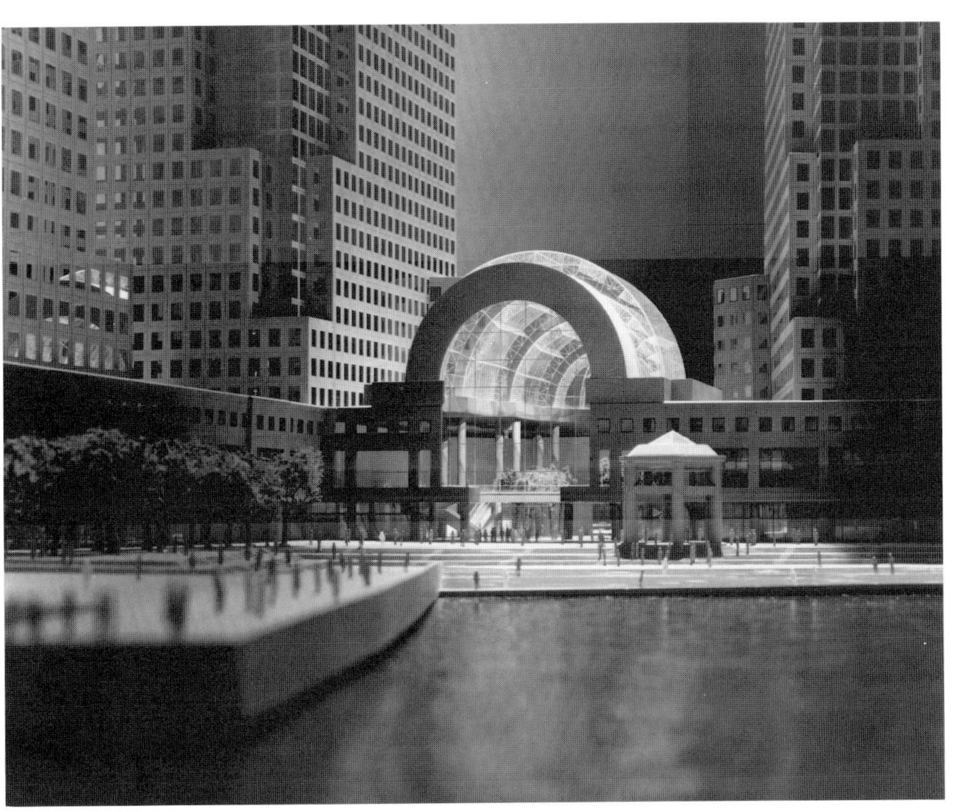

Cesar Pelli and Associates. Model for Battery Park City, World Financial Center. New York, New York, 1981. (copyright © Wolfgang Hoyt/ESTO).

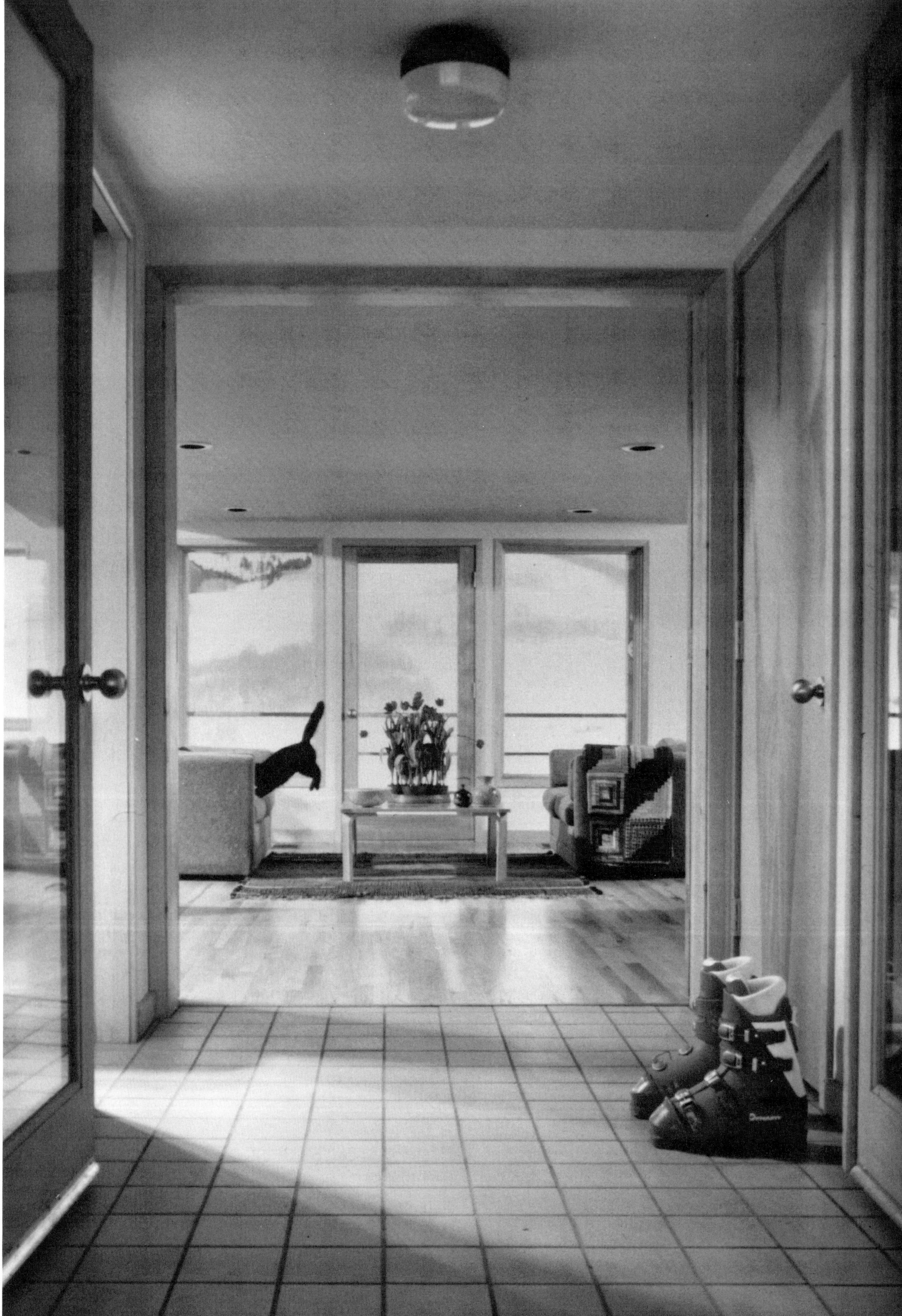

PETER AARON

While seven-eighths of our perceptions come through sight, the issue of lighting, the single most important factor that determines *how* we see, remains relatively obscure. Architects and designers know as well as theater designers that lighting can evoke a spectrum of moods as varied as its own—feelings of tranquility and relaxation, anxiety and apprehension can be reinforced, if not actually induced, by the lighting of a room as well as of a stage. Functional, emotional, and psychological, lighting is an imprecise science and until recently has tended to remain exactly that in its architectural applications. Recent technology, however, has brought new light—a wider range of fluorescents, tungsten-halogen, and mercury vapor sources—to the surface and space of contemporary architecture and design, and how the increasing variety of available light sources are chosen and put together do much to determine the final design of an interior.

Visually recording the subtle effects of light, by nature impalpable and elusive, is as difficult as defining them in the first place. Yet if architectural space can be structured with a substance so immaterial, the surface of a piece of film, marked by light and its absence, is surely the ideal medium for its expression. Just as an architect may structure his building with columns of light, photographer Peter Aaron composes his photographs with light.

A graduate of New York University's film school, Aaron manipulates light in his interior landscapes more as a cinematographer than still photographer. Studio photography, he points out, requires soft light augmented by strobes; lighting for film and interiors is made effective through multiple light sources and, rather than additional strobes, uses incandescent lights. It is these multiple light sources and their varied effects on space that Aaron transcribes so precisely. His visual documentation of architecture often suggests that the space has been structured by light, rather than by the more material elements that we conventionally think of as shaping space.

It is not only Aaron's handling of light that reflects a background in cinematography, but how he records architectural space. Although buildings themselves may move only under extreme circumstances, the spaces in a building connect and separate, flow and remain static. While the photography of an interior may technically be still photography, the grasp of how spaces form and interconnect can exploit the technical skills used in filmmaking. It is this sense of spatial movement

FACING PAGE: Nagle, Hartray and Associates. Salzman House. Crested Butte, Colorado, 1982 (copyright © Peter Aaron/ESTO).

that architectural photography shares with film, and one that Aaron recognizes, both intuitively and through formal training as a cinematographer.

Aaron turned to architectural photography after leaving film school to find work in the field of documentary-filmmaking limited; he recognized architectural photography as a profession demanding similar skills in the manipulation of light and composition. Aaron's subsequent apprenticeship with Ezra Stoller is clear both in his approach and in the final visual document; like Stoller, his intent is to represent the architect's intent, "to give an absolutely true impression of what's there." While his manipulation of light may be complex, its purpose is simply to reproduce on film what the architect installed in the building. And like Stoller, Aaron puts a high value on the photographer/architect relationship; establishing the trust of the architect is necessary to an understanding of the building. Which is not to say that he prefers to work on the site with the architect. Aaron suggests that architects tend to "see in three dimensions much better than they see in two —they're trying to capture in photographs things that cannot be seen well in two dimensions. Once I've established a working plan, I like to be left on my own. But this is only after we've reached this mutual trust."

To observe for himself what can be seen well in two dimensions, Aaron spends the first hours on a shoot simply observing the space, methodically apprais-ing its surfaces and structures and the way they are defined by light. His study of floor plans, building plans, and models determines the time of day that will yield the light most appropriate for the few angles the photographs will finally be shot from, and only then does he unpack his cameras. "Photographing requires seeing and if you just begin to shoot, you may not really see things. I delay the pictures until I feel I understand the space."

When Aaron is talking about understanding the space, he is talking about understanding the light. And understanding existing light is the keystone in Aa-ron's approach. Because it is his purpose to preserve the lighting specified by architect or designer, he is reluctant to use strobes or electronic flashes, the inten-sity of which tends to blanket the area and overpower the subtler effects that softer lighting may have on surface texture. "Strobes are very powerful and elusive light sources," he explains, "and if there's any way to shoot a space without them, I will."

Instead, to record the multiple light sources that the architect has often specified, and their subtle and diverse effects on the space, Aaron relies on a number of methods. Frequently, light sources are isolated and filtered indepen-dently. Especially in much recent postmodern architecture, in which the variety of light sources may include daylight, incandescent, fluorescent, and tungsten light sources (all of which are rarely compatible with one another, much less with the equal variety of subtle color tones on the surfaces surrounding them), separate exposures are the only means by which to convey an accurate impression. Fre-quently, a black cloth is hung over windows, and the space is photographed as though it were night; afterward the cloth is removed, and the same piece of film is reexposed with daylight. Another method simply makes the most of available light, using it when it is the brightest and eliminating the need for additional lighting. And the last is simply to shoot the space at night, eliminating the use of daylight altogether. While these methods themselves may not be so unconventional, what *is* unconventional is that Aaron determines which will be most effective without using a light meter, gauging the intensity and impact of light with his eye.

Aaron's compositions are also frequently distinguished by elevational angles in which the camera is parallel to the room. Ceiling and floor lines appear as horizontals at the top and bottom of the frame, and side walls are vertical parallels at the edges of the frame. Balance and composure are implicit in an elevational photograph. There is a sense of control and a stillness to them. Information is found and revealed quietly in layers. The viewer is drawn into the photograph through its various strata: a step leads to a doorway where they may be a table with a small still life, beyond which, perhaps, are a window and trees. Information is reported as a sequence. Direct shots such as these tend to give the facts in a straightforward way without distorting scale, a risk often run by diagonal compositions. And while the composition is symmetrical, it is a symmetry appropriate for contemporary architecture, much of which has as its trademark a graphic, almost two-dimensional presentation of space. Symmetrical itself, a balanced and equally symmetrical composition that mirrors the space as a series of layers seen head-on can be the most precise way to document it.

Architect Edward I. Mills of Voorsanger and Mills Associates in New York values Aaron's compositions for this directness and honesty. "These interior shots are the difficult ones," he explains. "In an exterior shot, the volume or the mass is able to complete itself. But an interior shot is never quite complete in that one ingredient—the wall behind you—is always missing. So it's far more difficult in interior shots to get a sense of the space as a whole." [1] One device Aaron uses to convey the space in its entirety, Mills suggests, is his use of a spatial foreground that introduces the viewer to the space. Rather than delineate the bottom edge of the photograph with objects—that, while adding to the composition of the photograph, might nevertheless obscure sight lines—Aaron tends to leave the expanse blank, a visual signal for the viewer to enter. "This makes for a clarity, a crispness to the work," concludes Mills.

That Aaron's compositions appear to have an almost painterly quality also reflects his background in film. While the foreground of Aaron's interiors may rarely be defined by objects, small still lifes do momentarily hold the eye there. A pair of boots, a table with a book, or pieces of decorative molding set in the foreground work to anchor the eye. Carefully composed, they suggest an interior landscape that is, again, layered. Says architect John Belle of the New York architectural firm Beyer Blinder Belle, "Aaron's photographs establish a clear relationship between objects in the foreground and those in the background. One takes you directly to the other." [2] And indeed, the photographs have been composed in such a way that the eye is drawn from front to rear, approaching the layers almost systematically. In the foreground of a photograph taken of the renovation of the New York Public Library, a sawhorse, broom, some old wires and hoses, and buckets compose a still life with a lyric presence of its own. Lesser stories or tableaus exist within the larger framework, an evocative framing device often used by cinematographers. Aaron is accompanied on sites by his associate Steven Horvath, whose background in painting and art history has contributed and helped to shape the painterly compositions of these interior still lifes.

Also evidence of Aaron's background in film is the ease with which he photographs people. While he admits to the obvious problems—"People move, which can be a problem in minute-and-a-half exposures, and the poses they strike can be awkward"—he is not reluctant to integrate people into architectural documentation. Not only does he photograph people for the more conventional purposes of outlining the use of a space or evoking a sense of its occupancy, but he is also prone to exploit the human figure for a more sculptural effect. In Aaron's photographs, the human form is not the mundane distraction it might easily become, but a more lyrical visual anchor or focus. A model's graceful slouch or a bystander's erect posture become pictorial elements in themselves, often bordering on the abstract. Likewise, an elevation photograph of a living room captures a cat leaping onto a sofa; while lighthearted and whimsical, the shape of the cat does not necessarily diminish the elegance of the space, but rather, adds a somewhat bizarre twist, a provocative juxtaposition to the otherwise austere lines of the room.

Aaron's skill in transcribing light and composing the details of quiet interior still lifes often yields photographs that have an esthetic merit of their own. That they are documents of architecture is not the only point they have to make. Often, they go beyond their utilitarianism to stand on their own esthetics as well as to reveal those of the building. While many of his colleagues hold that a beautiful photograph is the inadvertent by-product rather than purpose of an architectural photograph, Aaron states, "I'm proud of my work and feel it has as much merit as a good building. I'd like the photograph to be beautiful enough to be worthy of hanging on the wall, representing me as an artist as well as representing the building." Edward Mills concurs: "Aaron doesn't take details or oblique shots that simply dramatize the space without giving you any information about it. But by trying to explain the space, he often ends up with a beautiful photograph. In his work, you often have both." [3]

Photography of the nineteenth century reflected traditions of the painted canvas. Photographers, if they had not actually been painters, drew on conventions that had been established in drawing and painting. Contemporary photography is no more likely to exist in a vacuum, and one of the other mediums it most clearly acknowledges is cinematography, hardly surprising considering the technical kinship. It is a relationship that Aaron's photographs illustrate both in their studies of light and composition, and in their more subtle suggestion that architecture exists in a continuum. A building is not static, but a place in which people live and carry out their lives. While it is in the nature of film to take the viewer from one frame to another, Aaron's photographs suggest a similar continuum, a life outside the frame. Mills notes that there is a clear difference between the way photographer and architect perceive space: "An architect thinks of space as something expanding, and deals with it as something dynamic and functional. Its layering is sequential. A photographer is more likely to think of this layering in terms of composition. It tends to be more static. What is unusual about Aaron's work is that it can convey both." [4]

Likewise, architect John Belle observes that Aaron's work recognizes both a geographical and historical context. A private interest in historic preservation has led Aaron to document buildings before and during their restoration, and as Belle points out, "His interest and observations of architectural history give him a broader understanding. Rather than separating the architecture in the photograph, he clearly sets it in its context. It is a sense of continuity that he has refined in his formal training as a cinematographer." [5]

"The greatest compliment I've ever received," says Aaron, "is when someone tells me 'I've seen this room a hundred times, but I've never seen it like this.' " And this, perhaps, is the architectural photographer at his best, giving the viewer new eyes and a new way of seeing. With his innate understanding of light and how it creates its own space, structure, and surface, and his eye for composition, Aaron indeed frequently enables the viewer to see the space in a new way. More importantly, by observing architecture in a sense of continuum—both in the smaller physical spaces it contains and in the greater geographical and historical context by which it is contained itself—Aaron's photographs give us not only new eyes, but a larger, more total sensibility of architecture.

---

1. Conversation with author, May 1985.
2. Conversation with author, May 1985.
3. Conversation with author, May 1985.
4. Ibid.
5. Conversation with author, May 1985.

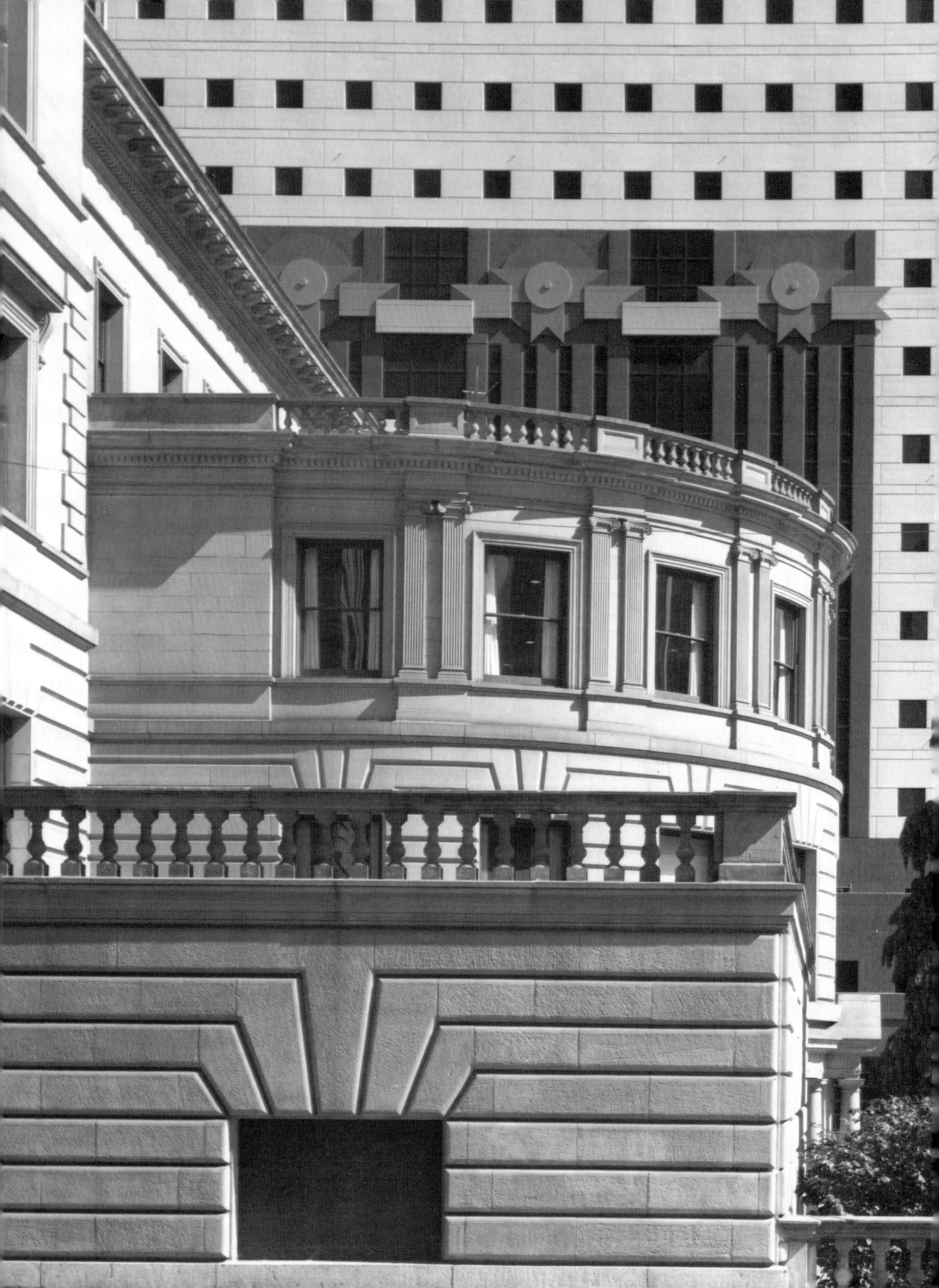

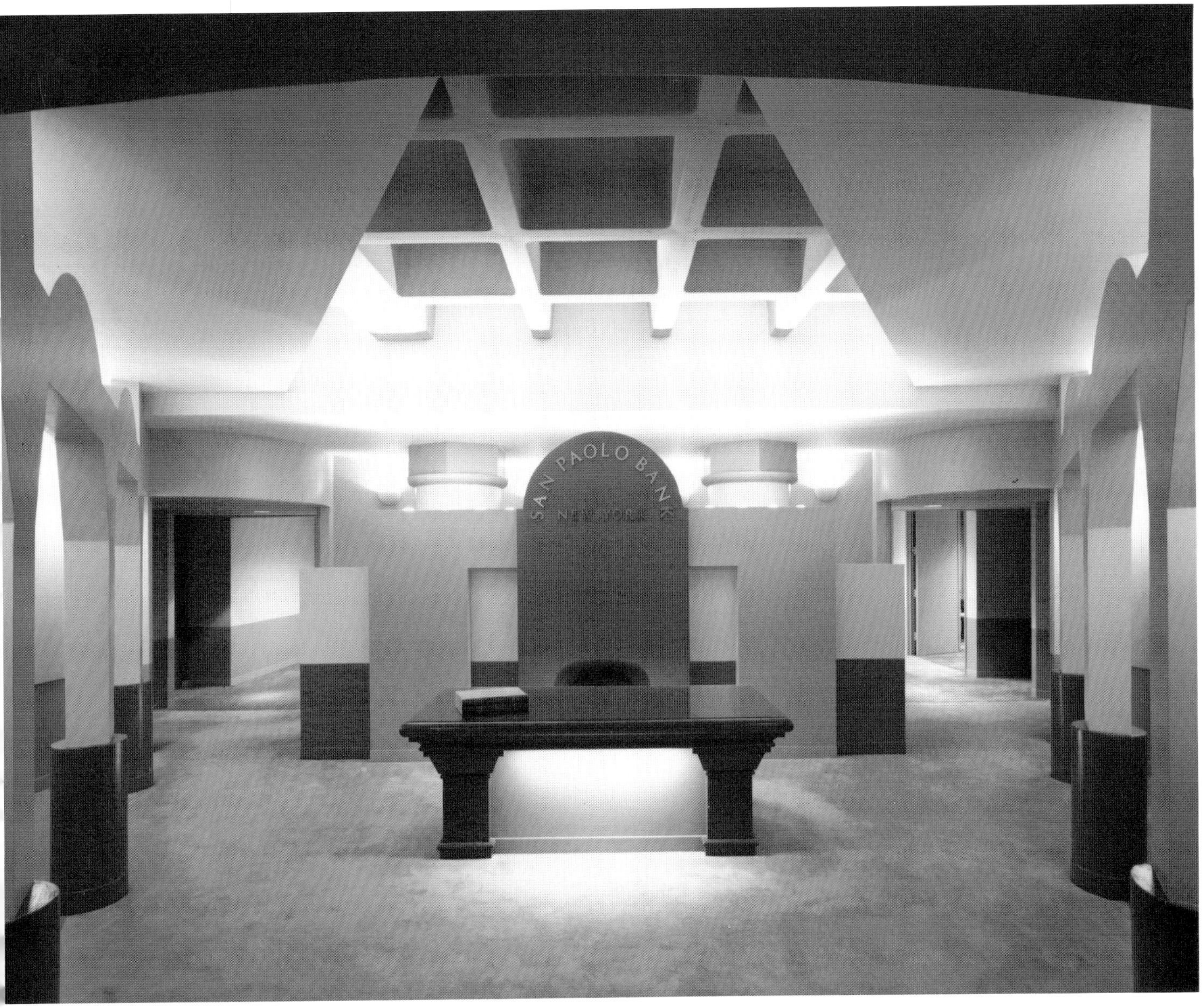

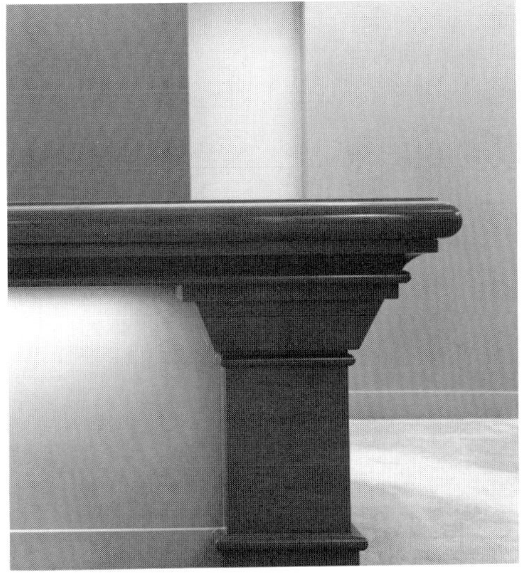

ABOVE AND LEFT: Voorsanger & Mills Associates. San Paolo Bank. New York, New York, 1981 (copyright © Peter Aaron/ESTO).

FACING PAGE: Michael Graves. Portland Public Service Building, as seen behind Beaux Arts City Hall Building. Portland, Oregon, 1982 (copyright © Peter Aaron/ESTO).

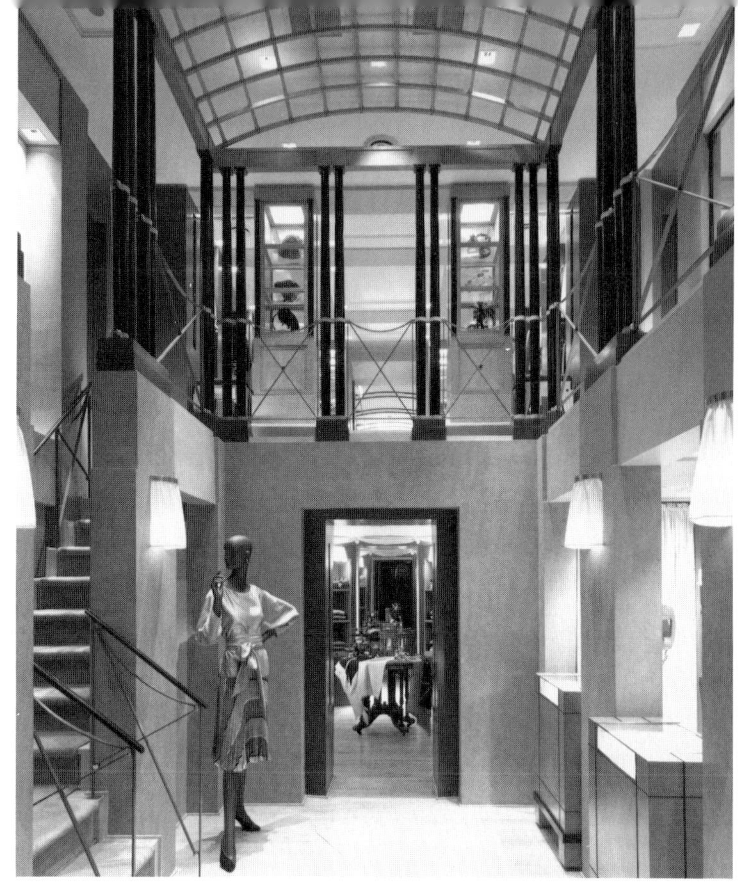

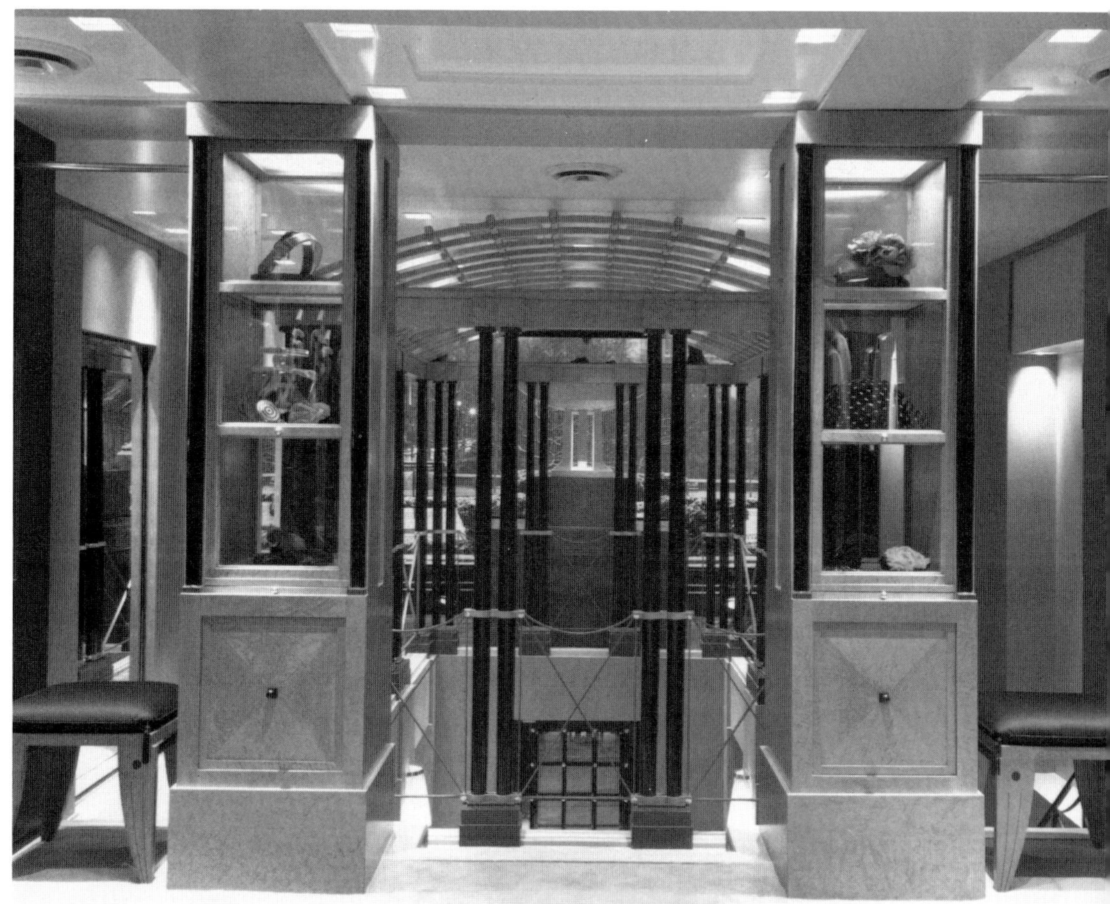

Michael Graves. Diane Von Furstenberg Boutique. New York, New York, 1985 (copyright © Peter Aaron/ESTO).

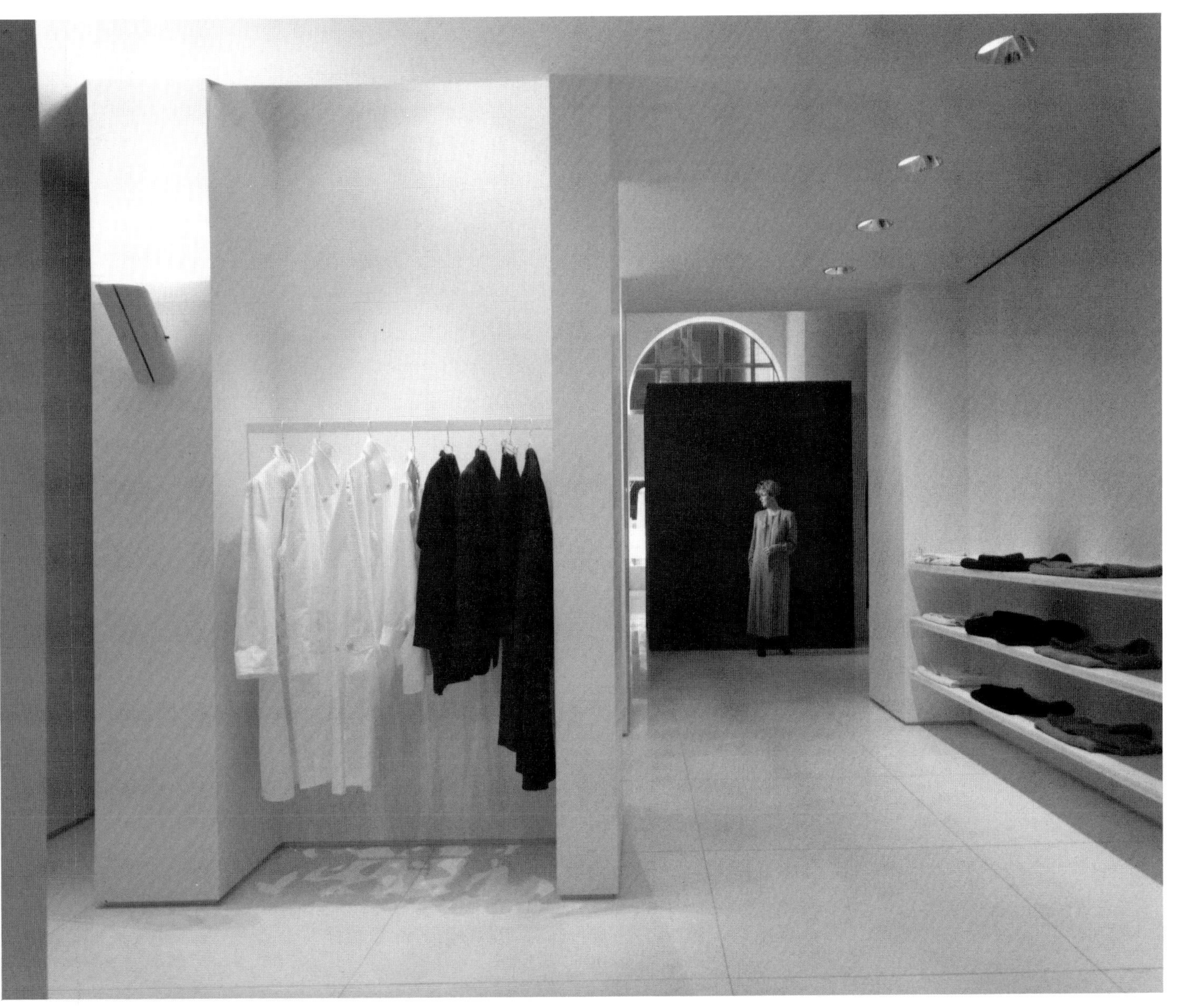

J. W. Smith.
Linda Dresner Boutique.
New York, New York, 1985
(copyright © Peter
Aaron/ESTO).

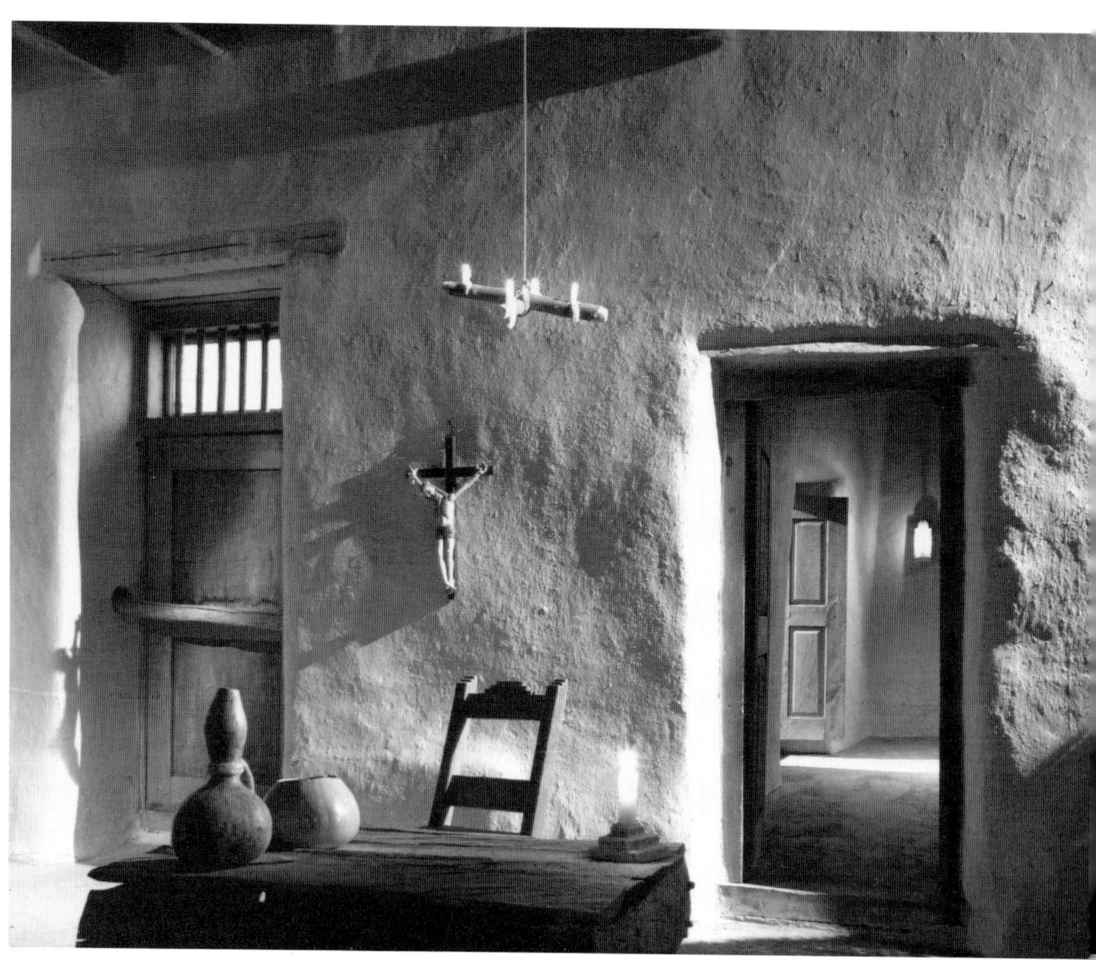

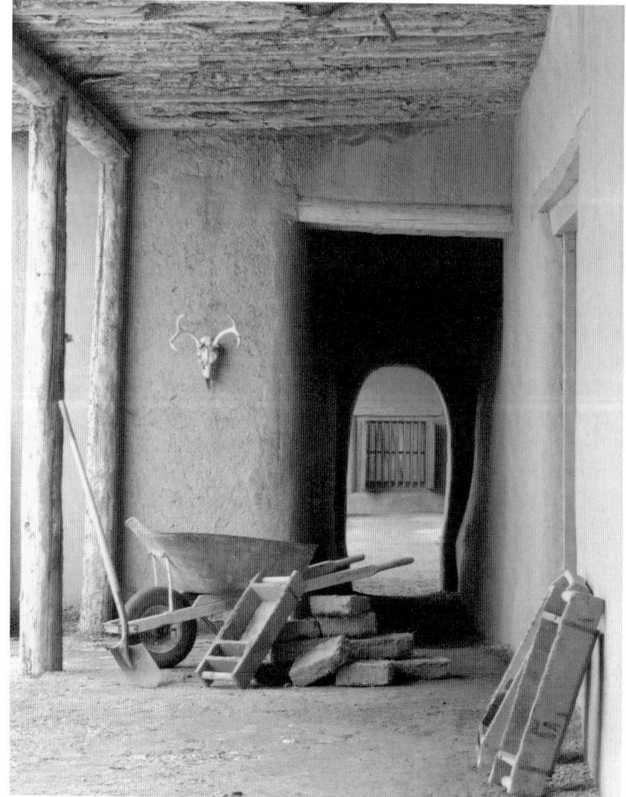

ABOVE AND LEFT: Bainbridge Bunting and Jack K. Boyer. The Kit Carson Foundation, Martinez Hacienda. Taos, New Mexico, 1984 (copyright © Peter Aaron/ESTO).

FACING PAGE: Galleria Vittorio Emanuelle. Milan, Italy, 1982 (copyright © Peter Aaron/ESTO).

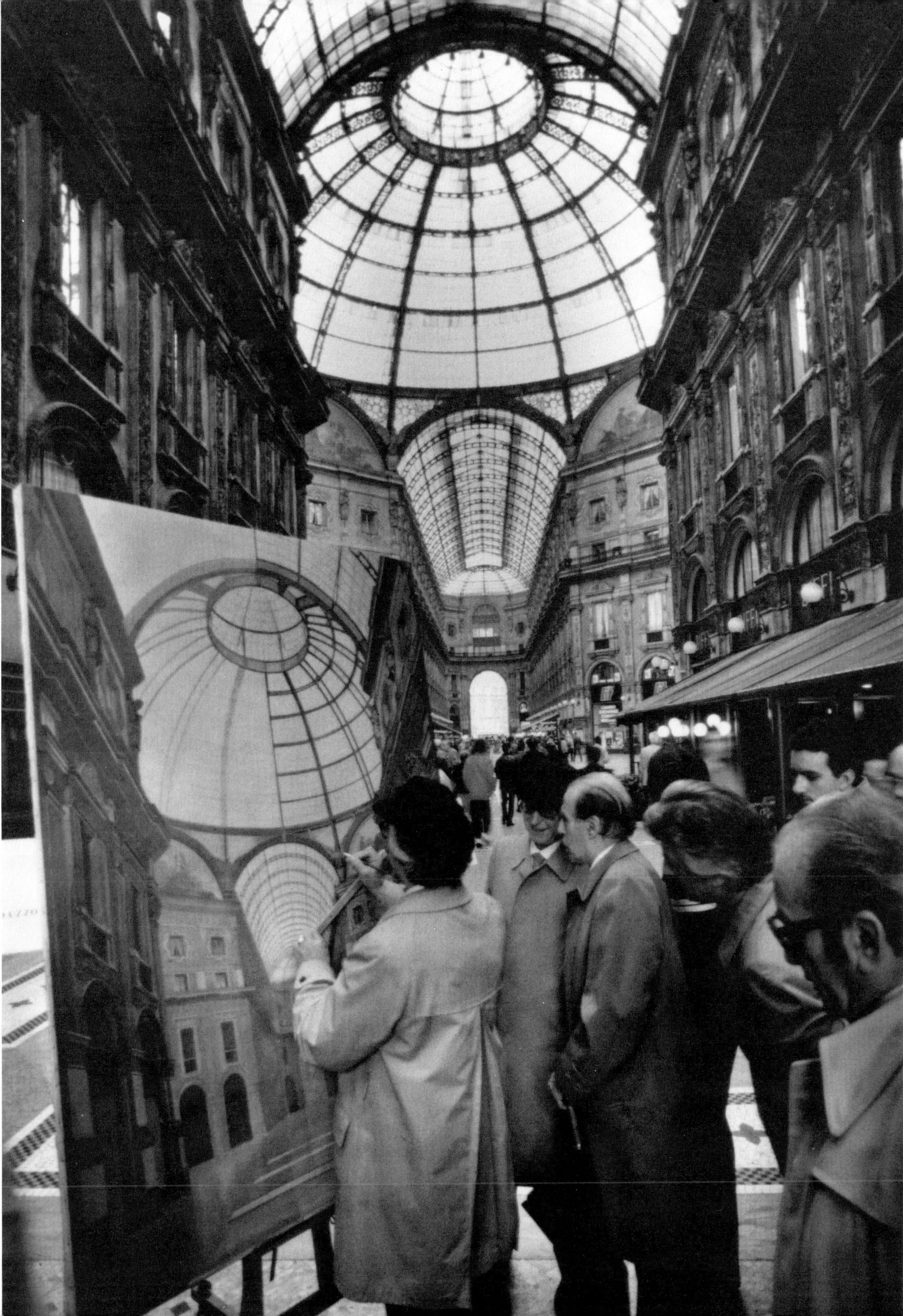

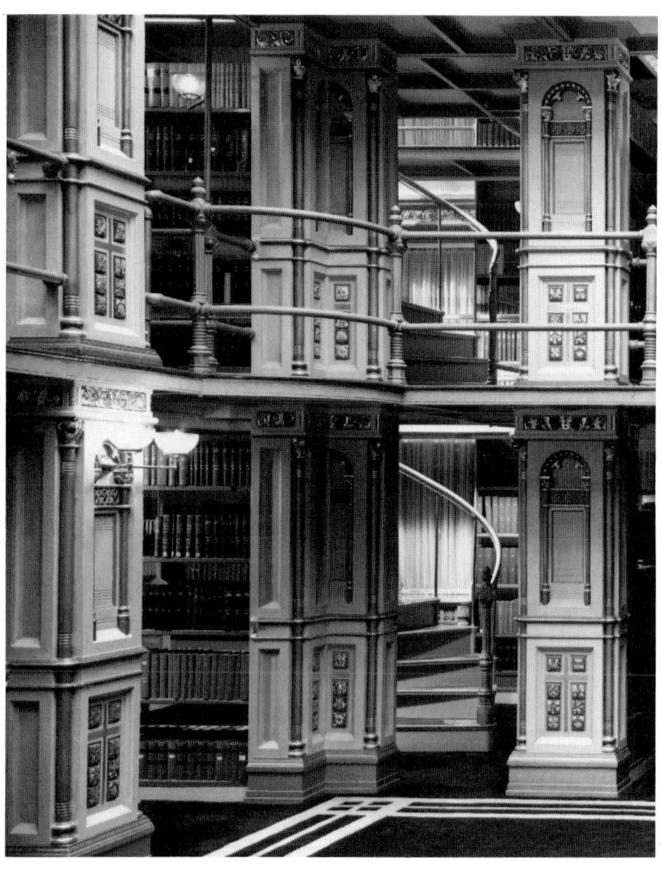

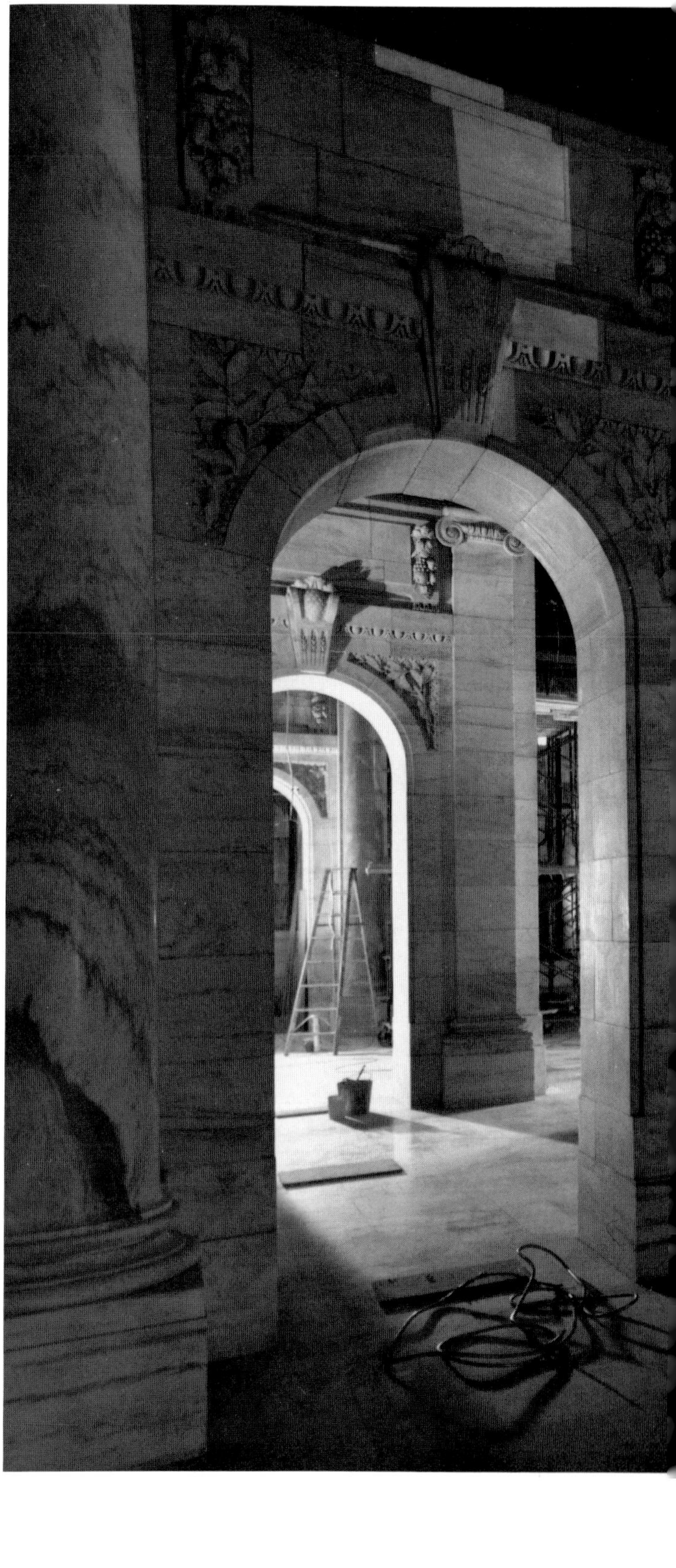

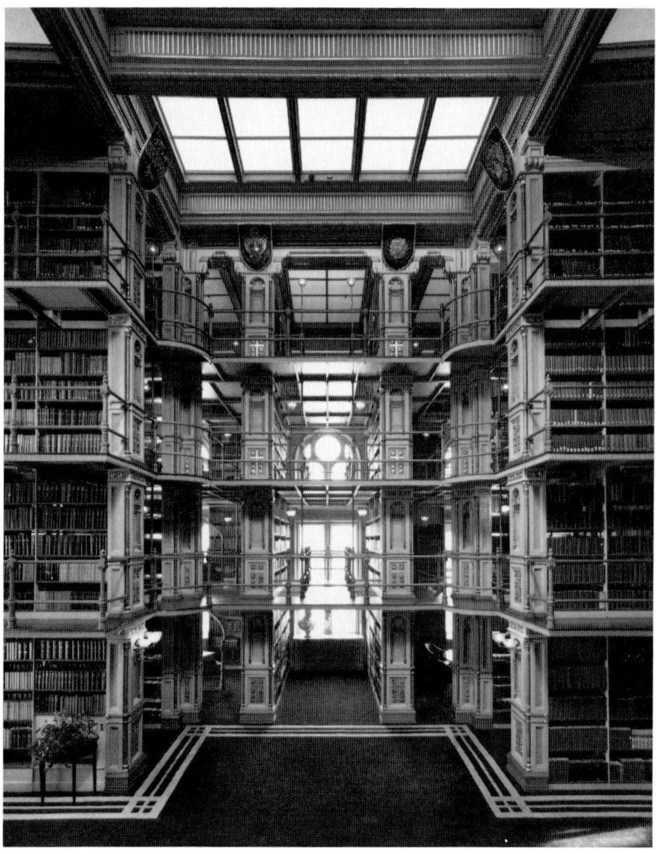

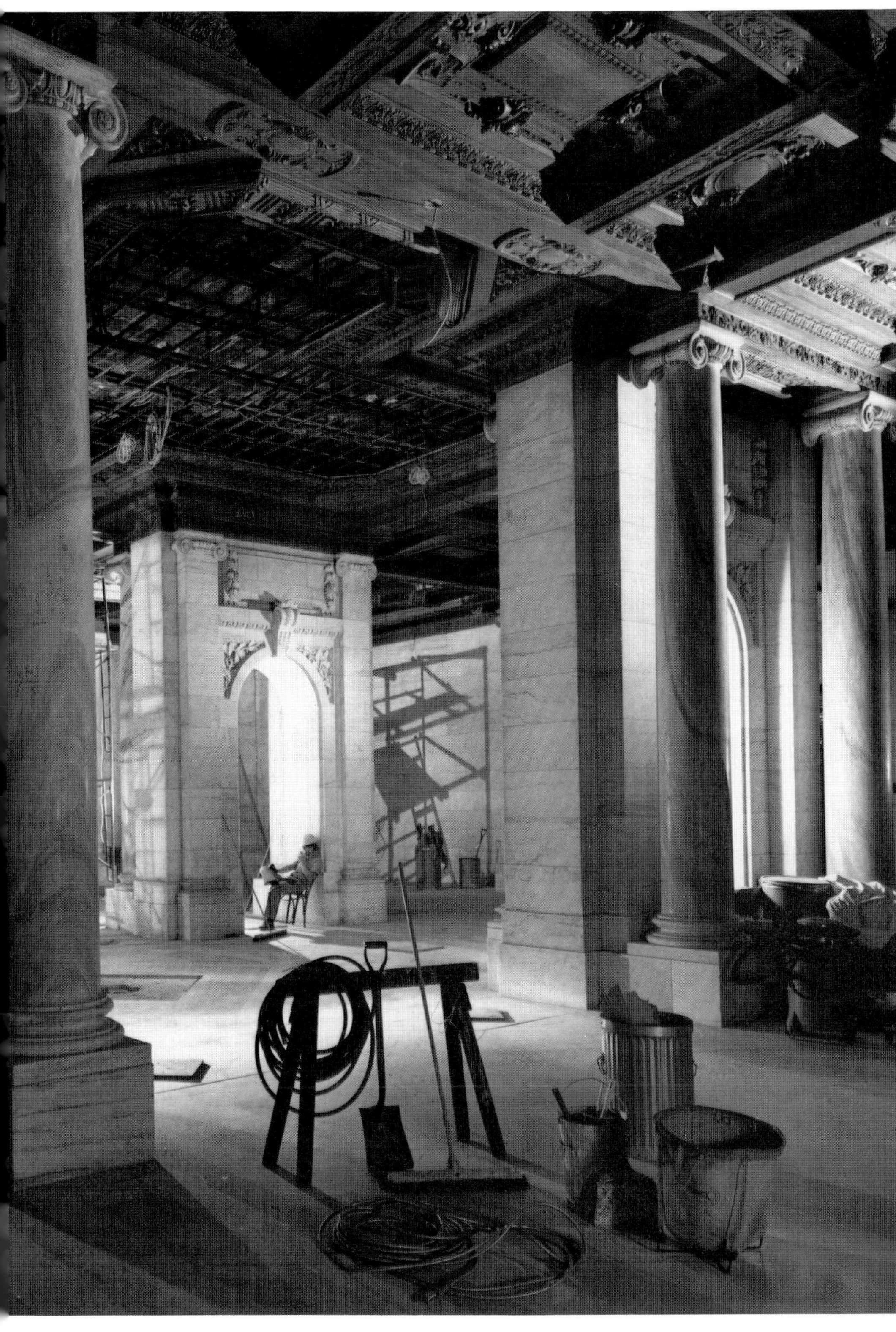

LEFT: Davis, Brody and Associates and Giorgio Cavaglieri, a joint venture. Gottesman Exhibition Hall, New York Public Library. New York, New York, 1984 (copyright © Peter Aaron/ESTO).

FACING PAGE: Environmental Planning and Research. Riggs Memorial Library, Georgetown University. Washington, D.C., 1983 (copyright © Peter Aaron/ESTO).

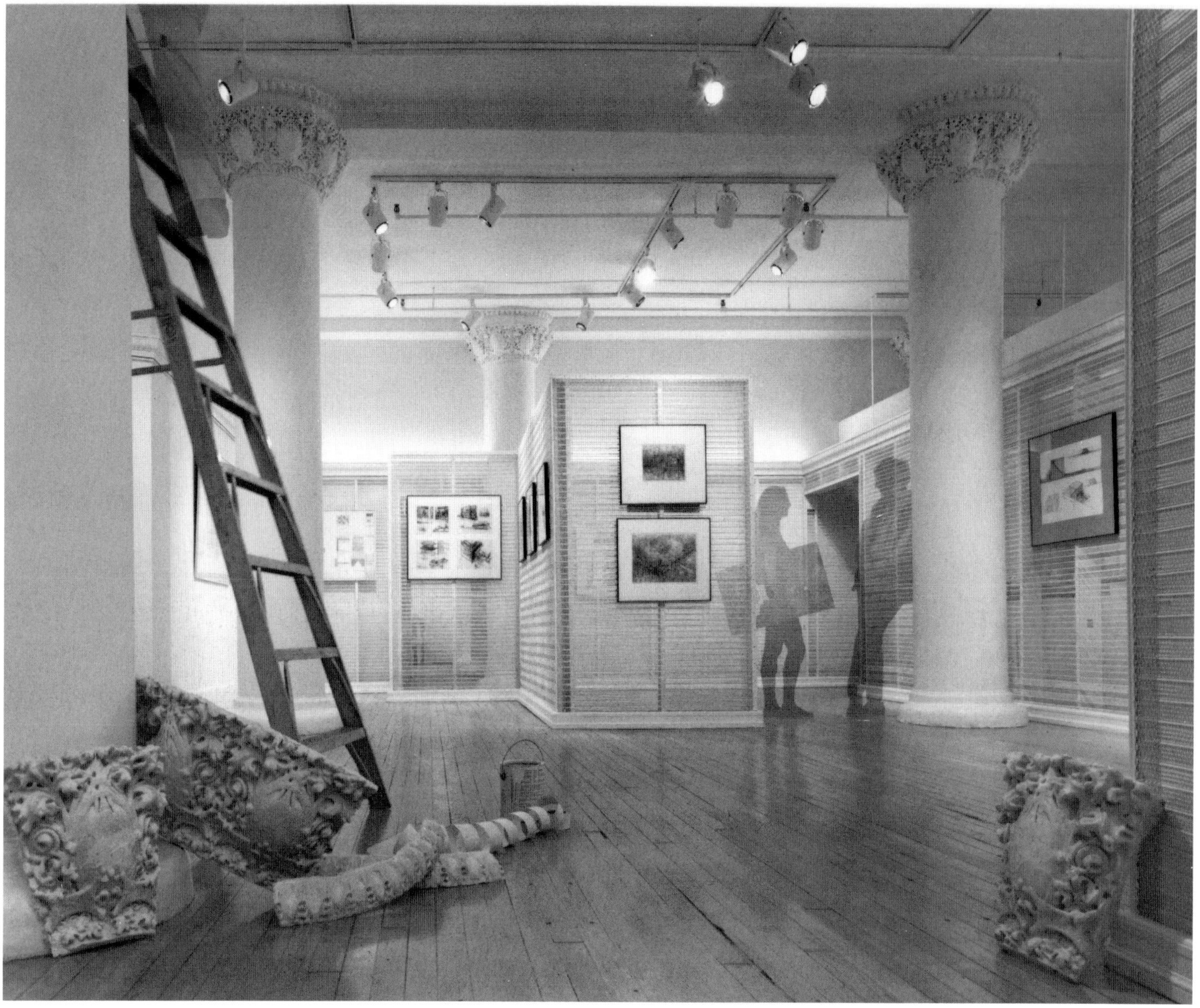

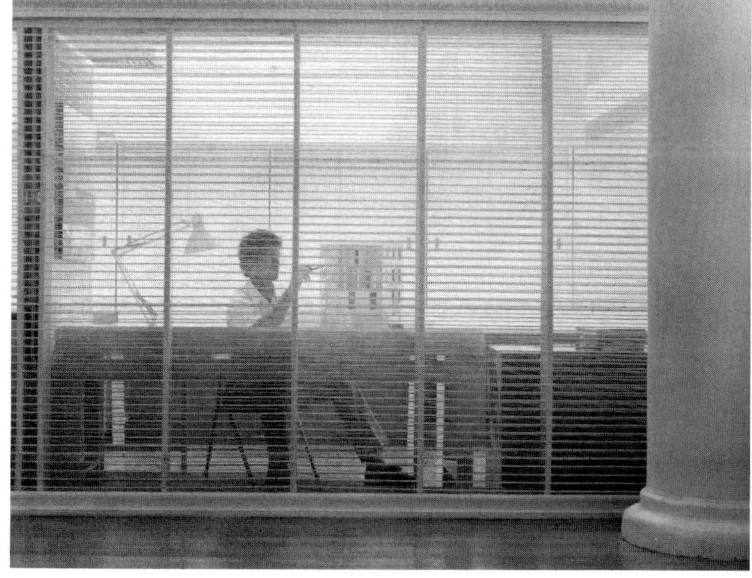

SITE Inc. SITE Offices.
New York, New York, 1984
(copyright © Peter
Aaron/ESTO).

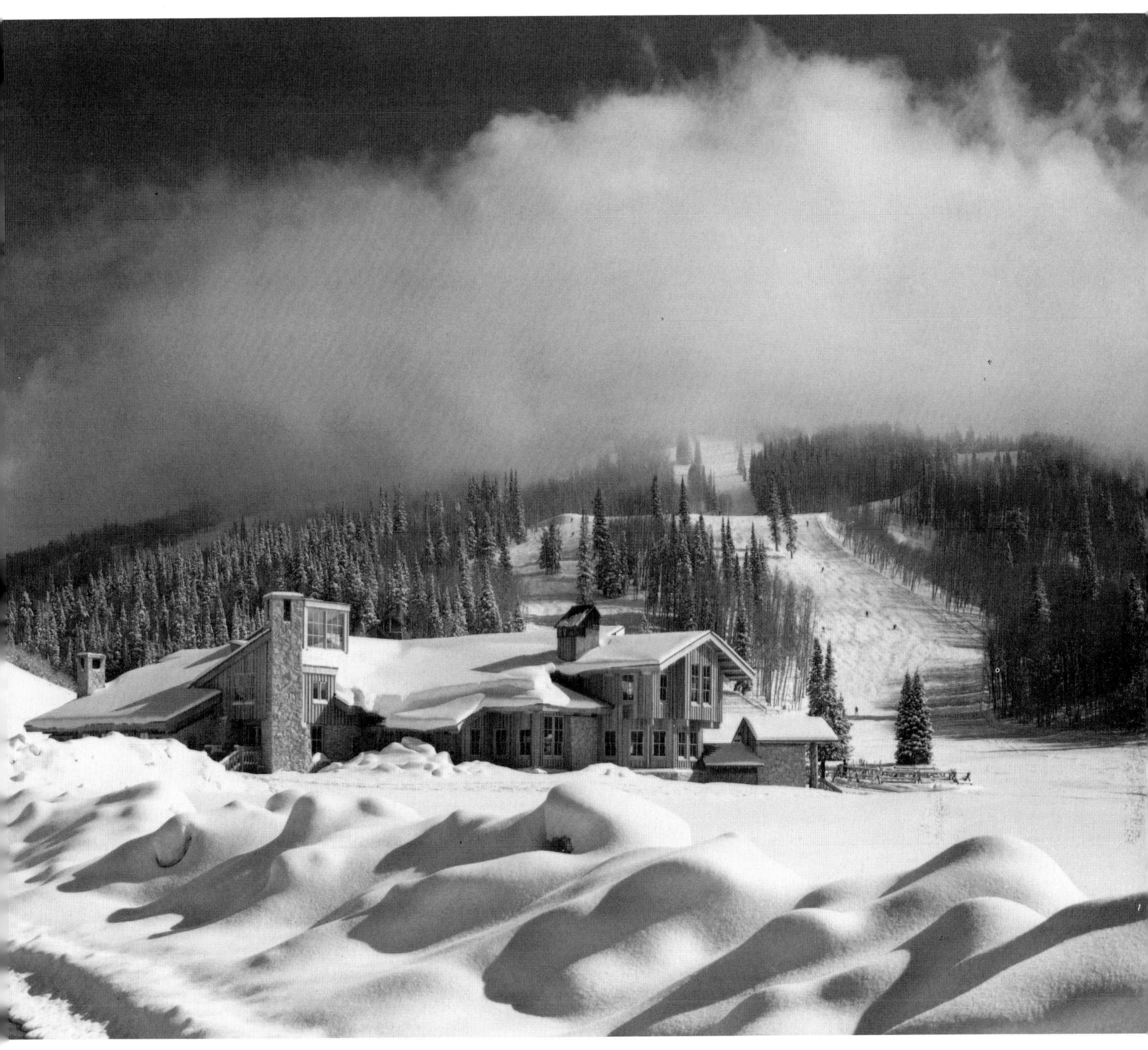

Esherick, Homsey, Dodge, and Davis. Silver Lake Lodge. Deer Valley, Utah, 1982 (copyright © Peter Aaron/ESTO).

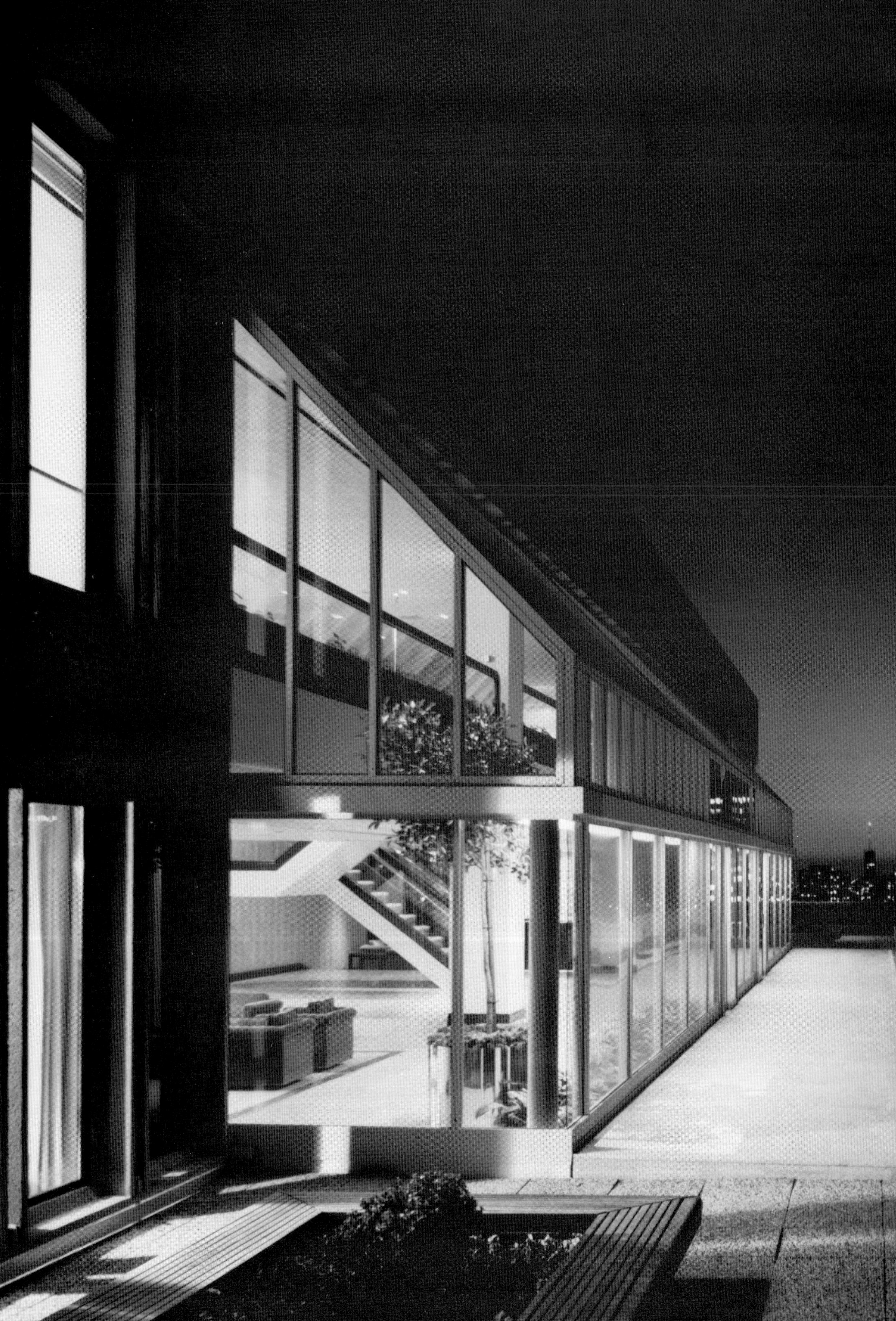

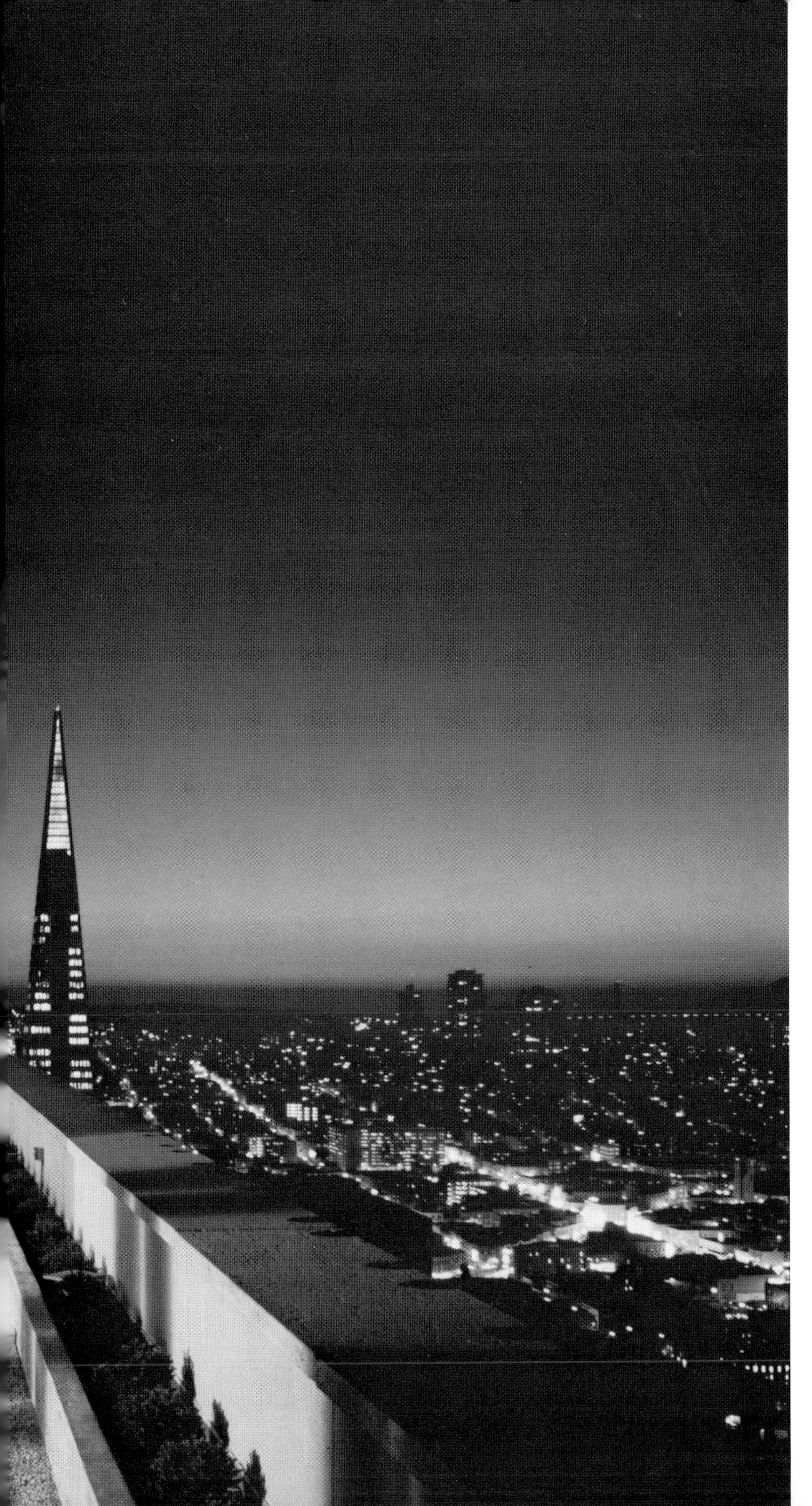

Environmental Planning and Research. Genstar Corporate Offices. San Francisco, California, 1982 (copyright © Peter Aaron/ESTO).

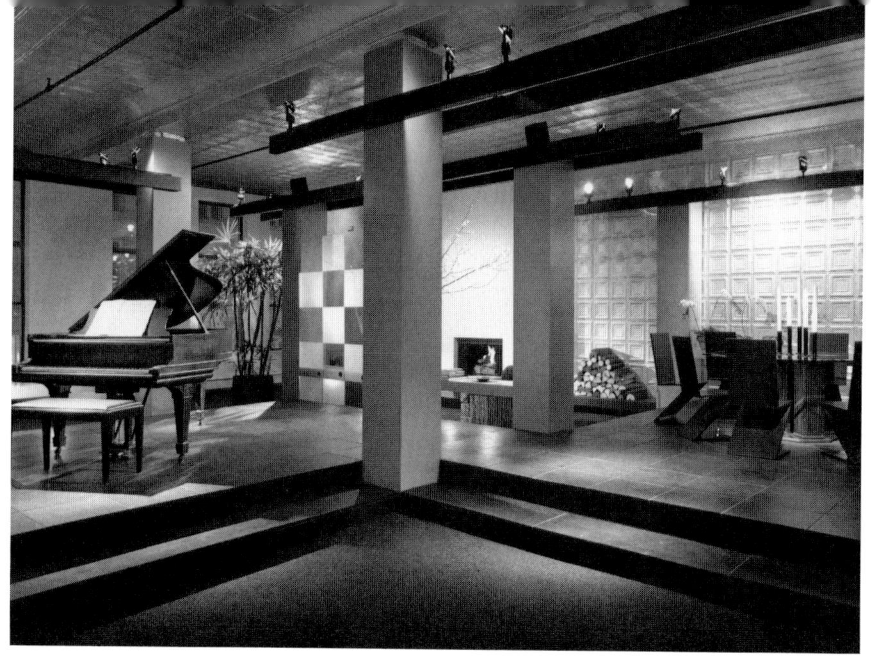

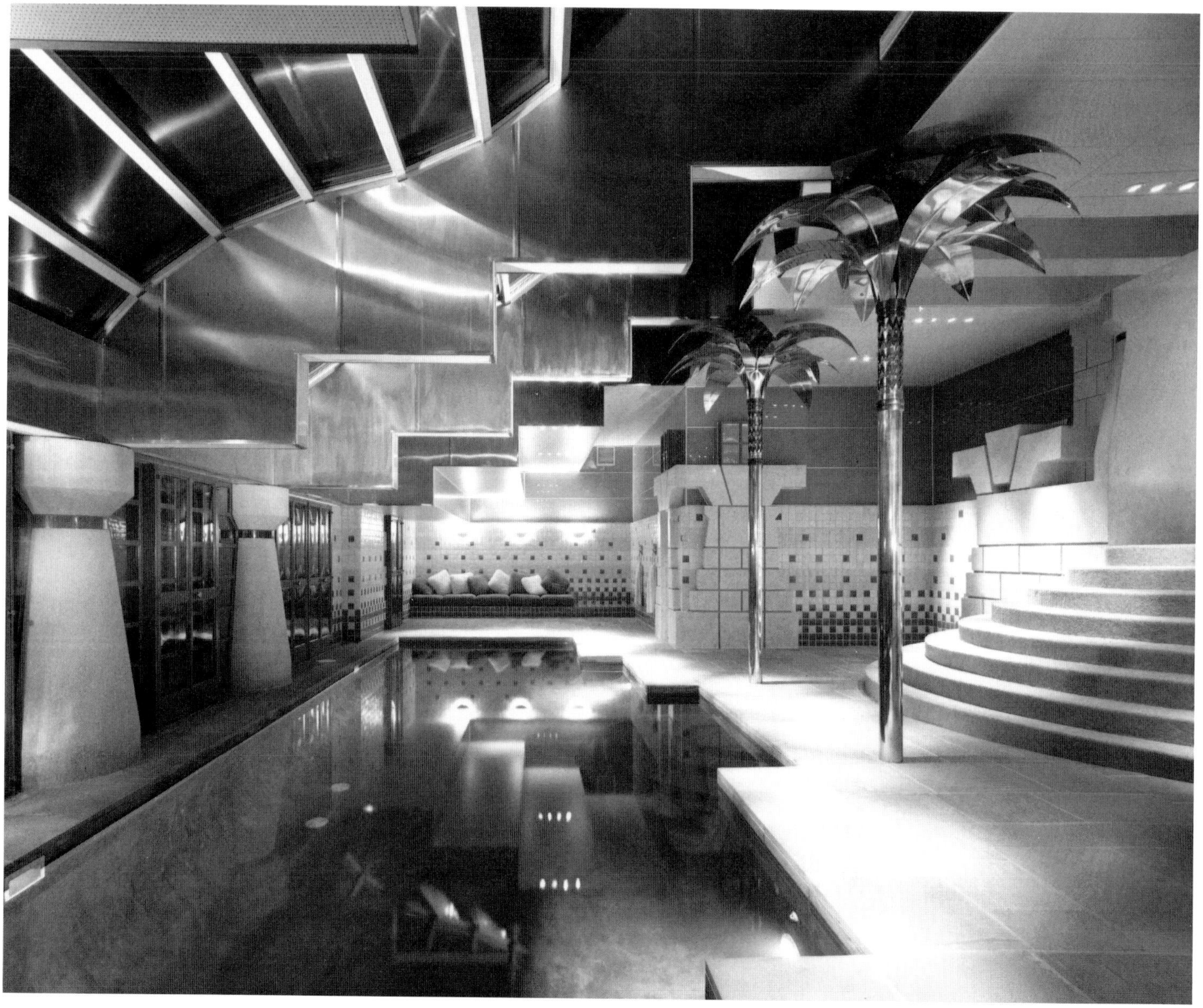

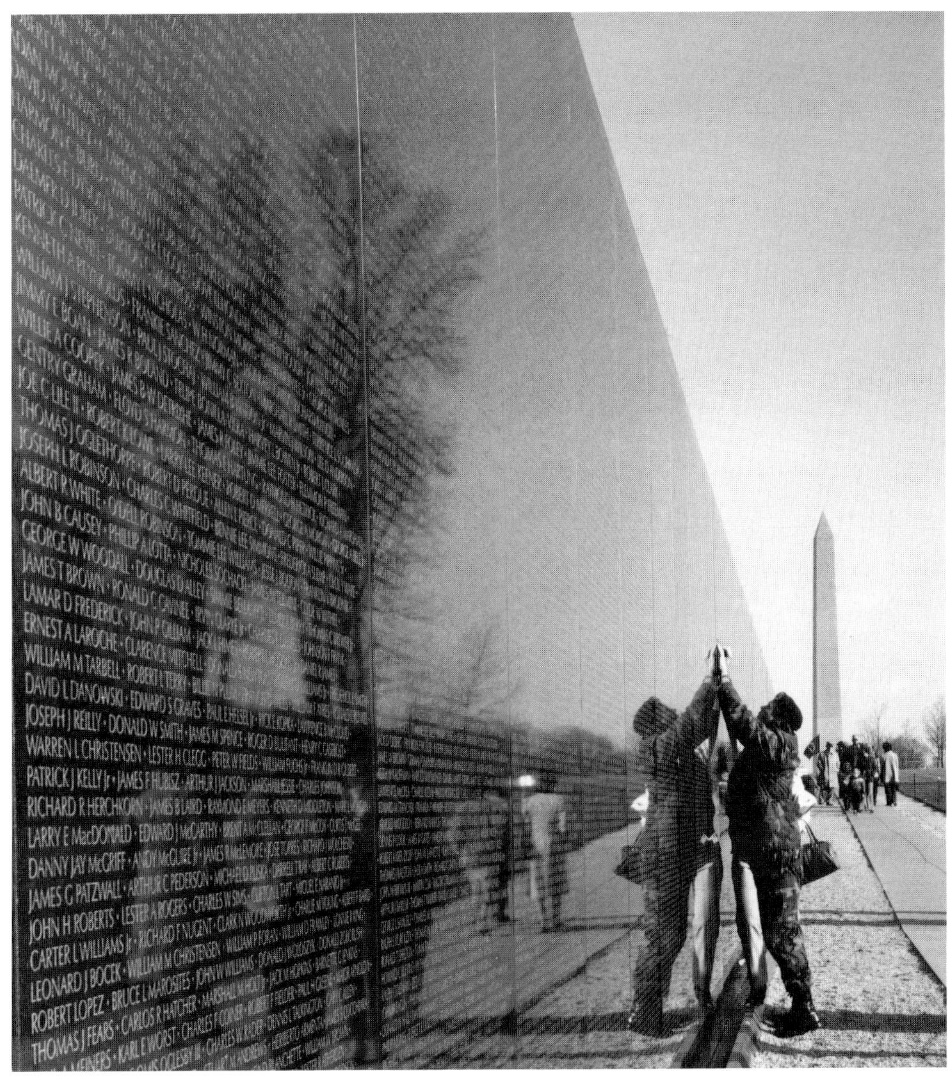

ABOVE: Maya Ying Lin.
Vietnam Veterans Memorial.
Washington, D.C., 1983
(copyright © Peter
Aaron/ESTO).

FACING PAGE (TOP):
Preston Phillips.
Private Residence.
New York, New York, 1984
(copyright © Peter
Aaron/ESTO).

FACING PAGE (BOTTOM):
Robert A. M. Stern.
Private Residence.
New Jersey, 1981
(copyright © Peter
Aaron/ESTO).

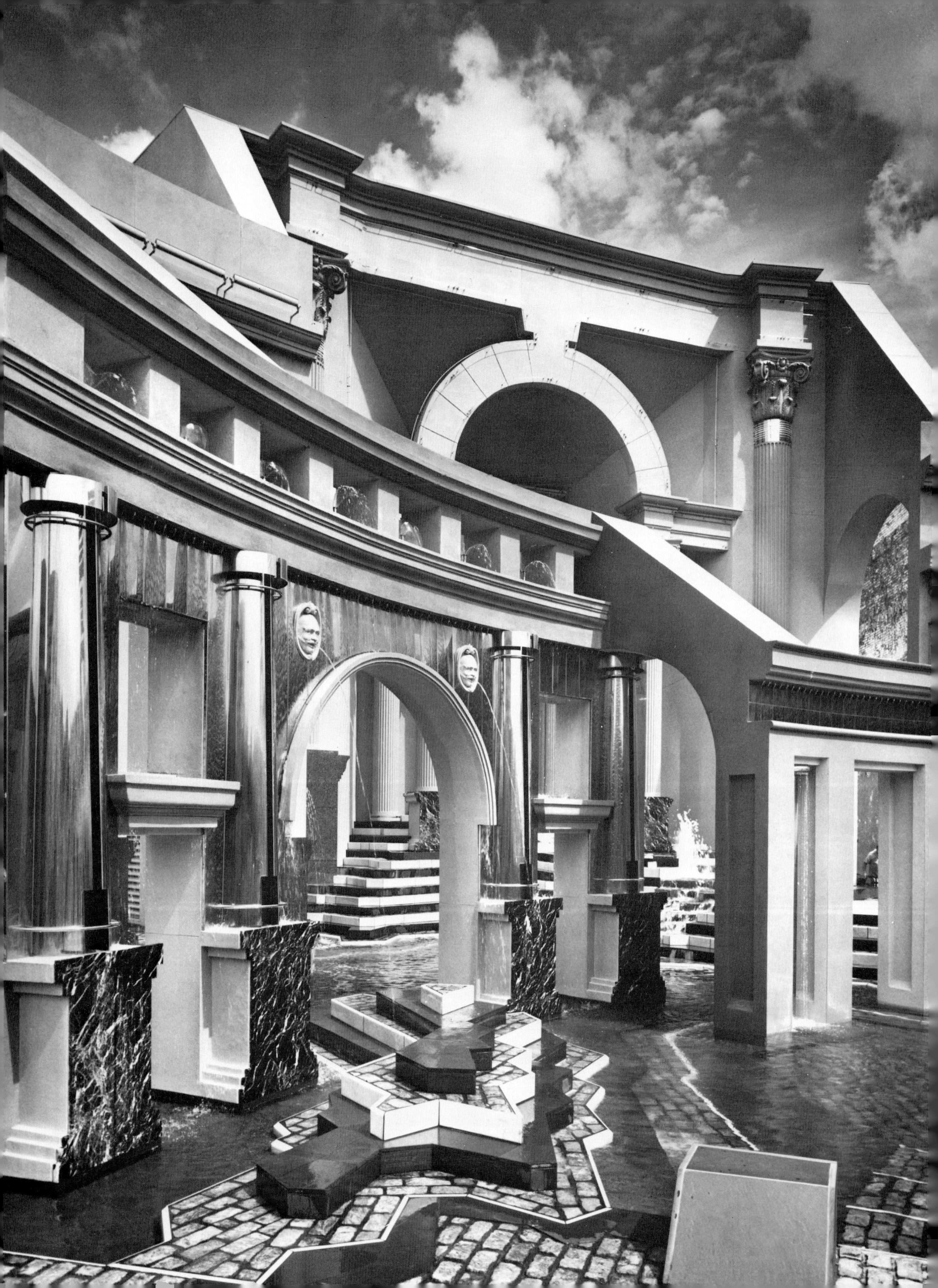

NORMAN MCGRATH

"I think that the whole basis for architectural photography has to do essentially with information," says Norman McGrath. "Its purpose is to convey the facts of the architecture." What is evident in McGrath's photographs, however, is that the facts of the architecture observed by the photographer do not necessarily repeat those noted by the architect. Not that there is any apparent conflict; rather, that the photographer as observer may compile his own data. It is data that supplements rather than contradicts that of the architect. The most successful photographs inform further; they add to the architect's body of information. McGrath's approach to architectural photography dismisses the notion that the photographer must choose between representing the intent of the architect or conveying his own interpretation.

The sympathy or sense of collaboration between architect and photographer is important to McGrath. "The more communication there is between the two, the better," he says. "If there is any conflict between architect and photographer, that's a real disadvantage to the photographer. It will be reflected in his approach towards getting the architect's input. And that's essential. It's not always immediately evident why a building is the way it is. If the architect can articulate that, it's important."

That McGrath values this dialogue is not surprising. His professional background as a structural engineer, first in Dublin and later in New York, made him conversant in the language of architecture. In Europe, however, the structural engineer, employed directly by the client, enjoys an equal relationship with the architect. Partly because the relationship was less advantageous to the engineer in this country, McGrath turned an avocation into a vocation, professionally photographing the buildings he had helped design. His background, however, remains evident in the photographs. It is hardly surprising that ceilings are the architectural element he finds most provocative. McGrath's operating premise states that structural honesty is a valid approach to architecture; even his more abstract photographs usually convey structural information about the building. His eye for detail is more than just pictorial.

It is also his background that especially qualifies McGrath to pursue facts beyond the obvious and his practice in structural engineering that gives particular legitimacy to his visual analysis of the building. While McGrath is sympathetic to

FACING PAGE: Charles Moore. Piazza d'Italia. New Orleans, Louisiana, 1978.

the architect's frequent request that the composition of the photograph resemble that of the rendering, he sees that work as a departure point only. "If the concept of the design has been predicated with this vision, the architect is quite likely to want a photograph taken from that same angle. But it shouldn't be anything more than a place to start."

Interior photography presents McGrath with far greater challenges than exterior. The variables of exterior photography, he points out, are the weather and light conditions, seasonal variables that tend to be predictable, and operable, if there is a reasonable deadline. "By and large, once you've selected the best angle for the building, it's a question of waiting for conditions to be right to photograph."

The artificial light and combined uses of artificial and natural daylight of interior photography offer more choices and, ultimately, more control. In most cases, the choices rest on how supplemental lighting can best be used to change the dark/light ratios. Lighting questions basic to interior photography have to do not with the quantity of overall light, but the contrast. Because film can only handle a limited range of contrast, how the photographer subdues the contrast will often determine the final value of the photograph. McGrath's light tends to be diffused in such a way that it is difficult to determine whether or not the photographer has introduced supplemental lighting.

McGrath uses light to inform; it is an approach that discredits the mood photography so evident in the contemporary design press in which dim lighting is used not to illustrate detail but to evoke mood—which may or may not have existed before the camera was set up. While these photographs may be long on visual excitement, they are noticeably short on information, and their effectiveness in a layout is largely determined by how they are balanced with more substantial documentation.

Interior photography is also limited simply by physical space. The photographer is all too often inside the space that he wants to photograph; he is unable to get the distance on his subject that exterior photography offers. "There," says McGrath, "you have a choice. You can photograph close up with a wide-angle lens, or from a middle distance with a normal lens, or from far away with a telephoto lens. And the results will be markedly different. But an interior doesn't offer those options; it's unusual that you can remove one wall to go back an extra twenty feet."

Wide-angle interior photography, done at close quarters, can yield highly distorted images. Foreground objects, especially those near the edges of the photograph, become exaggerated in size and shape; round objects or surfaces can have the rather disturbing effect of appearing to slide off the print; a diagonal shot taken with a wide-angle lens can often suggest that the entire room is sliding off the page. Wide-angle lenses can also tend to expand the distance between foreground and background objects; a living room might appear to have the spaciousness of Grand Central Station, not necessarily an unappealing feature, but surely, in most cases, an inaccurate one. McGrath limits his use of the wide-angle lens. He frequently relies upon an axial composition that will offset distortions and on one-point perspectives that bring with them a sense of symmetry. It is also the composition that will often convey the design precepts most clearly.

McGrath also uses objects and furnishings in the photograph in a suggestive rather than literal way. A chair or table, shown in its entirety, may occupy too great a position in the photograph; the arm of a chair and corner of a table are enough to get the idea across. Moreover, by only showing part of the object, the photographer is suggesting that there is more space in the room than meets the eye.

McGrath speaks of his work as being volumetric; his photographs evoke the experience of being inside the space. The viewer has little doubt as to the size of the room. "I think it's important that the viewer has a feeling for where the edges of the space are," he explains. Because the height of the space will do much to determine how it feels to be in it, McGrath's interior photographs usually include some portion of the ceiling or indication of where it is. And as often as not, the photograph will show three walls instead of the requisite two. Architect Hugh Hardy acknowledges this volumetric quality of McGrath's work. "In earlier years," he says, "many of our buildings had these multiple axes; they were less symmetrical than they tend to be today. They had multiple points of focus, and McGrath's photographs were able to capture this. He was able to get the camera to see these multiple perspectives without it being confusing. And you know how the camera lies." [1]

While McGrath's approach is informative and documentary, it is also interpretive. A photograph is, by his definition, an interpretation. Shots are composed and framed so as to enhance what he finds to be the strongest aspect of the design. "I want to try to take the very best of the design, and highlight it, though in a way that is neither theatrical nor obvious." And while even subtle interpretations may take liberties, McGrath suggests that these liberties are within the jurisdiction of the skilled photographer. His photographs rarely include human images, unless their purpose is to ground or give a sense of scale to an abstract composition. Yet there are times, he points out, when a sense of abstraction is legitimate; when the scale is mysterious or intriguing, and when this sense of intrigue is appropriate.

That McGrath's work strikes a balance between precise visual transcription and interpretation has been recognized by the American Institute of Architects. In conferring upon him a 1985 Institute Honor for distinguished achievement, the jury noted that his work is "consistently sensitive, documentary, and accurately interpretive no matter what the scale or the complexity of the project involved. He is a dedicated craftsman, a disciplined technician, and a photographer without overbearing stylistic preconceptions." [2]

Although McGrath rarely shoots specifically for a page format, he has found that when format is dictated, it can provoke, rather than restrain, inventiveness. This applies especially to cover format. Most cover photographs, he observes, are very nearly square; they also tend to have fairly uninterrupted, uniform tones, either near the top or the bottom for the publication's name and additional copy lines. Understandably, the architectural photographer is usually disinclined to compose a photograph that leaves the top or bottom third blank as it is a rather blatant deviation from his purpose to inform; but when he has the option to do so it can nurture a play with composition that may be less fruitful elsewhere. Such was the case with a photograph McGrath shot of the Citicorp headquarters in New

York City. Searching especially for a photograph that could be used on the cover of *Architectural Record,* McGrath moved his camera closer to the building than he had done for his previous documentation of the building. "I had always been intrigued by the view looking up to the tower, so I had always attempted to get back as far as I could. But as I got closer to it, I realized I had overlooked some of the possibilities." The ensuing photograph of the Citicorp tower is indeed eye catching and provocative, and though perhaps less documentary than the previous work, it nevertheless captures the dramatic upward trajectory of the building. Covers especially can give the photographer a wider visual latitude with composition and angle, and as the Citicorp photograph makes clear, this latitude can be enjoyed without undermining the more precise documentaion it introduces.

With an eye that is so focused on the structural underpinnings of the space, it is hardly surprising that McGrath puts a high value on black-and-white photography, which he often estimates to be the most effective vehicle for the design story. Especially if the design story is one of form—which it usually is—these forms will be conveyed most clearly and concisely in black-and-white. "When you reduce design to the ultimate, sometimes color can get in the way. It can just become a distraction."

The structural data of a space—the way a building has been layered, the angle of a cantilever, or the placement of columns supporting a mass of weight—frequently lends itself to abstract composition. The manipulations of light and shadow, space and mass, support and weight invite conceptual annotation. Yet in McGrath's eye, the abstract composition is not at the expense of fact.

"His is a genuine curiosity," says Hugh Hardy; and generally speaking, genuine curiosity is satisfied only by genuine fact. [3] In this case, it is the clear and incontestable facts of the architecture. In McGrath's collection of work, even the abstract compositions continue to give the viewer straightforward information about the building. "It's the equivalent of perfect pitch," McGrath says. "These elements balance. They don't look bizarre. And once you superimpose documentation onto the inherent desire to create a balanced composition, this is what decides the intrinsic merit of the photograph." That these elements coincide as often and as gracefully as they do is what most distinguishes McGrath's work.

---

1. Conversation with author, April 1985.
2. *Architecture,* April 1985, p. 18.
3. Conversation with author, April 1985.

FACING PAGE: Harrison & Abramowitz. Phoenix Mutual Life Insurance, Constitution Plaza. Hartford, Connecticut, 1964.

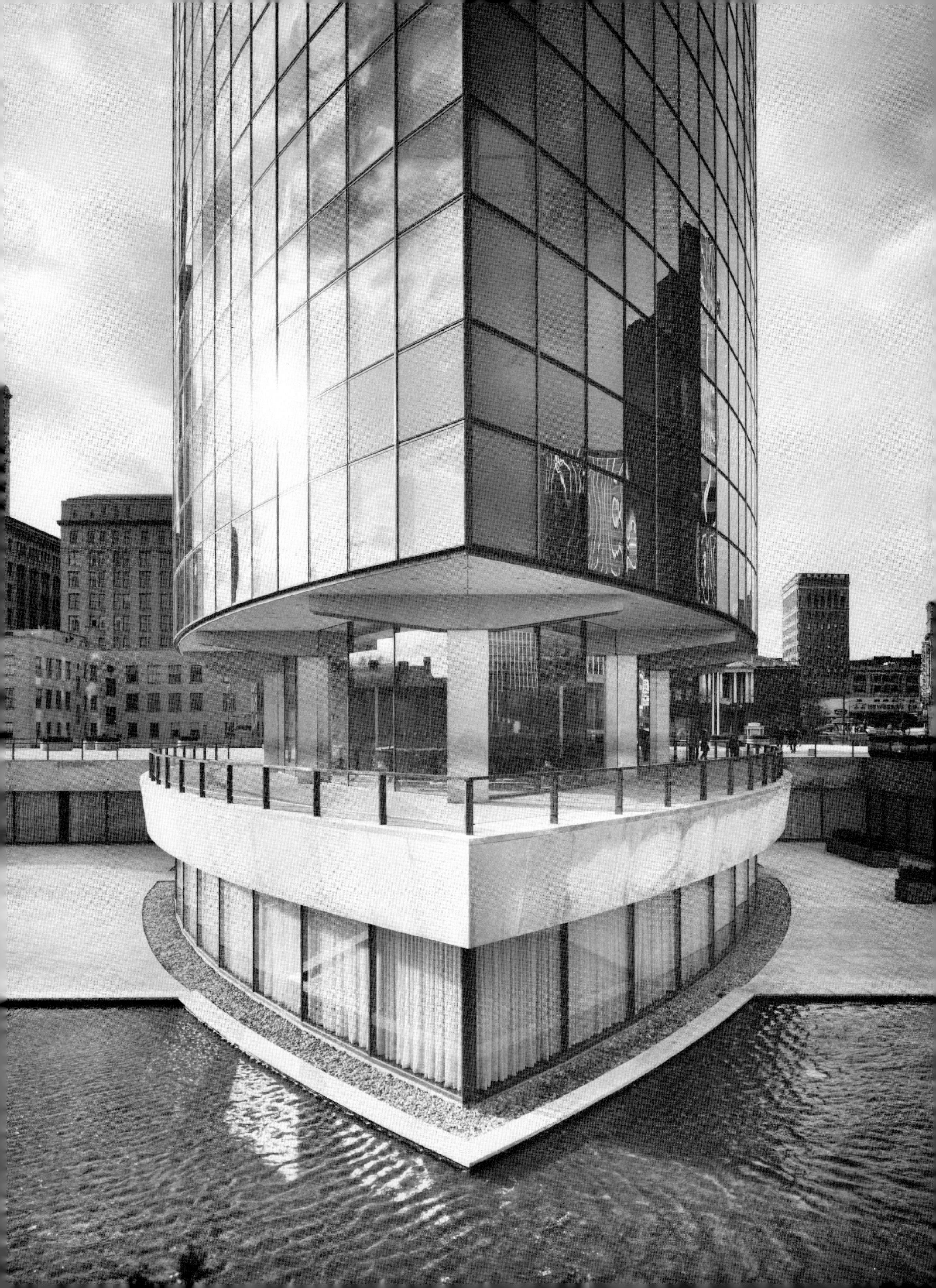

J.J. NEWBERRY CO.

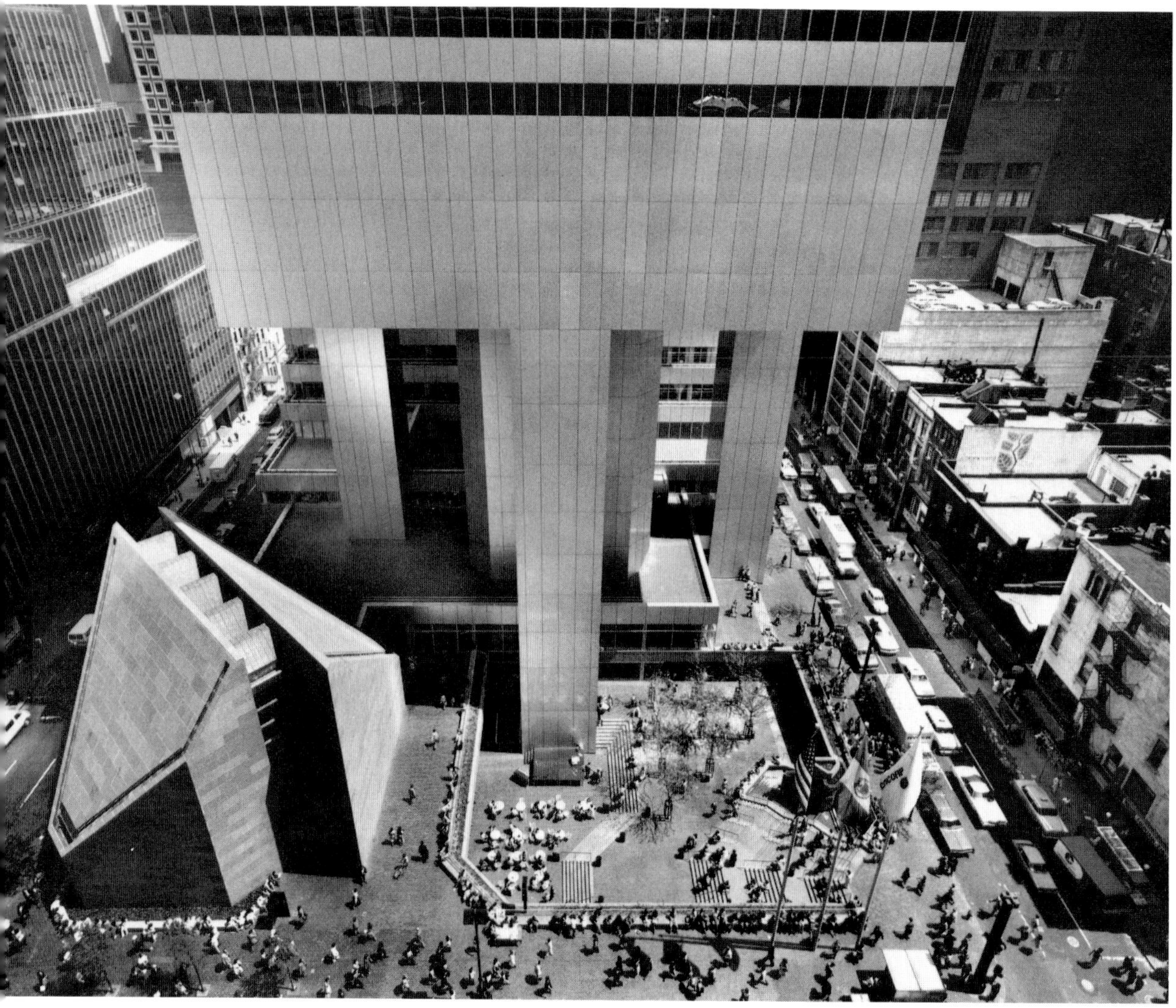

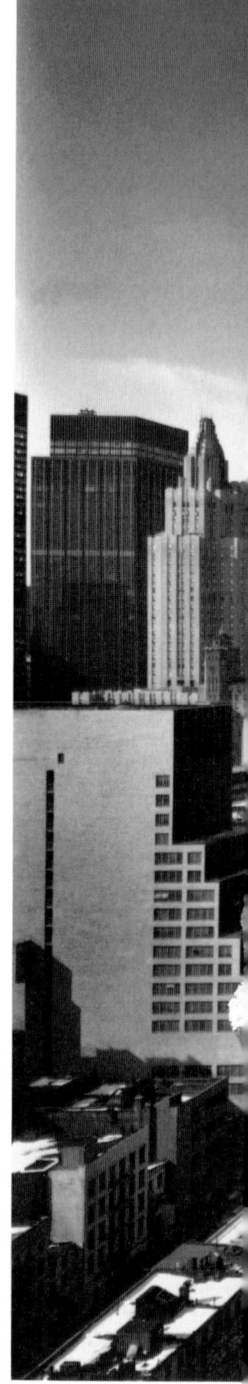

Hugh Stubbins and
Associates. Citicorp Center.
New York, New York, 1978.

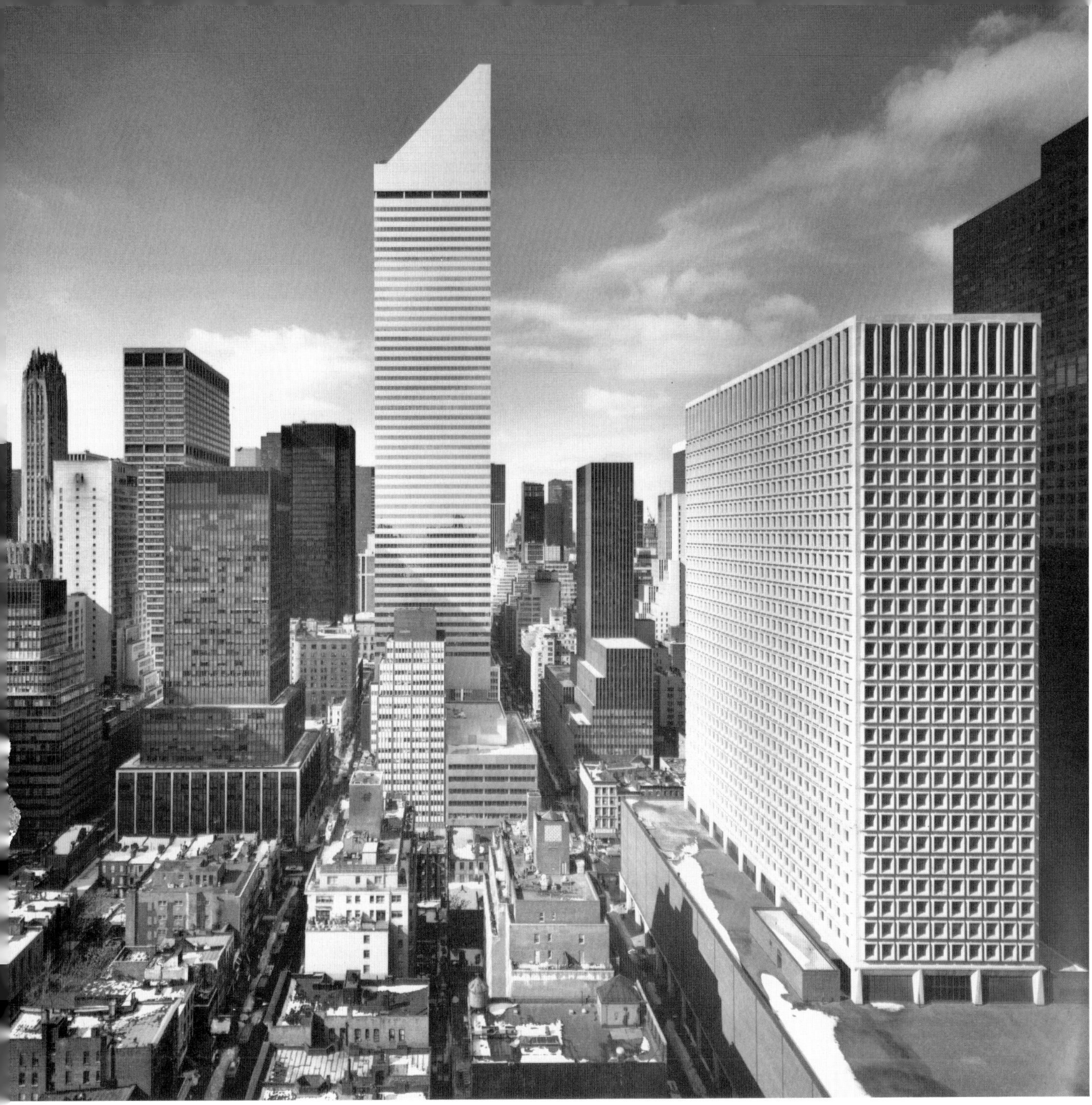

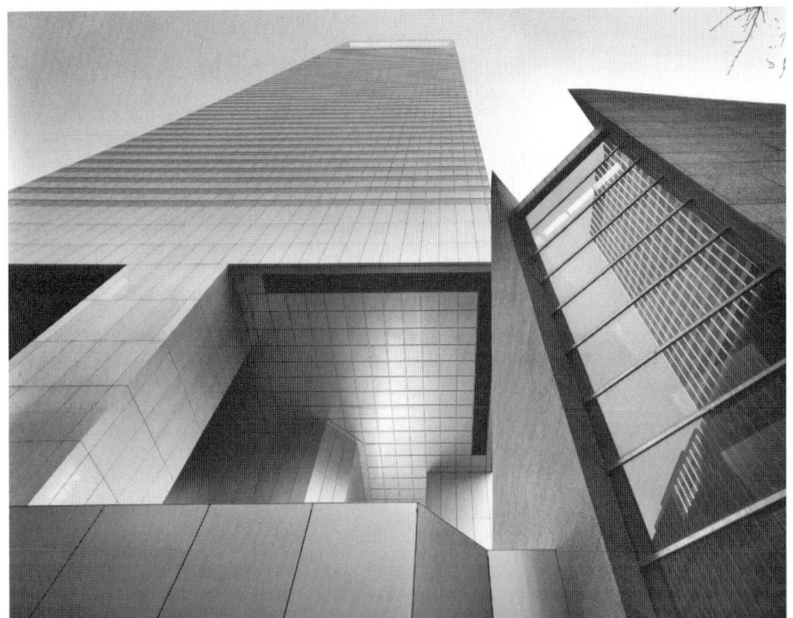

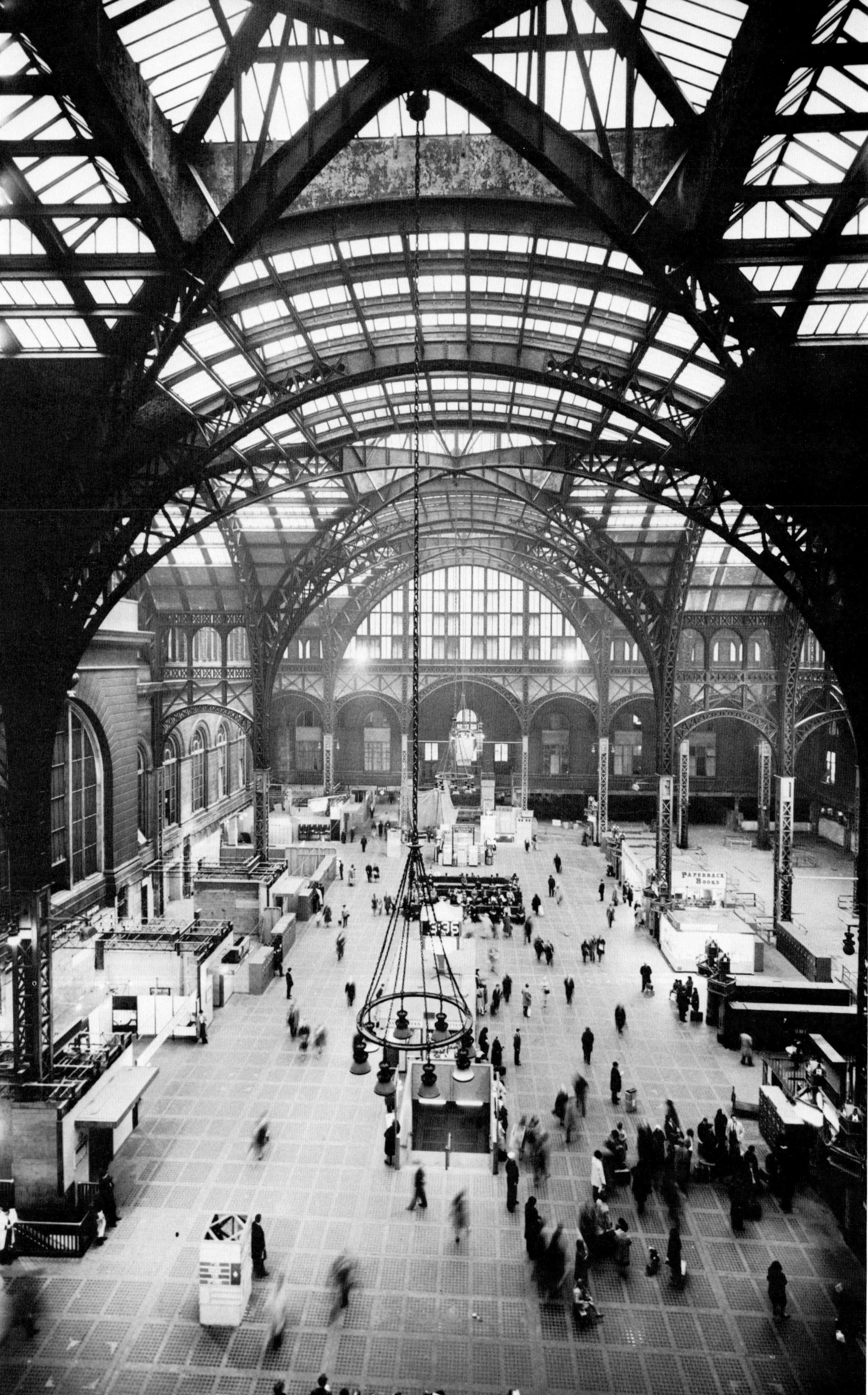
PAPERBACK
BOOKS

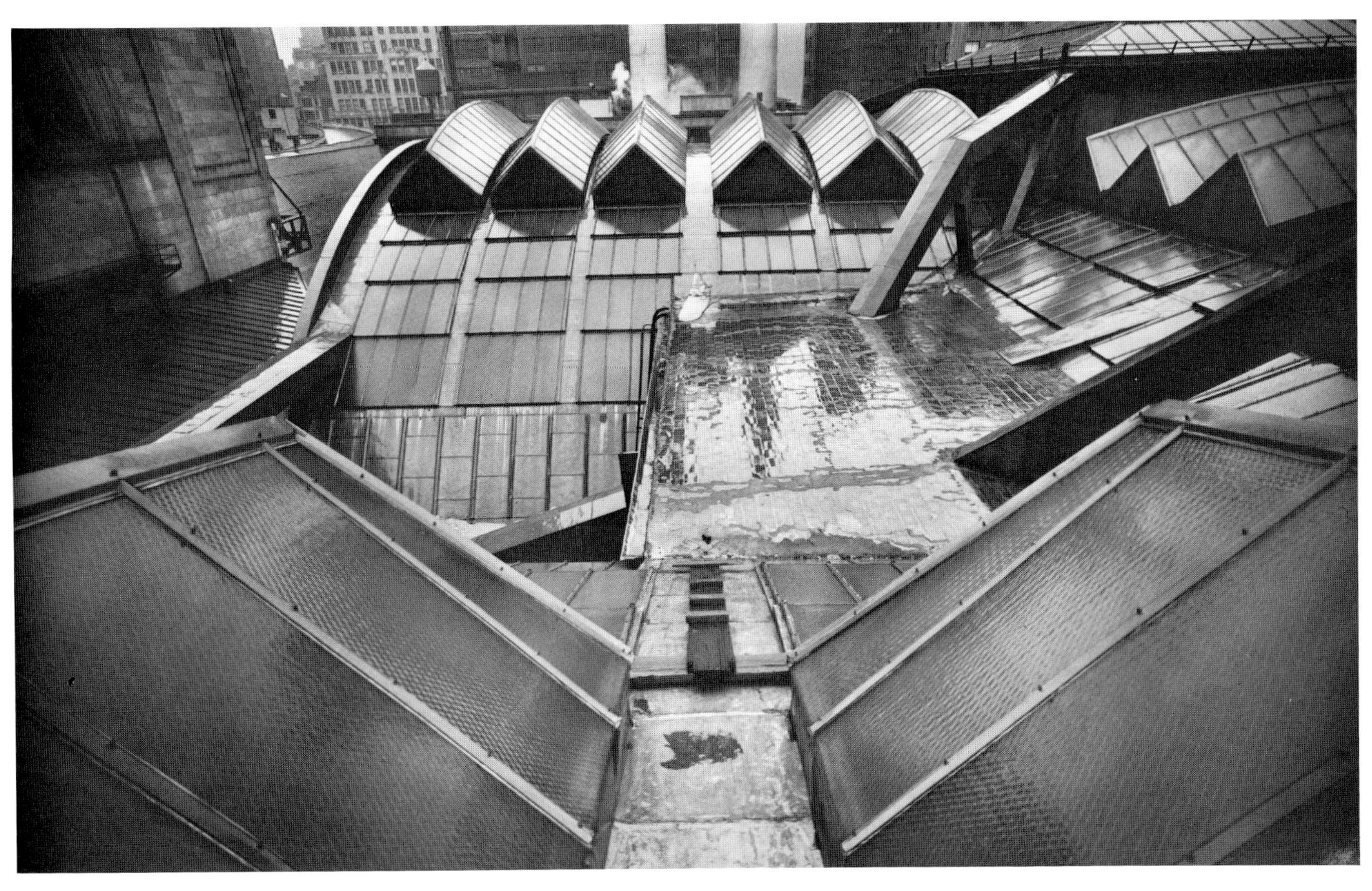

McKim, Mead & White.
Pennsylvania Station.
New York, New York, 1964.

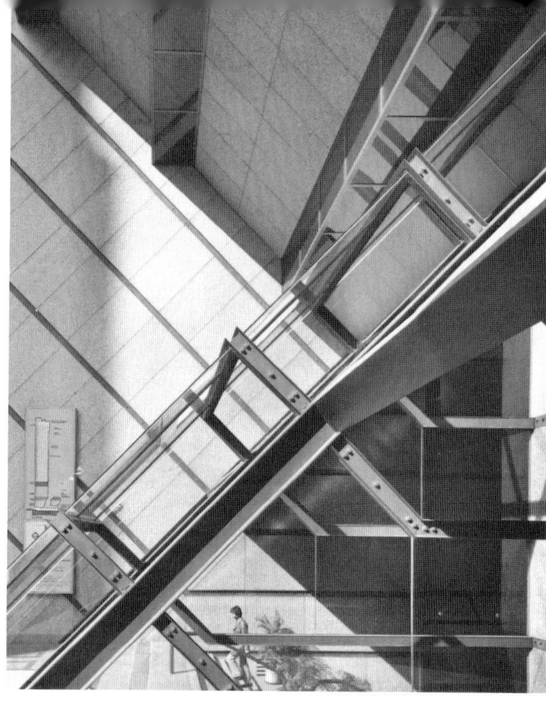

LEFT: David Kenneth Specter. Galleria. New York, New York, 1975.

BOTTOM: I. M. Pei. National Gallery, East Wing. Washington, D.C., 1978.

FACING PAGE: Roche Dinkeloo. Ford Foundation. New York, New York, 1976.

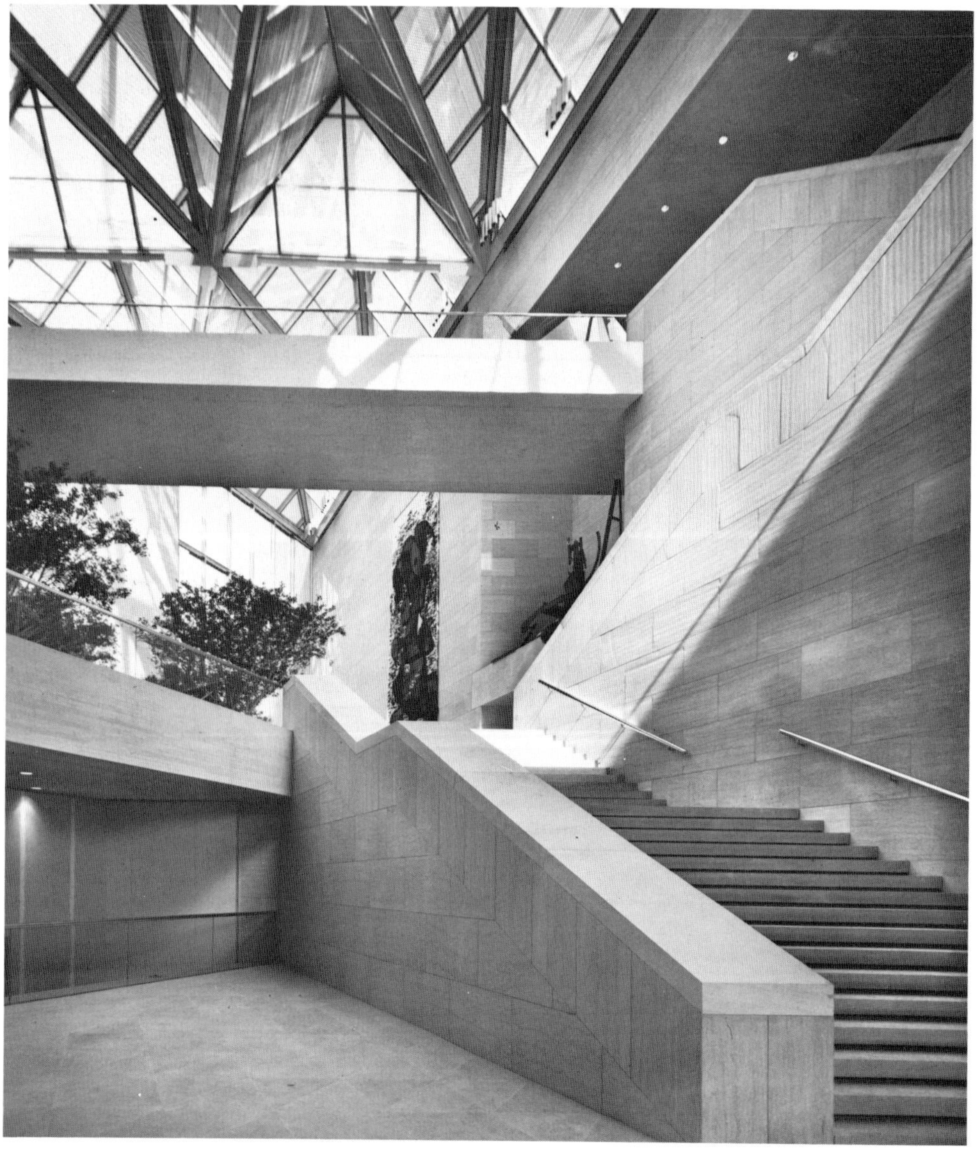

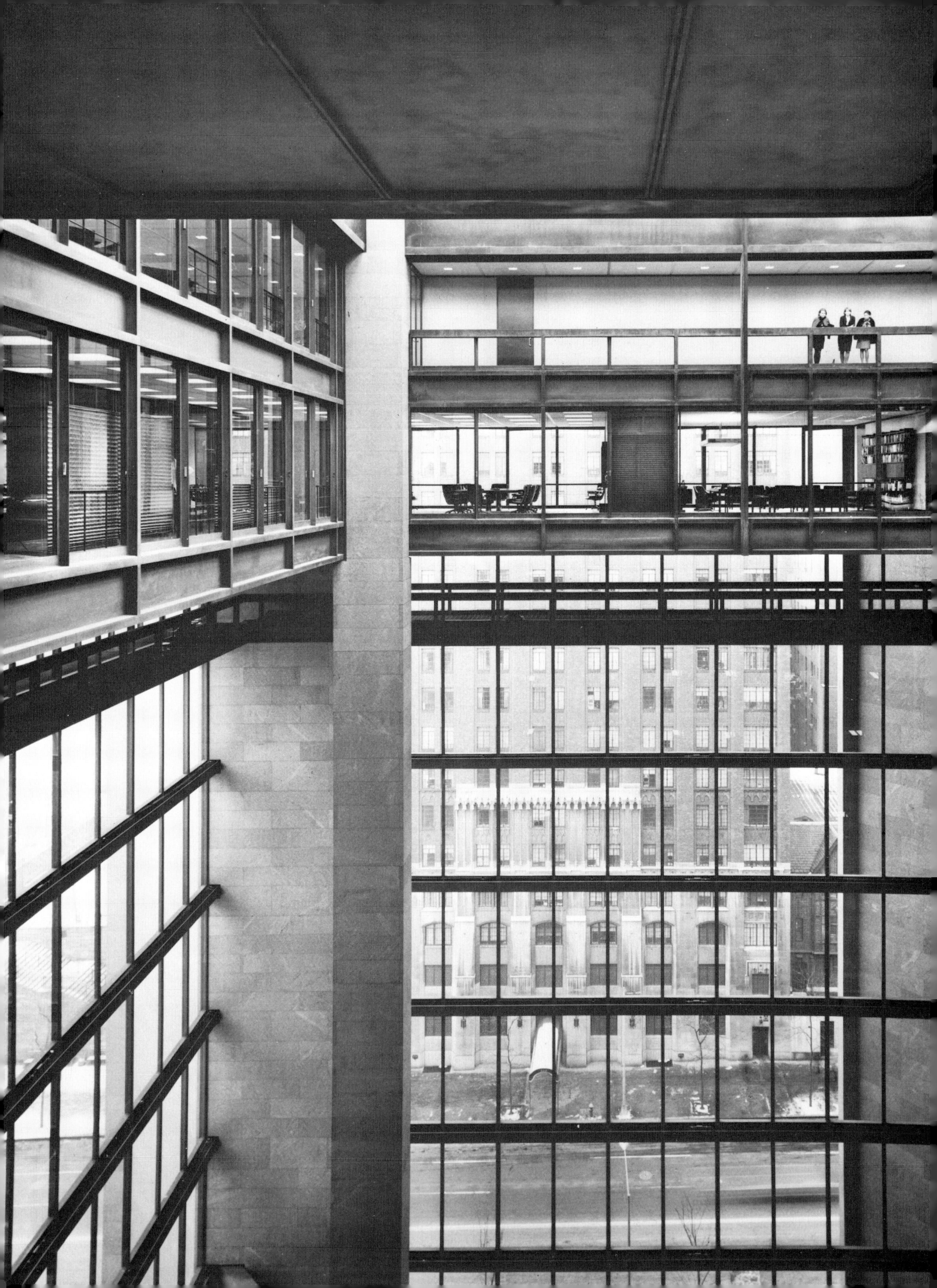

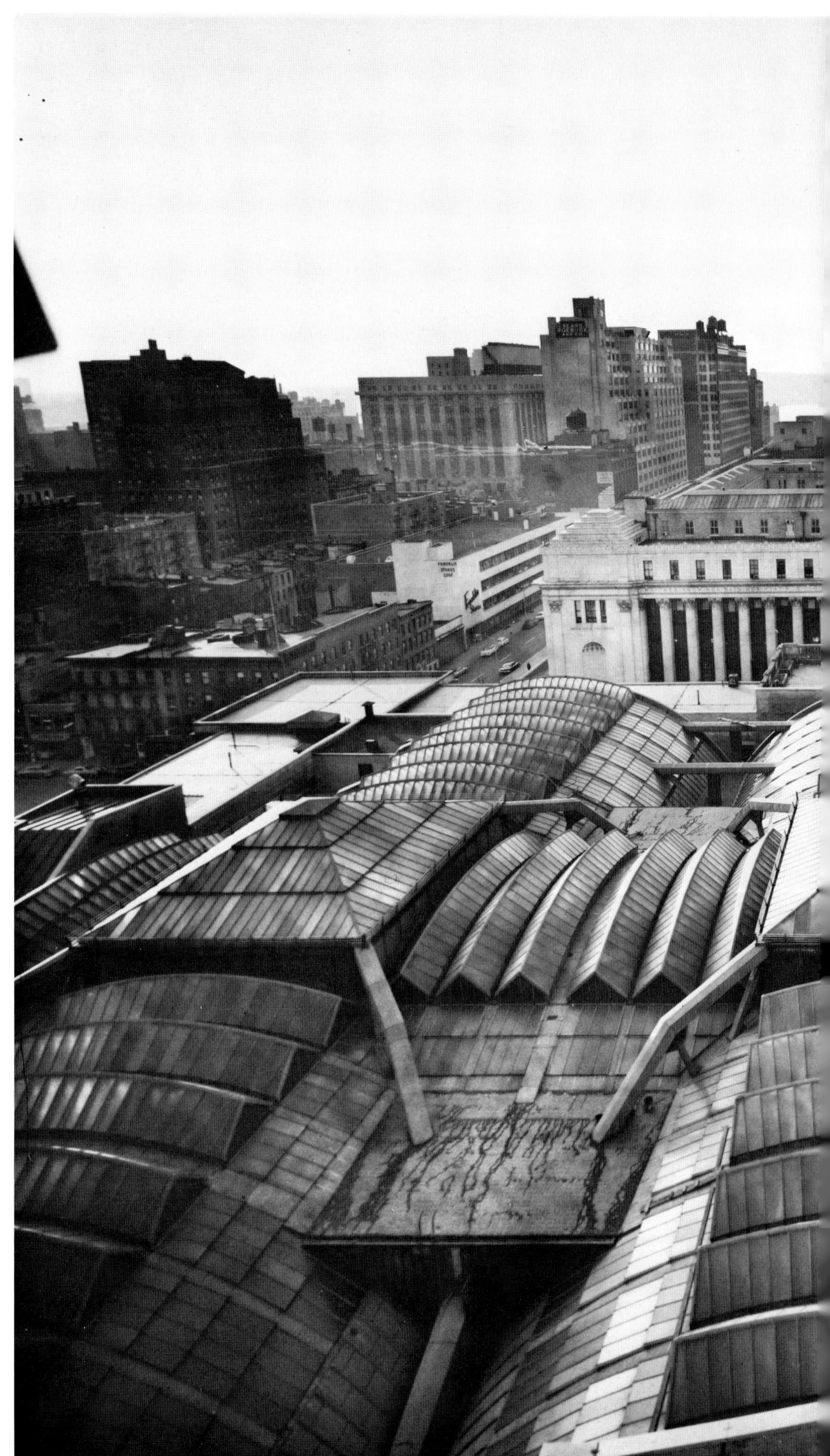

McKim, Mead & White.
Pennsylvania Station.
New York, New York, 1964.

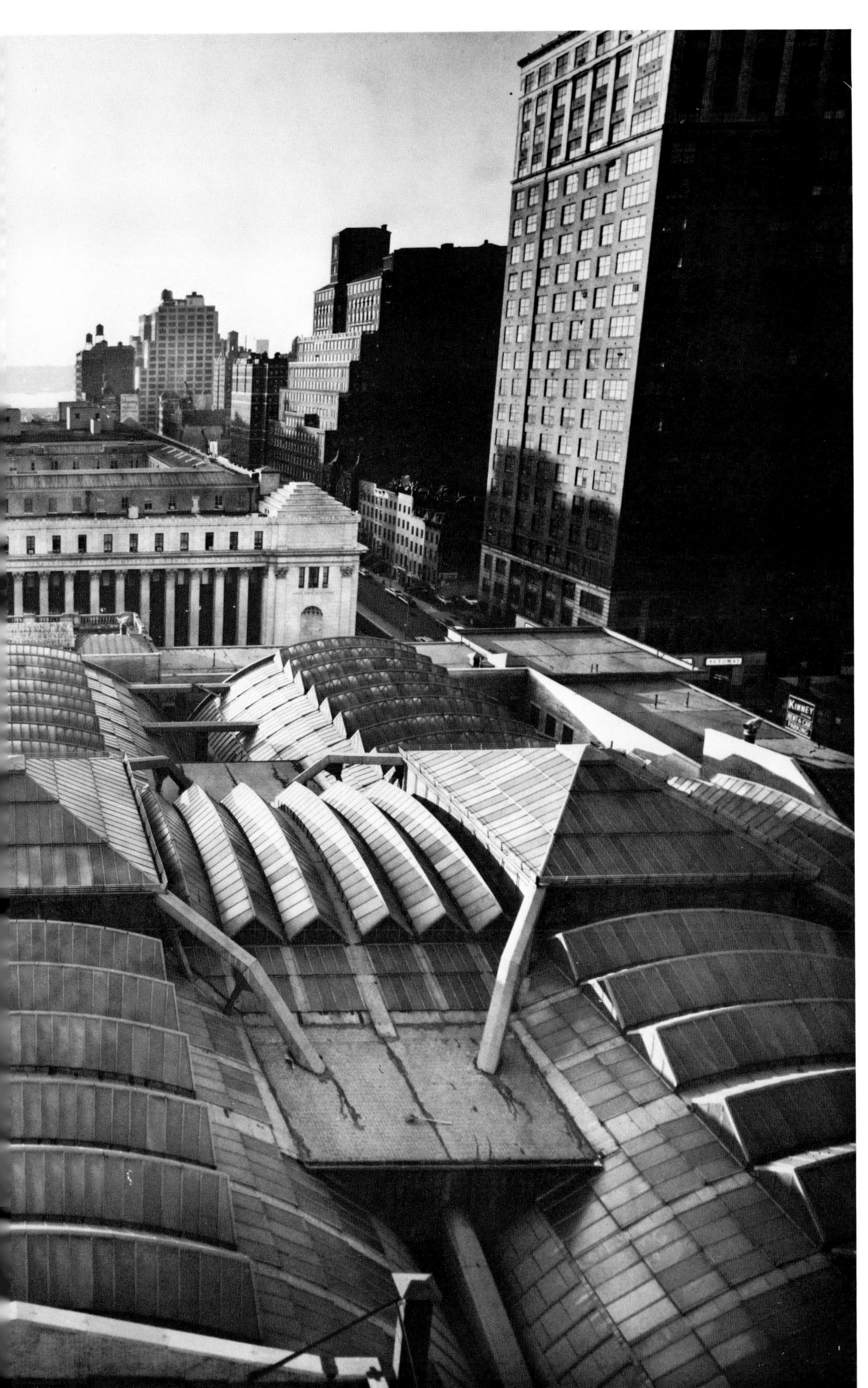
KINNEY

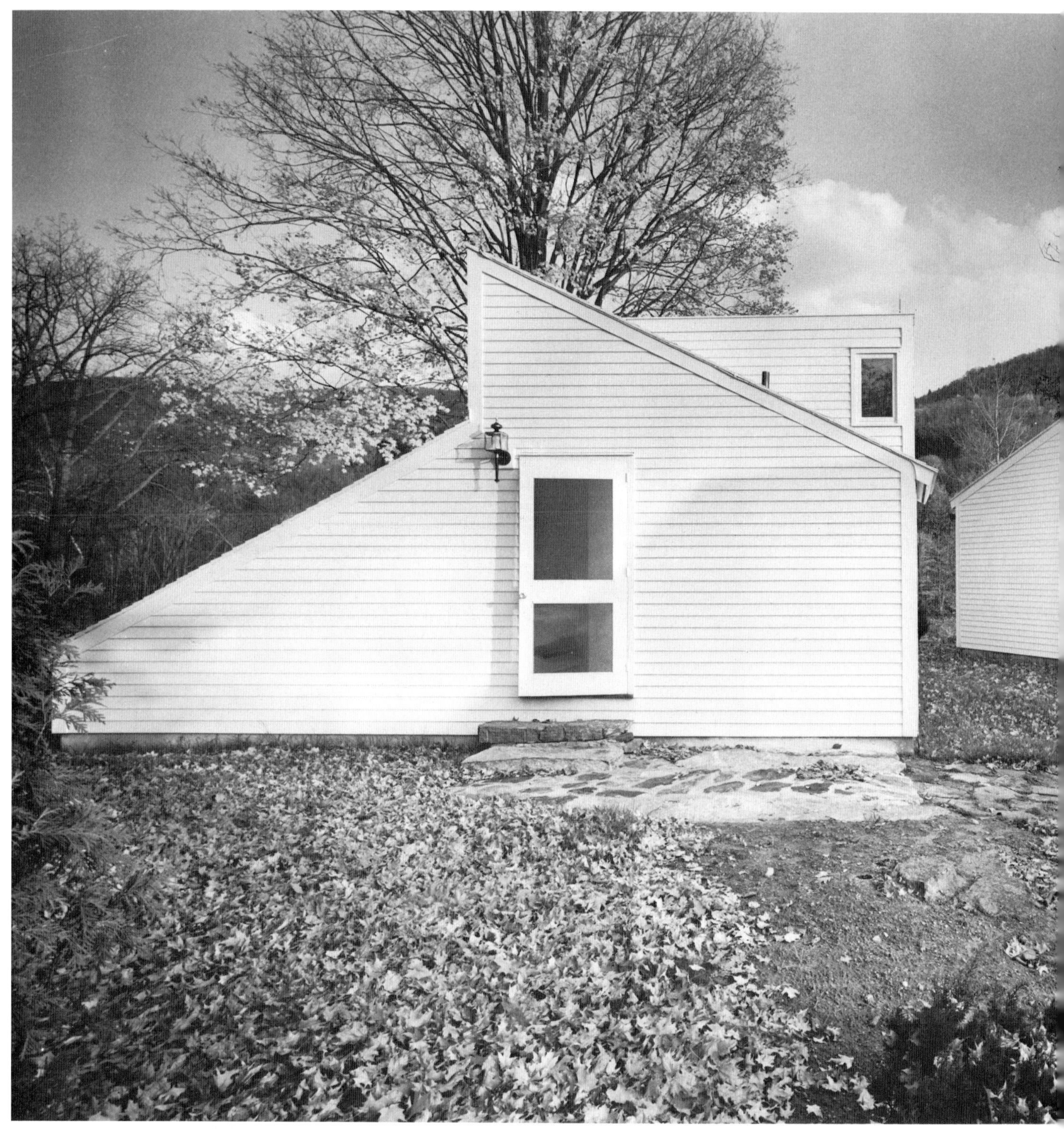

ABOVE: Hugh Hardy and Tim Prentice. Ingersoll Residence. Connecticut, 1965.

FACING PAGE: William Ehrlich. Ehrlich Residence. New York, New York, 1973.

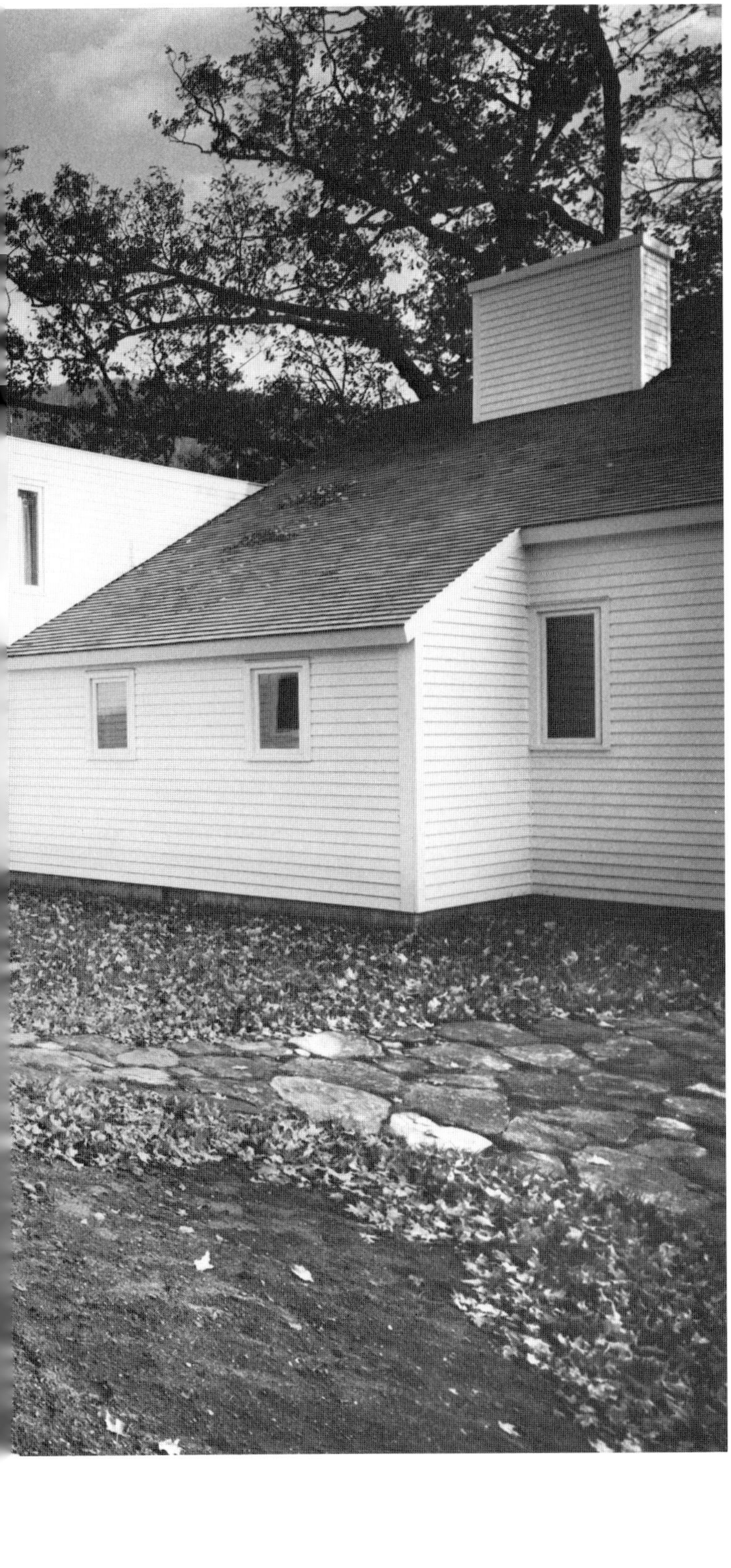

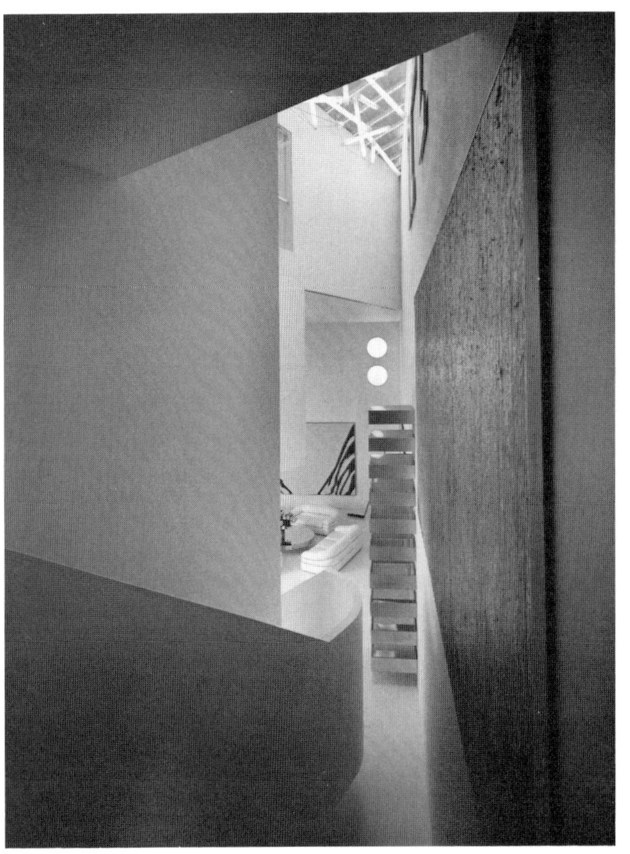

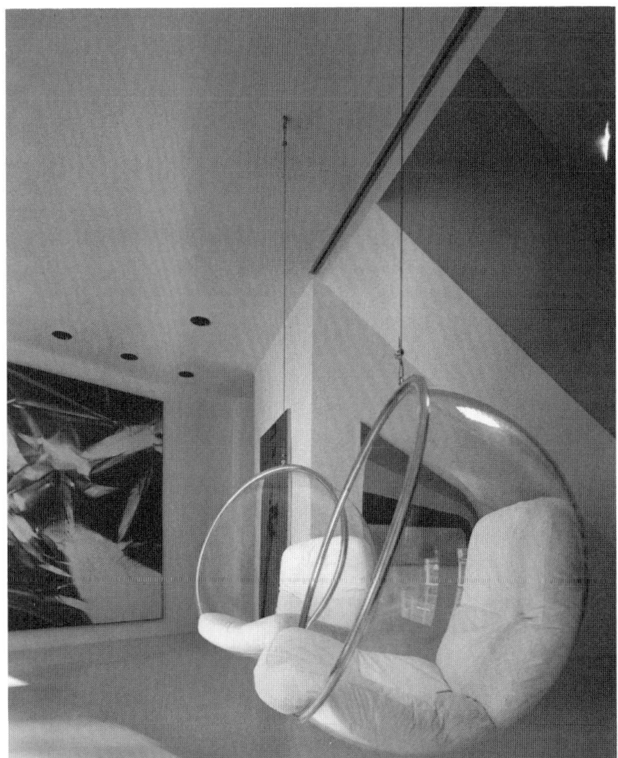

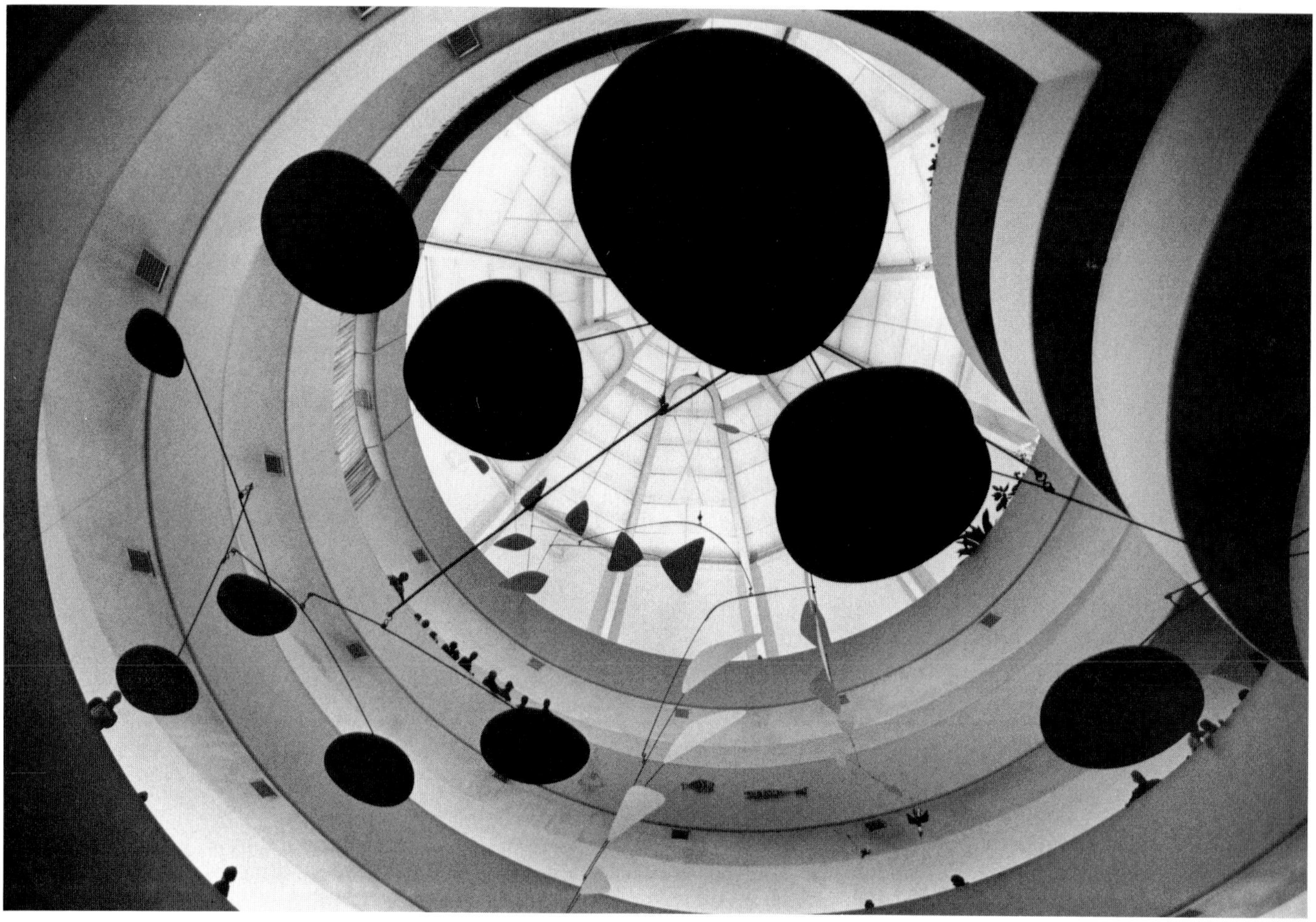

ABOVE: Frank Lloyd Wright. The Guggenheim Museum. New York, New York, 1967.

RIGHT: Port La Galère. Southern France, 1971.

FACING PAGE: Eero Saarinen. Dulles International Airport. Chantilly, Virginia, 1962.

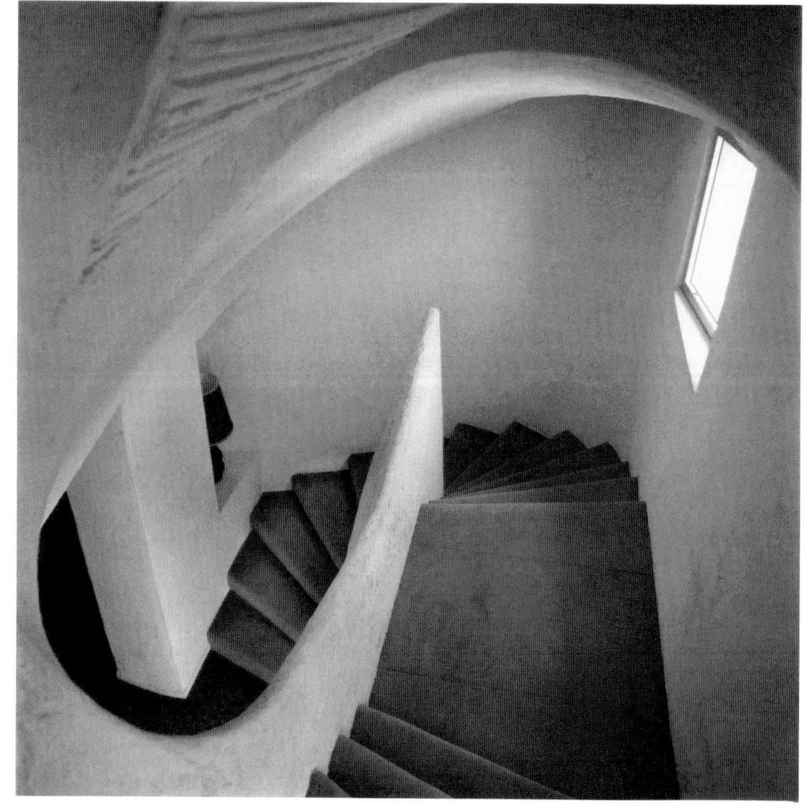

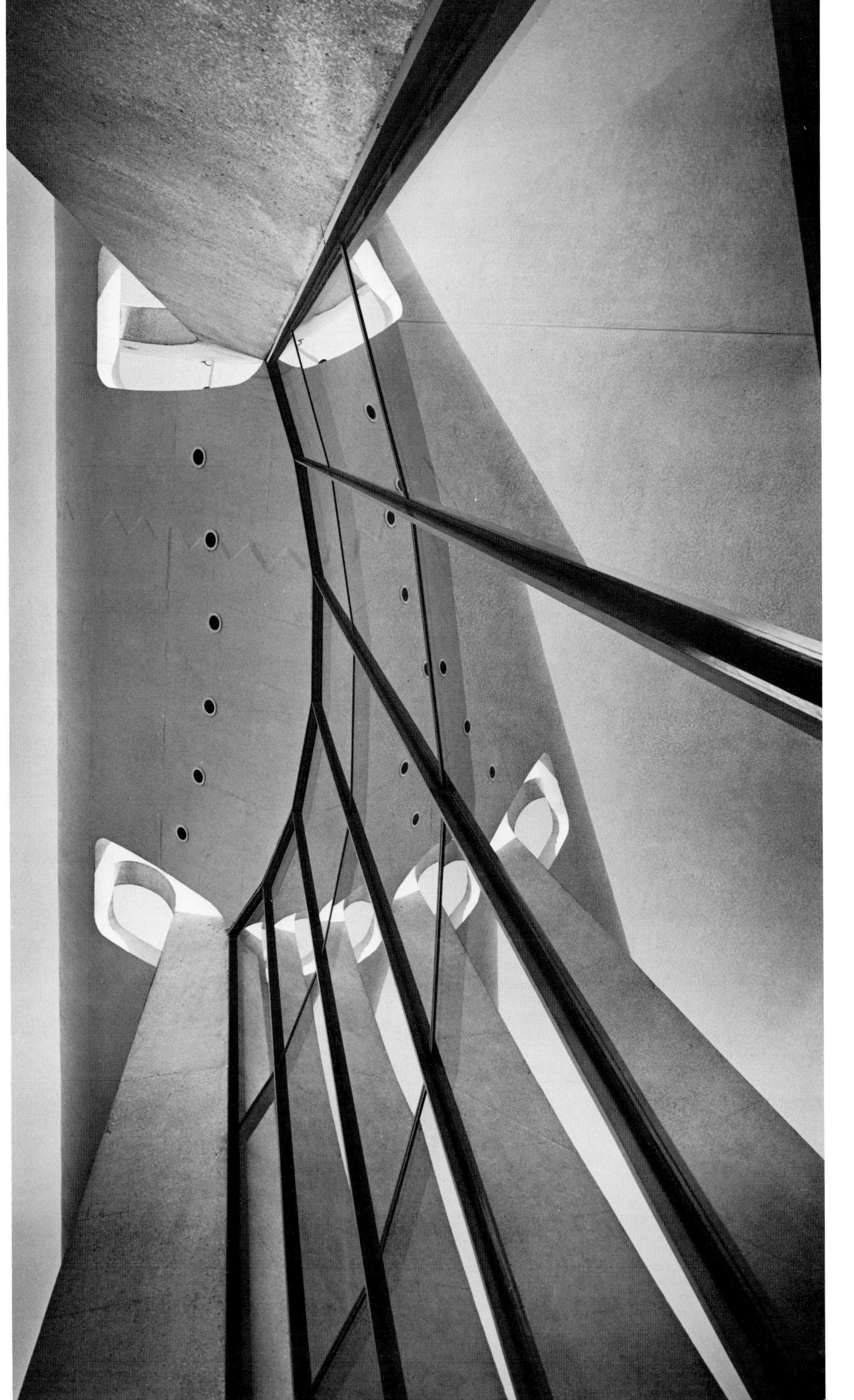

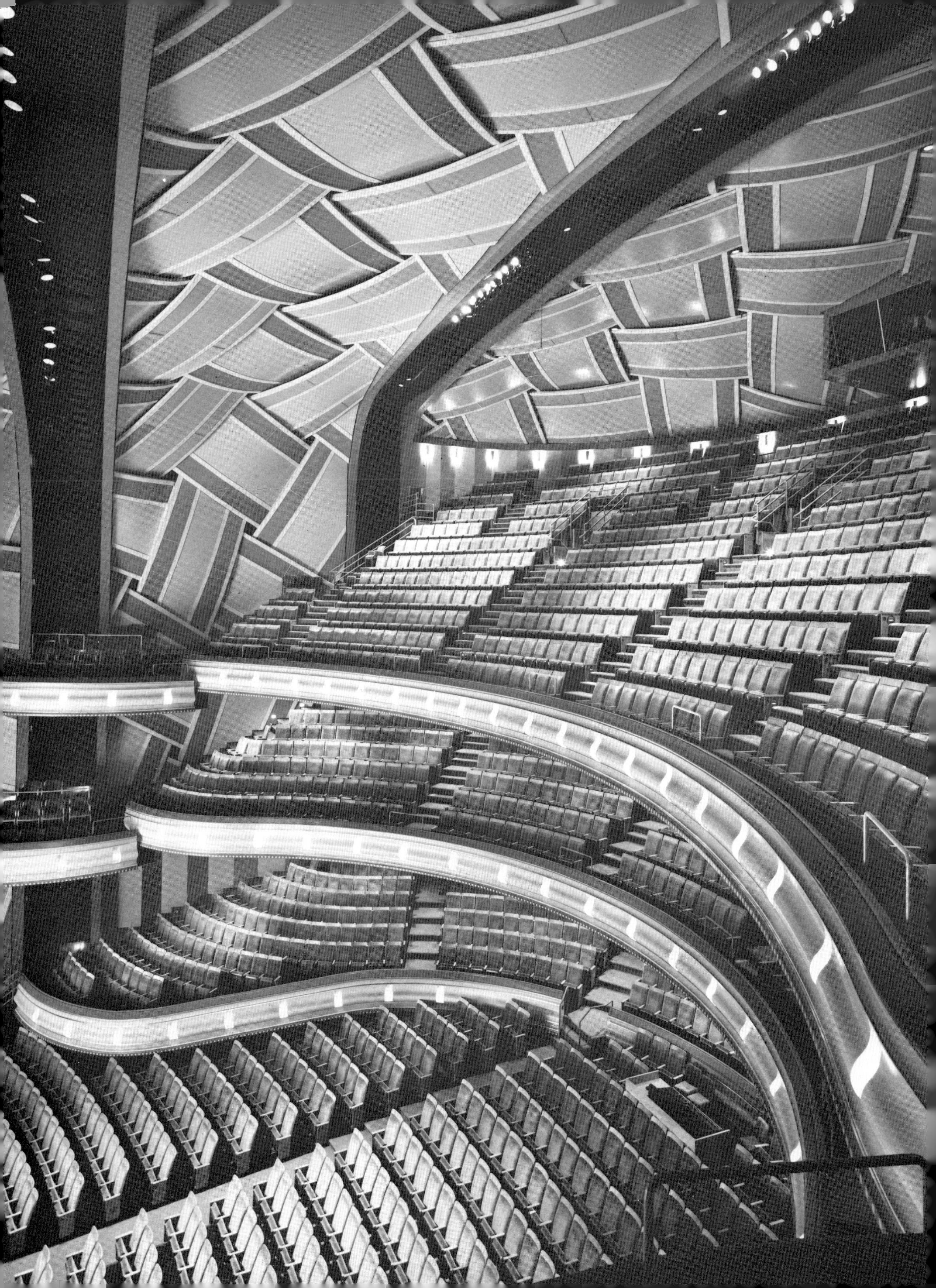

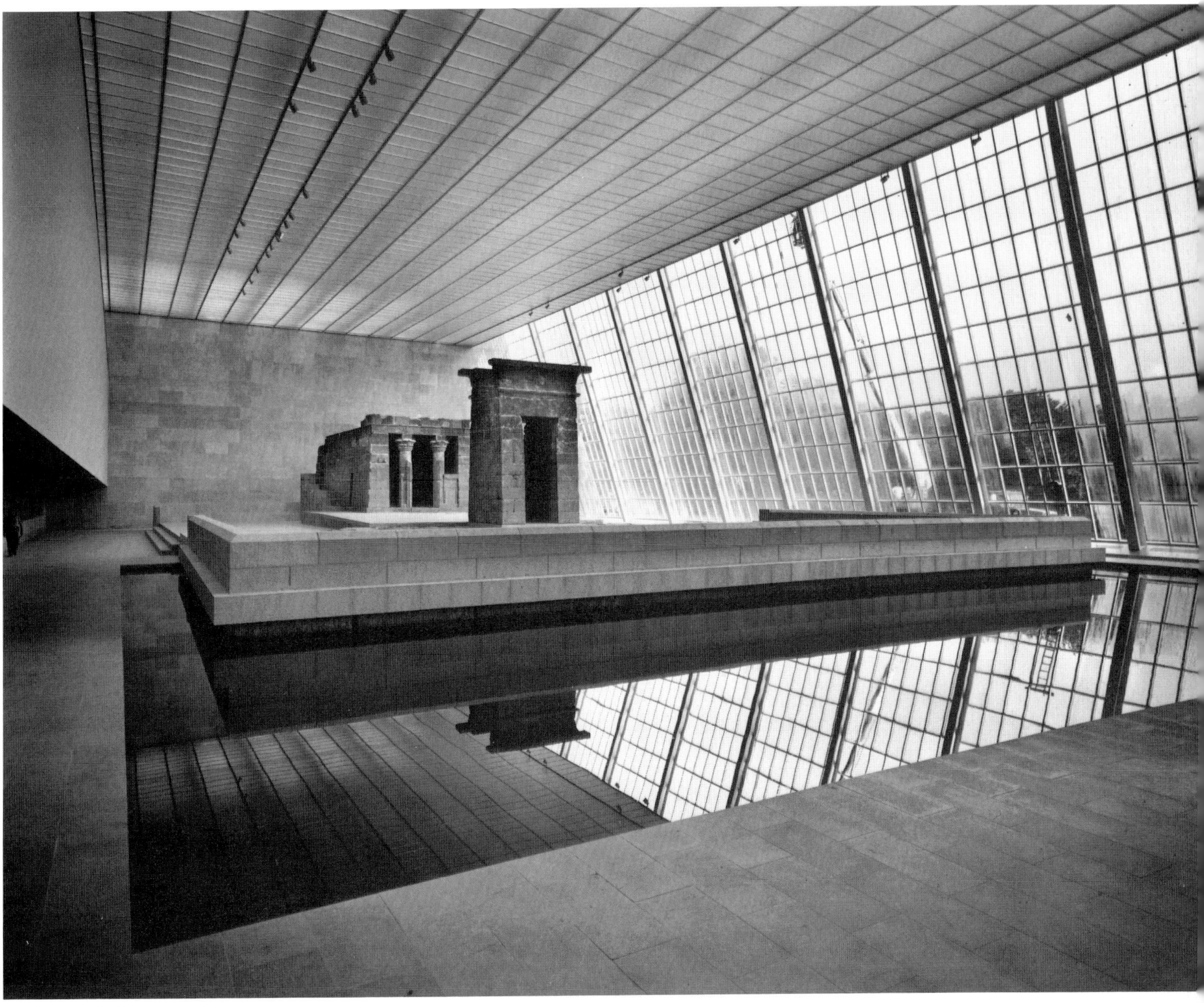

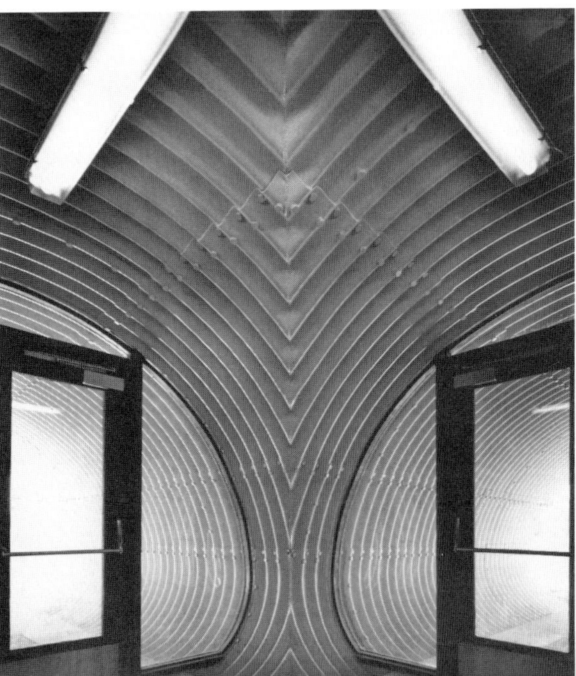

ABOVE: Temple of Dendur, The Metropolitan Museum of Art. New York, New York, 1978.

LEFT: Hardy Holzman Pfeiffer. Fireman's Training Center, Randalls' Island. New York, New York, 1975.

FACING PAGE: Hardy Holzman Pfeiffer Associates. Hult Performing Art Center. Eugene, Oregon, 1975.

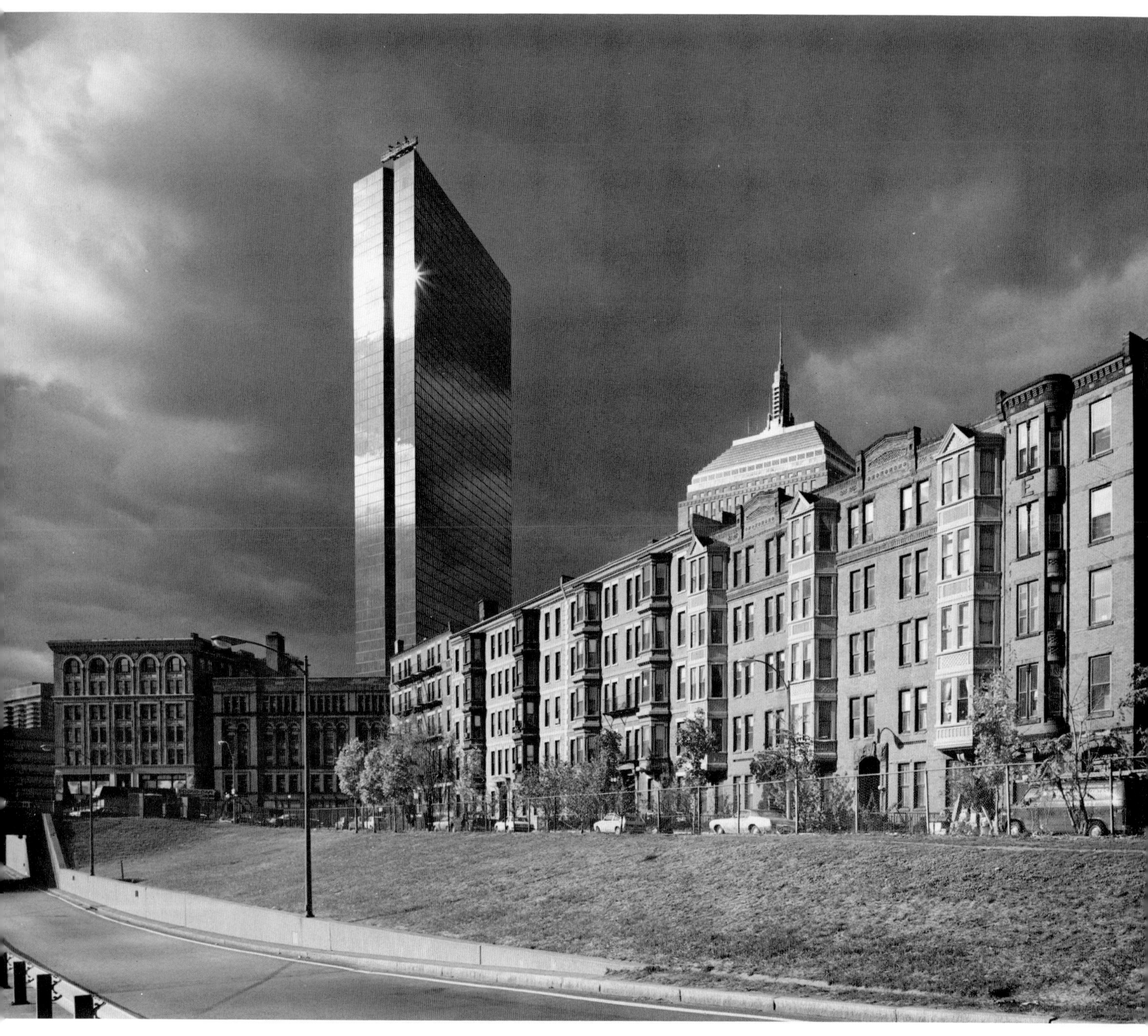

I. M. Pei and Partners; Henry N. Cobb, design partner. John Hancock Building. Boston, Massachusetts, 1980 (copyright © Steve Rosenthal).

STEVE ROSENTHAL

Because it is the intent of the architectural photograph to reveal the building as clearly and as accurately as possible, the building, as a result, often appears as pure object. Many architectural photographers speak of the process as one that puts the architecture first, the photograph second. The corollary frequently then is architecture as image and the building as pure object, existing pristine in its own world. As critic Robert Campbell has noted, "The problem is simple. From the point of view of getting good architecture, photography has been a bad influence. The reason is clear. The essence of photography is the act of framing. With your viewfinder, you put a frame around something, isolating it and giving it a special importance while suppressing everything outside the frame. Photography, in other words, is the removal of context." [1] While this approach may often represent and serve the intent of the architect, it says less of the way the building is used and perceived in its site by the people who use it.

Steve Rosenthal's photographs are marked by a more contextual approach. His work has been described by Campbell as "remarkably successful at capturing the whole experience of a building and especially of the quality of the architectural space inside it and around it." [2] It asks us to view architecture as something more organic and sets out to record the full potential of the building as a part of a larger world. It is difficult to crop his images, as their foreground and background provide the context invaluable to the perception of the architecture. Rosenthal's work resists the temptation to remove the architecture from its location or from its use; his presentation locates the building as part of a continuous whole.

It is Rosenthal's background as an architect, perhaps, that has allowed him this fluidity and given him this ability to place the building in its appropriate context. A graduate of the Harvard School of Design, Rosenthal worked for five years as an architect and designer for Cambridge Seven Associates and the Architects Collaborative in Cambridge. "But I realized I felt more comfortable dealing in two dimensions than in three dimensions," he explains. "And I realized that I would be a much better photographer than I would be an architect. I have the ability to translate three dimensions into two, rather than going the other way, which is what you do as an architect, going from plans and sections to construction. But having an architect's training was really very helpful in giving me that kind of intuitive understanding of space."

Rosenthal does indeed speak the architect's language, and largely for this reason, 90 percent of his work is for architects. But it is a situation, he points out, that works both ways. In previous years, simply because there were more architectural magazines, a competitive energy had been nurtured among them. Publications would commission photographers and compete to publish the most illuminating, and often provocative, photographs of a given building. But with fewer magazines on the contemporary marketplace than existed twenty years ago, there is less competition, and the result is that the magazines that do exist will usually publish photographs submitted to them by the architect. Which means, Rosenthal concludes, that the image eventually published is exactly the image the architect wishes the public to see.

Rosenthal exploits the advantages to this, though, which allow and encourage the photographer to convey the intent of the architect. Rosenthal's photographs have been credited with doing so, most notably by a 1984 Institute Honor from the American Institute of Architects. Citing his work, the jury noted that Rosenthal "understands site, program, structure, style, materials, cost, context. His broad understanding enables him to respond to architecture as a whole."

Rosenthal speaks of his own work as treading a fine line. To one side is embellishment and contrivance, to the other, disinterested documentation. And the tool that he uses most precisely in treading this line is light. Rosenthal manipulates light in such a way that the film captures what the eye sees. His photographs have a pictorial honesty that comes with his acknowledgment that the photograph is often the only way people may know a building. "There's a responsibility involved; the photograph often becomes a substitute for the building."

"I try first just to understand the building and why it is the way it is—the materials, the scale, the height, its site, the way it was organized, and why it turned out the way it did." Often these things are obvious. Just as often, they are not, and Rosenthal refers to drawings, renderings, other photographs. If the building is nearby, he spends time on the site before the shoot. Discussions with the architect, interior designer, graphic designer, and whoever else may have some interest in the photograph as well as some knowledge of the building, all contribute further to his understanding of the architecture.

Rosenthal's photographs mean to expose not only the space, but how it has been organized and how the smaller spaces have been put together and connect, both in their more abstract design concept and in actual construction. By analyzing the space, Rosenthal is also analyzing the circumstances under which it could best be photographed, which in most cases is the quality of light. He takes into account the altitude of the sun and its position in the sky. In New England, for example, in the early winter, the sun rises in the southeast and sets in the southwest. Because the sun is much lower, its light is much harsher, striking objects at almost a perpendicular angle; during summer months, the sun is higher, and its light grazes surfaces more softly.

Foliage is another dictate of season. Its own textures and the contrasts created by its shadows can often work as a desirable design element within the photograph. In a heavily wooded site, however, an excess of foliage can contribute to a jumble of patterns that may camouflage or obscure details of the architecture. If the shadows are underexposed and the highlights overexposed, both the continuity and detail of materials can easily be lost.

In interior jobs, especially, the play with light is often a critical balancing act. The color of daylight is always different from the color of the interior incandescent or fluorescent lighting, and film tends to exaggerate the difference, rather than subdue it, as the eye does. Rosenthal first tries to diminish the contrast; and although the space may be entirely relit, the objective is to maintain the same effect of lighting that the designer or architect intended.

The harsh greens and yellows of fluorescent lighting are particularly incompatible with other light sources, daylight and incandescent. While the problem is generally solved in shooting with multiple light sources, or making the different light sources compatible with filters, color correction is occasionally done in the darkroom, where the harsher green hues can be neutralized. In large, expansive interior spaces that cannot be adequately relit by the photographer, the light manipulation may also be done in the darkroom.

In some locations, the view from the building is imperative to establishing context. In such a case, in an effort to expose the view, the interior light is manipulated to diminish the contrast with the exterior, natural light.

The irony, of course, is that the objective of this often complex manipulation is simply to reveal what is there to begin with. While photographers in other fields may use the feats of darkroom technology, it is usually to heighten or otherwise dramatize their subject matter. The architectural photographer, however, relies upon these same controls to document, as honestly as possible, what is existing. "The human eye is able to handle a much greater range of contrast than the film can," says Rosenthal. Recording this range on film so that it appears as naturally as it does to the eye demands the same precision and imagination usually associated with work that is less strictly representational.

While light is perhaps the most effective and most valuable tool in this process of manipulation, there are others. "Just as your eye is aware of the contrast, and accommodates it," Rosenthal explains, "you're also aware of other things that are in the space that may not be in the frame of the picture. And anything that's outside the frame may as well not be there. So the question is how you get this ambience into the photograph." In interior photography especially, furniture, furnishings, and whatever objects may be in the space may be rearranged to reveal not only the architecture, but the feel or sense of the space. "You want to feel as though you can walk across the room," says Rosenthal, "which sometimes means that you have to move furniture around."

The wide-angle lens used in most interior photography may also suggest—or demand—that objects be rearranged. Although the wide-angle lens will accommodate more within the frame, it also tends to distort curved shapes and the depth of space, the latter by dramatically elongating it; objects closer to the camera may appear to be particularly distorted. In such instances, a room may be totally rearranged but with the objective, again, that the new arrangement retain the original feeling, be it one of spaciousness and openness or of seclusion and privacy.

Rosenthal's use of people also distinguishes his work. The reluctance of most architectural photographers to use people in their photographs is due to a number of legitimate reasons. Primarily, a photograph with a person in it all too often becomes a photograph of that person. If the human presence does not actually become the focus of the photograph, it can easily distract from the architecture. While people are clearly not the subject of an architectural photograph, too easily they become exactly that. Which is all the more unfortunate, Rosenthal points out, because people can tend to look wooden and stiff when posed. Especially in long exposures, the poses they strike can appear mannered. Also, for obvious reasons of fashion and appearance, the person can easily date the photograph. And while it is occasionally argued that the human figure endows the architecture with a sense of scale, the more persuasive argument is that if the architecture needs the human figure to convey a sense of scale, it has not been well resolved. Suggestions that people in architectural photographs evoke a human element, a sense of warmth, or other intangible qualities can be answered similarly.

While Rosenthal hardly uses people in his work as instant evocations of these qualities, his fine-tuned attention to how a space might be perceived and occupied often leads him to show the space as it is used. He especially encourages the use of people in photographing spaces whose sense and feeling is utterly flavored by how they are used. The documentation of a schoolroom, for example, is incomplete without a photograph of children in it. Likewise, the documentation of a public plaza would demand the photograph of the site as it is being used. "The use of people depends *completely* upon the project," says Rosenthal. "While there may not be any point in it in a studied interior, you do need people in any kind of candid approach toward public spaces." Rosenthal adds that while the use of the human figure to convey scale can sometimes be a gimmick, at other times the angle or composition of a single photograph may not represent the building's scale clearly. In such cases, then, it can be clarified by the human figure.

Rosenthal occasionally relies upon graphic as well as photographic solutions. Villa Victoria was the subject of a photograph taken from the top of Prudential Center in Boston, but from that vantage point, it merged with its surroundings and became nearly indistinguishable. Rosenthal's solution, then, was to splice two separate photographs together: the building from a high-contrast photograph was superimposed on low-contrast surroundings. The device allowed the subject of the photograph to stand out noticeably without appearing overly dramatic or contrived.

Although the use of such graphics are the exception rather than the rule, they again point out that the manipulated photograph can be documentary as well as interpretive; that technical manipulation can yield not forced contrivances, but straightforward and revealing documents. That the honesty of the final document is often the result of skilled manipulation is one of the subtle ironies that informs Rosenthal's work, making his photographs authentic rather than artificial records of place.

"When people say the building looks better in the photograph, I don't necessarily take it as any compliment," says Rosenthal. "I find it really a little disappointing; it makes me feel as though I'm engaged in something a little bit dishonest. Without trying to deceive, I'm trying to show things the way they really are, in their best light and under the best conditions." That he has done so is amply evident in the body of work and the professional recognition it has received. Rosenthal's photographs tell us that documenting architecture accurately relies upon the precise technical skill that will reproduce the facts of the place, but more so, on the interpretive, imaginative, and intuitive skill that will record the less tangible sense of it. Both of these skills are apparent in his work, and together they make for an authentic photograph; one that considers not only the image of the building, but its site, use, and location; not only place, but placement.

---

1. Robert Campbell, "Architecture," *Boston Globe,* 14 February 1984, p. 56.
2. Ibid.

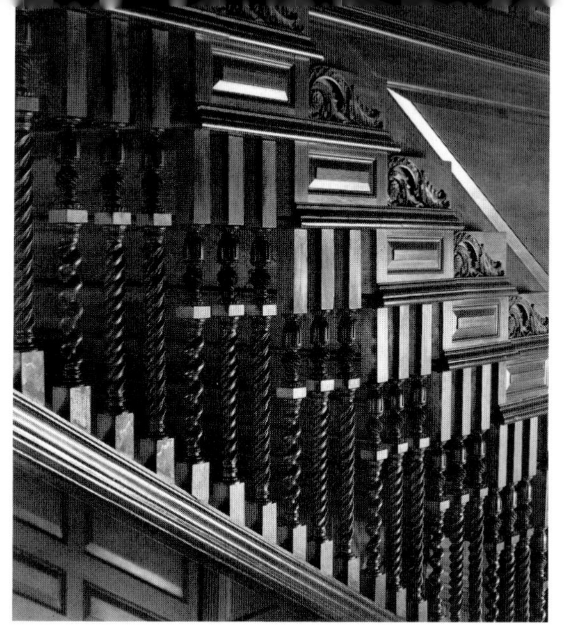

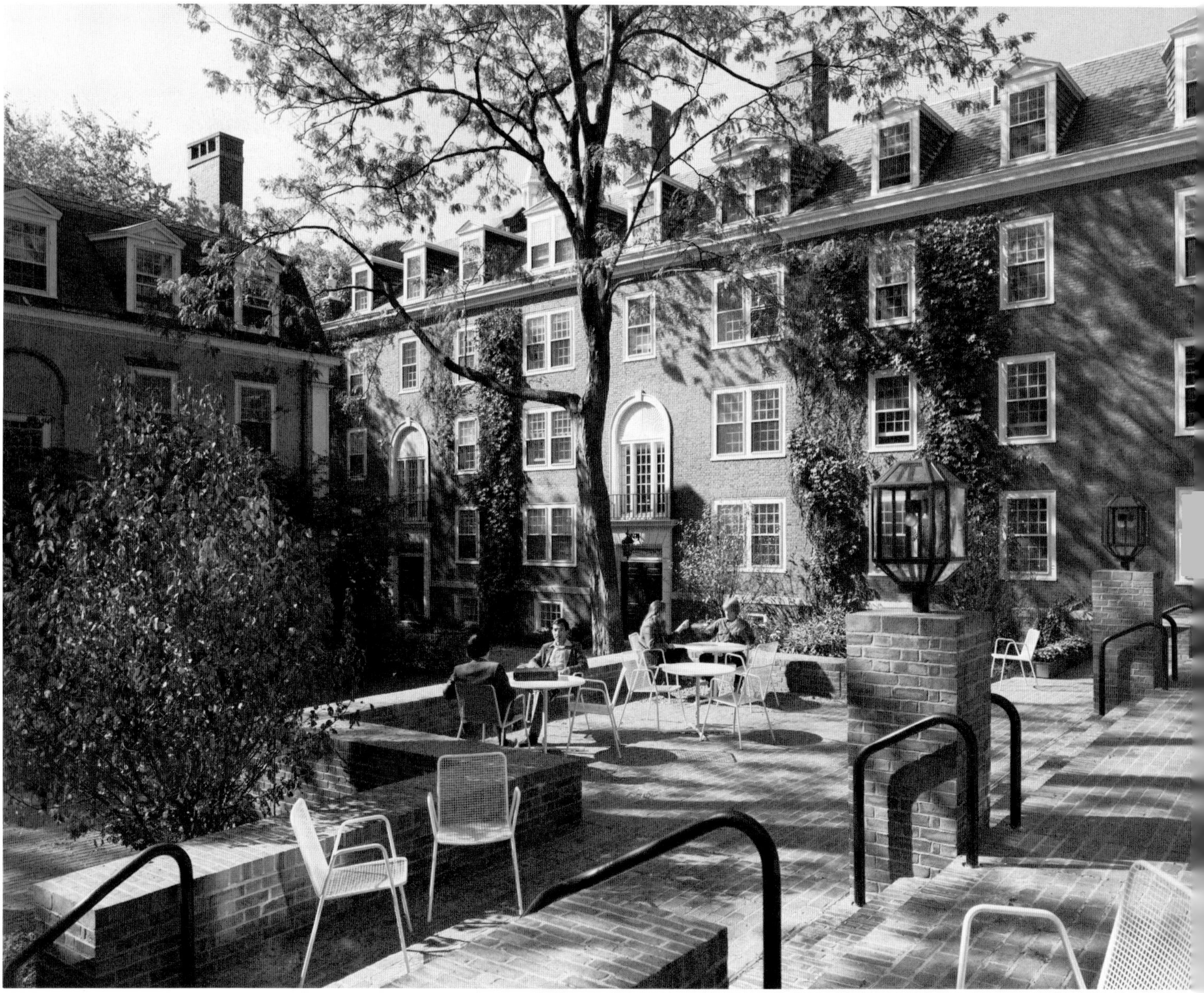

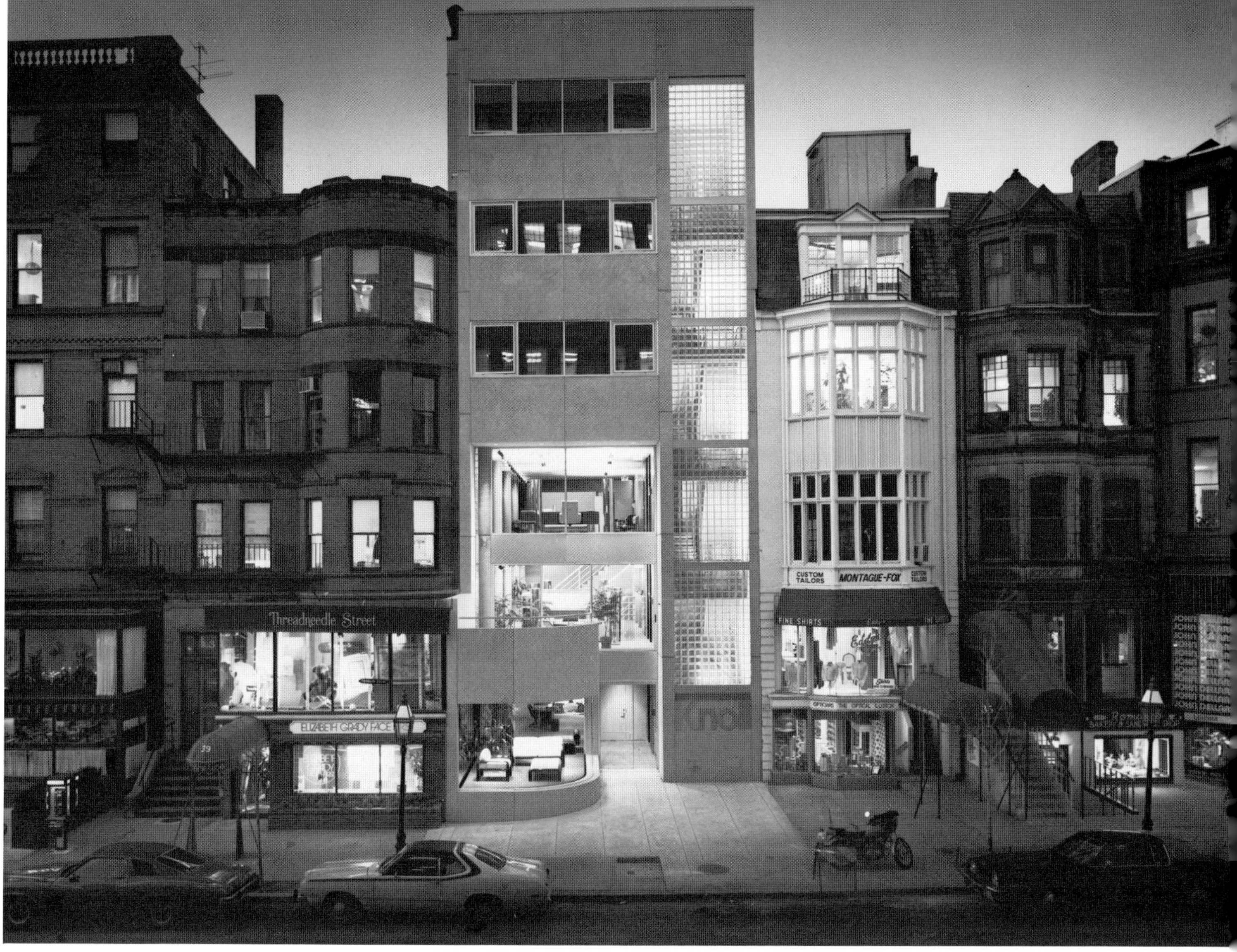

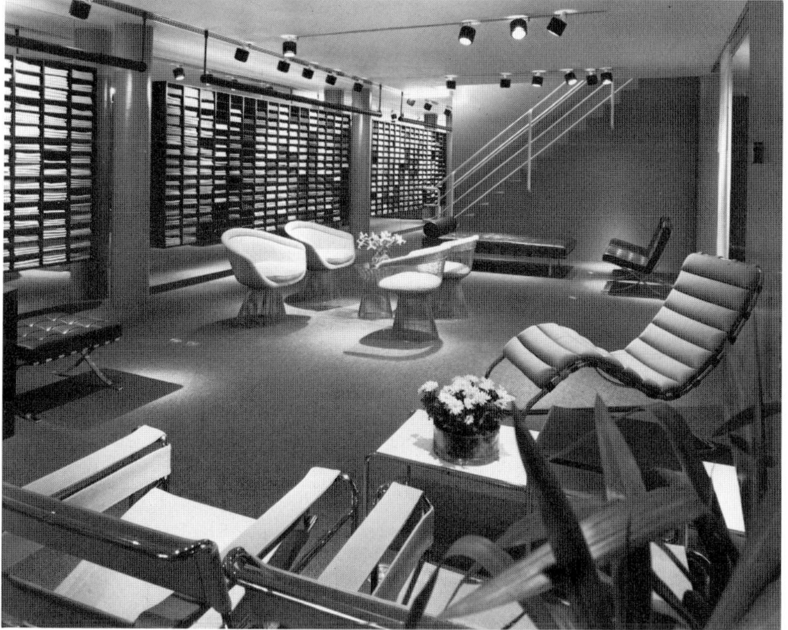

ABOVE AND LEFT:
Gwathmey-Siegel and Associates. Knoll Offices and Showroom. Boston, Massachusetts, 1980 (copyright © Steve Rosenthal).

FACING PAGE (TOP):
Lee Mansion. Marblehead, Massachusetts, 1982 (copyright © Steve Rosenthal).

FACING PAGE (BOTTOM):
Architectural Resources Cambridge. Chase Hall, Harvard Business School. Cambridge, Massachusetts, 1982 (copyright © Steve Rosenthal).

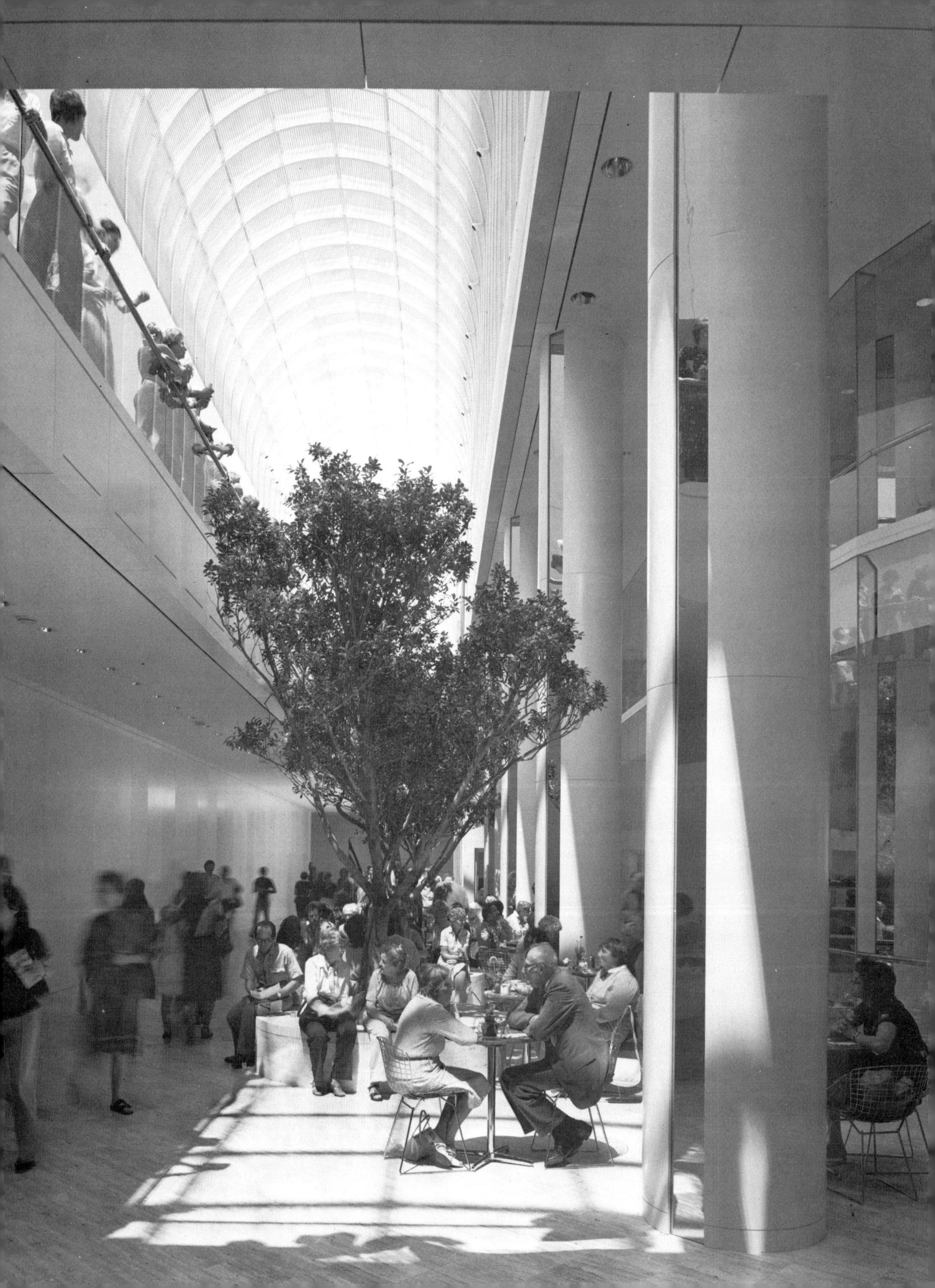

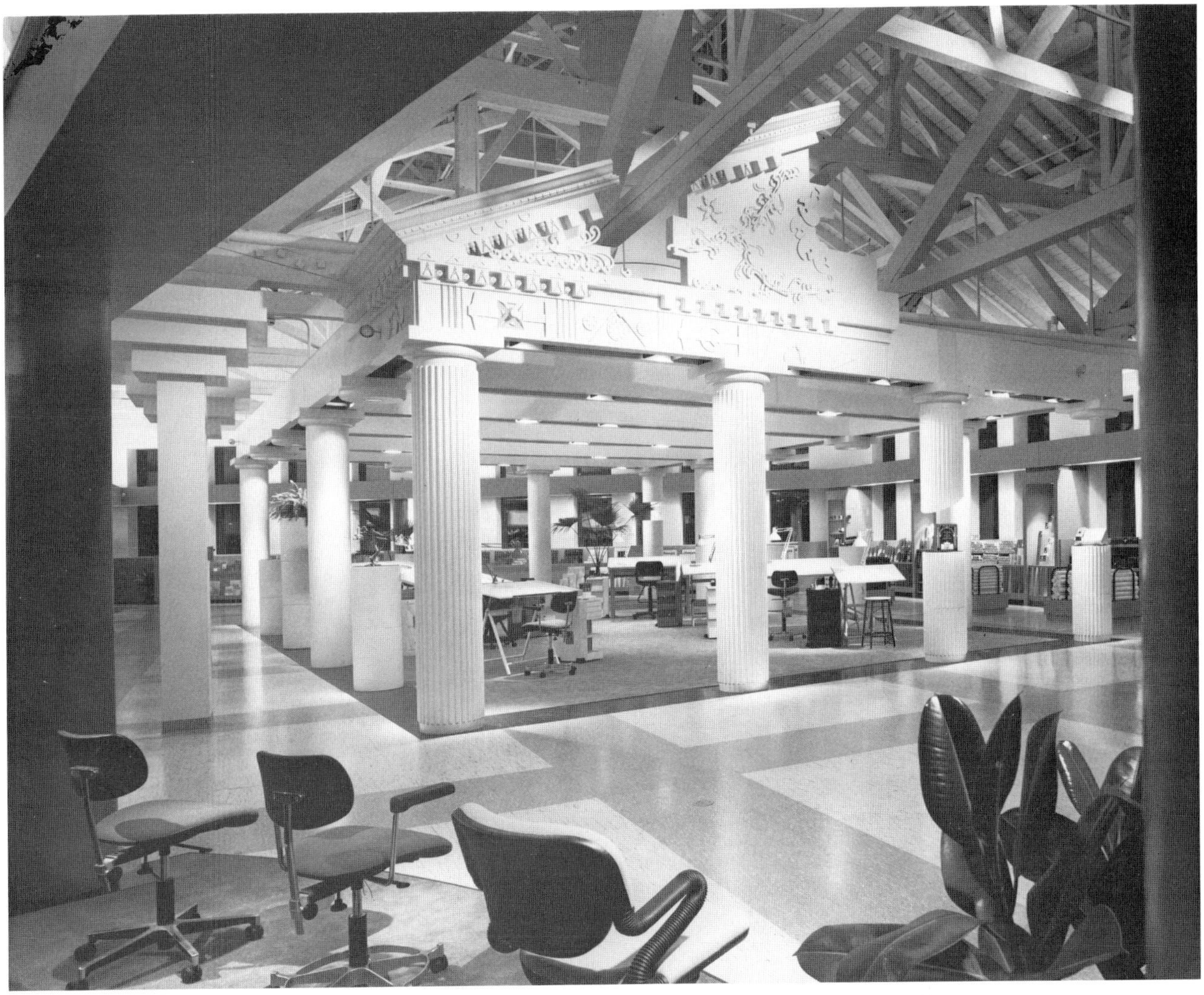

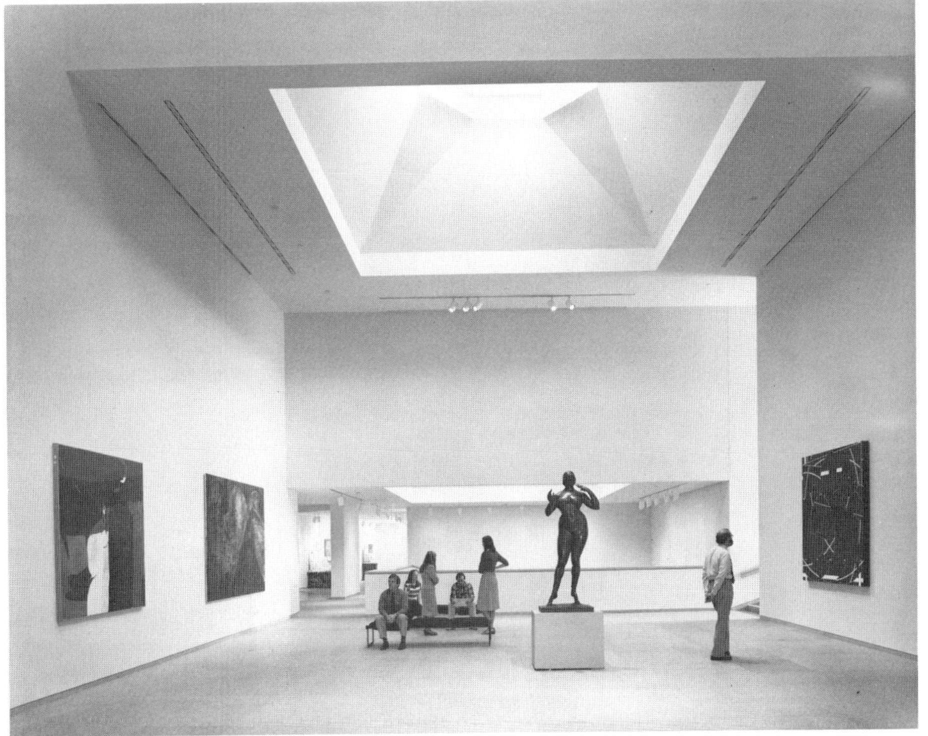

ABOVE: Olson-Lewis. Charrette. New Haven, Connecticut, 1982 (copyright © Steve Rosenthal).

LEFT: I. M. Pei and Partners; Henry N. Cobb, design partner. Portland Museum of Art. Portland, Maine, 1983 (copyright © Steve Rosenthal).

FACING PAGE: I. M. Pei and Partners. Museum of Fine Arts, West Wing Addition. Boston, Massachusetts, 1981 (copyright © Steve Rosenthal).

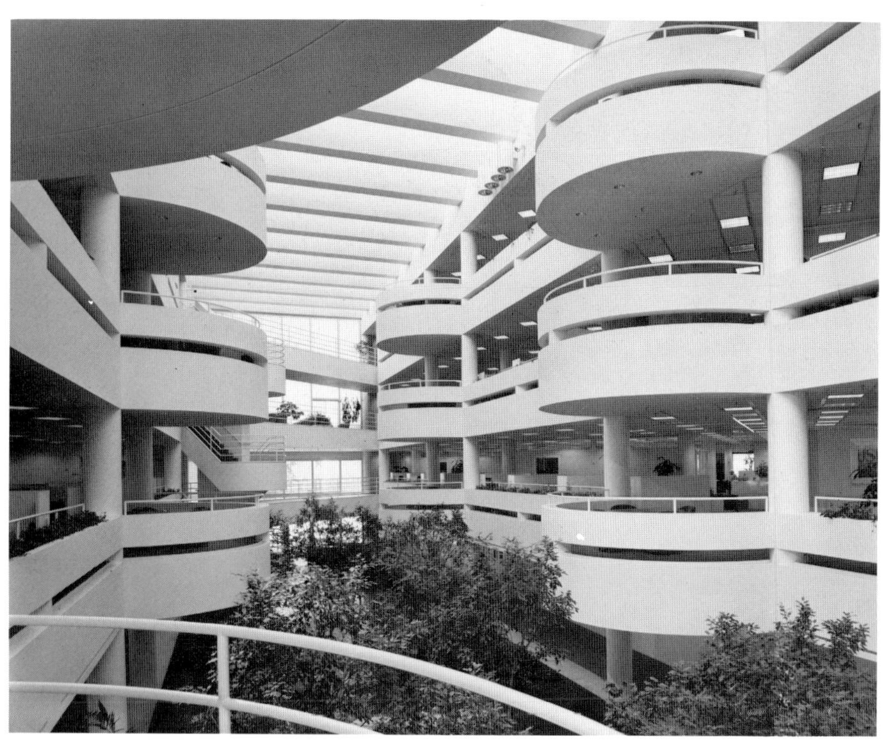

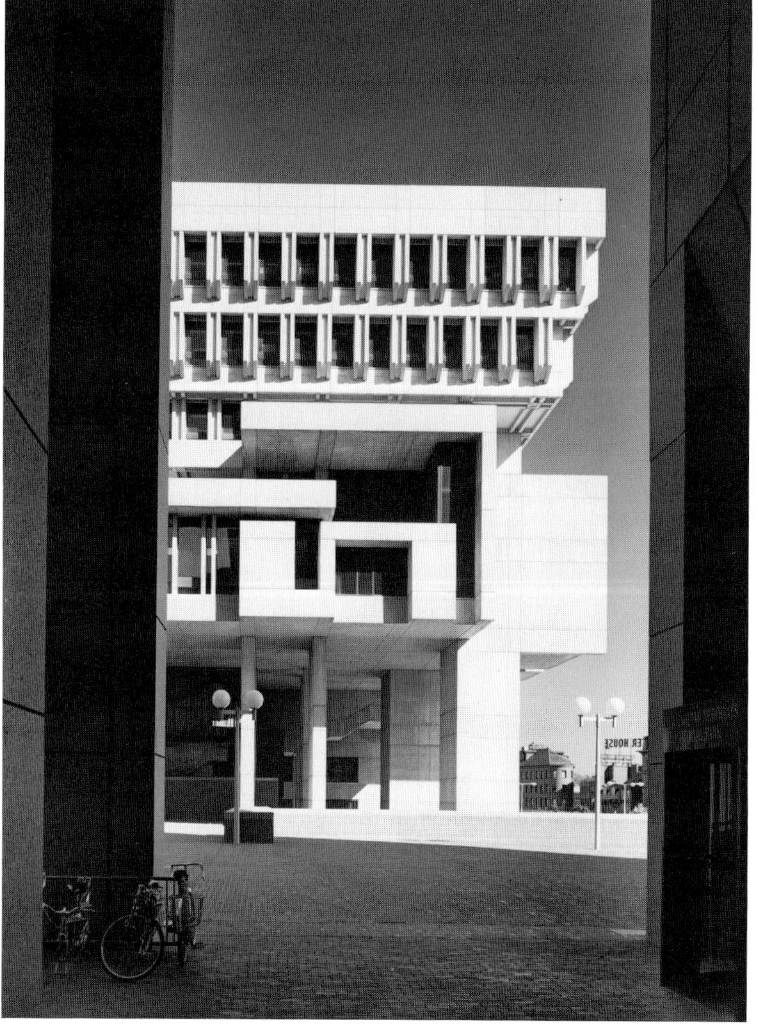

ER HOUSE

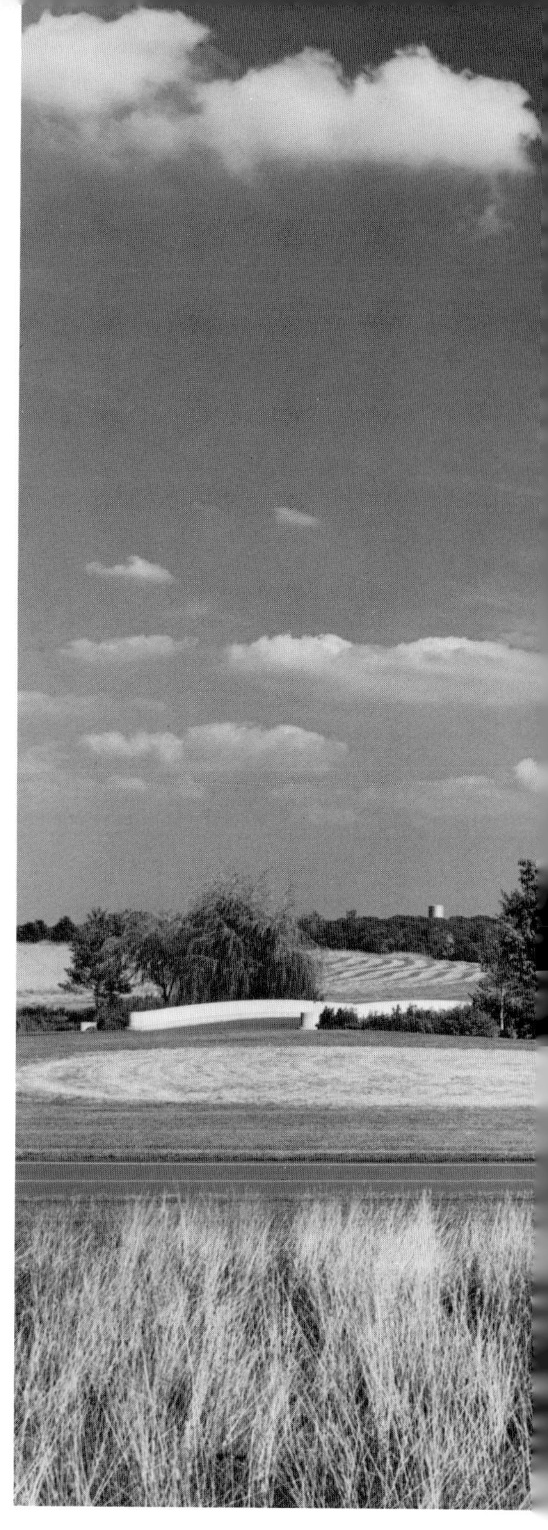

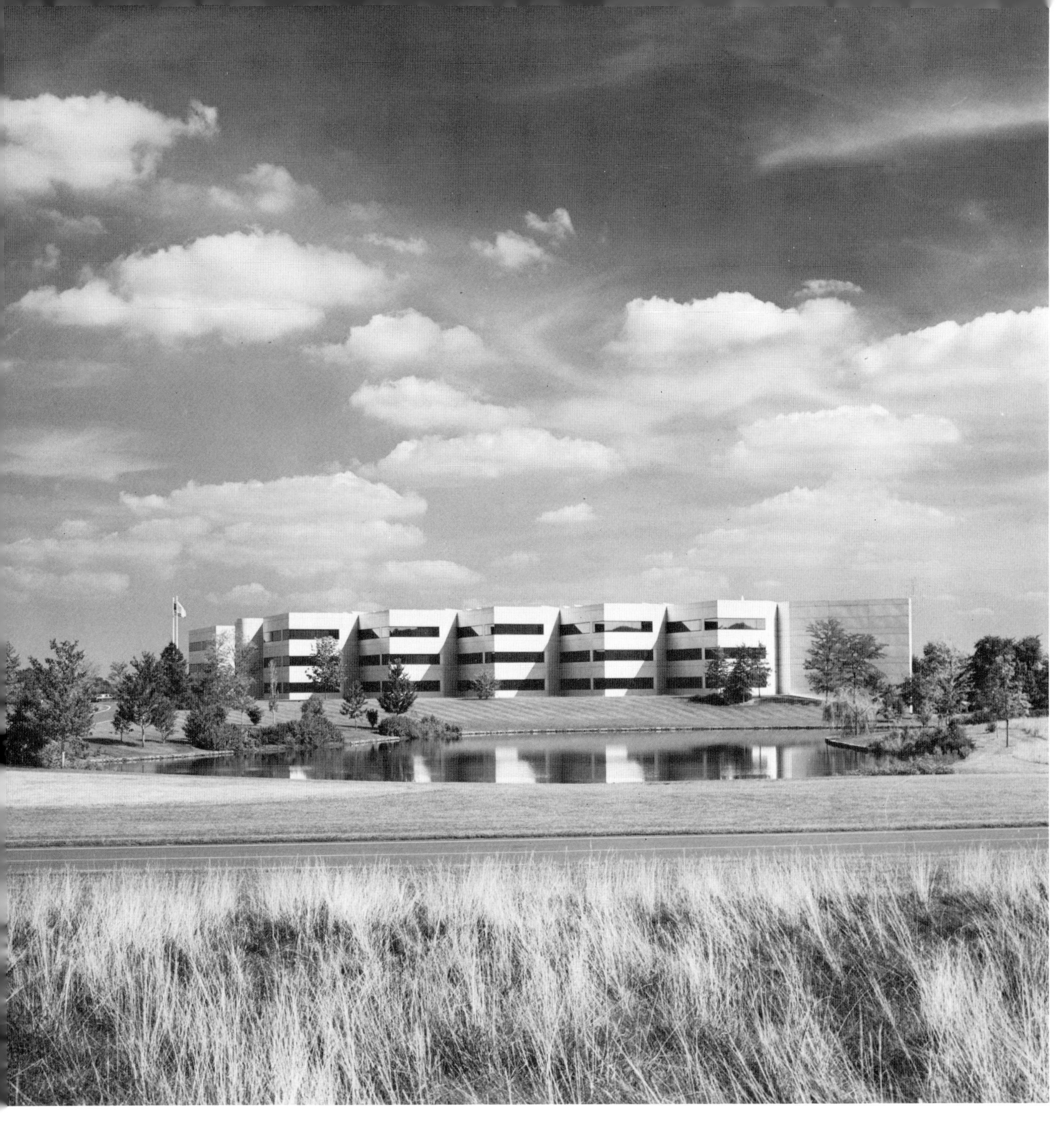

FACING PAGE (TOP) AND ABOVE: I. M. Pei and Partners; Henry N. Cobb, design partner. Office Building. 1984 (copyright © Steve Rosenthal).

FACING PAGE (BOTTOM): Kallman, McKinnell and Wood. Boston City Hall. Boston, Massachusetts, 1974 (copyright © Steve Rosenthal).

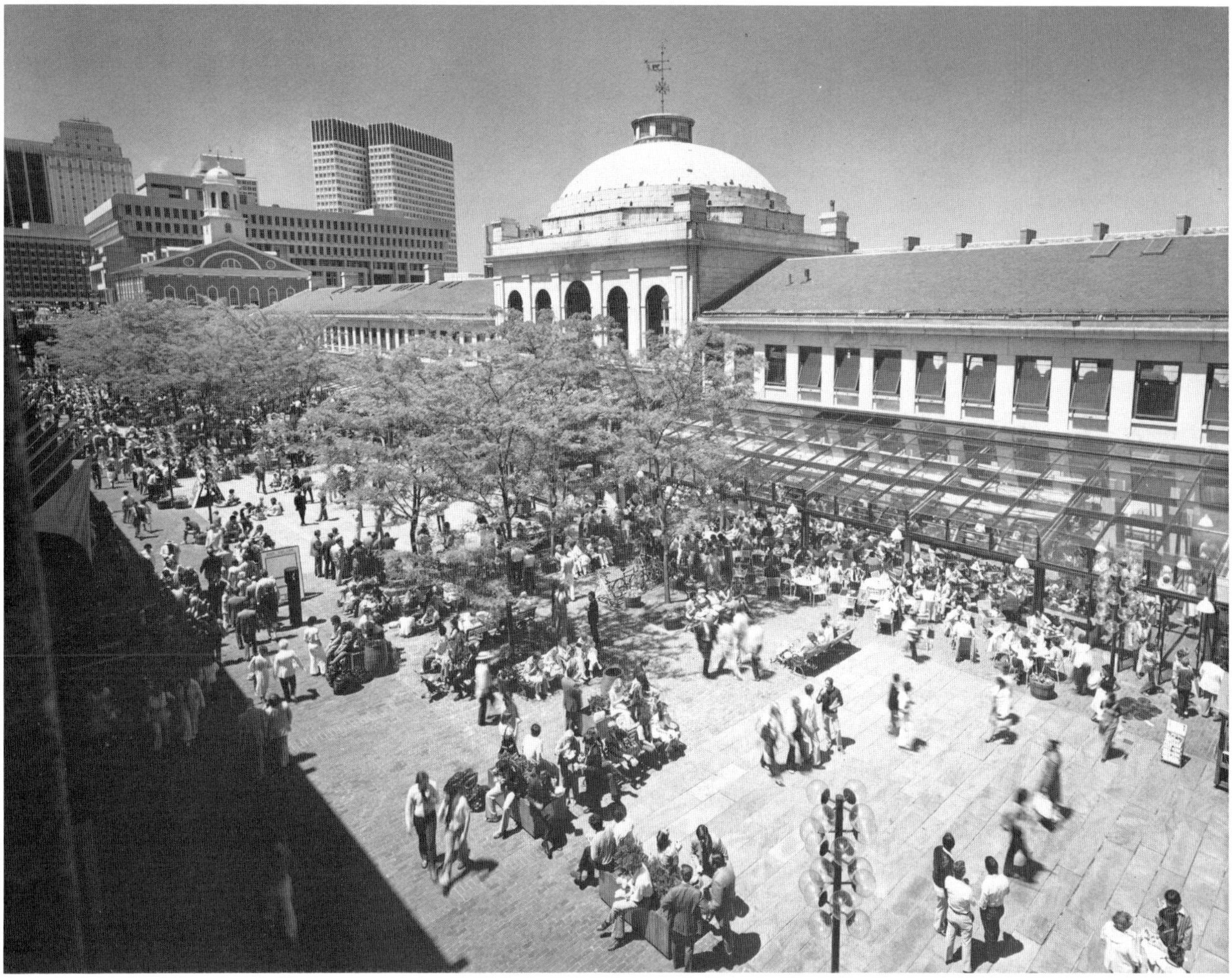

ABOVE: Benjamin Thompson and Associates. Faneuil Hall Marketplace. Boston, Massachusetts, 1977 (copyright © Steve Rosenthal).

RIGHT: Benjamin Thompson and Associates. Fulton Market, South Street Seaport. New York, New York, 1983 (copyright © Steve Rosenthal).

FACING PAGE: John Sharratt and Associates. Villa Victoria. Boston, Massachusetts, 1977 (copyright © Steve Rosenthal).

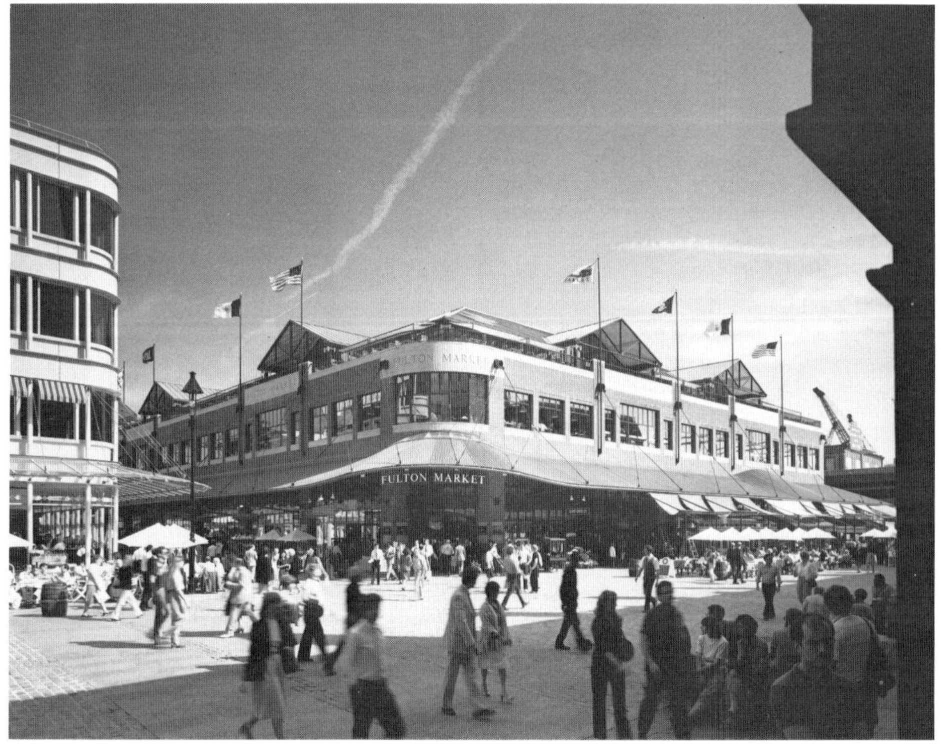

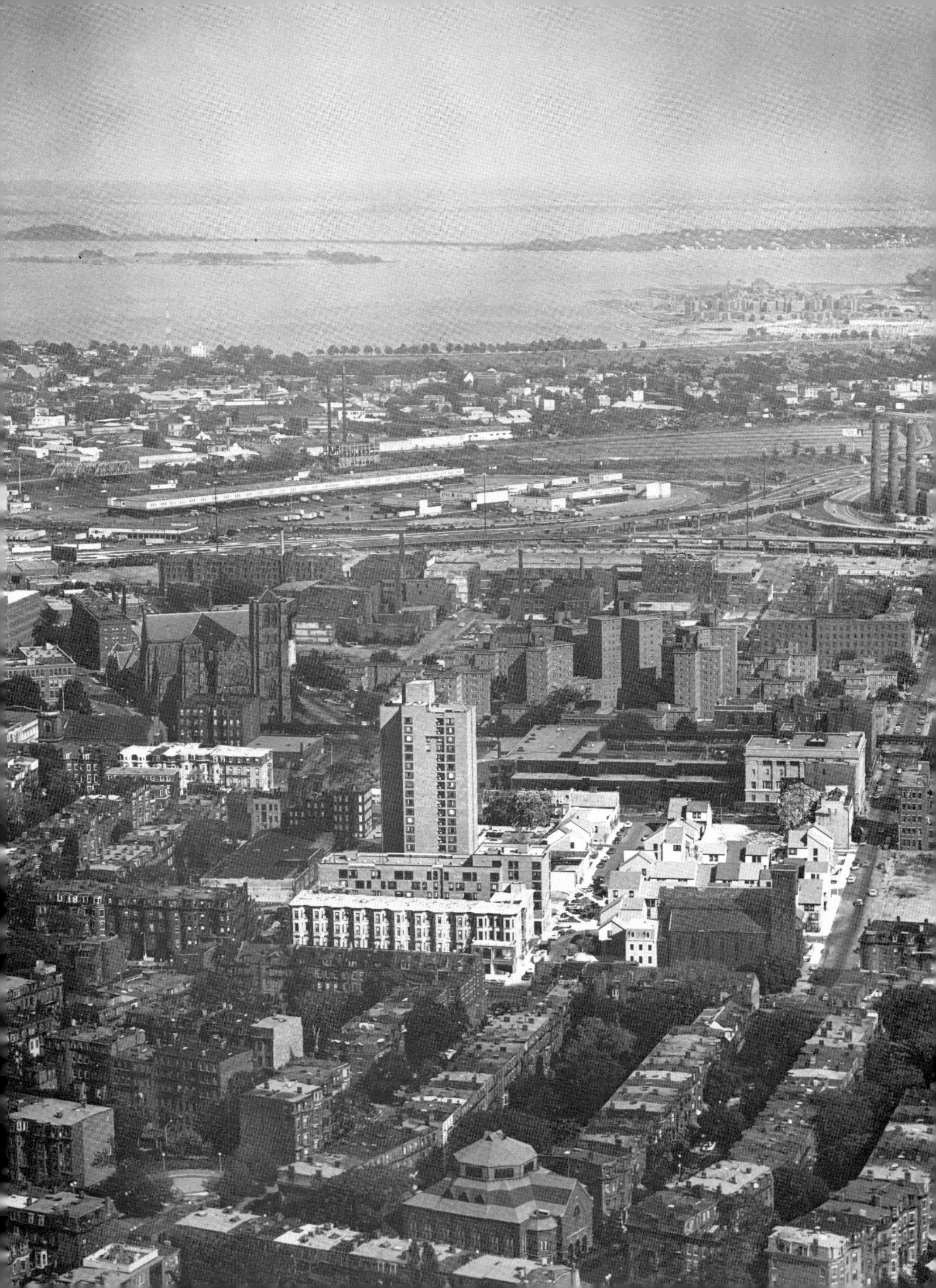

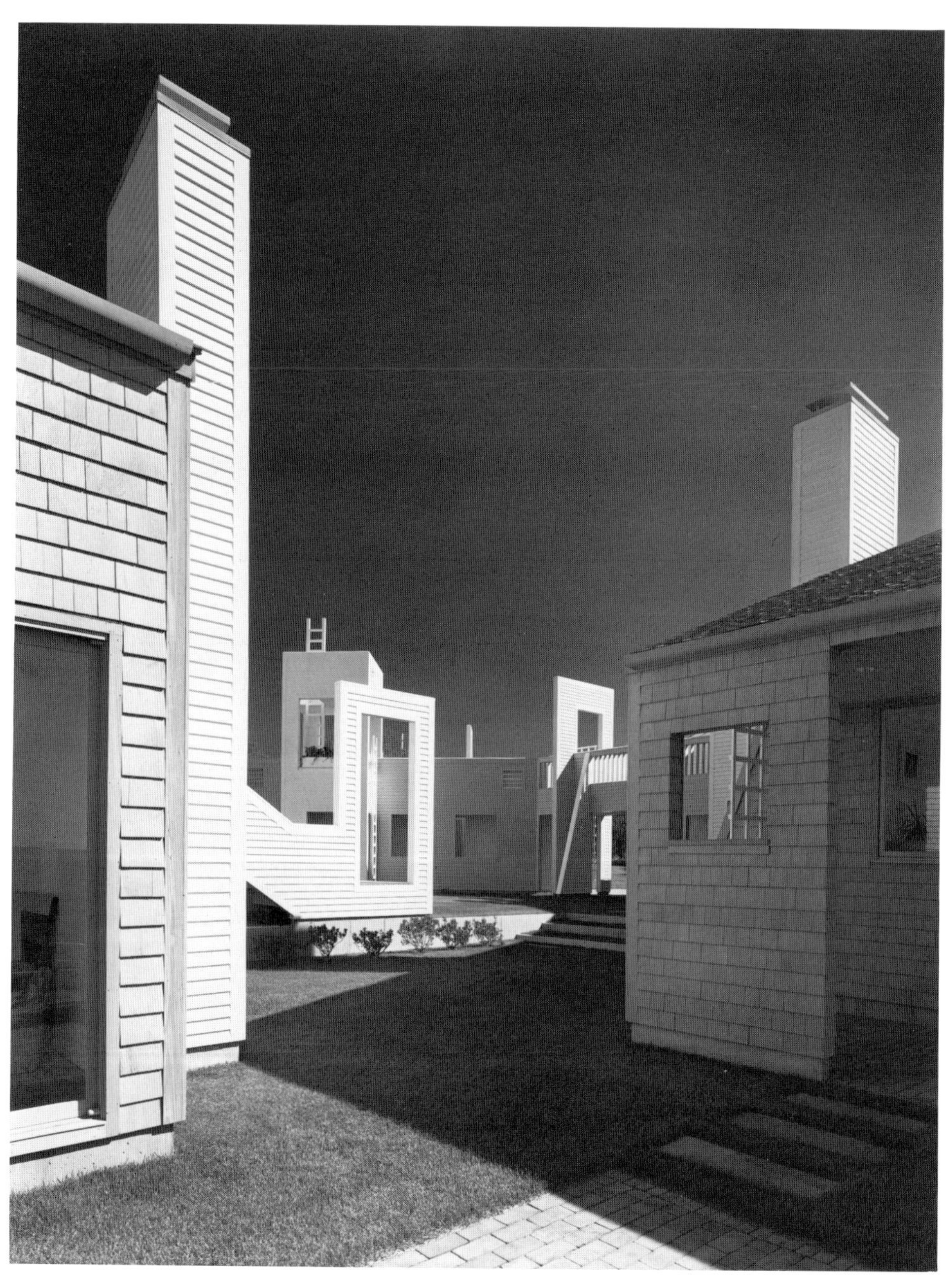

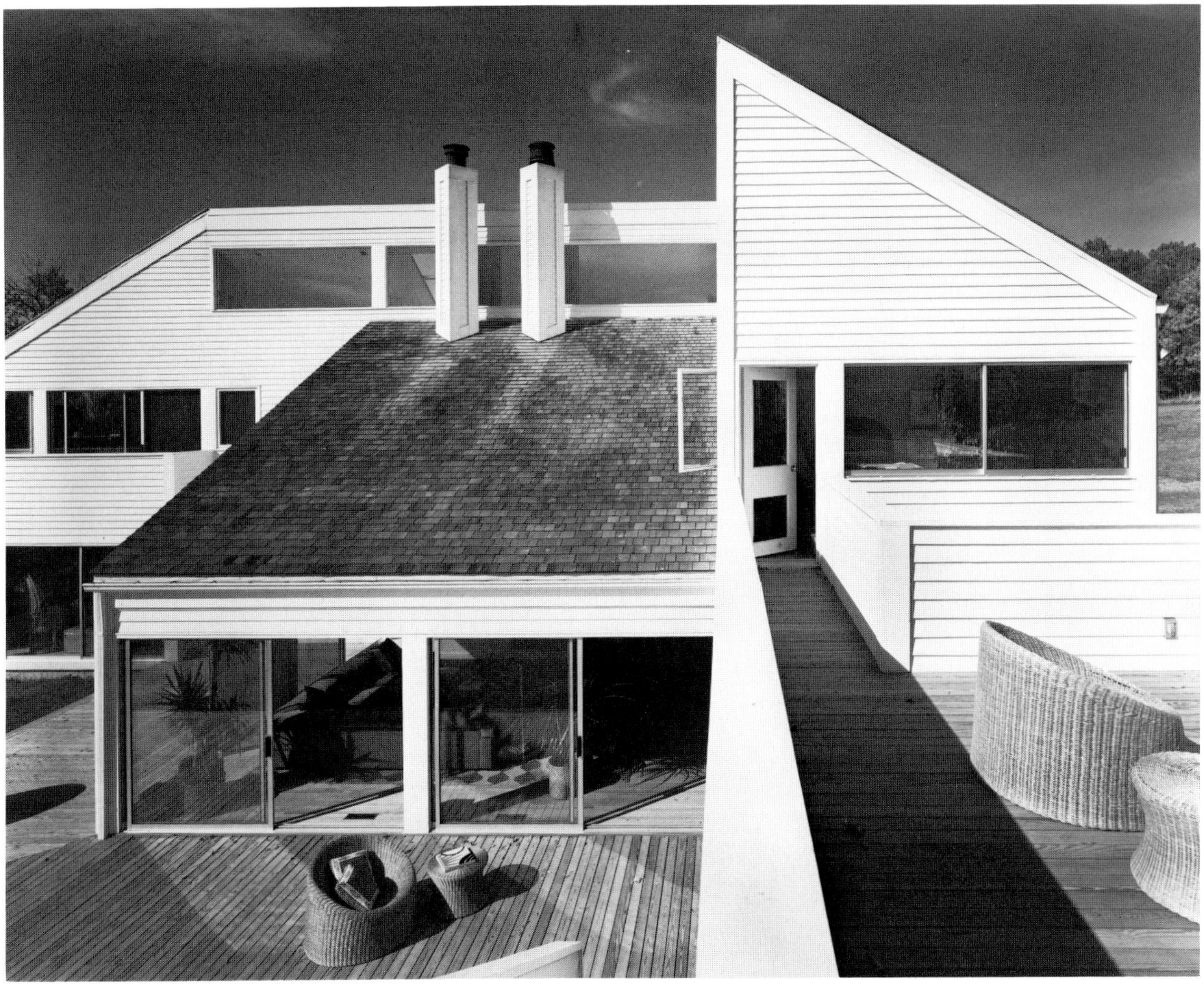

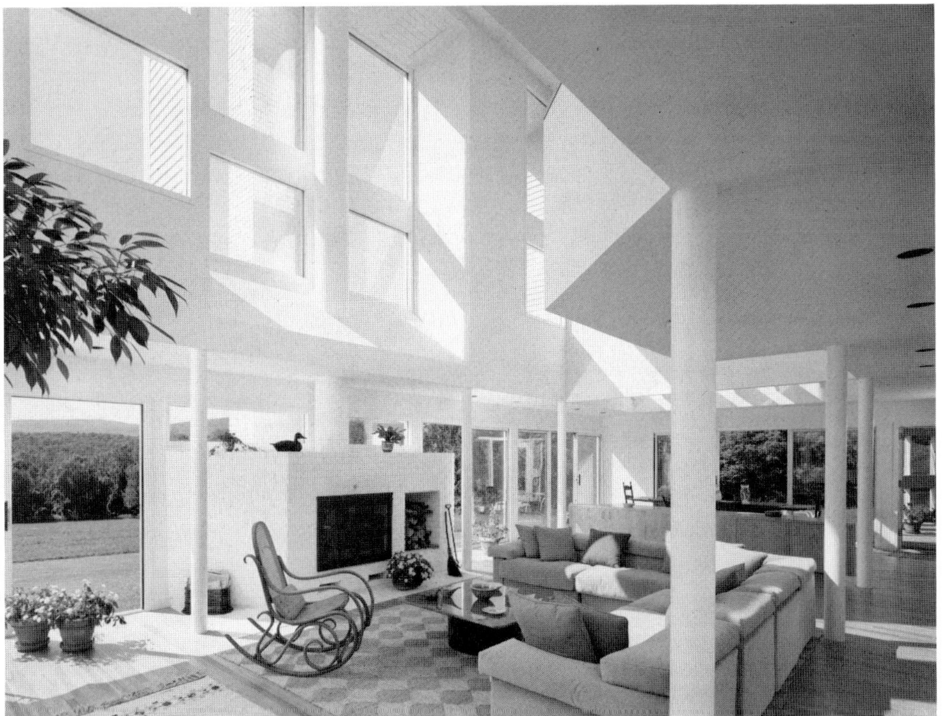

ABOVE: Crissman and Solomon
Private Residence. 1978
(copyright © Steve Rosenthal).

LEFT: Crissman and Solomon.
Private Residence. 1983
(copyright © Steve Rosenthal).

FACING PAGE: Graham Gund
and Associates.
Private Residence. 1978
(copyright © Steve Rosenthal).

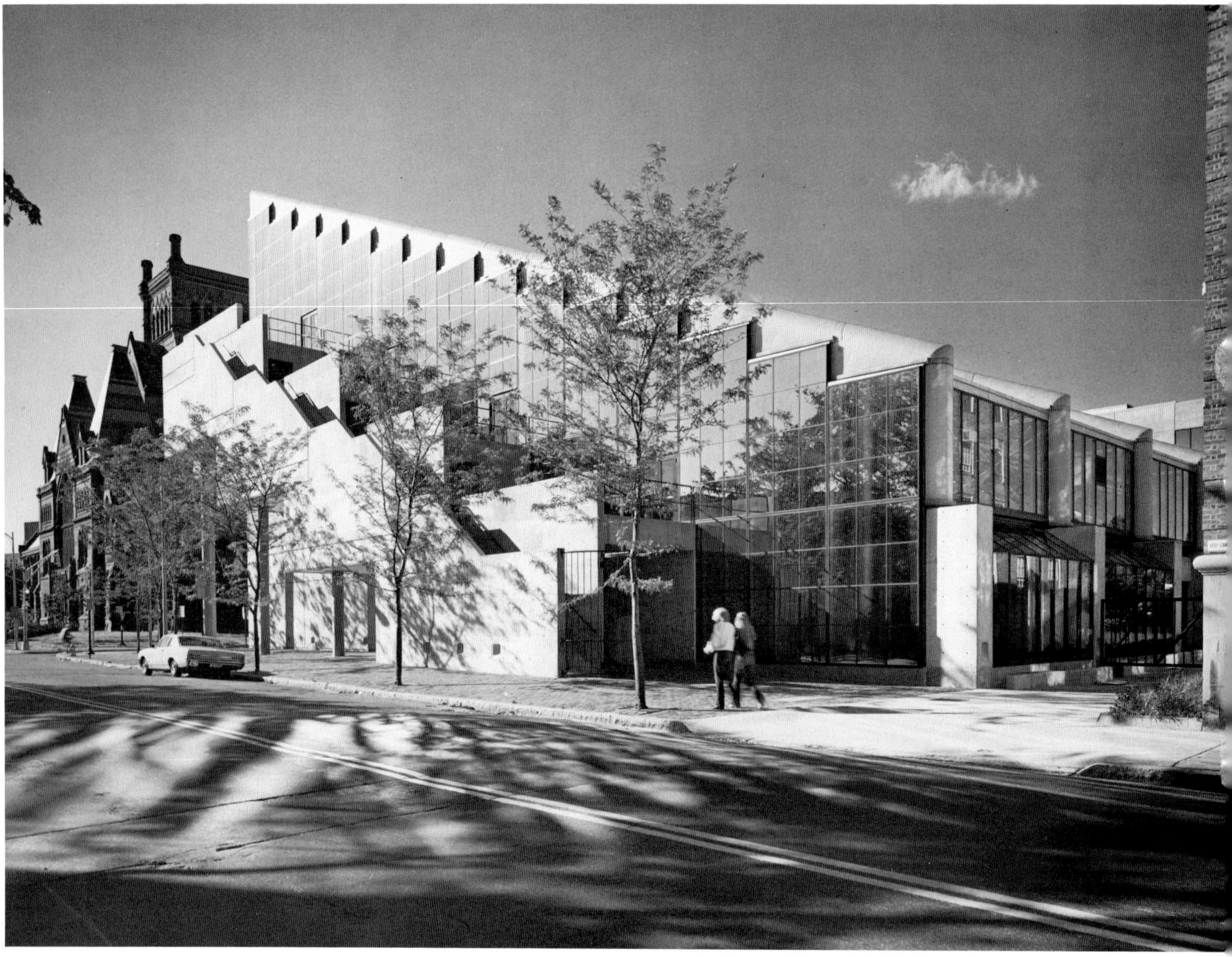

ABOVE: John Andrews, Architects. Gund Hall, Harvard University. Cambridge, Massachusetts, 1972 (copyright © Steve Rosenthal).

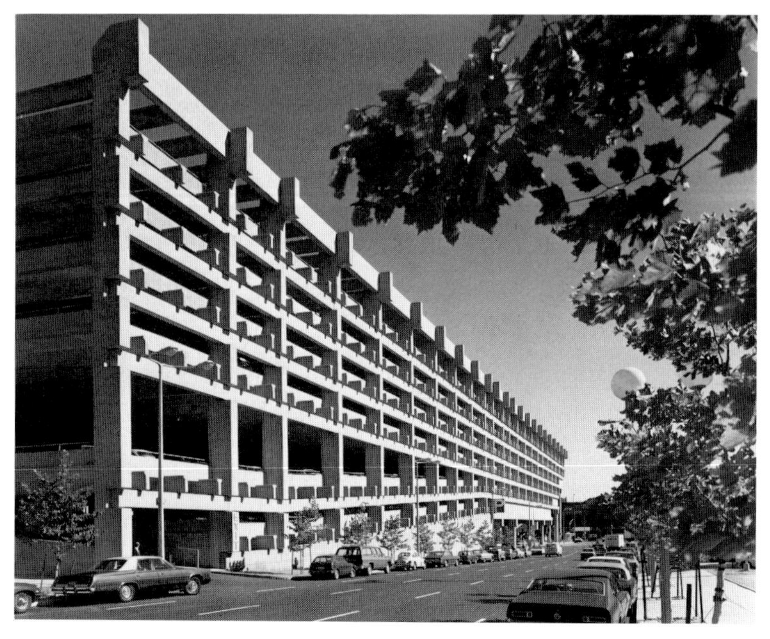

RIGHT: Kallman, McKinnell and Wood. Government Center Garage. Boston, Massachusetts, 1977 (copyright © Steve Rosenthal).

FACING PAGE: Sert, Jackson and Associates. Harvard University Science Center. Boston, Massachusetts, 1973 (copyright © Steve Rosenthal).

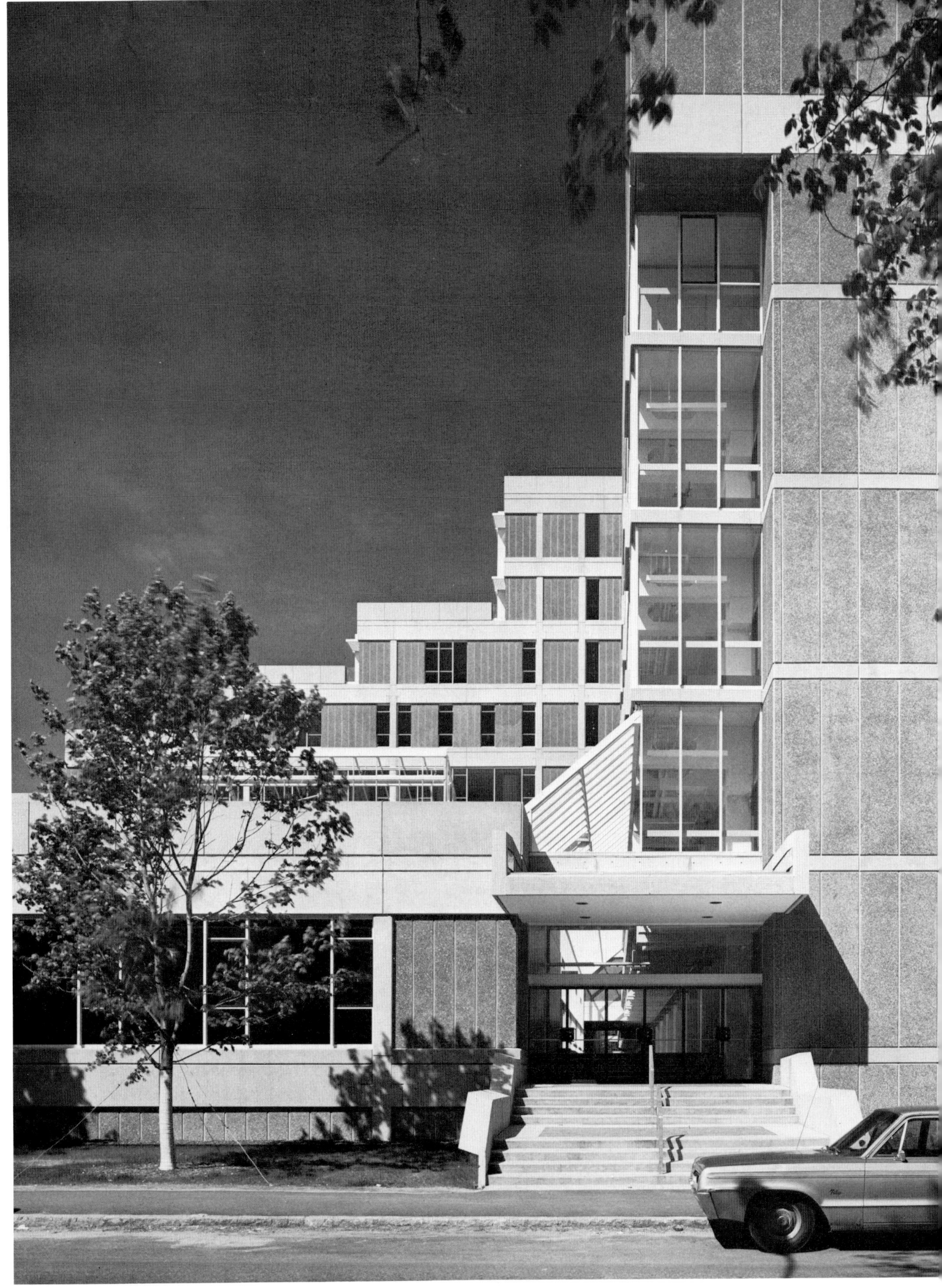

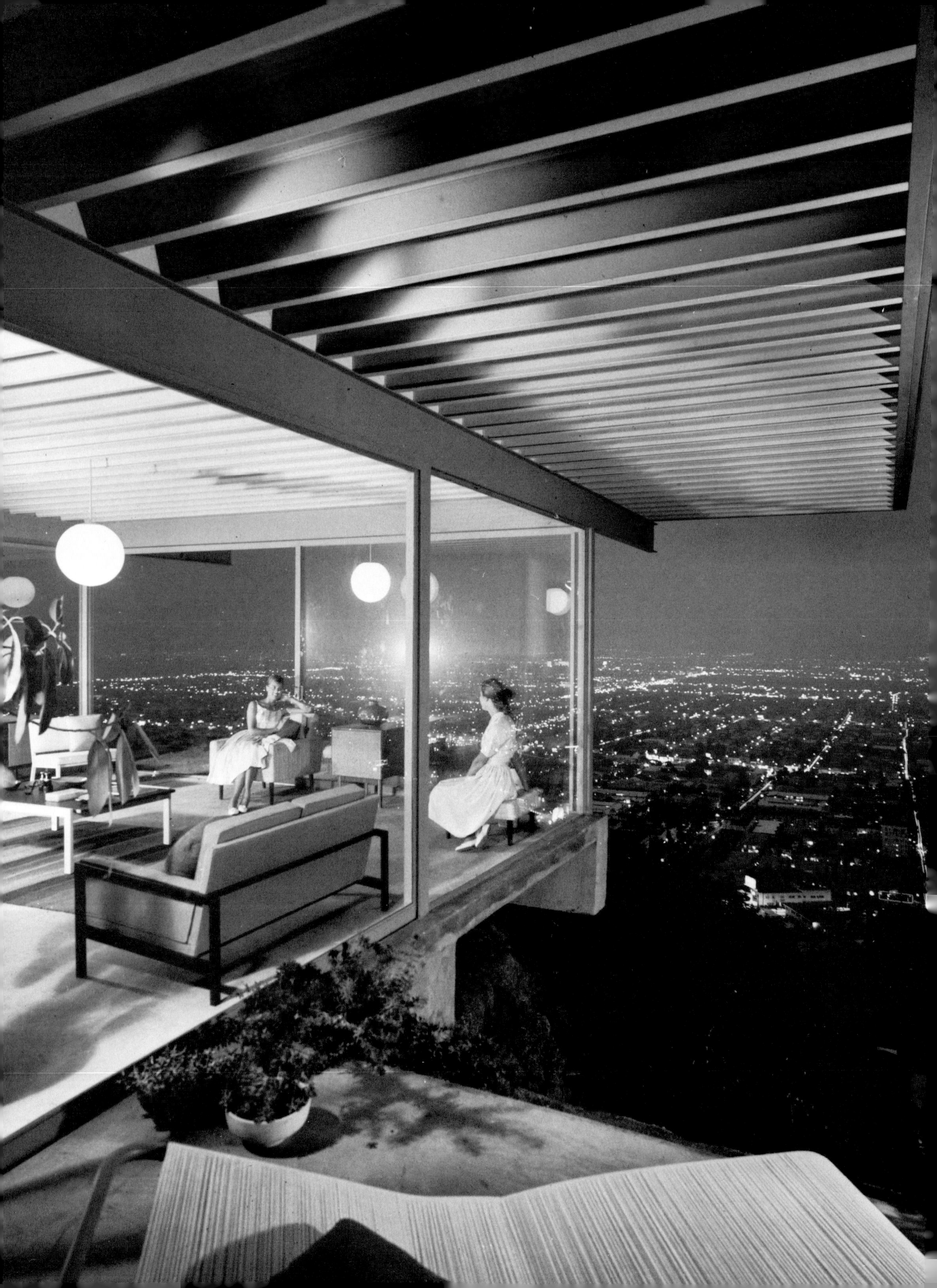

JULIUS SHULMAN

"The subtle interplay of light and shadow on a building is the paint an architectural photographer uses on his canvas of film," says Julius Shulman. "A shadow in a photograph is almost subliminal, an introduction to the mystique of vision." [1] That Shulman uses the painted canvas as a metaphor for his work is appropriate. "Every inch of my composition has to be graphic," he says, "a strong composition which does not necessarily have information, but is a graphic construction of forms and lines. It spells out something which attracts the eye."

Shulman's work is indeed informed by a graphic sensibility. He works to make his photographs appeal to the eye on two levels; the first is as a concise architectural statement. "You want to show the edge of the building; you show the top and the bottom, and the left and right sides. That's the architectural statement. But then," he says, "you begin to change the lenses and play with the graphic detail." And the visual abstractions that occur at this point invite the eye, not by their factual account of the building, but by their strong visual interplay of form, space, and line.

The purpose in the photography of architecture, Shulman observes, is to make, not a photographic statement, but a design statement. For this reason, he tries to work closely with the architect to reach an initial understanding of the building. It is a dialogue that Shulman first established with architect Richard J. Neutra, in 1936, when he took his first architectural photograph of a residence designed by Neutra; this dialogue was continued throughout the architect's lifetime. But Shulman emphasizes that its purpose is more to get a grasp of the architecture than to learn how to photograph it: while the architect may not know how to fill the frame or compose, he knows the building. "What the architect may not know," he says, "is how to apply the rules of composition, how to find that composition which delineates or defines the design. What is the edge of the building you're going to show? How much space do you need at the top and bottom? And what is the context of the scene? What elements of design are present, and how do they all fit together to make a design statement?"

It is a kind of thinking, he concludes, that has to do with neither camera nor light meter: just as the photographer learns to define and delineate the essence of the design, he also learns to experience and read light. "For me," says Shulman,

FACING PAGE: Pierre Koenig. *Arts and Architecture Magazine's* Case Study House Number 22. Hollywood, California, 1960.

"the impact of light on the eyeball is enough to determine exposure." That is, these are calculations made without photographic equipment.

Yet once Shulman starts looking through the lens, he often relies upon photographic techniques that may idealize the initial image or design statement. A strong graphic composition may not simply render the architecture, but may sometimes transform it. It is a transformation, he states, that is always done in such a way as to support what was originally there. It is not exaggeration so much as idealization. His photographs mean "not to glamorize, but to glorify." And while his dramatic technical manipulations are sometimes charged with "making the building look better than it really is," Shulman finds this transformation a legitimate convention of the profession. "The photographer has the potential of transcendation; he can transcend what's there. He can transfigure it and transform it. By transfiguration, I mean I can take that picture on a glorious day with infrared black-and-white film, and the sky will sing out."

It is Shulman's use of infrared film that most often transfigures his images. Photographs taken with infrared film record the invisible infrared radiation of heat. And when orange or red filters are used, the way color is reproduced in black-and-white is radically altered. Blues become almost black, reds are light, and greens almost white. It is a shift of values that Shulman uses "to emphasize and dramatize areas and subjects that normally would not be as exciting or as prominent." [2]

Infrared film can achieve an especially dramatic effect in black-and-white compositions. Most photographers agree that black-and-white film, in its emphasis on form and tone, conveys the intrinsic design qualities of a building more clearly and directly than color. To Shulman, it is communicative and honest, and when augmented with infrared film, is an even more powerful means of representation. Grays and blacks are deepened, and whites seem almost to glow. Infrared film also tends to eliminate haze and, in so doing, allows even weak sunlight to delineate the building. This quality of infrared film, then, along with its intensification of tone, can heighten the effect of a silhouette against a sky, as it does in the photograph of the United Covenant Presbyterian Church, or exaggerate the strong verticals and horizontals of the building's structure, as it does in the photograph of the Hunt Food International Headquarters. Again, both are instances in which the photographer has chosen to transfigure the architecture. And this, says Shulman, is "within the area of knowledge, experience, and inclination of the photographer. If I like the architect and am impressed by the building and the way the building works, I want to transfigure it, to glorify it."

Shulman's best-known photograph, perhaps, is that of the Kaufmann House designed by architect Richard J. Neutra in Palm Springs. Taken at twilight, the photograph records the house in its relationship to the mountains behind it, ranges that fade and blend into one another especially in the early evening light. Because he was using existing architectural lighting and floorlamps, Shulman took a series of different exposures, turning on and off the lights in the various parts of the house. By doing so, however, he also built up the exposure in the sky. To compensate for this overexposure, he instructed his darkroom technicians to burn in the sky to restore its darkness. "And that," he says, "is what you call poetic justice or license. You can call it manipulation, or transfiguration, because the house didn't look that way to the naked eye."

As well as film and darkroom manipulation, Shulman also exploits the more natural dramas of the landscape. A darkening sky, the texture of storm clouds, the dusky silhouette of mountains—Shulman observes that the natural is very often spectacular. And when it is, his work suggests, it can transfigure the architecture. Why take a photograph when the sky is bleak, he asks. Why not wait for clouds to pass over that might add a texture and movement to the flat plane of sky, casting shadows that might help to further delineate the forms in the architecture as well as enhancing the photograph's overall graphic composition?

His photograph of Philip Johnson's Crystal Cathedral is a case in point. "I took it in a lightning and thunder storm, in the rain," he says. "I had packed up all my equipment and was driving away, when I looked in my rearview mirror and saw the building in this violent rain storm. It was 7:15 at night, and the sky was overcast and black. And I saw, in the mirror, this break in the clouds. I got out of the car, pulled out my camera and was standing there, soaking wet, with the camera covered with my focusing cloth, and took a five minute exposure." What came out of the accidental rearview glimpse, he says, was a glorification of the architecture.

Shulman's photographs, then, record accident as well as observation. They are a careful synthesis of the two. Perhaps in recognition of what Shulman calls "the mystique of vision," they absorb and appreciate the accidental. While they consider the facts of the building, they also may note, and use to a pictorial advantage, changes in the sky, a sudden shadow, a breath of wind. "I say this all the time," Shulman repeats. "Photography is accidental. But you still have to be in the right place at the right time to be able to record that accidental situation—and through your technique and willingness to observe, be able to apply it."

But it is not only technique and attentiveness that Shulman lists as ingredients essential to the profession, but a sense of freedom. Shulman's fifty years in the profession of photographing architecture have granted him a seniority enjoyed by only a few others. And throughout his career, what he has perhaps valued above all has been "the sense of freedom and willingness, and a fearlessness, to listen and talk to people, to understand the building, and to grasp the essence of design that distinguishes each project." But it is a freedom that also clearly extends itself beyond the initial understanding of the building to its representation; a sense of liberty that begins by nurturing an unrestricted perception of the architecture and ends, often, in its transfiguration.

"I'm on the side of the architecture," Shulman explains. "I'm on the side of good environment. Therefore, if I feel a building has a certain quality which contributes to the society or to the community or to the client, I want the architect to be given credit. I'm not trying to exaggerate his work, but to idealize it." Clearly, Shulman's photographs are provocative and compelling expressions of this sense of liberty.

---

1. Julius Shulman, *The Photography of Architecture and Design* (New York: Whitney Library of Design, 1977), p.51.
2. Ibid., p. 69.

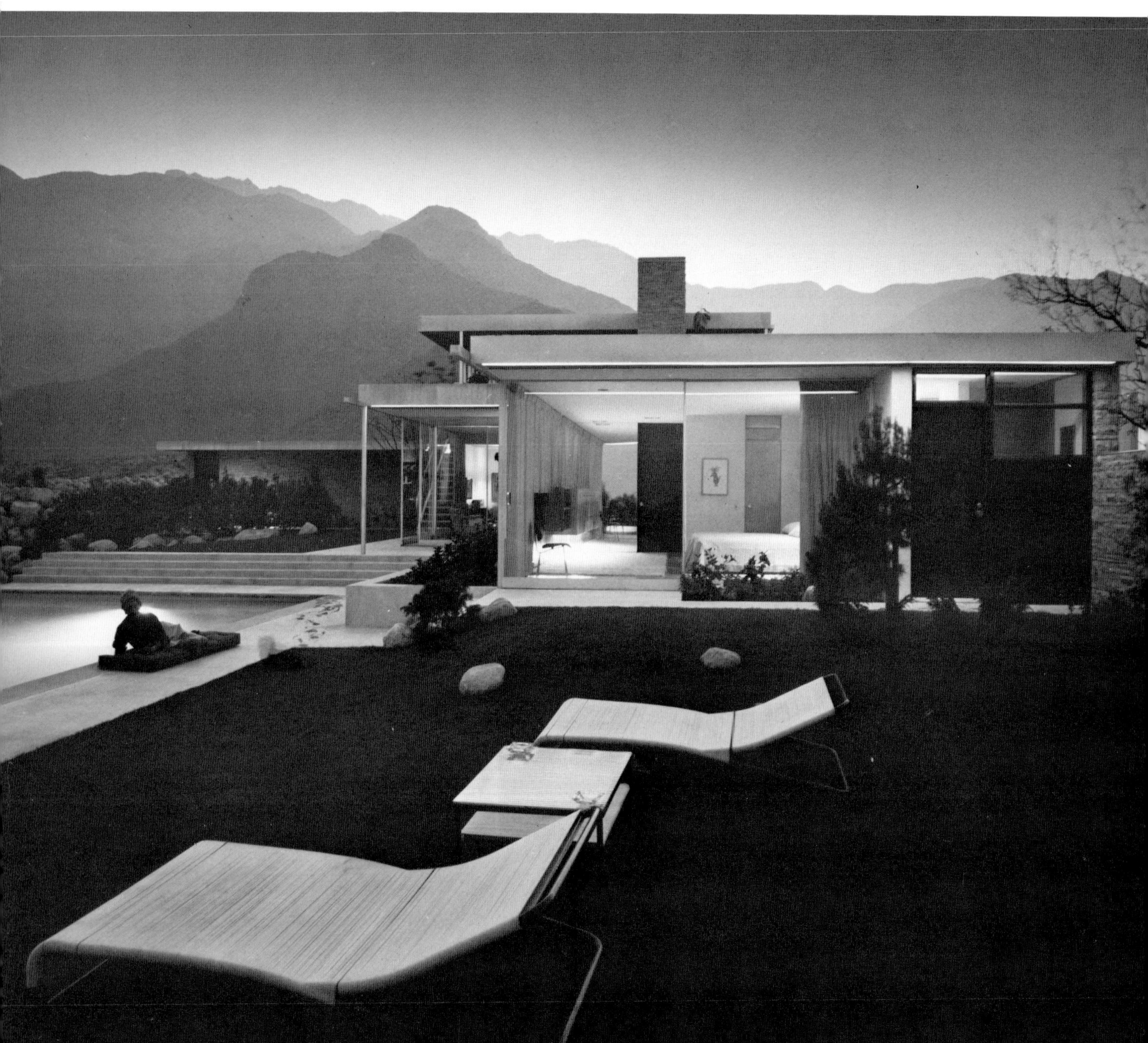

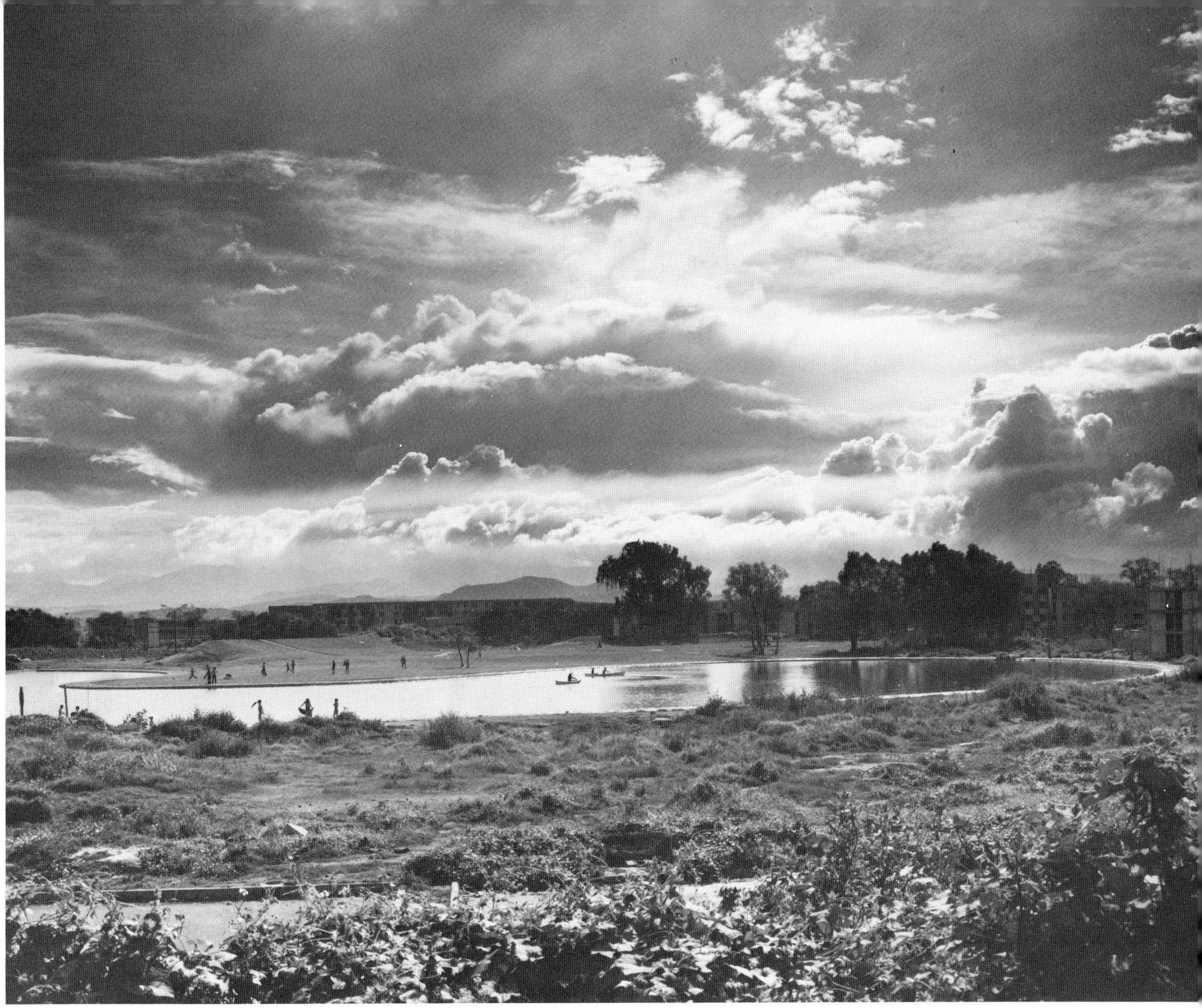

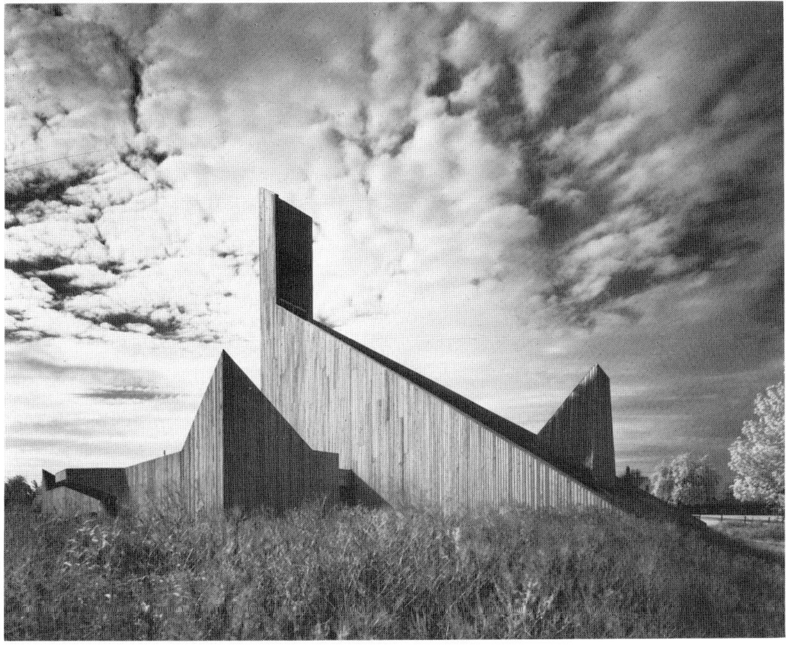

ABOVE: Ricardo Legorreta. El Rosario Housing Project. Mexico City, Mexico, 1976.

LEFT: Crites & McConnell Architects. United Covenant Presbyterian Church. Danville, Iowa, 1967.

FACING PAGE: Richard J. Neutra. Kaufmann Residence. Palm Springs, California, 1947.

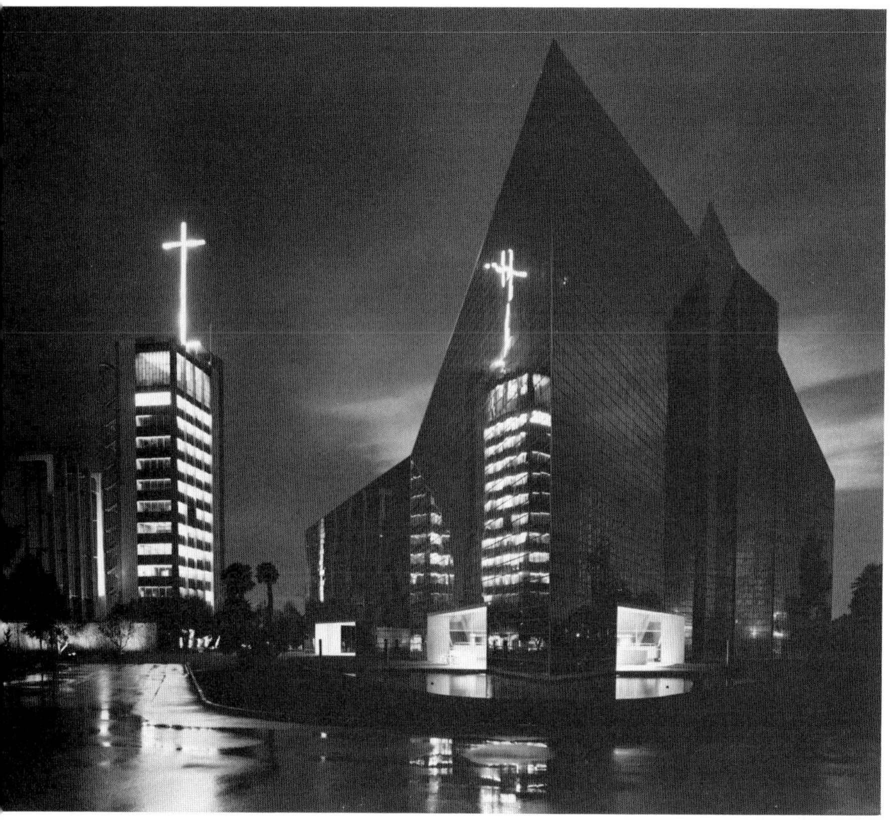

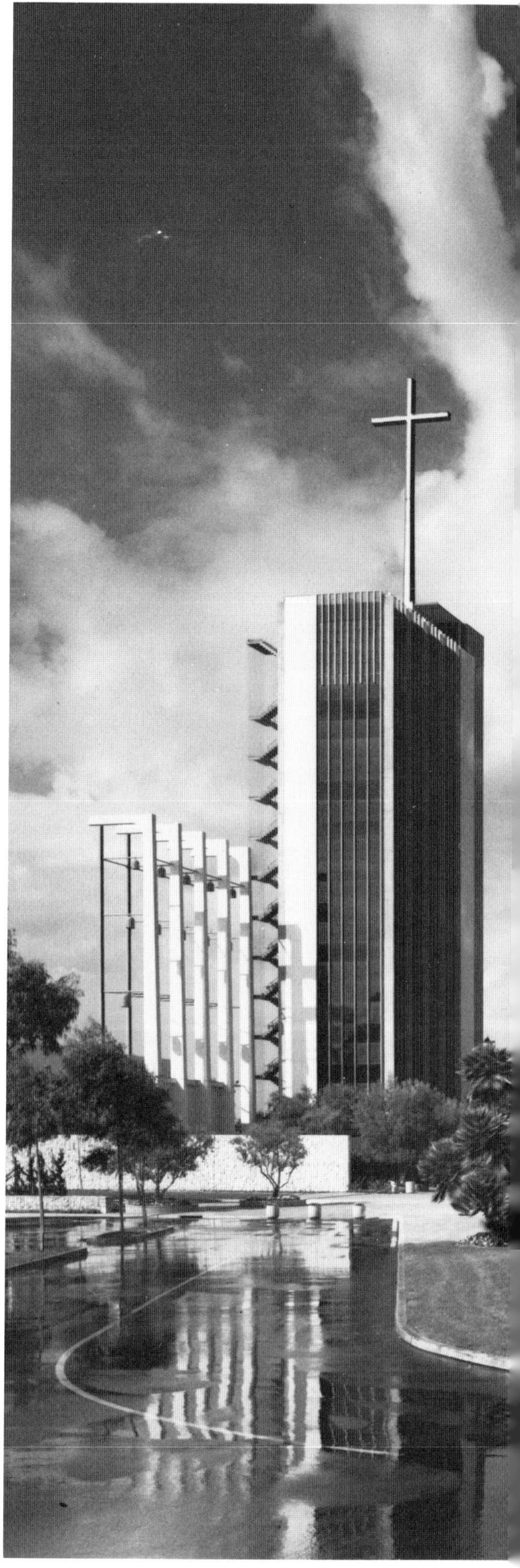

Johnson-Burgee Architects.
Crystal Cathedral.
Garden Grove, California,
1984.

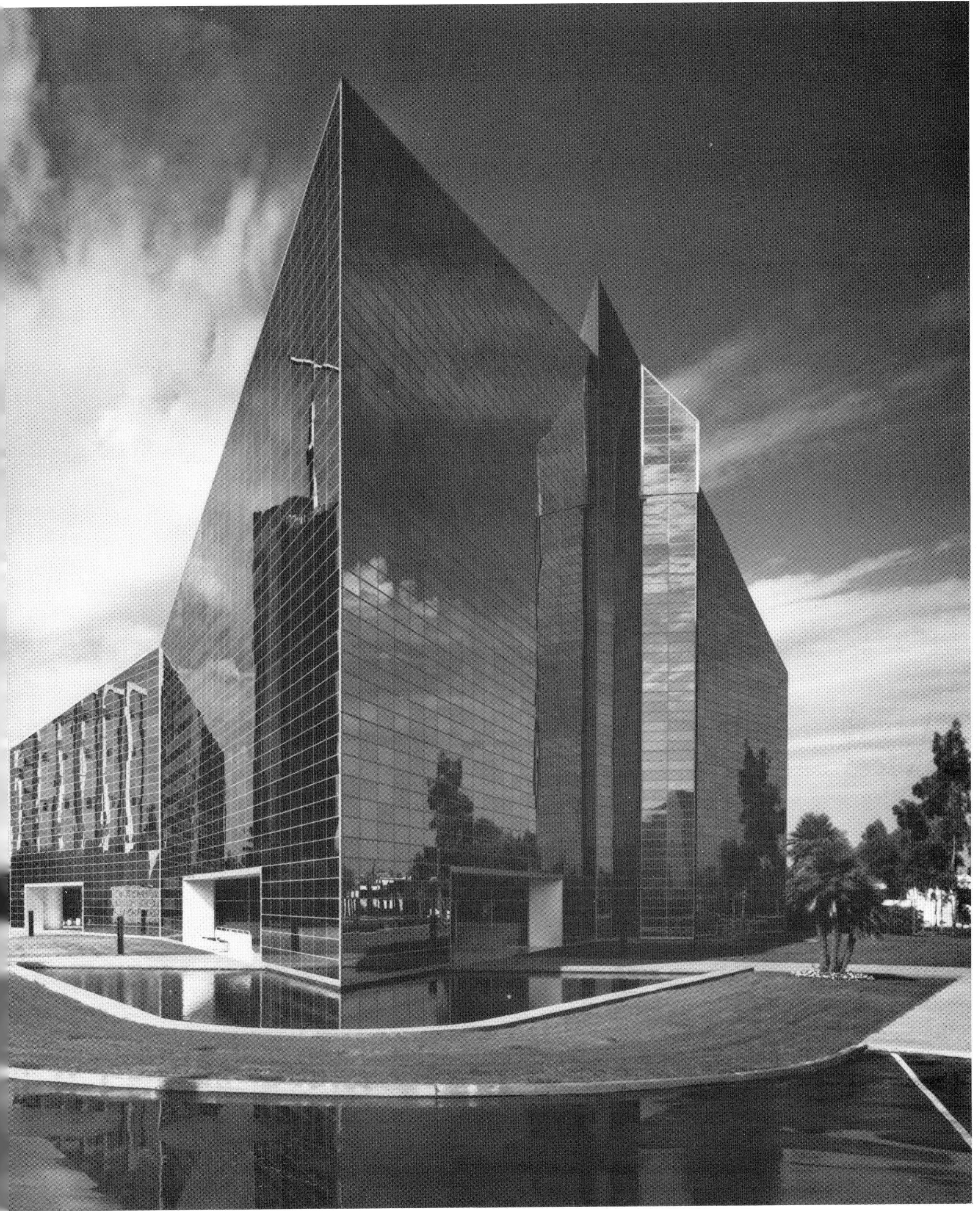

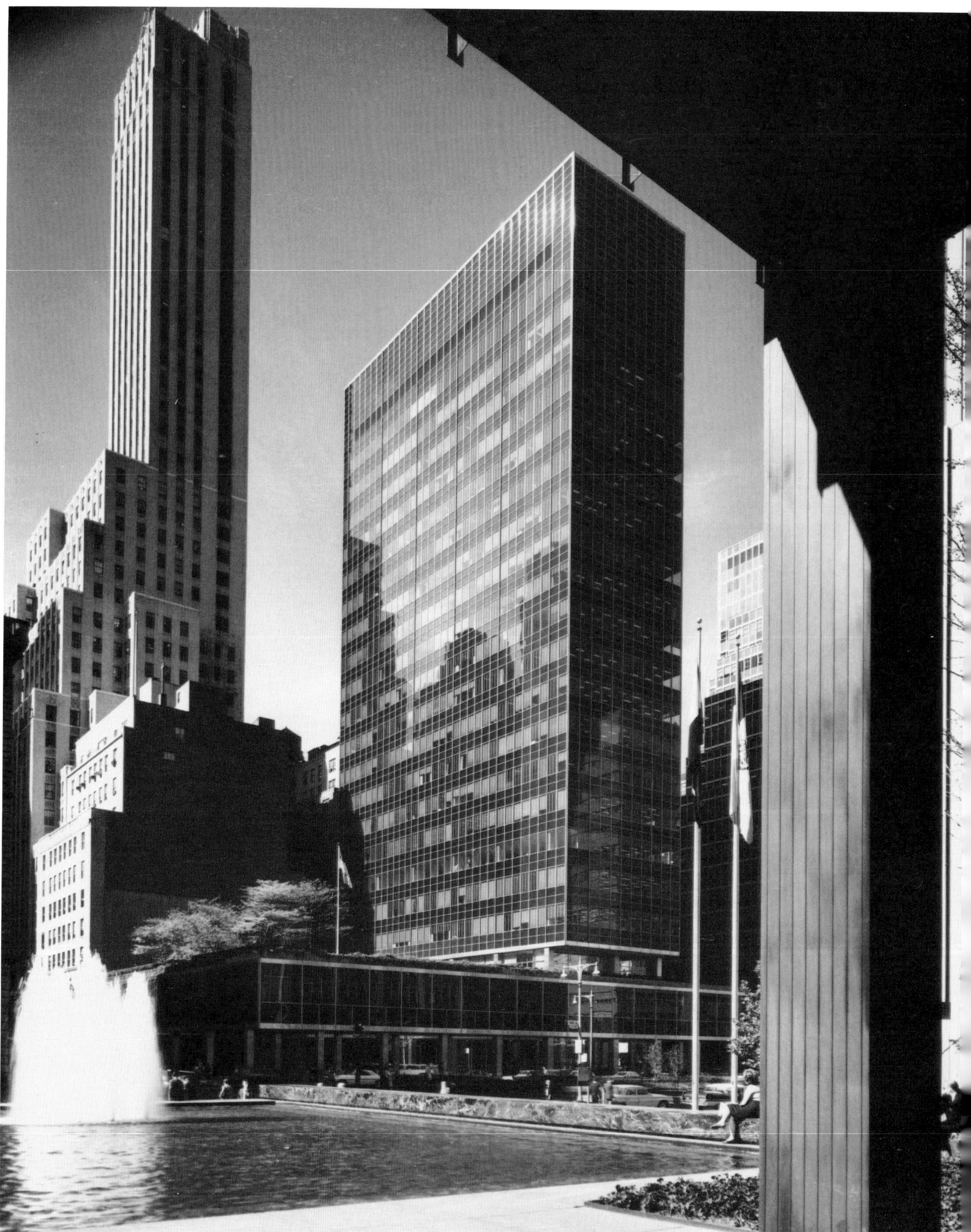

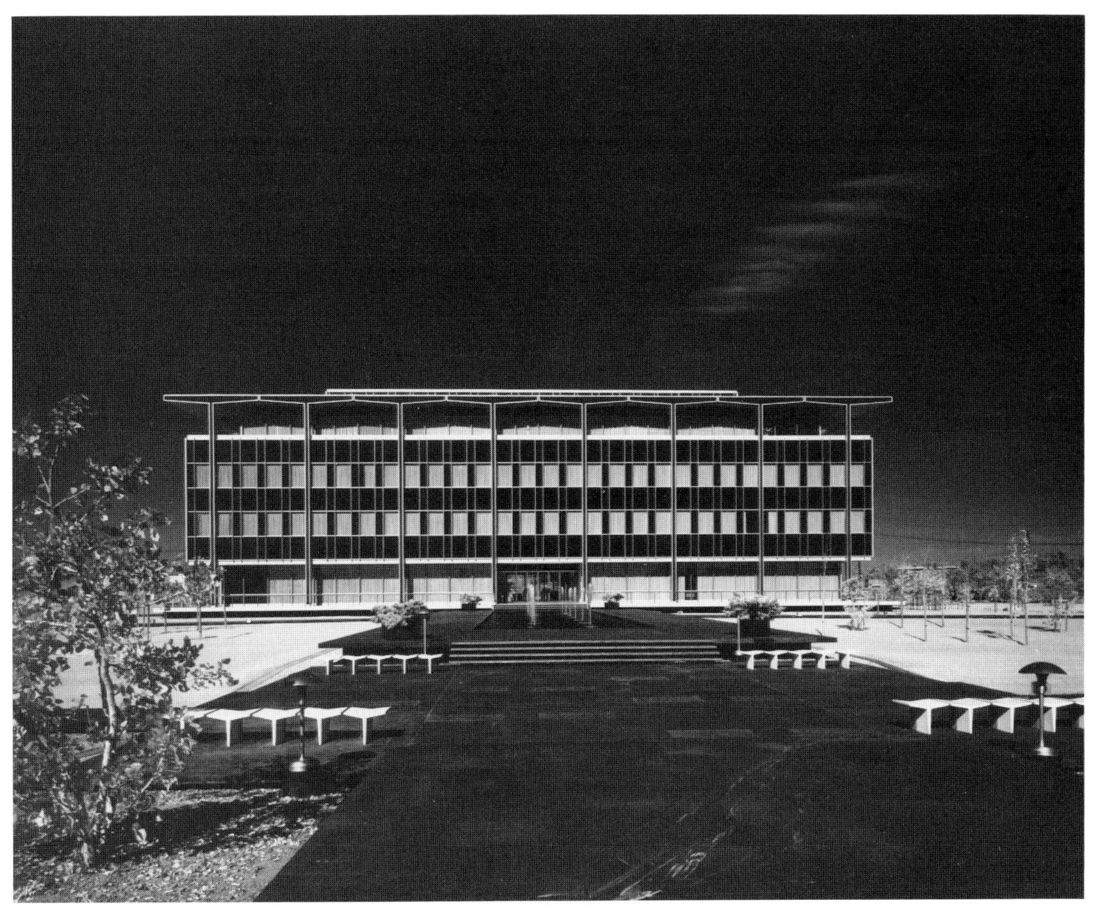

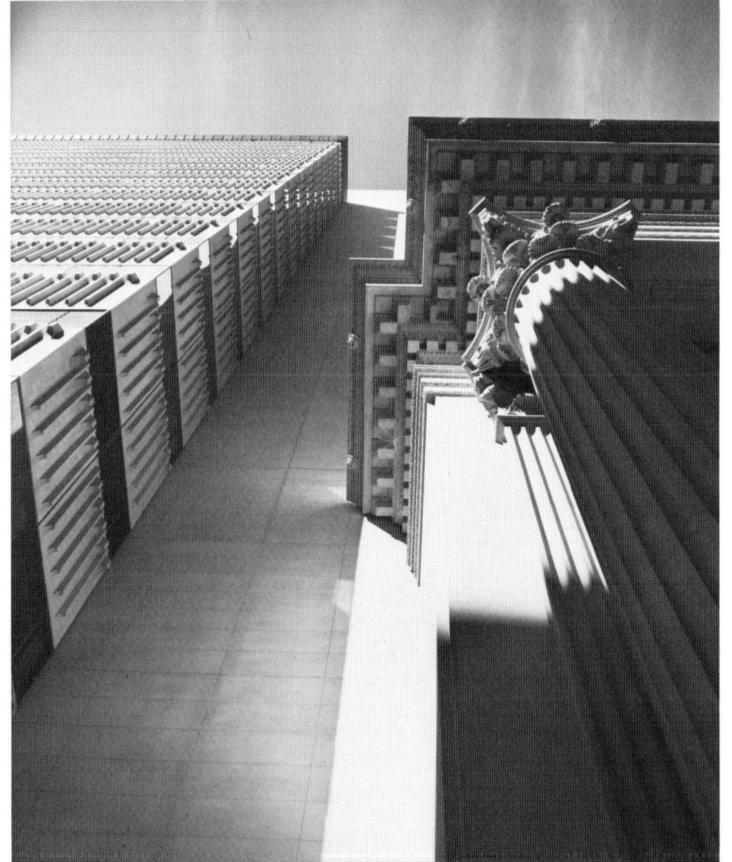

ABOVE: William L. Pereira & Associates. Hunt Foods. Fullerton, California, 1962.

LEFT: Anshen-Allen Architects. Bank of California. San Francisco, California, 1969.

FACING PAGE: Skidmore, Owings & Merrill. Lever House. New York, New York, 1959.

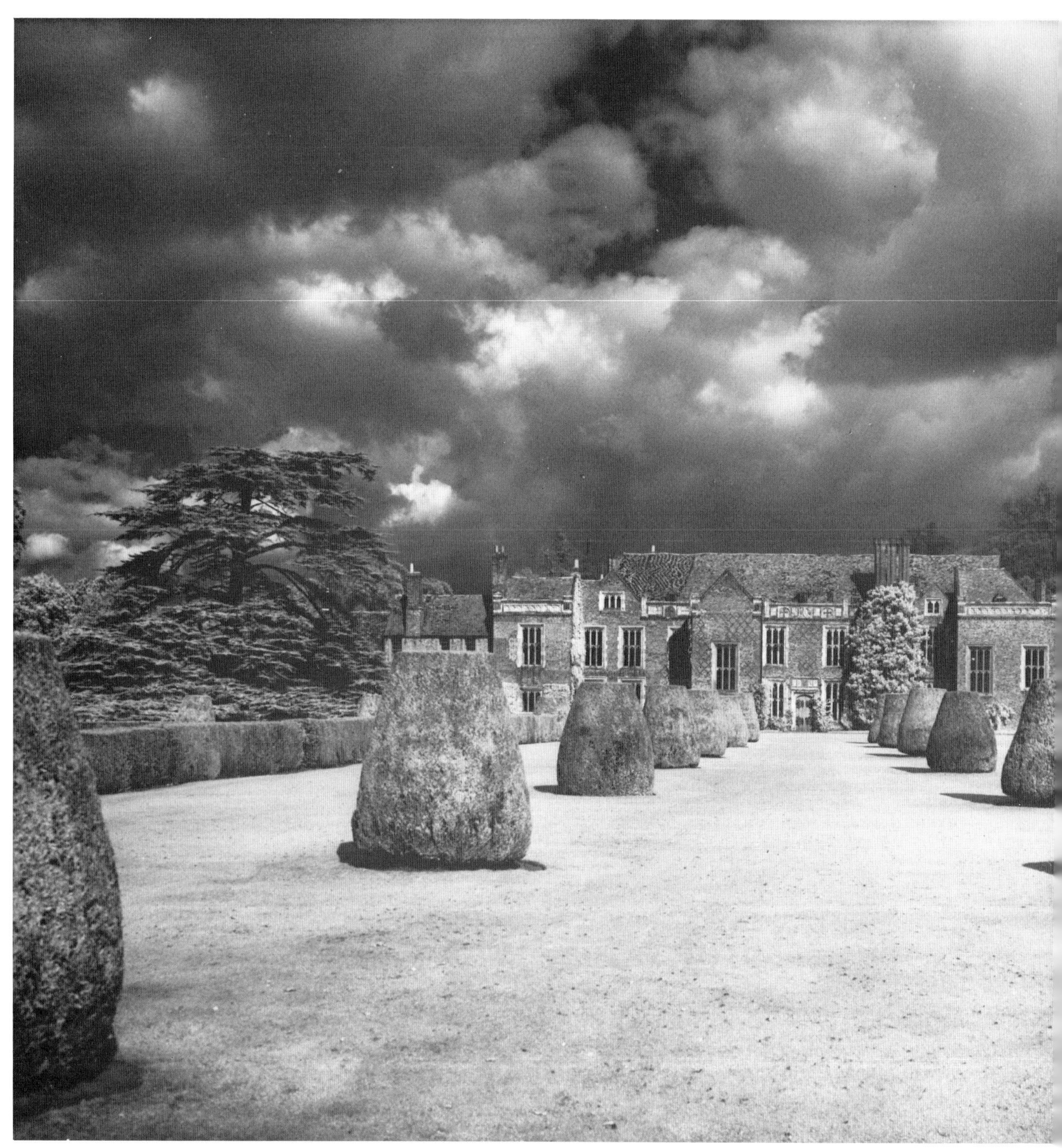

FACING PAGE (TOP) AND ABOVE:
J. Paul Getty Estate.
Sutton Place, England,
1964.

FACING PAGE (BOTTOM):
Langdon/Wilson Architects.
CNA Building. Los Angeles,
California, 1972.

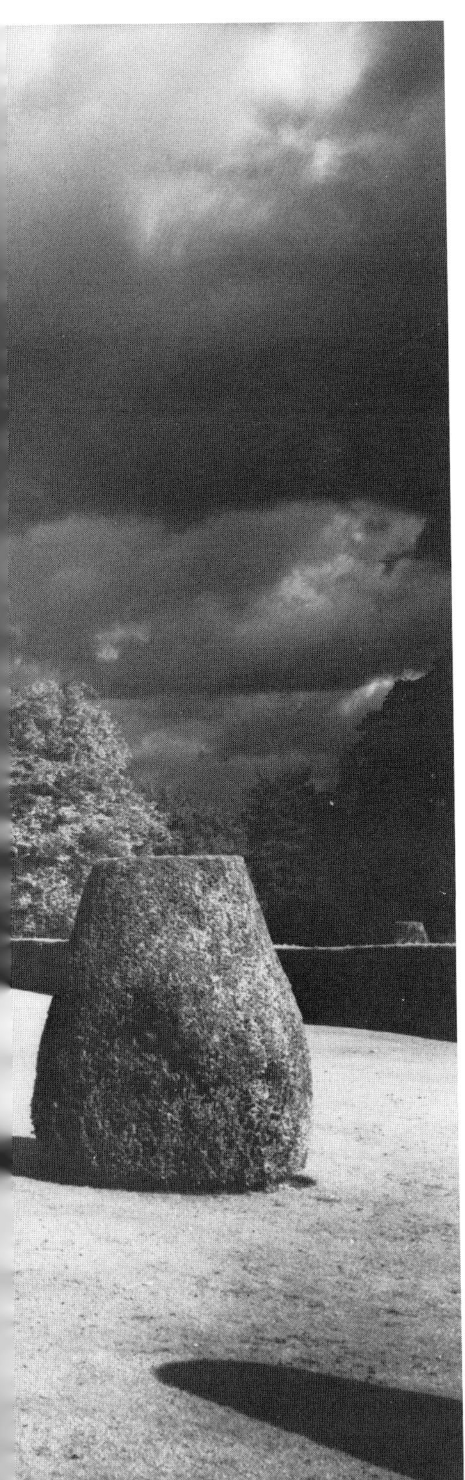

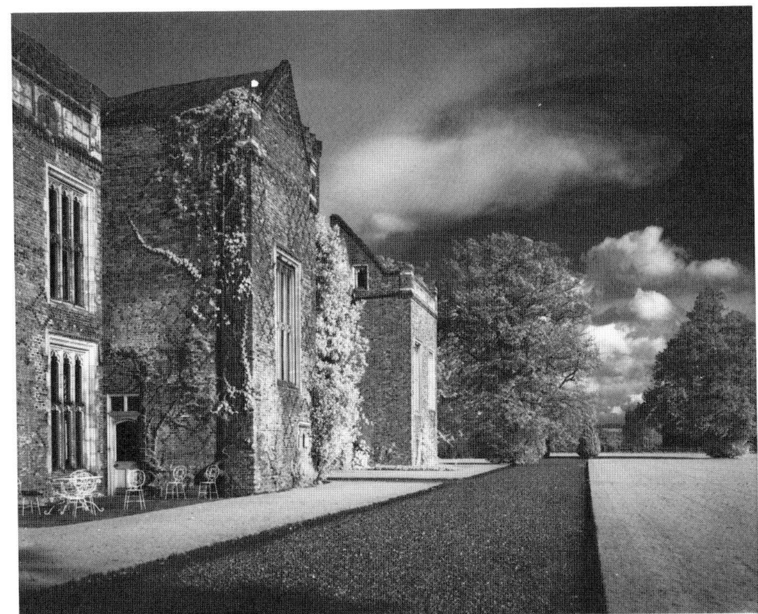

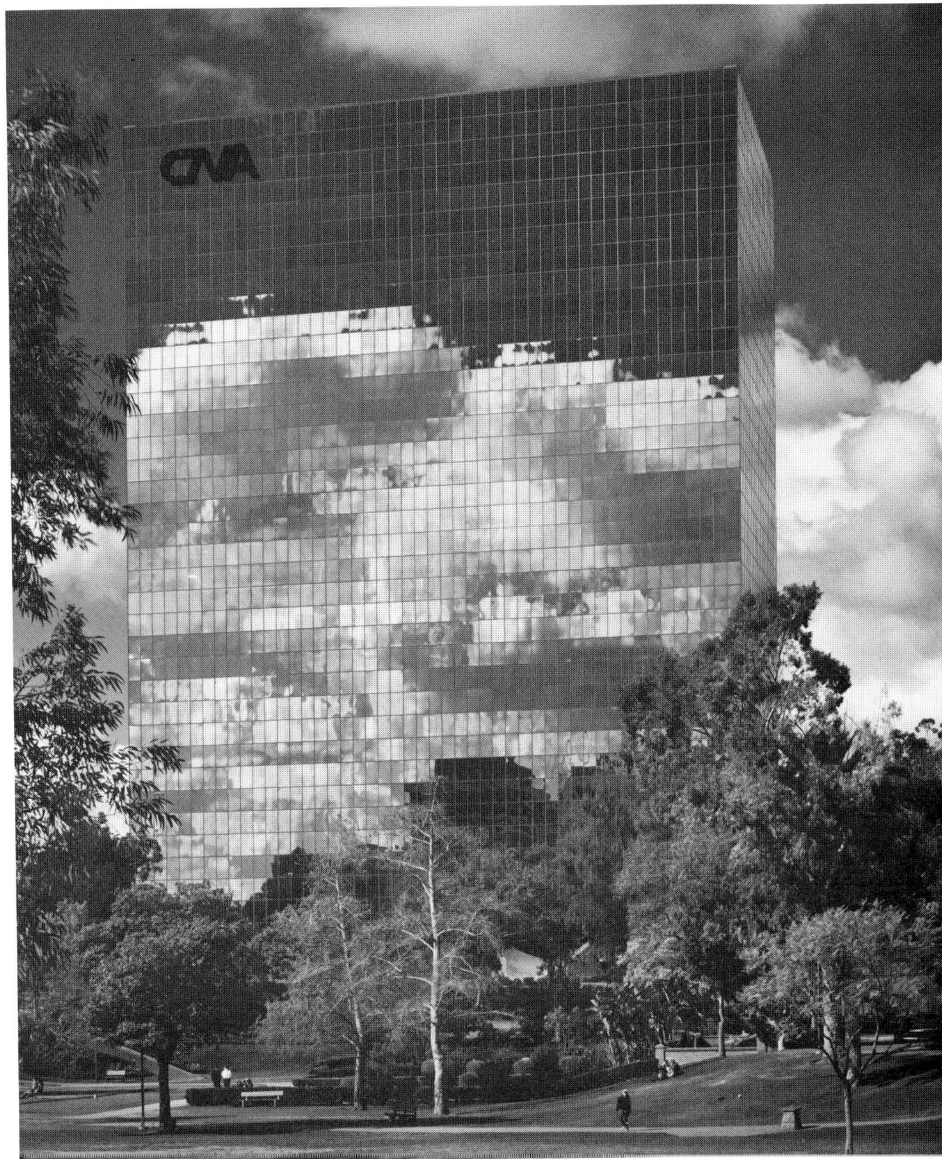
CNA

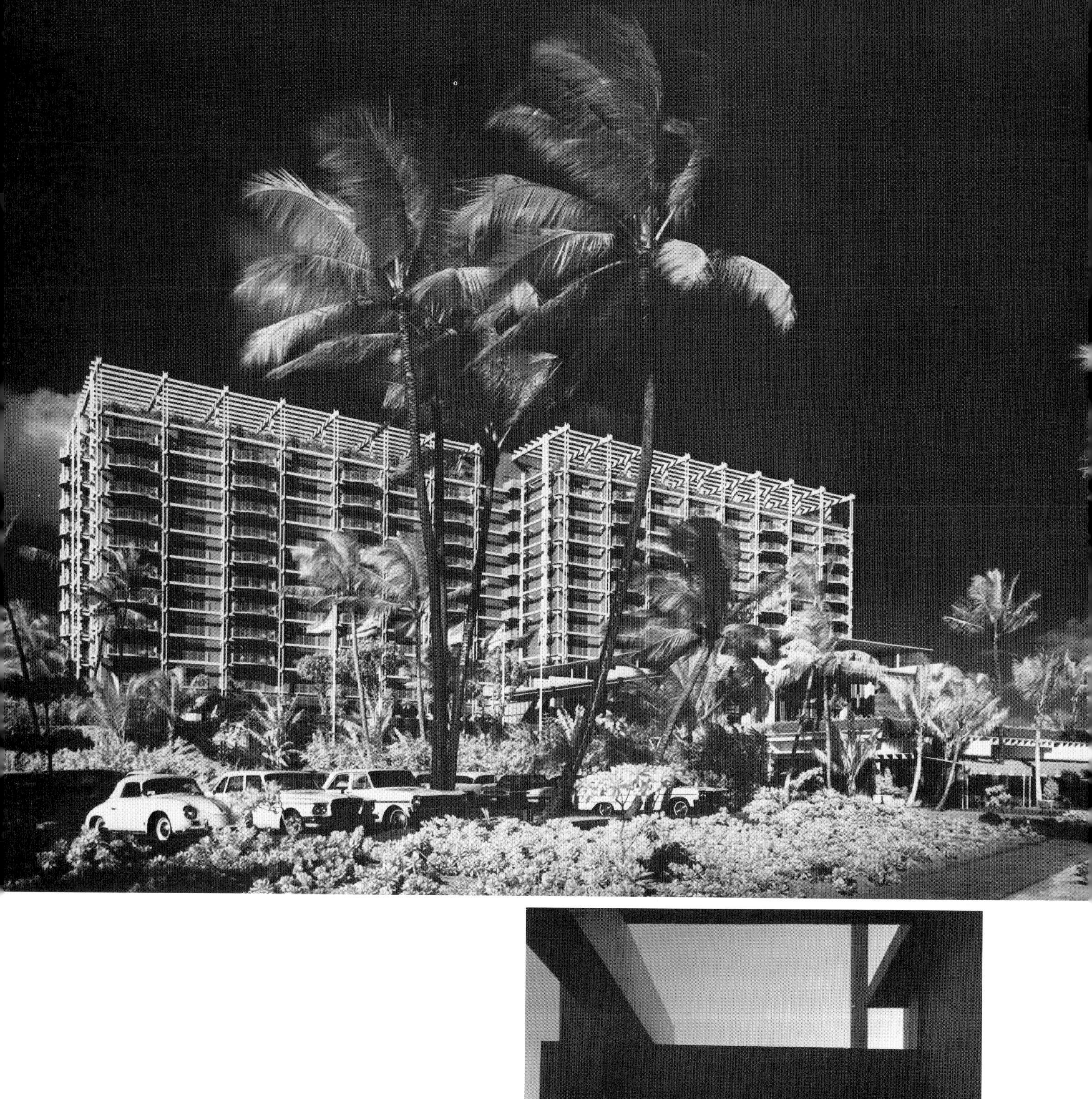

Killingsworth/Brady & Associates. Kahala Hilton Hotel. Honolulu, Hawaii, 1964.

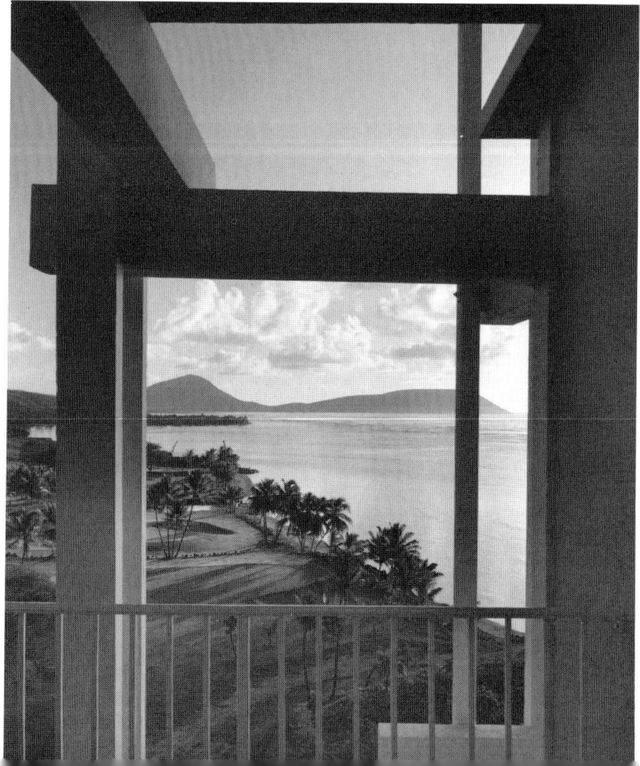

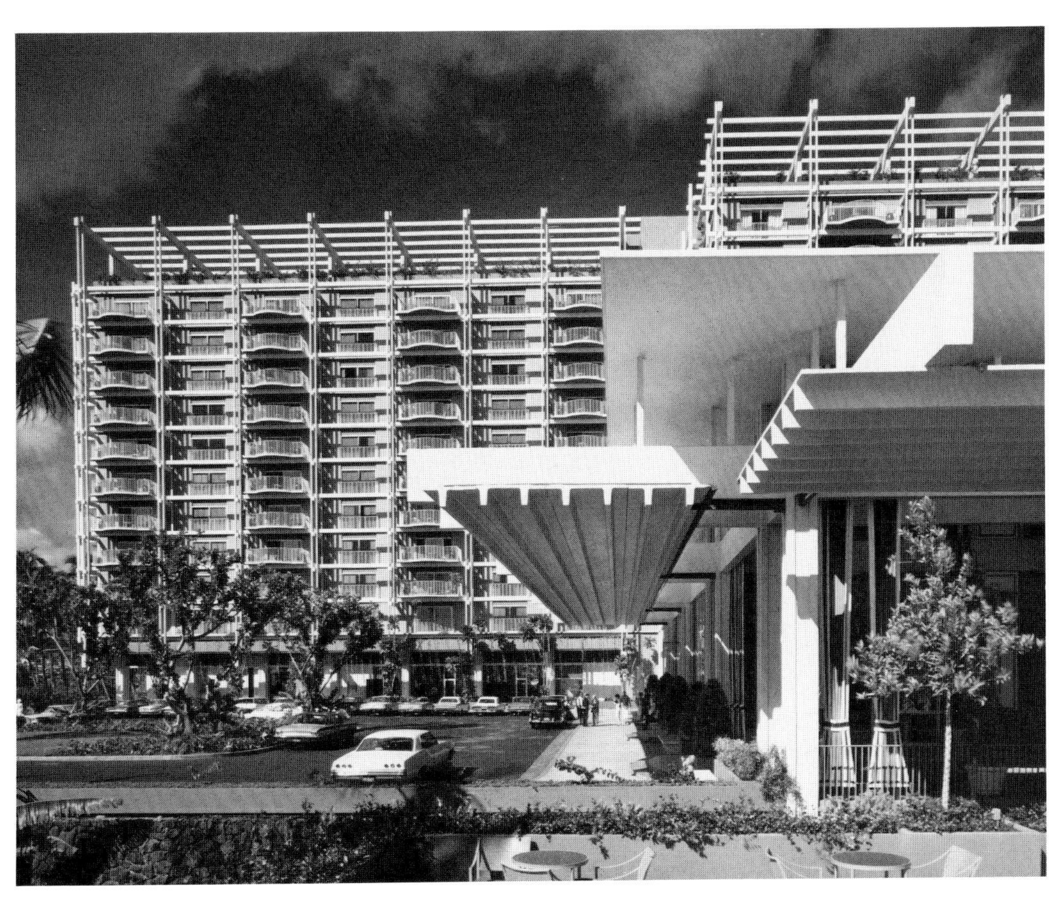

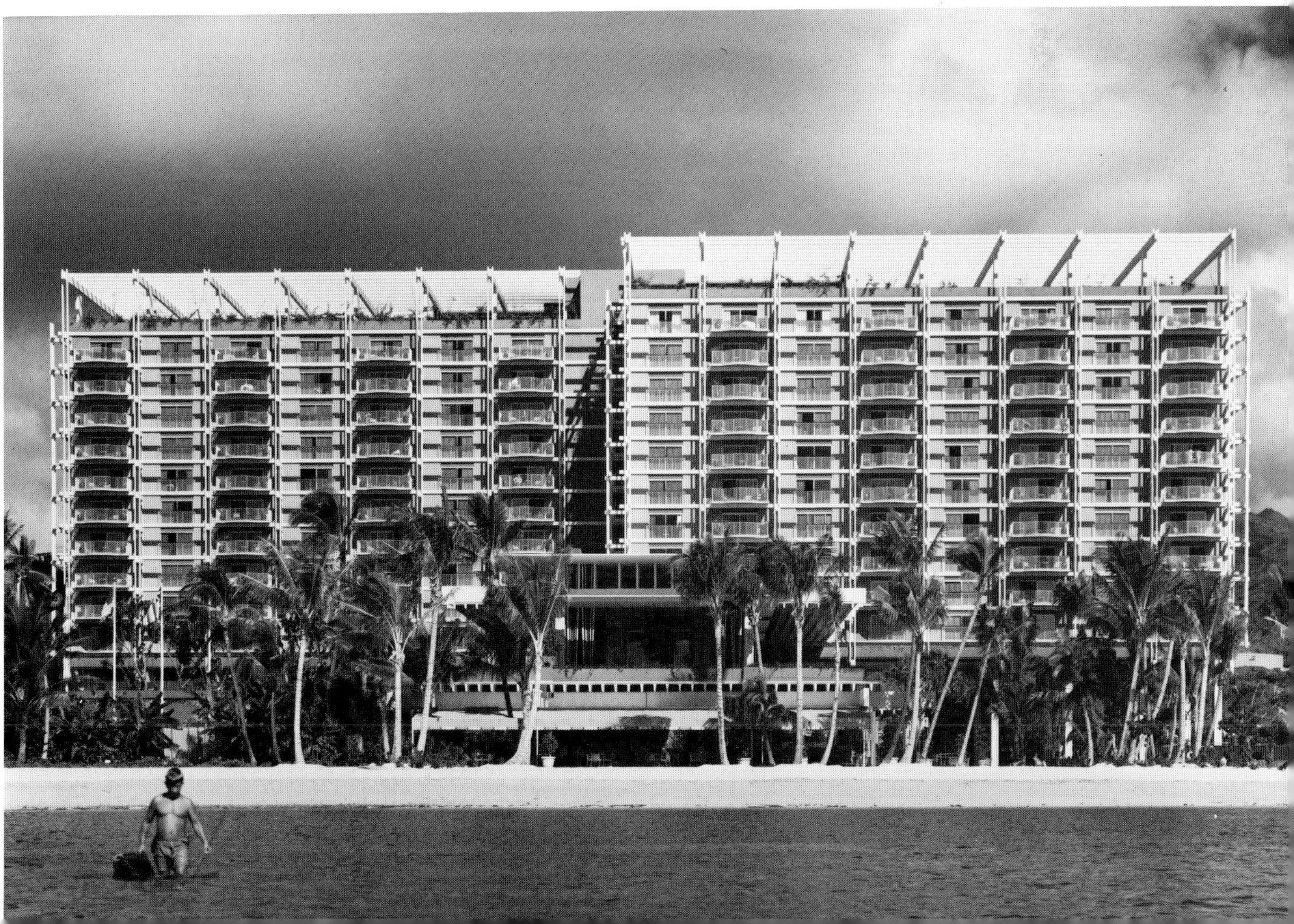

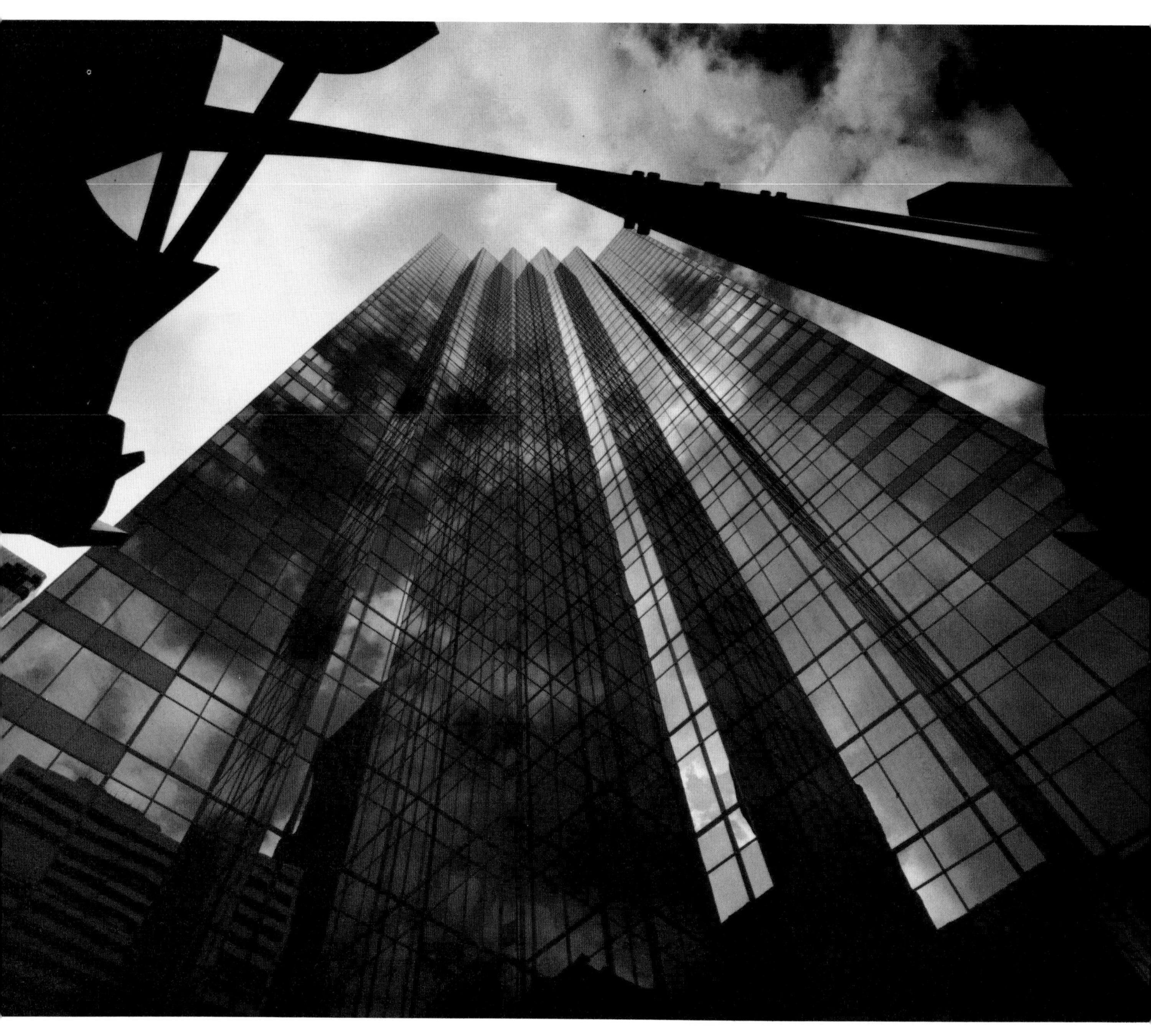

Skidmore, Owings & Merrill. Madison Plaza. Chicago, Illinois, 1983 (courtesy of Bill Hedrich, Hedrich-Blessing).

BILL HEDRICH

" 'Biggest' was preferred, and the 'biggest in the world' was the braggart phrase on every tongue. Chicago had had the biggest conflagration in the world. It was the biggest grain and lumber market 'in the world.' It slaughtered more hogs than any city 'in the world.' It was the greatest railroad center, the greatest this, the greatest that." [1]

So observed architect Louis Sullivan, and indeed, Chicago at the turn of the century was not the sophisticated midwestern metropolis it is today, but an energetic boomtown with its stockyard industry and a location that delegated it the country's agricultural crossroad. Its expansion was rapid, and its spirit was dynamic, and one that was abundantly reflected in the city's architecture. Gertrude Stein observed too in the thirties that "the central part is a beautiful city. They told us that the modern high buildings had been invented in Chicago and not in New York. That is interesting. It is interesting that it should have been done where there was plenty of land to build on and put in New York where it is narrow and so must be of necessity. Choice is always more pleasing than anything necessary." [2]

And indeed, the architecture of Chicago represented an architecture of invention, a frontier architecture. The buildings of Louis Sullivan, Frank Lloyd Wright, Holabird and Root, and Burnham and Roche, as well as those of their students, were built to meet the city's rapidly expanding commercial demands, and by the thirties, Chicago offered a generous compendium of their achievements. The lake and prairie landscape, in its immense power and beauty, indeed proved to be a setting appropriate to their work.

It was perhaps natural, then, that the firm of Hedrich-Blessing should be established in Chicago in 1929 to document the vigor and power of the city's architecture. The firm was founded by Ken Hedrich and Hank Blessing, who were joined in 1930 by Ed Hedrich as bookkeeper, printer, manager, and occasional photographer, and by Bill Hedrich in 1931 as photographer. It has expanded since then to include a staff of eight photographers who no longer simply document the landmarks of their own urban confines, but those of a more international landscape.

"Architectural photography archaeologizes the past and validates the present, and in these respects the firm of Hedrich-Blessing is in keeping with photographic tradition," writes Robert A. Sobieszek in his introduction to a collection of the firm's work. [3] If Hedrich-Blessing's work has kept with photographic tradition, then the work of Bill Hedrich, one of the founding brothers, is surely representative of this tradition. As a fifty-five-year veteran of architectural photography, Bill Hedrich shows a portfolio of work that both reflects the direction taken by the profession, as well as one that has often actually determined it.

Bill Hedrich's photographs reflect the evolutions in architectural style that have occurred over the last half century. The sense of high drama implicit in early International Style architecture is eloquently recorded, as is the more restrained elegance of the buildings that were constructed after the Second World War. Throughout, the photographs display an esteem for their subject; they are precise in their documentation, accurate both in their observances of lesser details as well as in their record of grander schemes. Yet they acknowledge without deferring. While his photographs may interpret, they are interpretations based on the understanding of and genuine regard for his subject matter, rather than the desire to impose a personal viewpoint.

Hedrich's seniority in the profession has given him an uncommon perspective. "In the early days," he recalls, "we put an emphasis on light and shadow; we'd think of these as our tools. We used more spotlights. Today, we try to build up more overall lighting with umbrellas and by using more available light. We try to simplify the lighting to give it a more open, honest look. We try to keep it at a more modest level." The effect of these changes on the photographs is clear: whereas the earlier photographs tended to be more dramatic, idealizing the architecture, more recent work is more straightforward and direct, with less photographic embellishment. This is not to say that any less attention has been paid to lighting, but simply that it has been used to a different end; that the lighting used by the photographer corresponds to or complements what the architect specified rather than highlighting or dramatizing it in any way.

"We also tend to use more one-point perspectives in our current work," Hedrich adds, "which seems to show the architecture in a more straightforward way." Just as lighting was used to heighten the innate drama of the earlier work, so too were two-point perspectives, the angularity of which usually achieved a more assertive or emphatic effect.

Yet Hedrich stresses the point that the photography of architecture observes no hard and fast rules. How a building is visually recorded has to do with its individual qualities rather than with photographic trend, and it is this flexibility that in part has earned Hedrich-Blessing its reputation. Architecture that is itself exaggerated and dramatic can, at times, best be recorded without additional embellishment, while the more reserved geometries of other buildings can be more memorably recorded with a play or emphasis on their angularity.

Nevertheless, that the early work did heighten the drama of the architecture it sought to represent is not to say that it misrepresented it or falsified it in any way. Architecture of the thirties and forties had itself set a dramatic tone, and that the tone of its representation corresponded was not inappropriate.

Bill Hedrich's photograph of Fallingwater, the house designed by Frank Lloyd Wright in 1936 for Edgar Kaufmann, is one of the best-known architectural photographs ever taken and is a lucid case in point. Taken from a standpoint slightly below the house and waterfall, its viewpoint is almost reverential. The planes of the house appear to float serenely, and somewhat miraculously, above the rocks. Even Wright, on first seeing the photograph, found it slightly "acrobatic." [4] Nevertheless, despite the sense of drama, what gives the photograph its real importance is its record of site. Fallingwater is remarkable not only for its small symphony of planes, but for its synthesis of nature and architecture. The rough stone walls and floors of the house make for visual and tactile associations with its site. And the impression that architecture and geography have been fused here is substantiated by the photograph; while it may seem to revere, it also captures the physical sense of architecture emerging from a landscape of rock.

Photography, by its very nature, concentrates on what is visual. It is difficult for a photograph to capture other impressions—tactile qualities, the sound, and smell of a building. Most of all, it is difficult for the camera to capture the simultaneity of these impressions. Yet what is uncommon about Bill Hedrich's photograph of Fallingwater is that it *does* seem to suggest a broader range of senses and impressions that contribute to our entire experience of a building, here a house appearing to emerge quite naturally from a quarry of rock. While some photographs may beautify their subject to the point of manipulating the truth, photographs such as this clarify in their beauty. In this instance, it is a clarification not simply of the architecture, but of architecture in its relation to site.

Another significant change in direction Hedrich has observed in the documentation of architecture has to do with the presence of the architect. Hedrich puts a high value on the creative alliance between photographer and architect. In his early days, he points out, the architect was present on all shoots, and it was an invaluable presence: "It helps to keep in mind the architect's own demands and own desires. No two architects are alike. I remember Mies van der Rohe would like clear, white skies, without any clouds. He wanted the emphasis on his stark modular steel and glass buildings. But then you work with a more contemporary architect like Harry Weese, who might ask you to photograph the building just the way it is. If there's a telephone pole there, he'd say, then leave it in."

Perhaps because Hedrich's seniority has permitted him to spend so much of his location time with some of this century's most renowned and prolific architects, he regrets the more limited participation of architects in contemporary photography. That the architect is absent on most shoots makes the experience of the building a fraction less complete for the photographer. "Having the architect on the site made an enormous difference," he recalls. "And I miss it enormously because I know how much he can contribute."

While Hedrich's remarks may at first seem to substantiate the popular notion that the architectural photographer is, at best, handmaiden and translator to the architect, what is clear in the work is that the presence of the architect does not necessarily serve to direct photography in any forceful way so much as simply to enrich it. That is to say, the photographer arrives on the site with his own data and insights, and these are nurtured, questioned, strengthened, and otherwise refined through his alliance with the architect.

Hedrich's deliberate and methodical approach to lighting, which distinguishes much of his work, is a case in point. Hedrich emphasizes the point that lighting and composition determine one another. "I emphasize the choice of angle," he says, "not for the angle itself and its end result, but because the choice of the angle will also dictate the choice of lighting. To choose the wrong angle will compromise the lighting." What he does initially, then, is establish a fairly uniform foundation of light with umbrellas, maintaining the authentic tone of the interior. Significant details are then spotlighted. "After all," he explains, "there are certain details the architect worked on, that he wanted to feature, and it's up to us to interpret those significant details."

"Contemporary architecture is clean and disciplined," he concludes. "We try to keep our lighting in the same spirit. There's a purity in contemporary photography, and there's a real difference between purity of lighting and sterility. The difference is the emphasis on design. We must remember why we're there, which is to interpret design and architecture and to reflect what the architect designed."

And it is this consistent balance of interpretive faculties with reportorial honesty that remains conspicuous in Bill Hedrich's work. "You must interpret their buildings with your camera, but you must be truthful," he states. In defining the responsibility of the architectural photographer, Robert A. Sobieszek, director of photographic collections at the George Eastman House, observes that "the photographer certainly interprets—in a sense he or she cannot do otherwise—but the interpretation is, in essence, a conjunction between the photographer's vision of the architecture and his or her respect for another's artisanry." [5] That the photographer must constantly appreciate and exploit this conjunction is what gives architectural photography its great complexity. It is also a conjunction that Bill Hedrich's work has located repeatedly throughout his career.

---

1. John Szarkowski, *The Idea of Louis Sullivan* (Minneapolis: University of Minnesota Press, 1956), p. 74.
2. Joel Snyder, "Some Thoughts on Photography and Architecture," *Archetype* (Spring 1981), p. 15.
3. Robert A. Sobieszek, ed., *The Architectural Photography of Hedrich-Blessing* (New York: Holt, Rinehart and Winston, 1984), p. 3.
4. Ibid., p. 9.
5. Ibid., p. 6.

FACING PAGE: David Haid & Associates. Private Residence. Highland Park, Illinois, 1974 (courtesy of Bill Hedrich, Hedrich-Blessing).

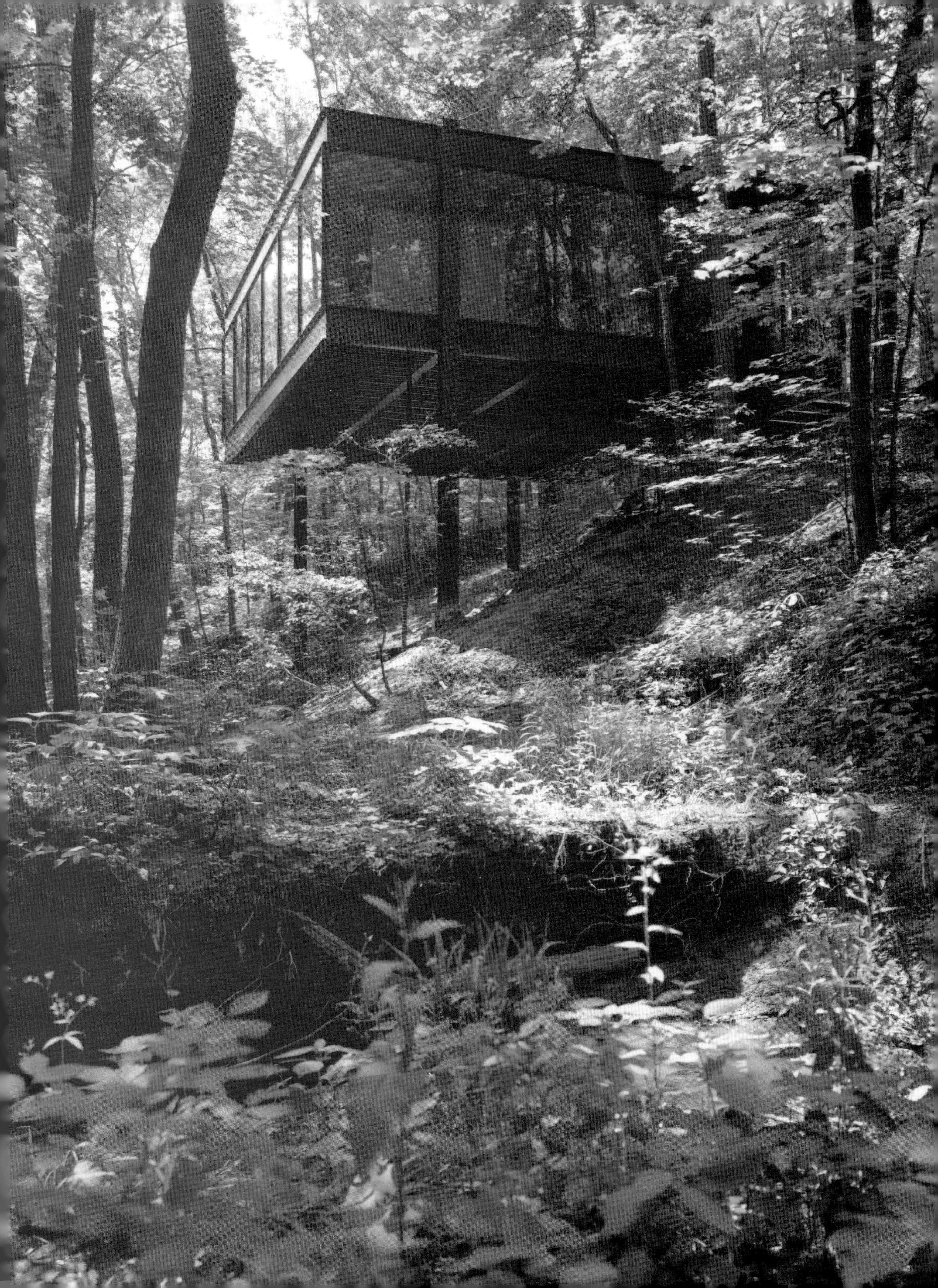

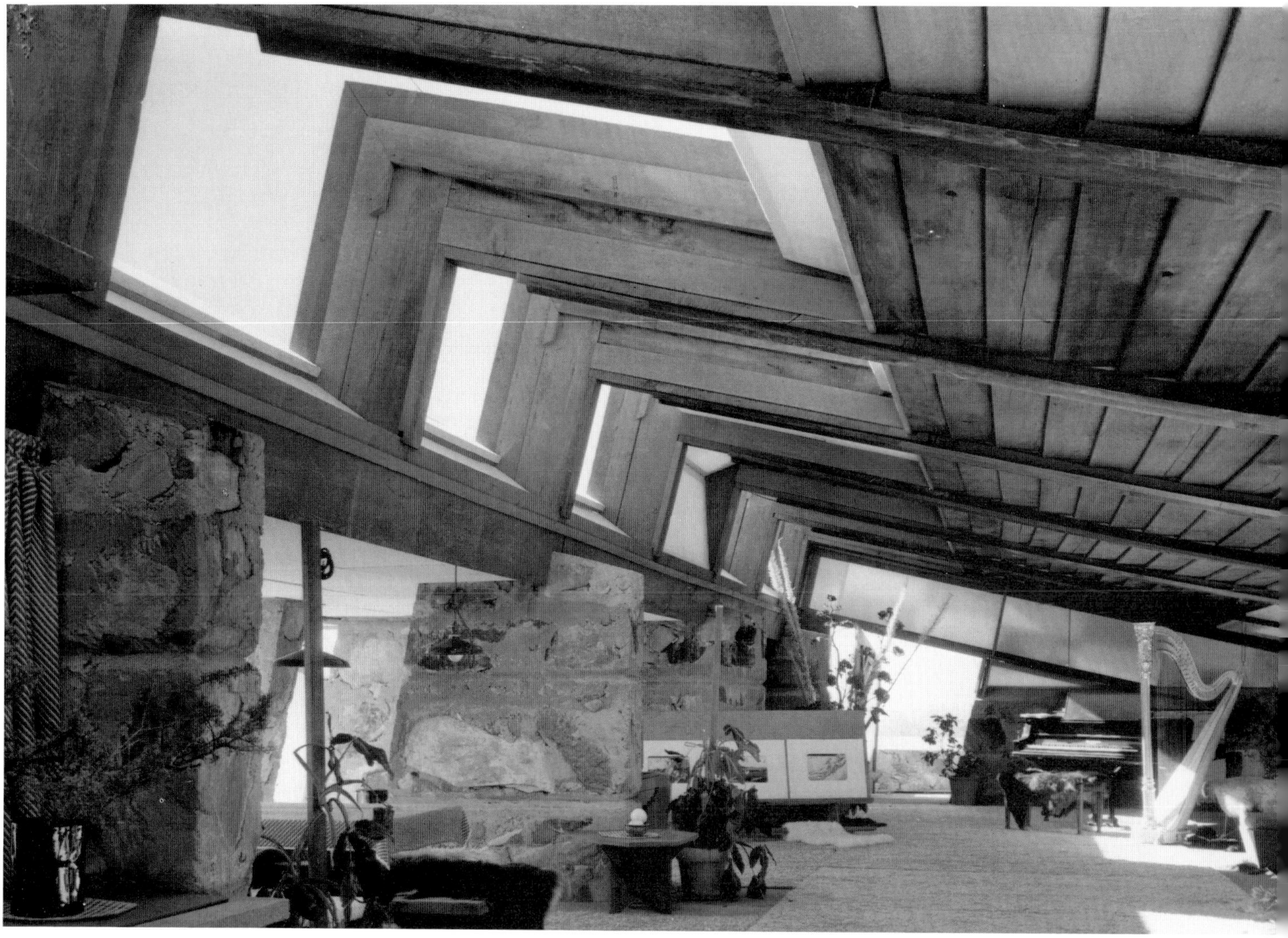

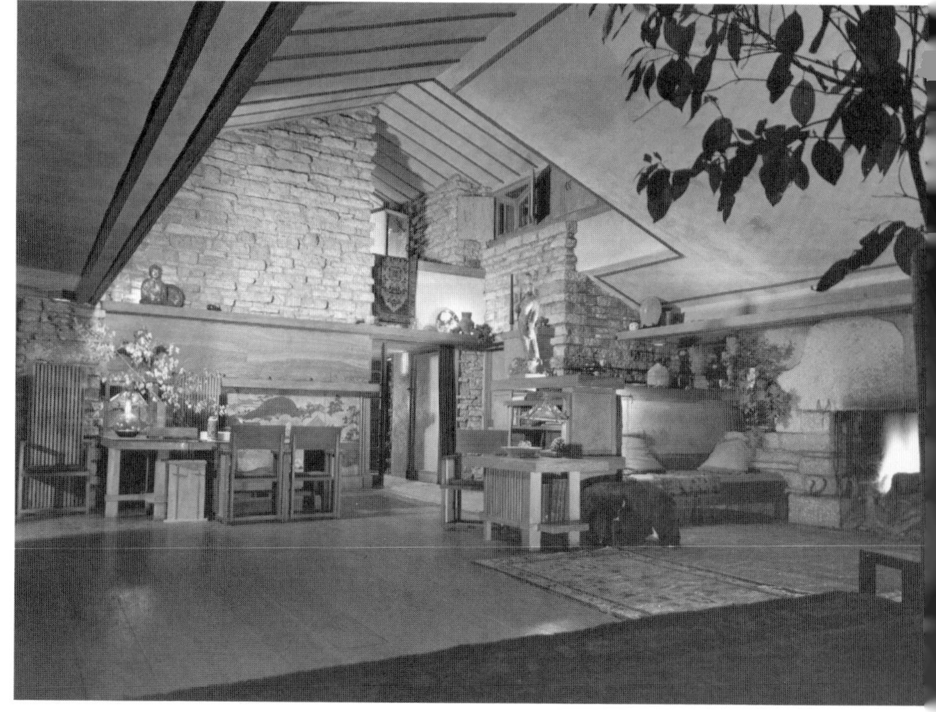

ABOVE: Frank Lloyd Wright. Taliesin West. Scottsdale Arizona, 1942 (courtesy of Bill Hedrich, Hedrich-Blessing).

RIGHT: Frank Lloyd Wright. Taliesin East. Spring Green, Wisconsin, 1937 (courtesy of Bill Hedrich, Hedrich-Blessing).

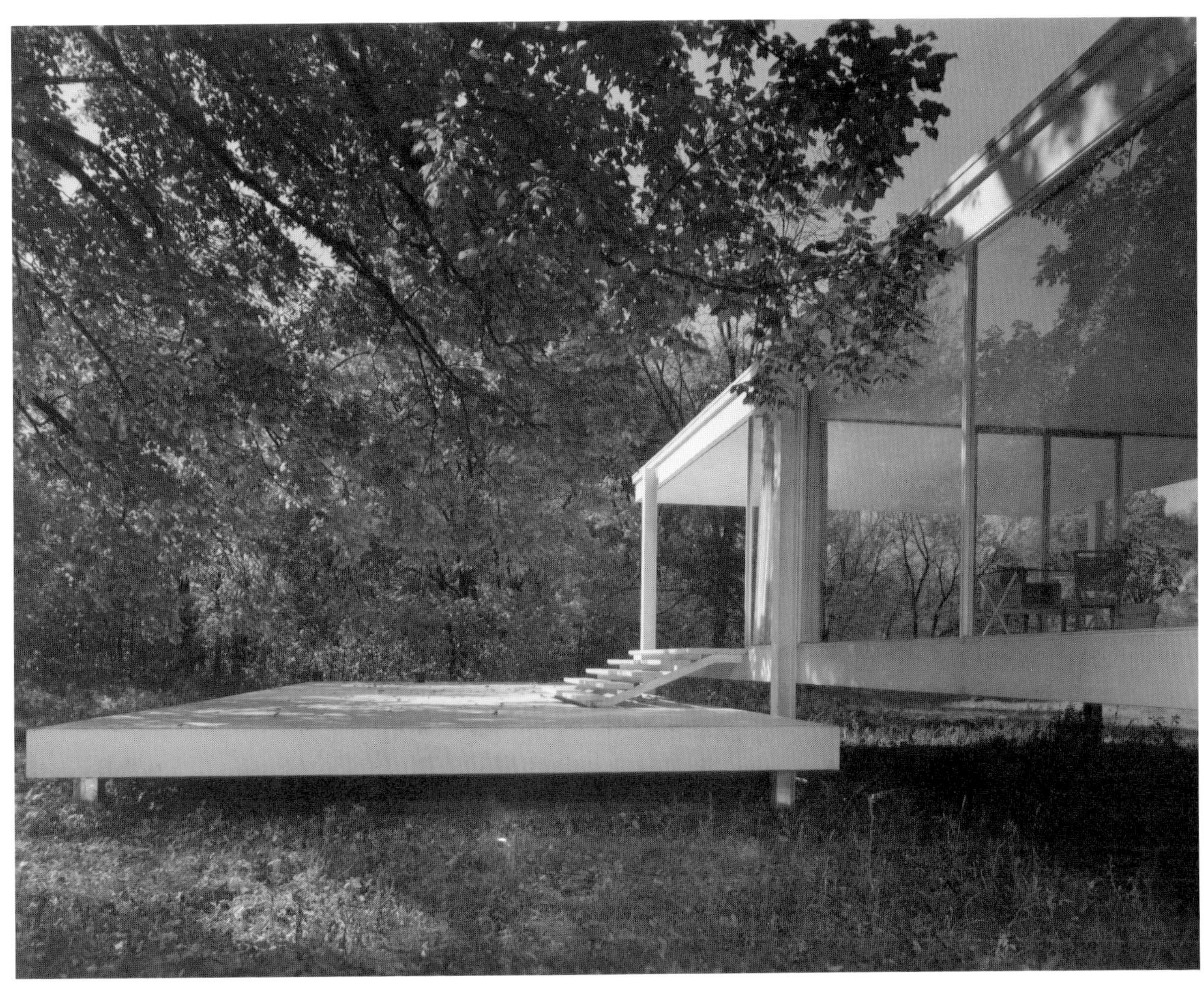

Ludwig Mies van der Rohe. Farnsworth House. Plano, Illinois, 1951 (courtesy of Bill Hedrich, Hedrich-Blessing).

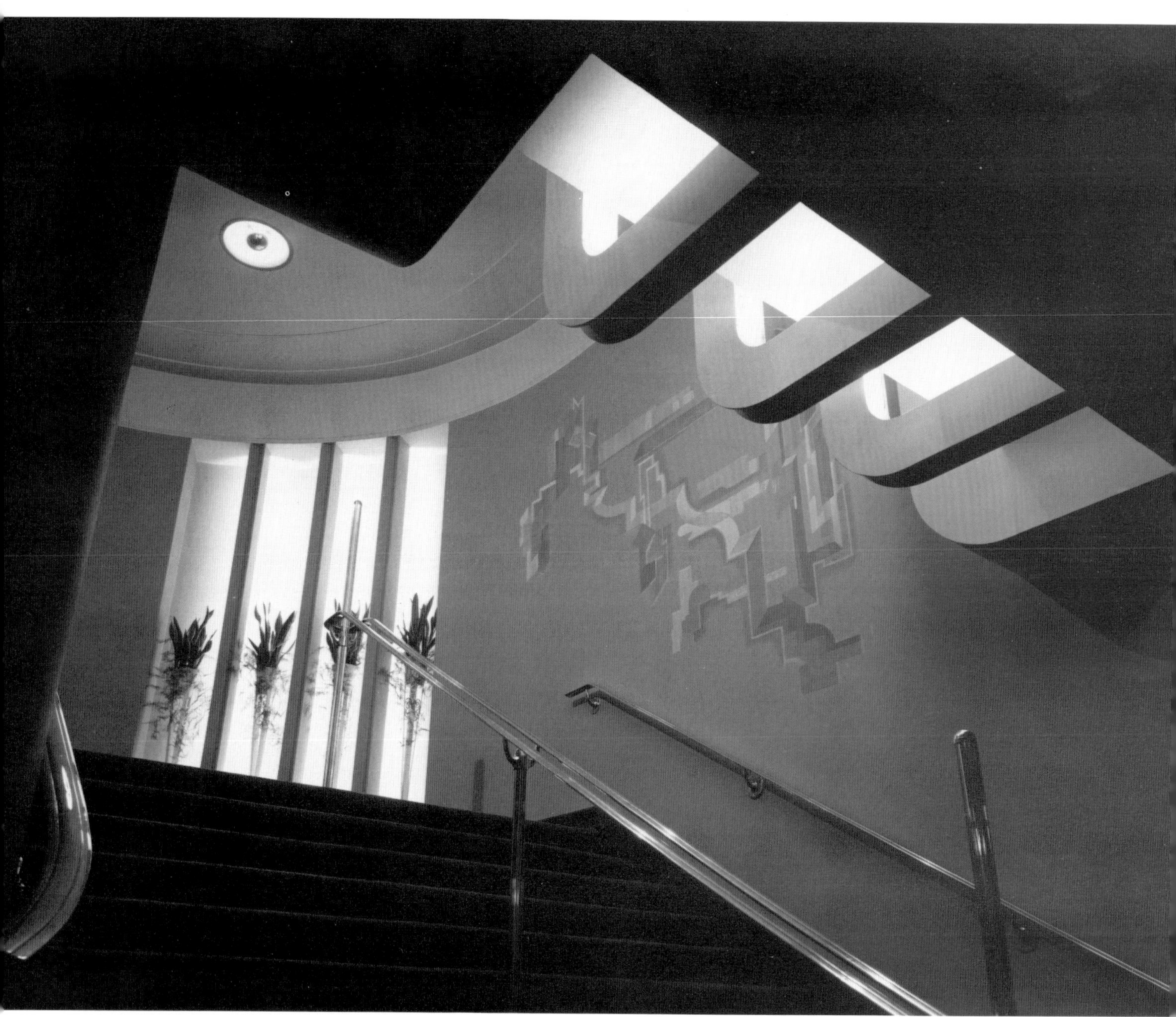

Pereira & Pereira.
Esquire Theatre. Chicago,
Illinois, 1938 (courtesy of
Bill Hedrich, Hedrich-
Blessing).

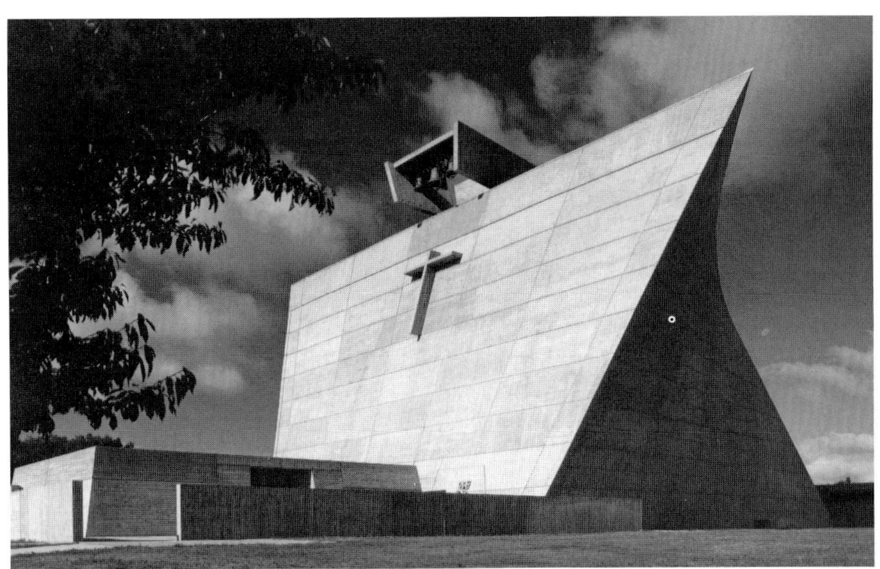

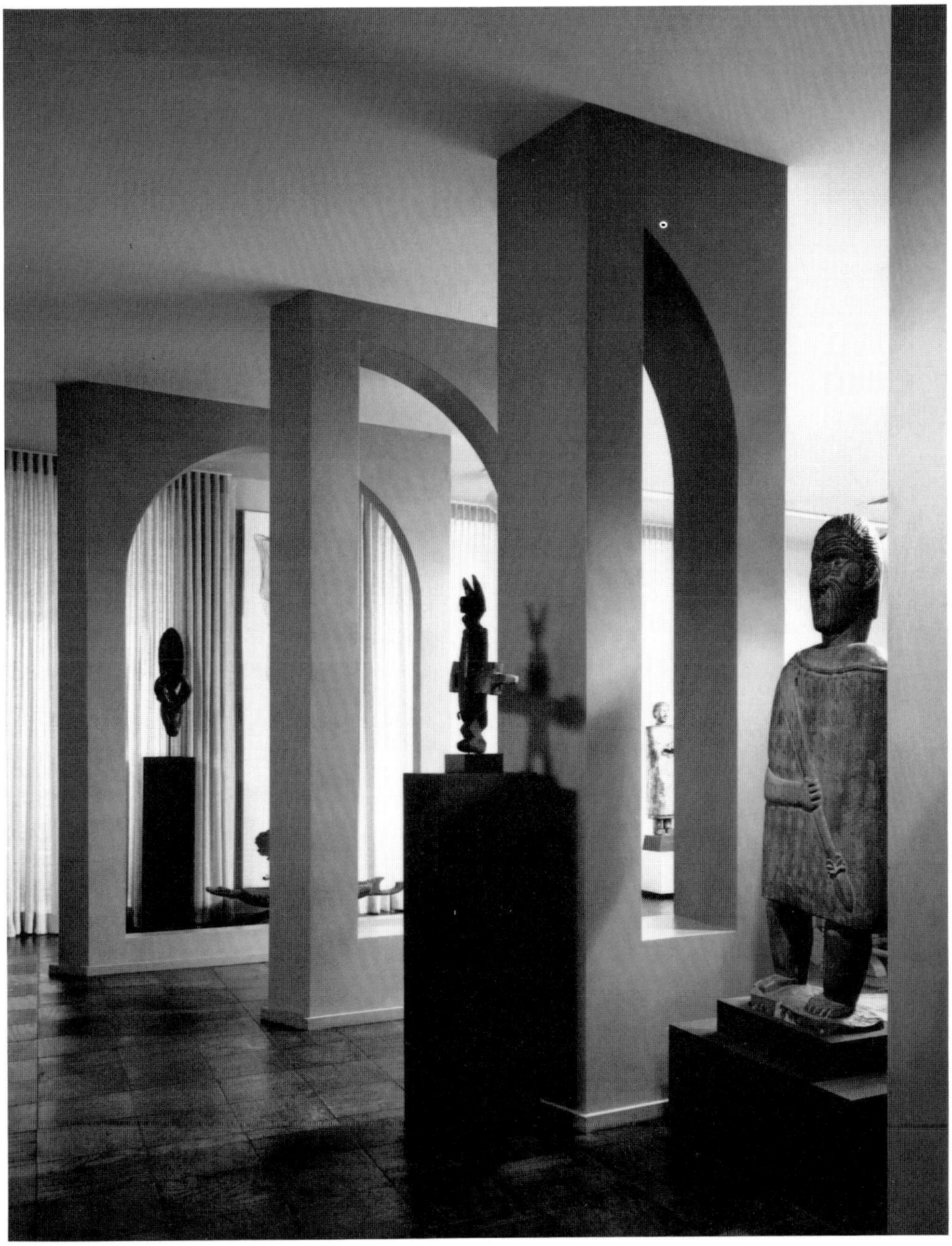

ABOVE: Marcel Breuer and Herbert Beckhard. St. Francis de Sales Church. Muskegon, Michigan, 1966 (courtesy of Bill Hedrich, Hedrich-Blessing).

LEFT: J. D. Bloodgood & Associates. Brady Apartment. Des Moines, Iowa, 1980 (courtesy of Bill Hedrich, Hedrich-Blessing).

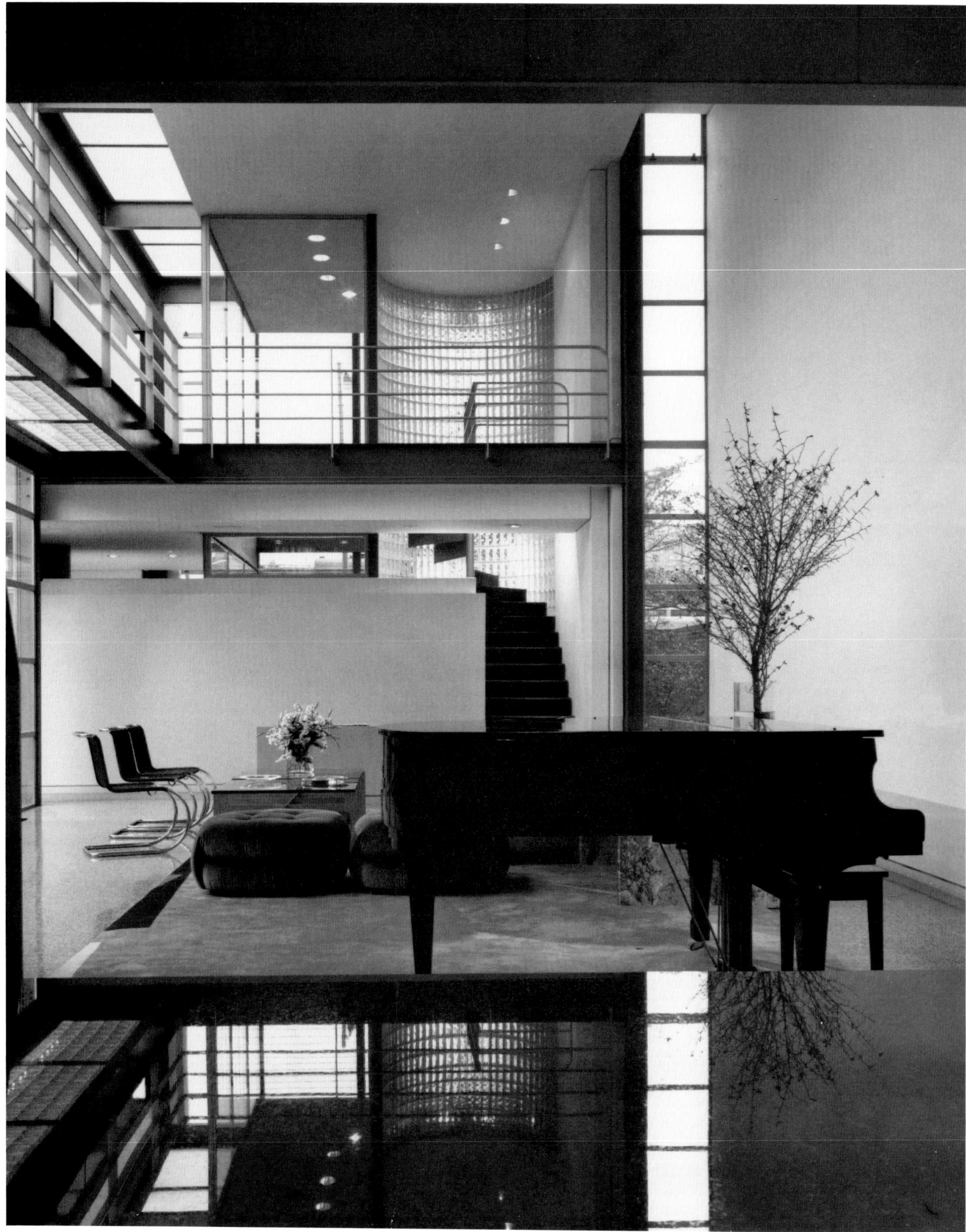

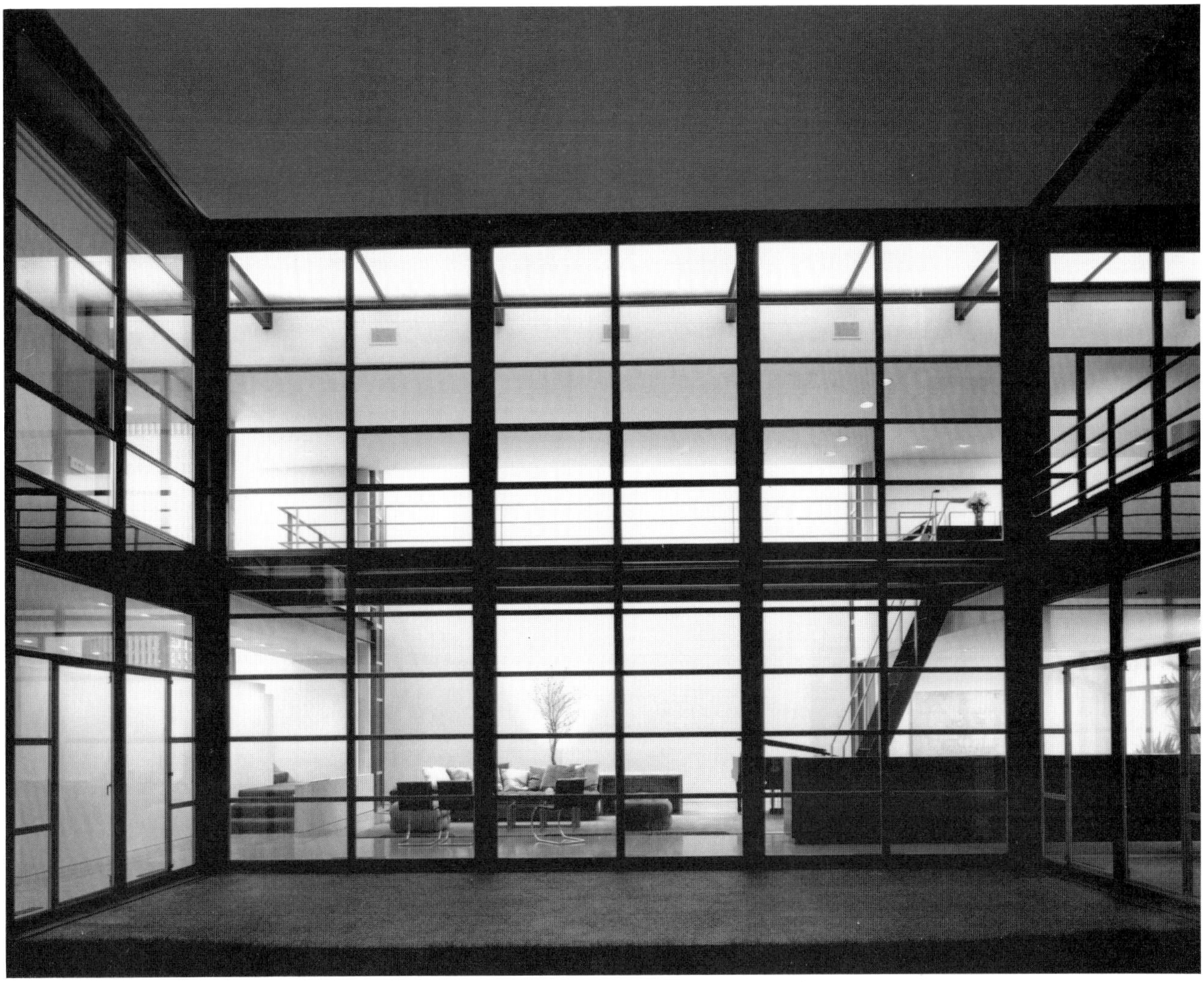

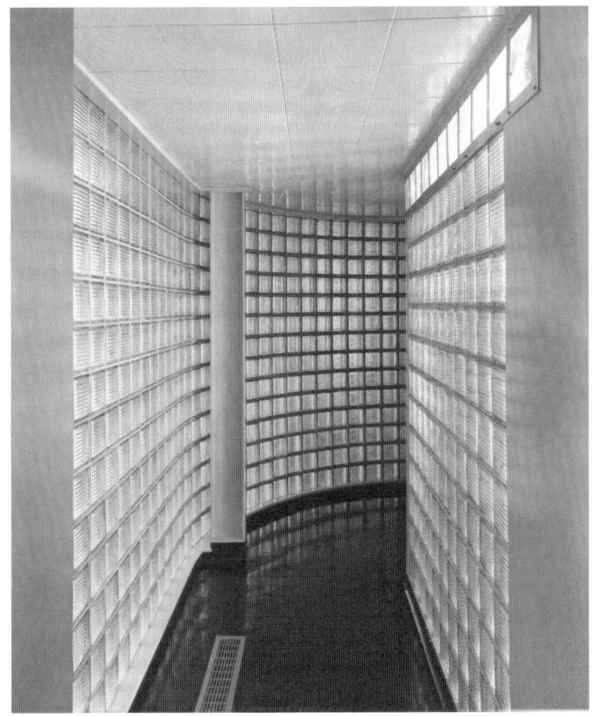

LEFT: George Fred Keck and William Keck. Cahn Residence. Lake Forest, Illinois, 1938 (courtesy of Bill Hedrich, Hedrich-Blessing).

FACING PAGE AND ABOVE: Krueck & Olson. Private Residence. Chicago, Illinois,1981 (courtesy of Bill Hedrich, Hedrich-Blessing).

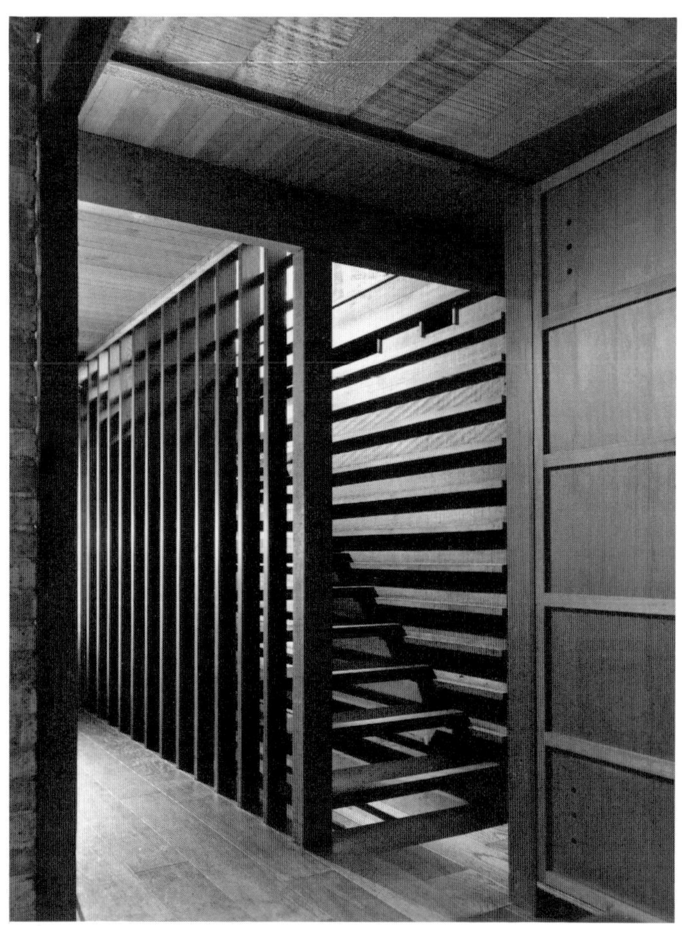

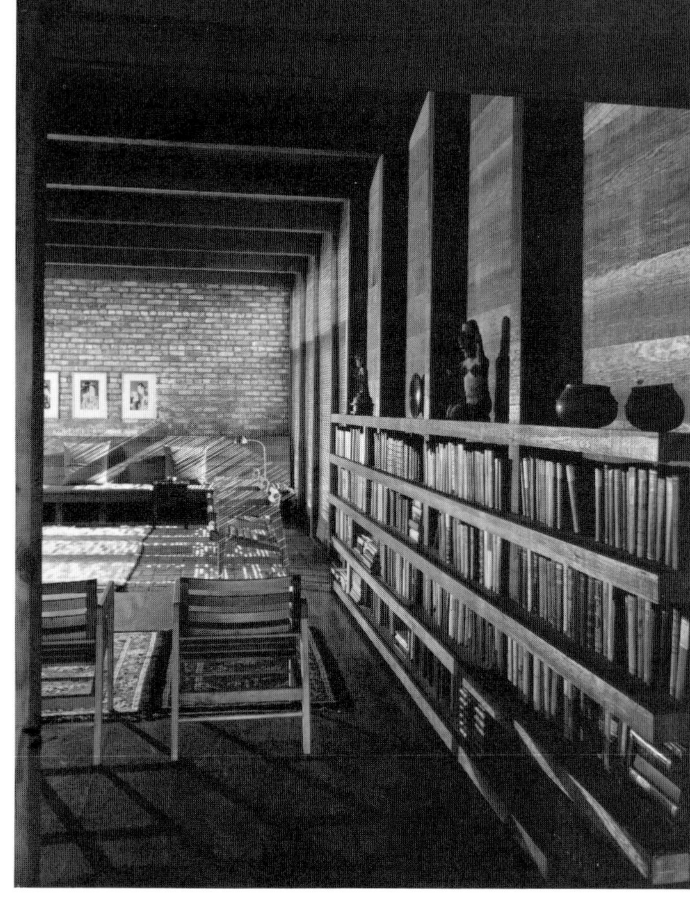

ABOVE: Paul Schweikher. Rinaldo Residence. Downers Grove, Illinois, 1946 (courtesy of Bill Hedrich, Hedrich-Blessing).

RIGHT: Paul Schweikher. Schweikher Residence. Downers Grove, Illinois, 1946 (courtesy of Bill Hedrich, Hedrich-Blessing).

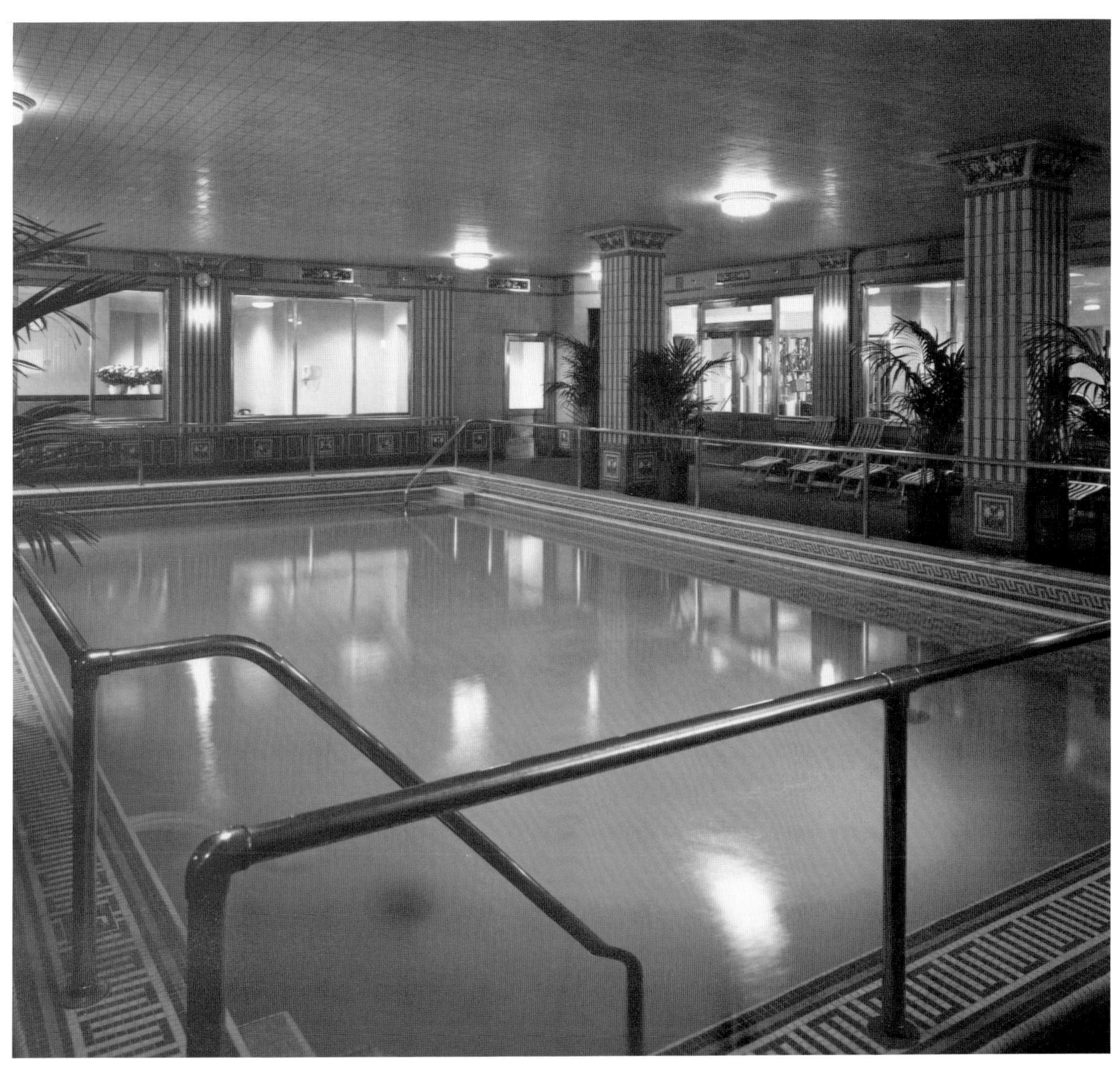

Schultze & Weaver.
The Biltmore Hotel.
Los Angeles, California,
1981 (courtesy of Bill
Hedrich, Hedrich-Blessing).

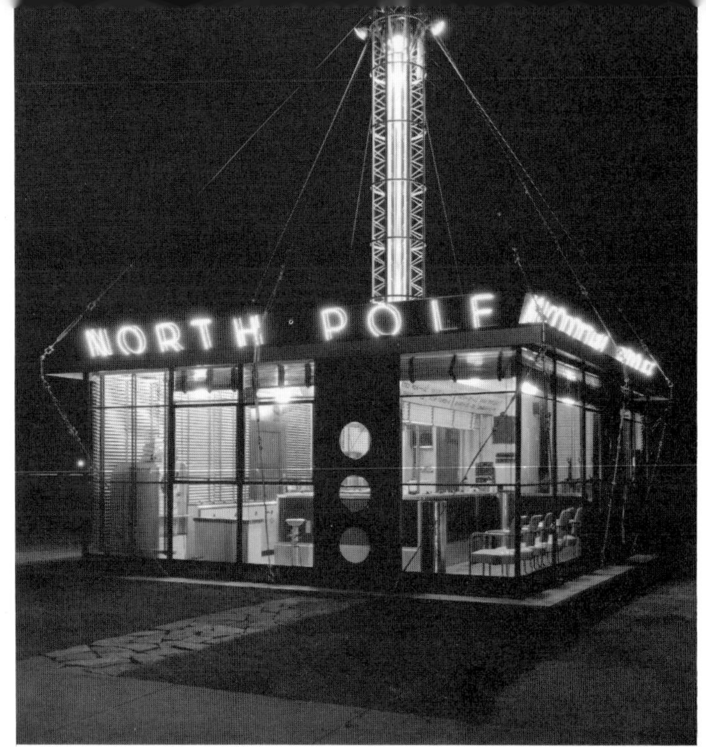

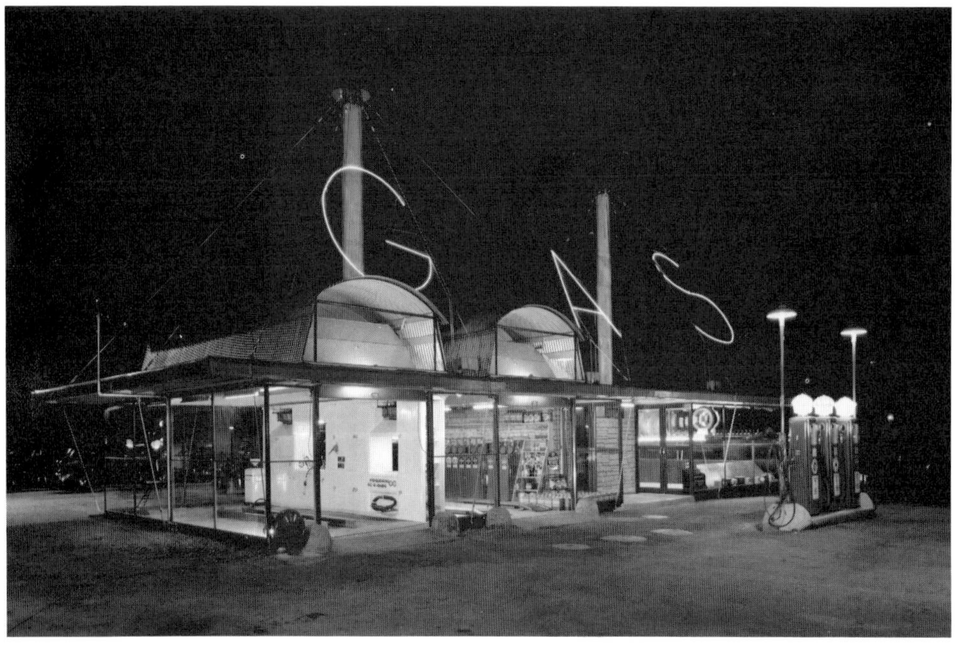

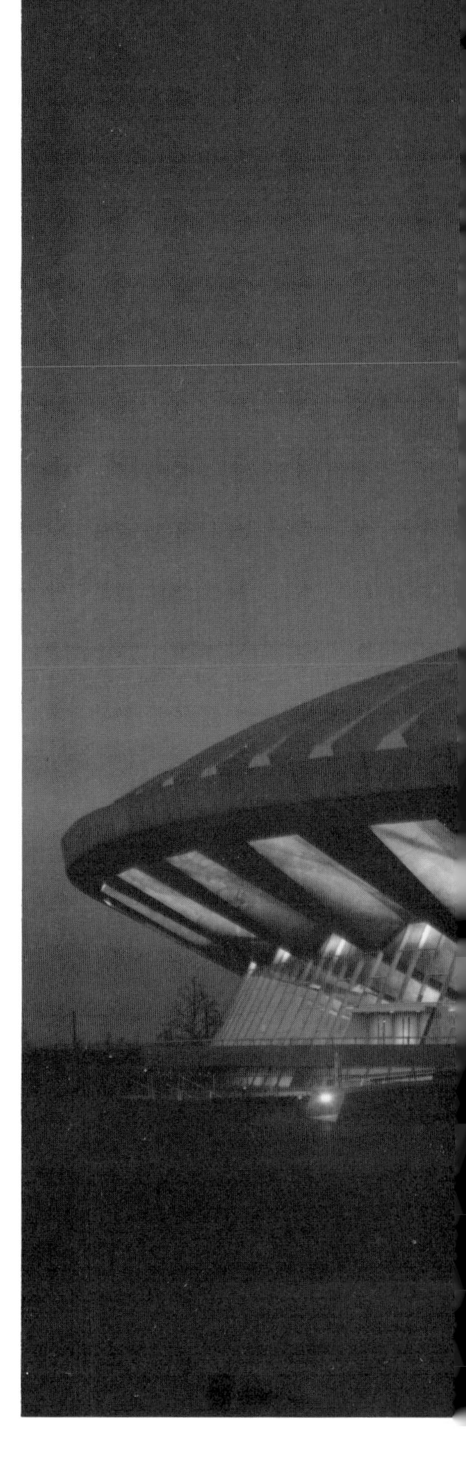

TOP: Bertrand Goldberg. "North Pole" Ice Cream Parlor. River Forest, Illinois, 1938 (courtesy of Bill Hedrich, Hedrich-Blessing).

BOTTOM: Bertrand Goldberg. Gas Station. Chicago, Illinois, 1940 (courtesy of Bill Hedrich, Hedrich-Blessing).

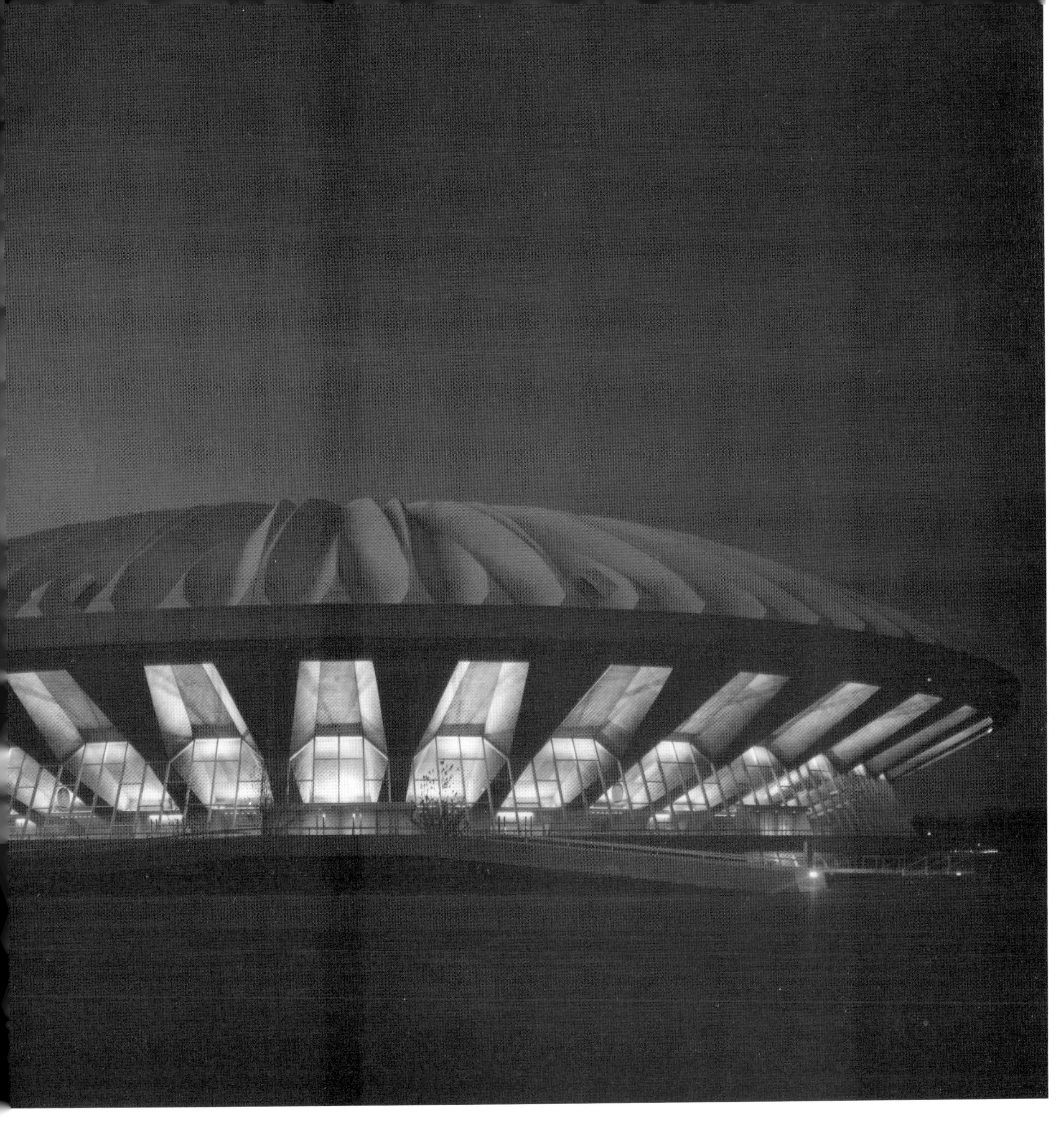

Harrison & Abramowitz.
Assembly Hall,
The University of Illinois.
Champagne, Illinois, 1962
(courtesy of Bill Hedrich,
Hedrich-Blessing).

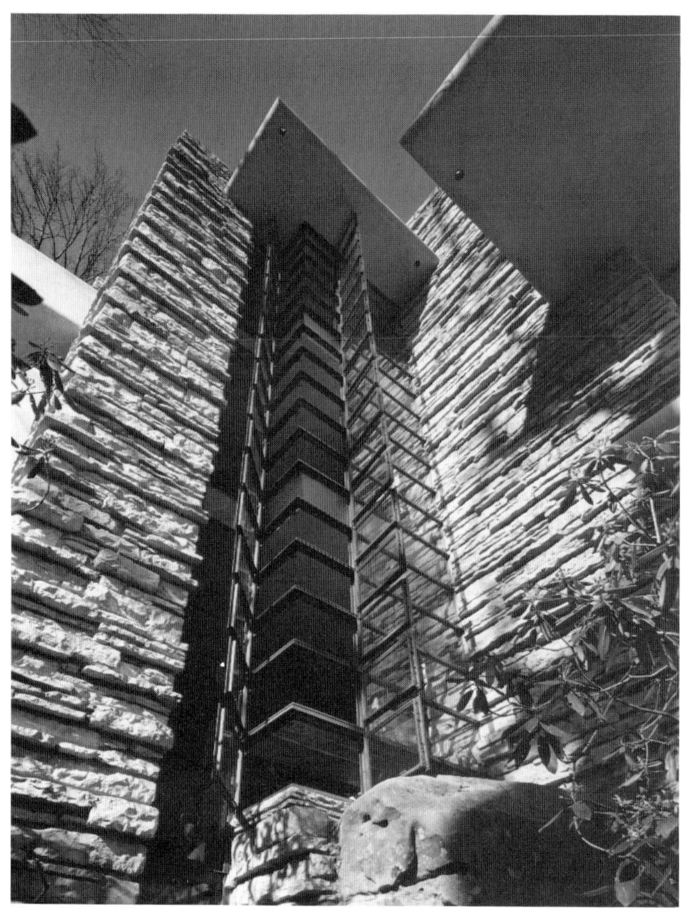

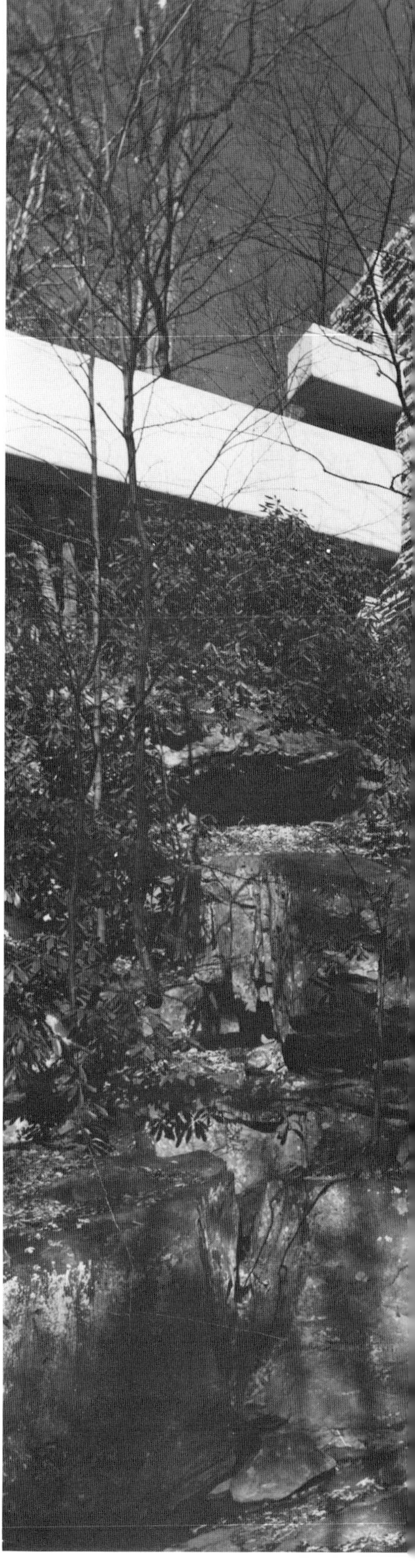

Frank Lloyd Wright. Fallingwater. Bear Run, Pennsylvania, 1937 (courtesy of Bill Hedrich, Hedrich-Blessing).

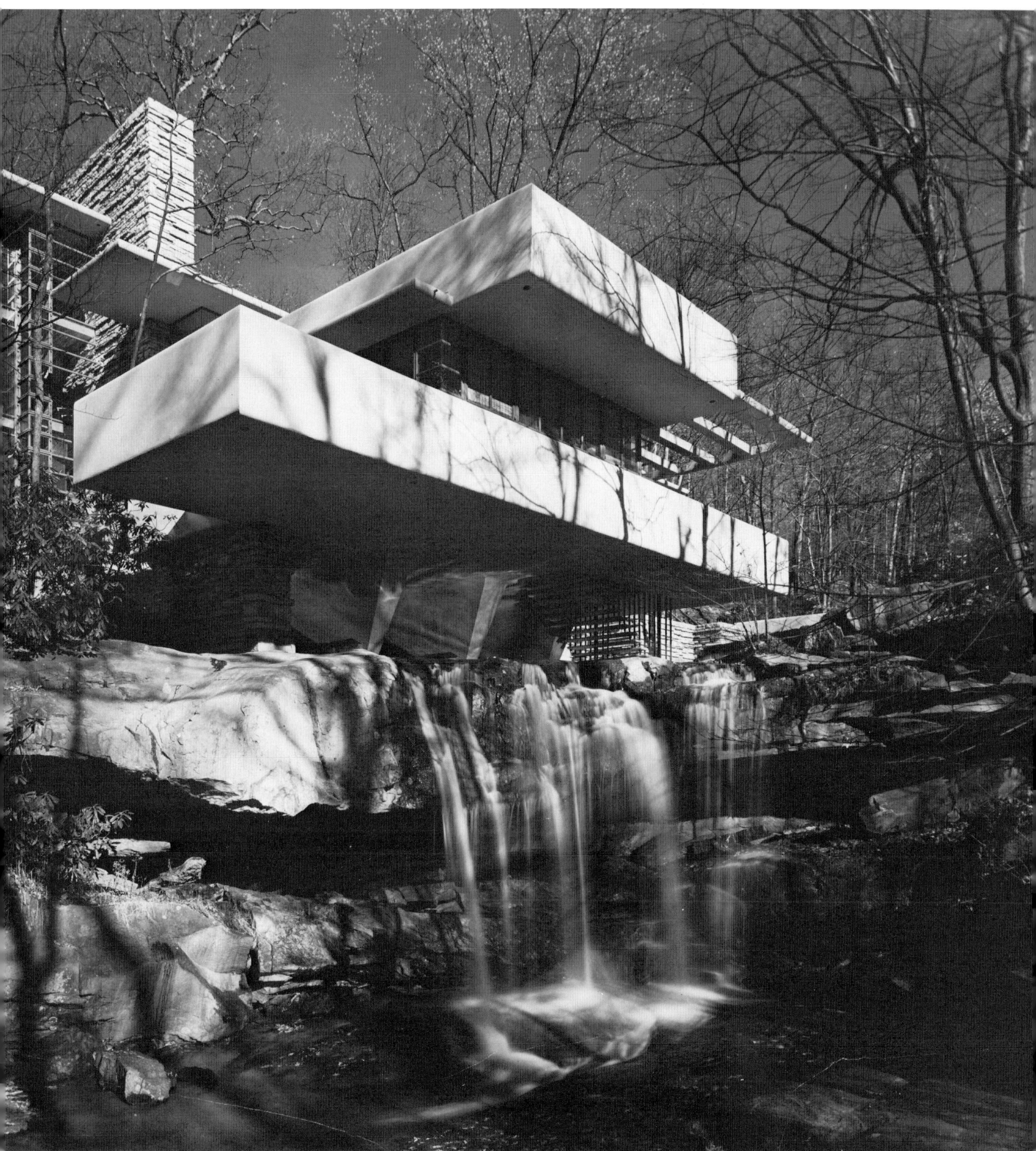

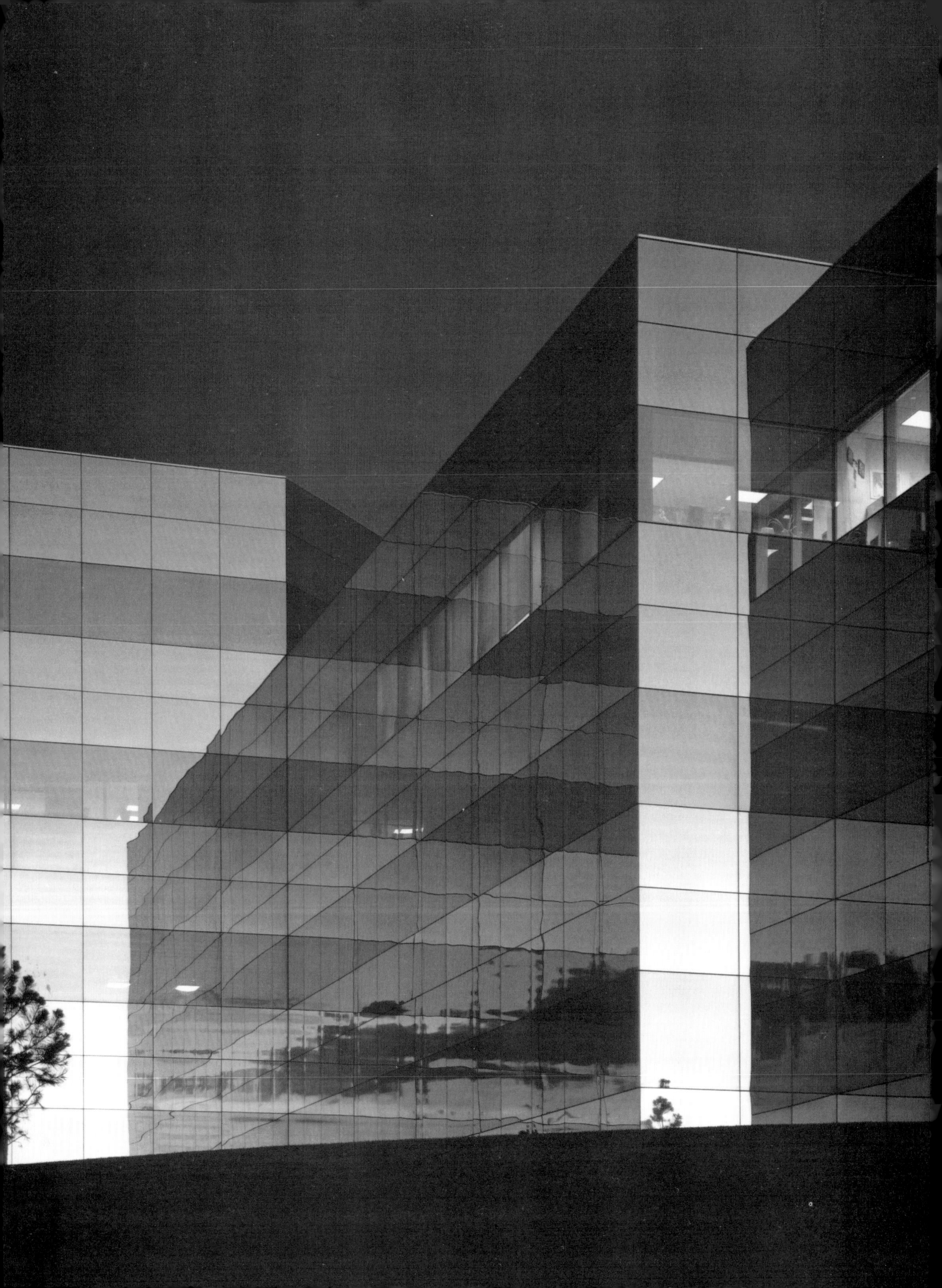

NICK MERRICK

"I've always been interested in how men interacted with their environments," says Nick Merrick. "I'm interested in how men build things." It was as staff photographer on an archaeological excavation in the city of Cyrene, Libya, in 1973 that Merrick first found photographic documentation an effective means with which to investigate these questions. The artifacts of the Greek and Roman ruins offered Merrick an historical perspective on the constructions of the built world. A short step away was the photography of architecture that allowed, clearly, a more immediate visual grasp. And his portfolio of subsequent work indeed provides a precise visual transcription of the structures—both material and abstract—found in the built world.

Merrick's visual investigations are not limited to commissioned work; rather, his commercial architectural work has struck an esthetic balance with his own, more personal portfolio of photographs. While the two remain distinctly separate, they continue to provoke and nurture one another, creating both a balance and a broadness of vision.

While Merrick continues to separate his work into categories of commerce and art, what is perhaps unique is that once he has done so, he often proceeds to blur their distinctions. That the purpose of many of his photographs is to meet the demands of a client is not always enough to distinguish them from those taken as more personal and private expressions. "To me," Merrick says, "if a photograph has succeeded in giving information that absolutely has to be told, then it's not a bad photograph." That the images inform is basic to all his work. "Unfortunately," he says, "I recognize the fact that there is a line between commercial and art photography. But I'm trying to bring the two together."

How he does so reveals much about the way he works. Merrick's approach is formal; his training has been to investigate and record the design ideas expressed by the building, and it is a formal investigation that he applies in his personal as well as commissioned work. The construction of several steel-frame buildings in Chicago was the subject of a recent noncommissioned series. "My commercial work had gotten me visually interested in how buildings are put together during construction," he explains. The grids, then, of the steel structures are recorded not as pictorial or decorative constructions, but as a more formal system that delineates both the physical density of the building, and the more abstract design concepts

FACING PAGE: C.W. Fentress & Associates. 116 Inverness. Denver, Colorado, 1984 (courtesy of Nick Merrick, Hedrich-Blessing).

on which it has been based. They document an anatomy of architecture. Nevertheless, such photographs remain more personally motivated; greater liberties are taken with their information. "While the lines between art and commercial photographs might remain hazy, the latter might emphasize the emotional aspect more."

While the steel structures of the buildings he frequently photographs professionally have motivated his personal work, the personal work is as supportive of his commercial work. The subject of another recent noncommissioned series was the Grecian landscape, fields that over the centuries had been worked heavily for what little vegetation the Mediterranean climate and geography permit. Carved into mountainsides, the fields assume a form all their own, suspended in a place between the natural and built worlds. While Merrick's photographs are an inquiry of the relationships between man and his land and are not connected to architecture in any direct way, they do continue to probe man's maneuverings in the built environment.

Moreover, the technical approach he had adopted to record the landscape has contributed and helped to shape his architectural documentation. "In working on that series," he continues, "I had gotten interested in shooting with a longer lens, a semitelephoto lens that worked to foreshorten the landscape. Information was distributed very evenly over the entire surface of the photograph." This quality of uniform spatial information was carried into the architectural photographs and it remains a quality that Merrick finds marks most of his current work. "Instead of one event in the photograph taking precedence," he says, "the pictures have a lot of smaller photographic events within the larger frame. And while these smaller events are interrelated, they are distributed evenly." It is an approach derived, in large part, from the recent series of landscape photographs.

Merrick's photographs are indeed a departure from the heightened dramatic approach where a single architectural event dominates the photograph. The single focus has been replaced by a more neutral sort of character where the graphic elements of the photograph have been arranged with a greater uniformity. "On a purely formal level of how a picture is constructed," Merrick explains, "where there is light and dark, how light interacts with texture, all of these little bits of information are distributed around the frame. Rather than seeing the image as a quick gesture where one strong sweeping line controls the whole picture, there are smaller gestures in eight or ten places around the picture."

The somewhat diffused sense of composition evident in Merrick's photographs is not simply an arbitrary esthetic choice; rather, it is one that he finds appropriate to his subject matter. "I don't feel my job is to document what an interior or building looks like," he says. "That doesn't interest me." What *does* interest me are the design ideas that the architect has used to organize the space, and how those are carried through in the smaller details." And it is the nearly uniform distribution of these details across the surface of the photograph that conveys the design ideas most concisely. The facts have been spread out; one leads to the other, and that to another, and the sum of the many parts yields a greater whole. "My favorite photographs," Merrick adds, "tend not to be overall building shots, but rather sections, in which a detail can speak for the whole." A photograph composed, then, as a series of such details is a narrative account of the space; they tend to be tightly layered, drawing the eye through the space in an organized, sequential movement. And they point out succinctly that it is often through the details that the flow of space is articulated.

Not surprisingly, Merrick's photographs are also heavily structured; their format is rigorous. The diffusion of design elements across the photograph's surface, and their subtle connections and interrelations are methodical and deliberate. Among his own associates, Merrick is known for the amount of time spent composing behind the camera. "How the items are distributed and how the various shapes are proportioned in the frame is everything," he says. "I spend a lot of time building the photograph. Pictures are not snapshots, but something that you study and build." There is little in the photographs that has been left to chance.

Merrick's photographs are structured so as to reflect the structures of the architecture; the composition of the photograph reflects the composition of the space. "I am trying," he says, "to allow the visual design ideas of the building to become the very same ideas that I will organize the picture upon." He adds that this is indeed possible when the photographer is working with an architect with ideas of strength and consistency. The balance or contrast of positive and negative space, light, surface texture, transparency, opacity, reflection, mass, and the illusion of mass—all of these are formal design qualities that can be translated directly from the architecture to the photograph; they can structure the photograph as well as the space.

This being the case, Merrick's work is, by nature, interpretive. As he admits himself, strict documentation interests him less than the visual grasp and translation of design precepts. But the interpretations are not such that the subject is rendered in a personal or subjective manner, nor is the material manipulated in any private rendition, as interpretation is so commonly thought to imply. Rather, it pursues and visually analyzes the design content of a building, choosing the salient design ideas and then recording those on film. It is interpretive in that it is selective. "It's a way," Merrick observes, "of allowing a portion of the building to stand for the whole." The photographs, then, are precise and sensitive abbreviations of the whole; and in so being, they present us with a concentrated version of an often more expansive design thesis.

When Merrick speaks of "building a photograph," he is speaking not only of the subtle relationships betwen details and design elements, but of the process of selection that has yielded their very presence in the photograph. The sensitivity and discrimination with which he makes choices are qualities that he attributes to Ken Hedrich, a founding partner of Hedrich-Blessing: "It's an approach to the photography of architecture that was really established by Ken, a more dramatic approach than the matter-of-fact documentary that dominated the profession in its early days. Ken suggested that the photographer really wait for the light and search for a sense of detail that might give a motive or a more feeling-oriented interpretation of the architecture."

As a senior photographer and partner of Hedrich-Blessing, Merrick continues to practice traditions established by the Chicago firm. The steady commitment to craft, the sharing of technical ideas and problem solving, and finally, the visual approach that permits the part to represent the whole are all qualities that distinguished the work of the firm in its early days, and they are ones maintained today by Merrick and his associates.

But as well as continuing tradition, Merrick has made individual marks in the profession. Robert A. Sobieszek points out that "new kinds of architecture call for new ideas in documenting them. New kinds of constructions and changes in how large buildings and urban locales are developed demand inventive ways of recording and communicating architectural ideas. And new materials available to the photographer lead to new visual possibilities of contributing to the photographic world of architecture." [1] Merrick's work clearly demonstrates these new visual possibilities. While the sensitivity of his interpretations is not unlike that of his predecessors, his vision is perhaps less dramatic. He has replaced the single, often theatrical focus with a more subtle layering of information. His work, perhaps, demands more of the viewer.

These more quiet interpretations mark Nick Merrick's work. A sense of deliberation and choice accompanies the photographs, as does a keen design analysis that continually prevents the images, despite their graphic strength or impact, from conflicting with or overpowering the simple facts of the architecture. That the photographer can interpret as well as transcribe is abundantly clear in his work. "With all the tools a photographer has available," he says, "there are ways to get the information and still be very selective. And in being selective, you can compose a photograph that works." That Merrick is knowledgeable and skilled in the use of these tools is evident in these pages.

---

1. Robert A. Sobieszek, ed., *The Architectural Photography of Hedrich-Blessing* (New York: Holt, Rinehart and Winston, 1984), p. 10.

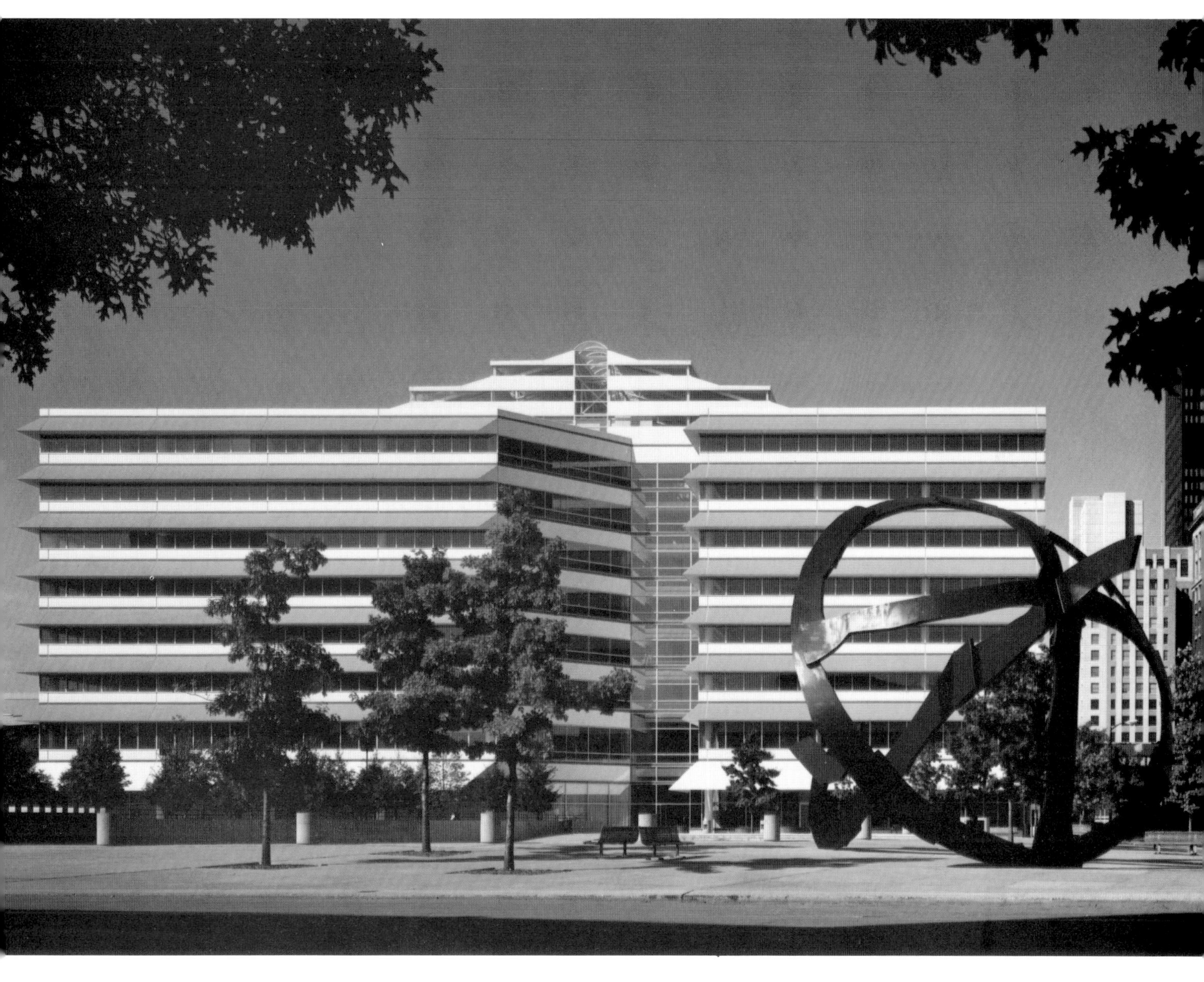

Skidmore, Owings & Merrill.
Capitol Square Building.
Des Moines, Iowa, 1983
(courtesy of Nick Merrick,
Hedrich-Blessing).

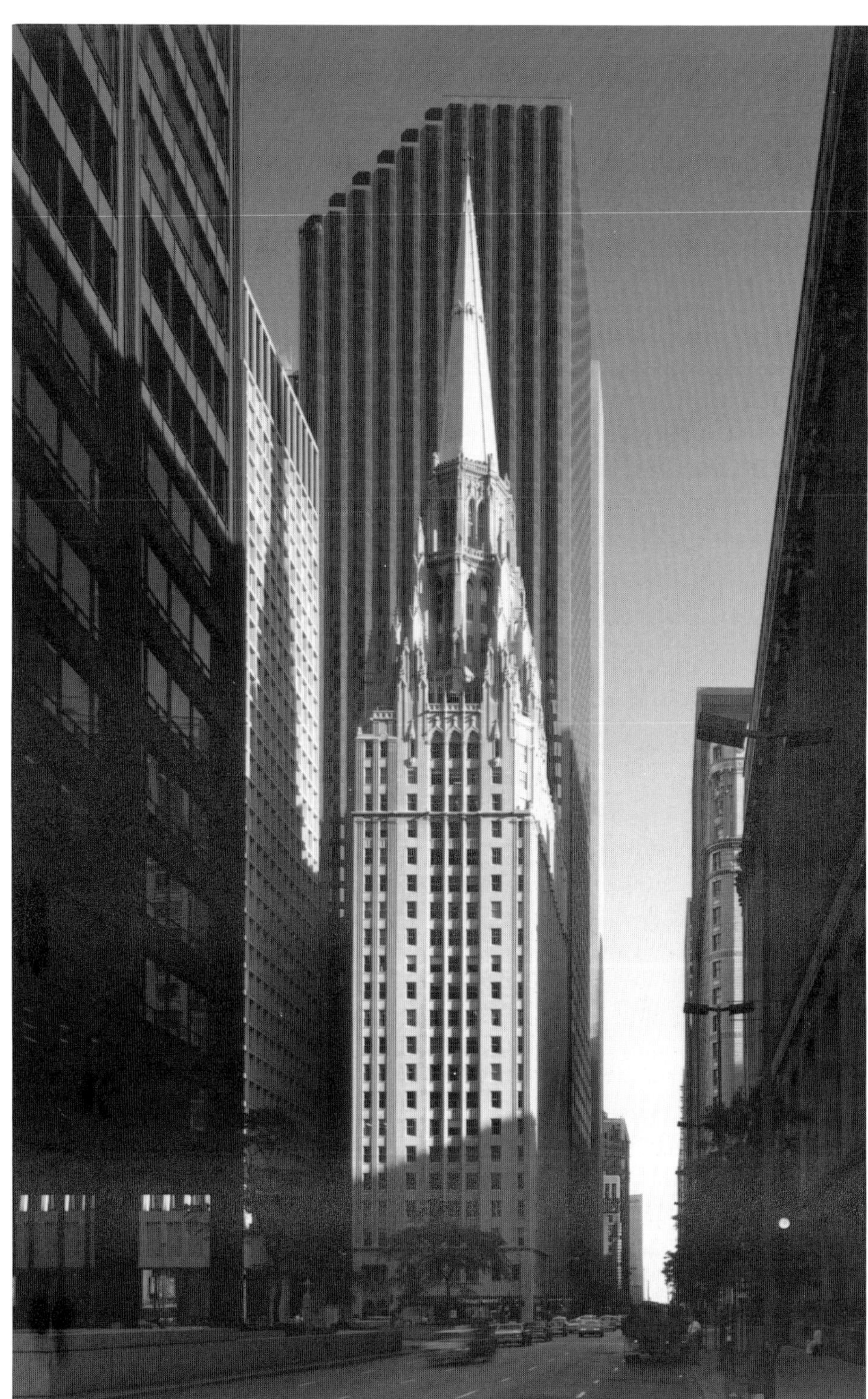

RIGHT: Skidmore, Owings & Merrill. Three First National Plaza. Chicago, Illinois, 1982 (courtesy of Nick Merrick, Hedrich-Blessing).

FACING PAGE: Skidmore, Owings & Merrill. Inland Steel Building. Chicago, Illinois, 1982 (courtesy of Nick Merrick, Hedrich-Blessing).

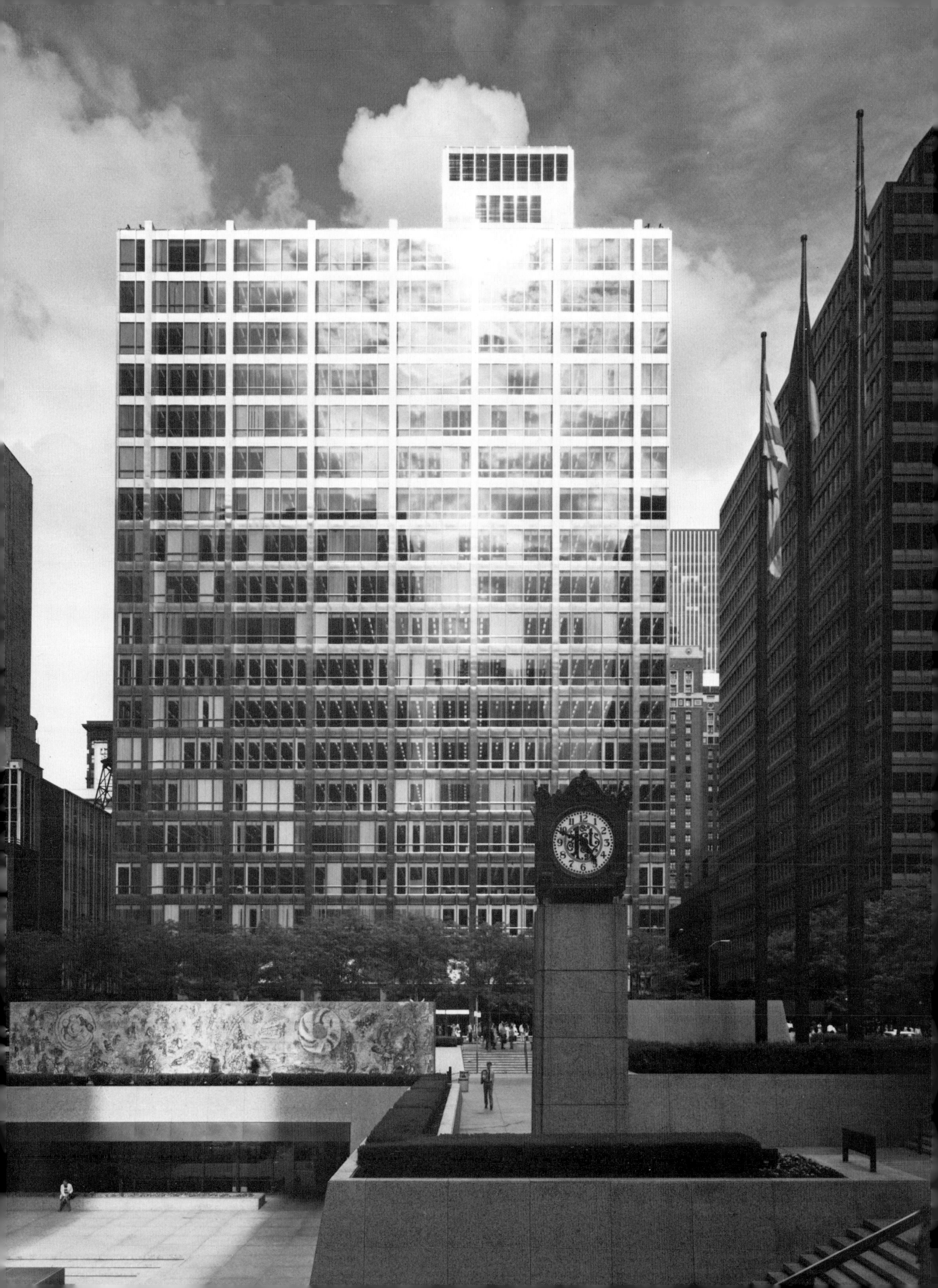

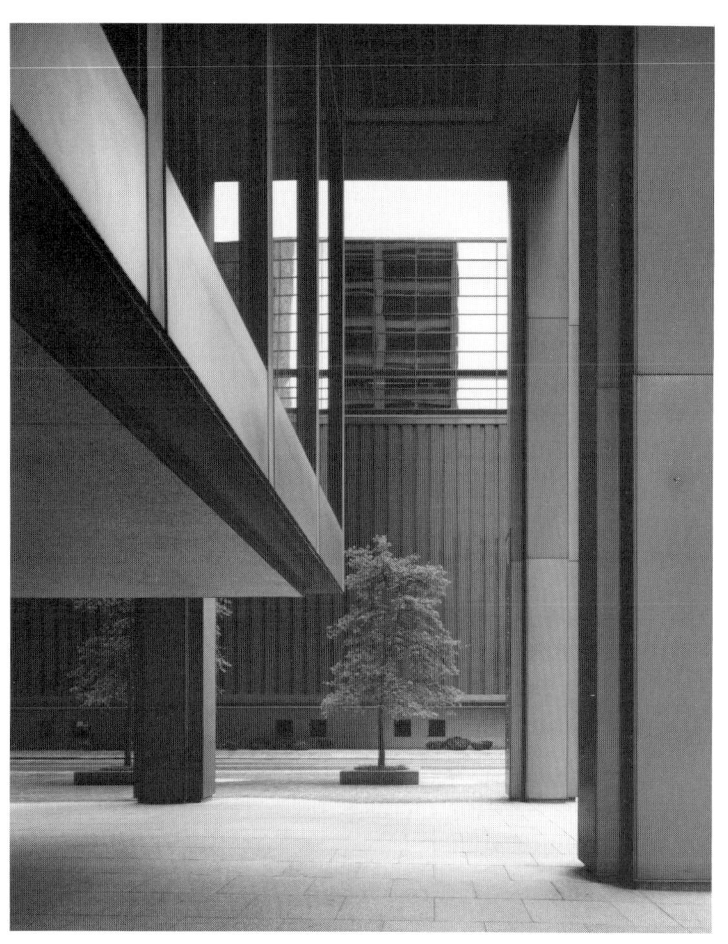

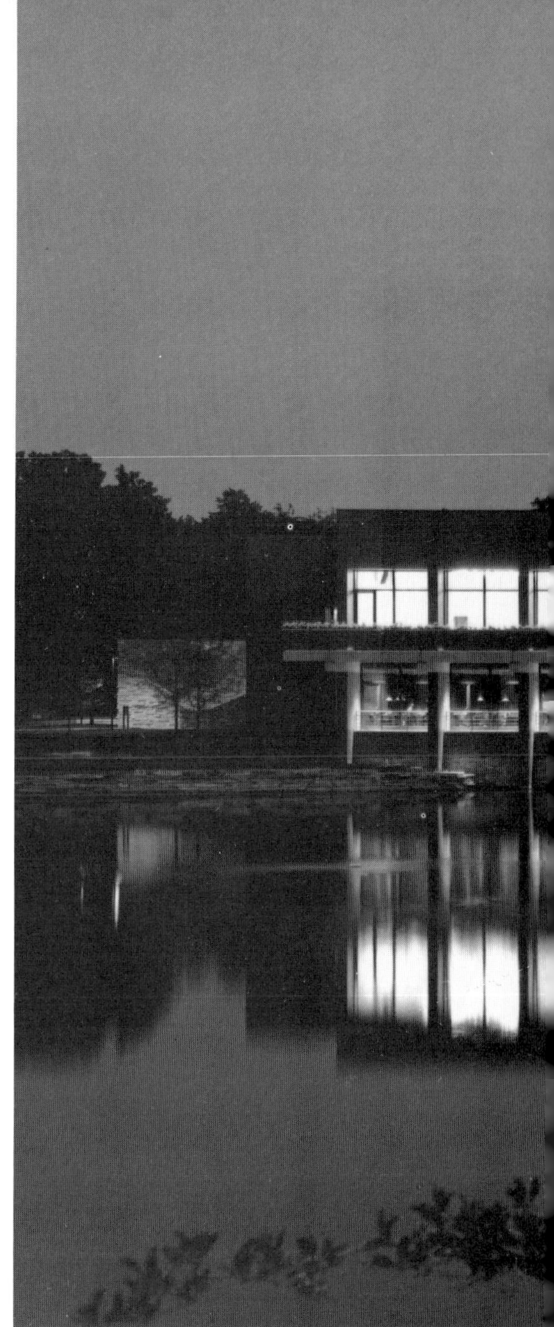

Skidmore, Owings & Merrill. Teneco Buildings. Houston, Texas, 1982 (courtesy of Nick Merrick, Hedrich-Blessing).

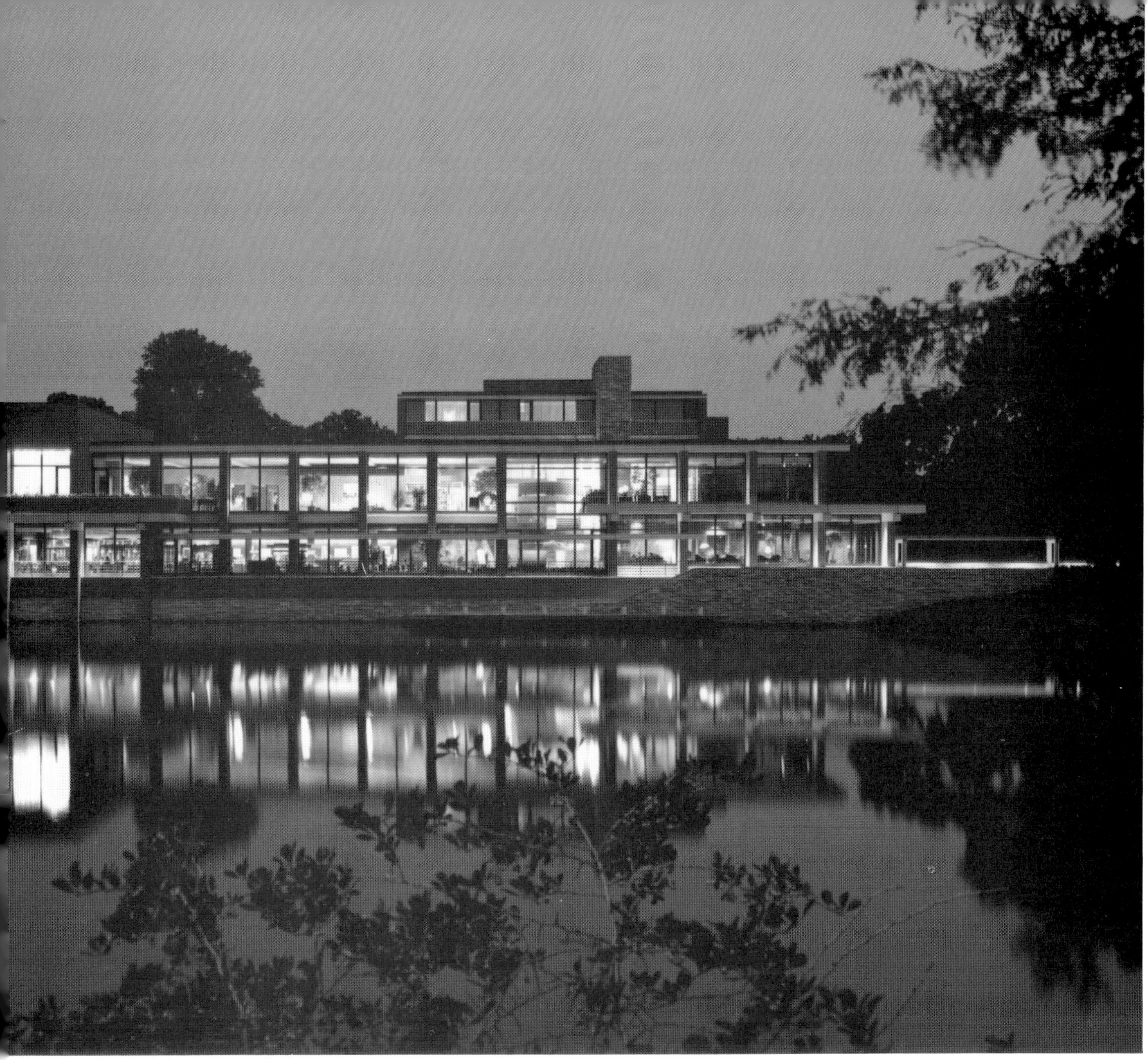

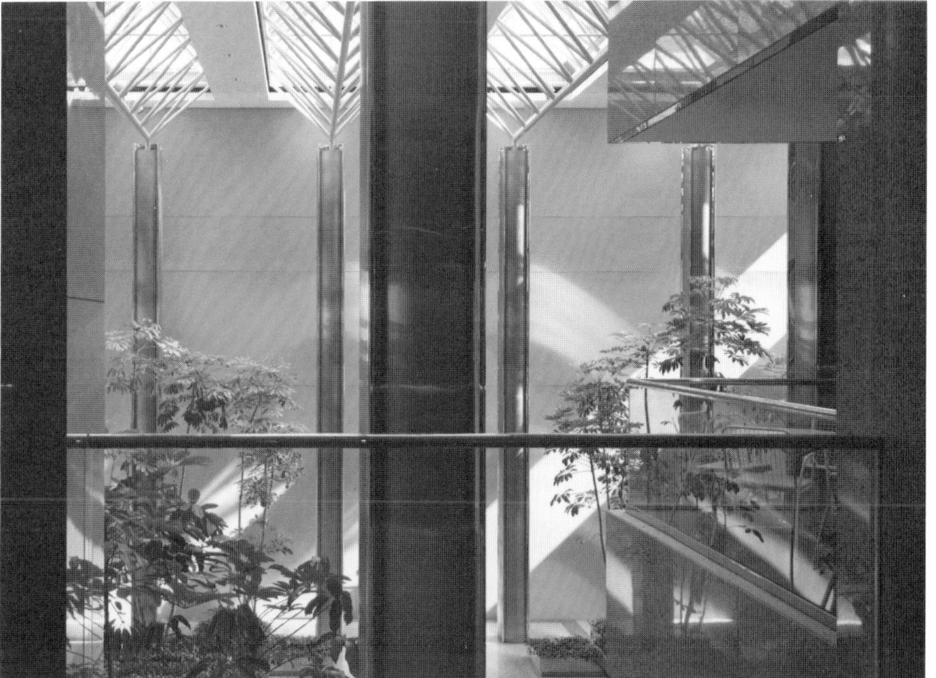

ABOVE: FCL & Associates. McDonald Training Center. Oakbrook, Illinois, 1984 (courtesy of Nick Merrick, Hedrich-Blessing).

LEFT: Skidmore, Owings & Merrill. CityPlace. Hartford, Connecticut, 1984 (courtesy of Nick Merrick, Hedrich-Blessing).

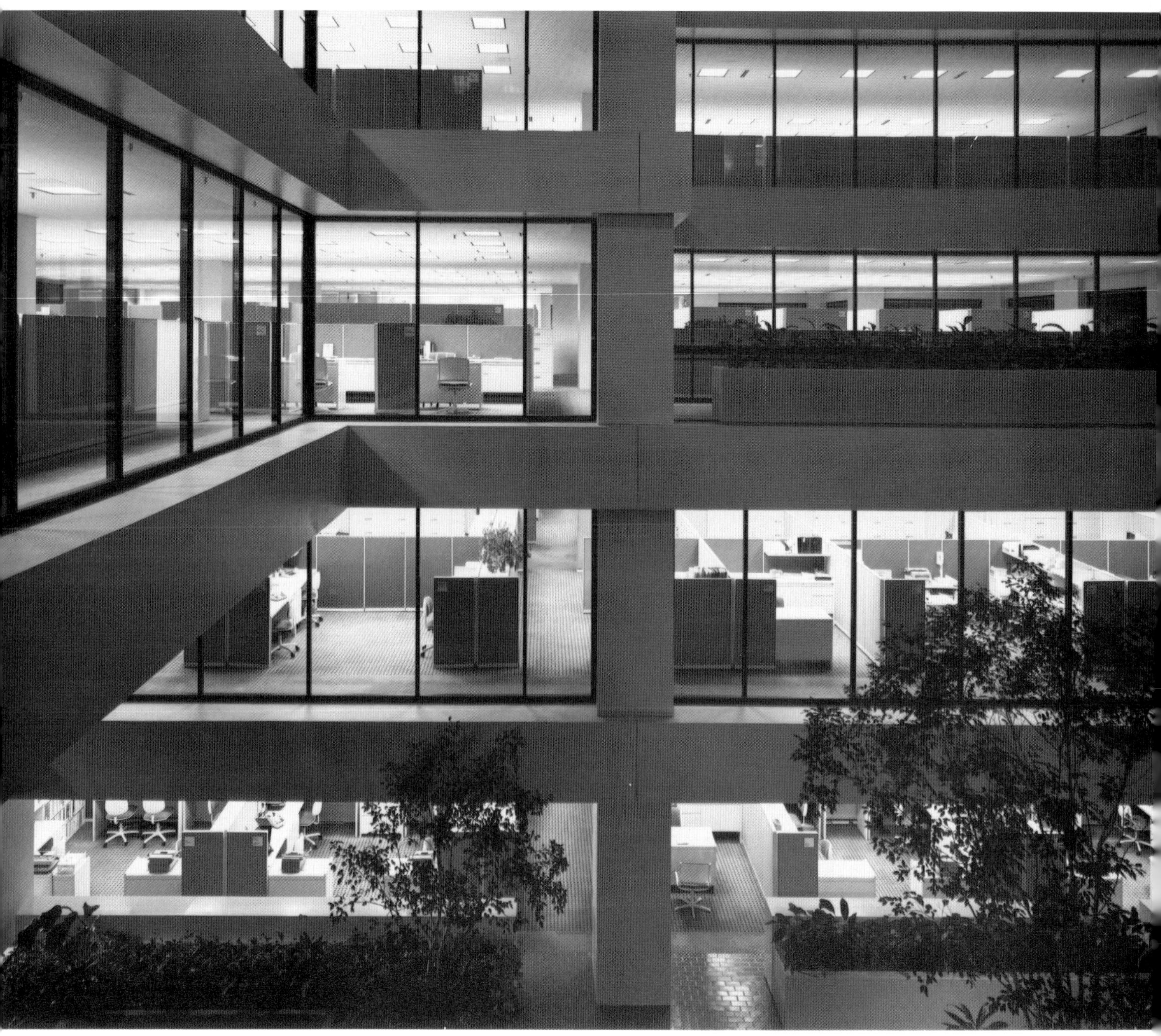

Skidmore, Owings & Merrill. Pan American Life Center, Corporate Headquarters. New Orleans, Louisiana, 1983 (courtesy of Nick Merrick, Hedrich-Blessing).

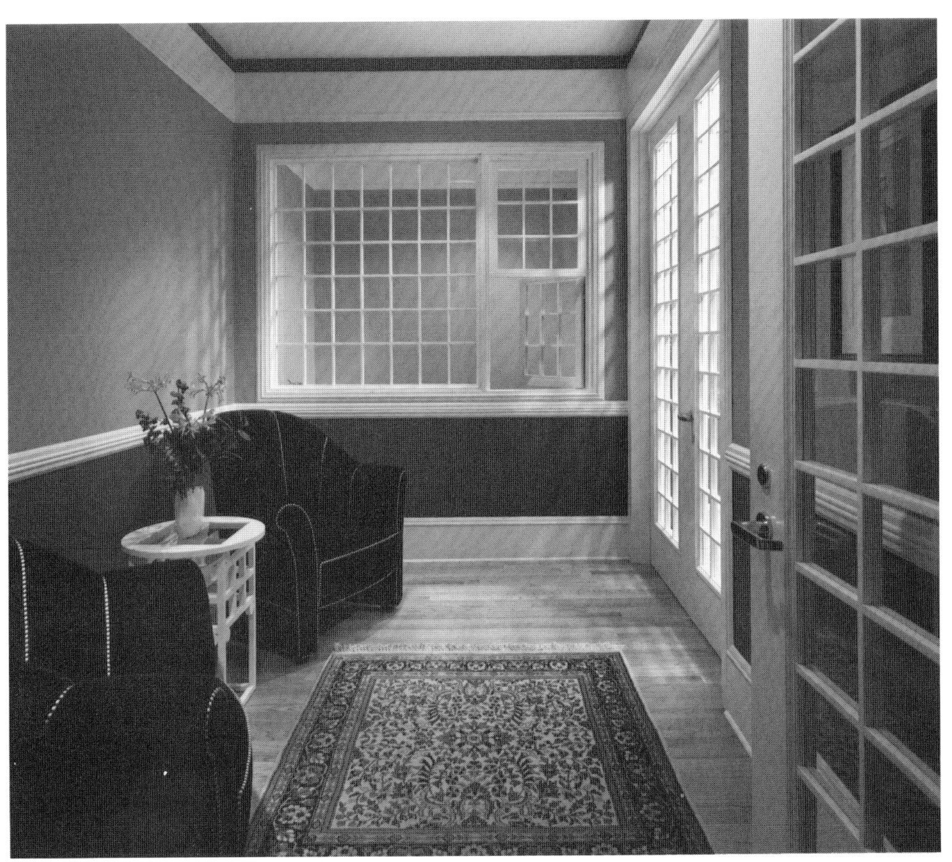

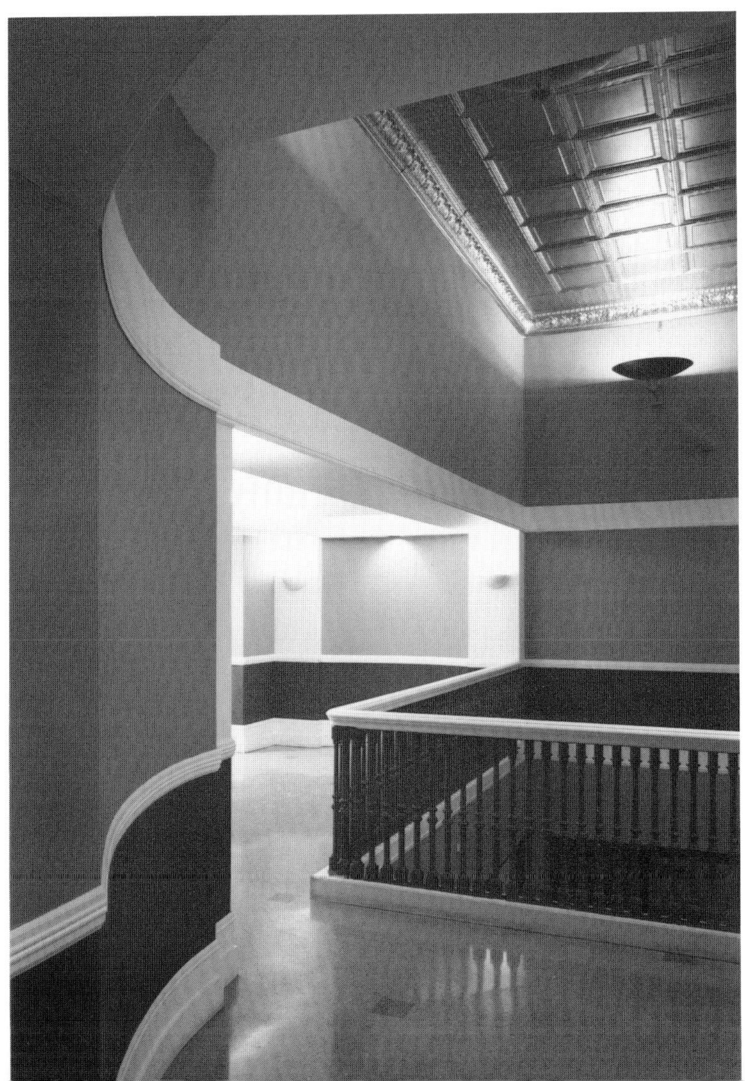

Stuart Cohen & Anders Neriem Architects. 175 Franklin Building. Chicago, Illinois, 1983 (courtesy of Nick Merrick, Hedrich-Blessing).

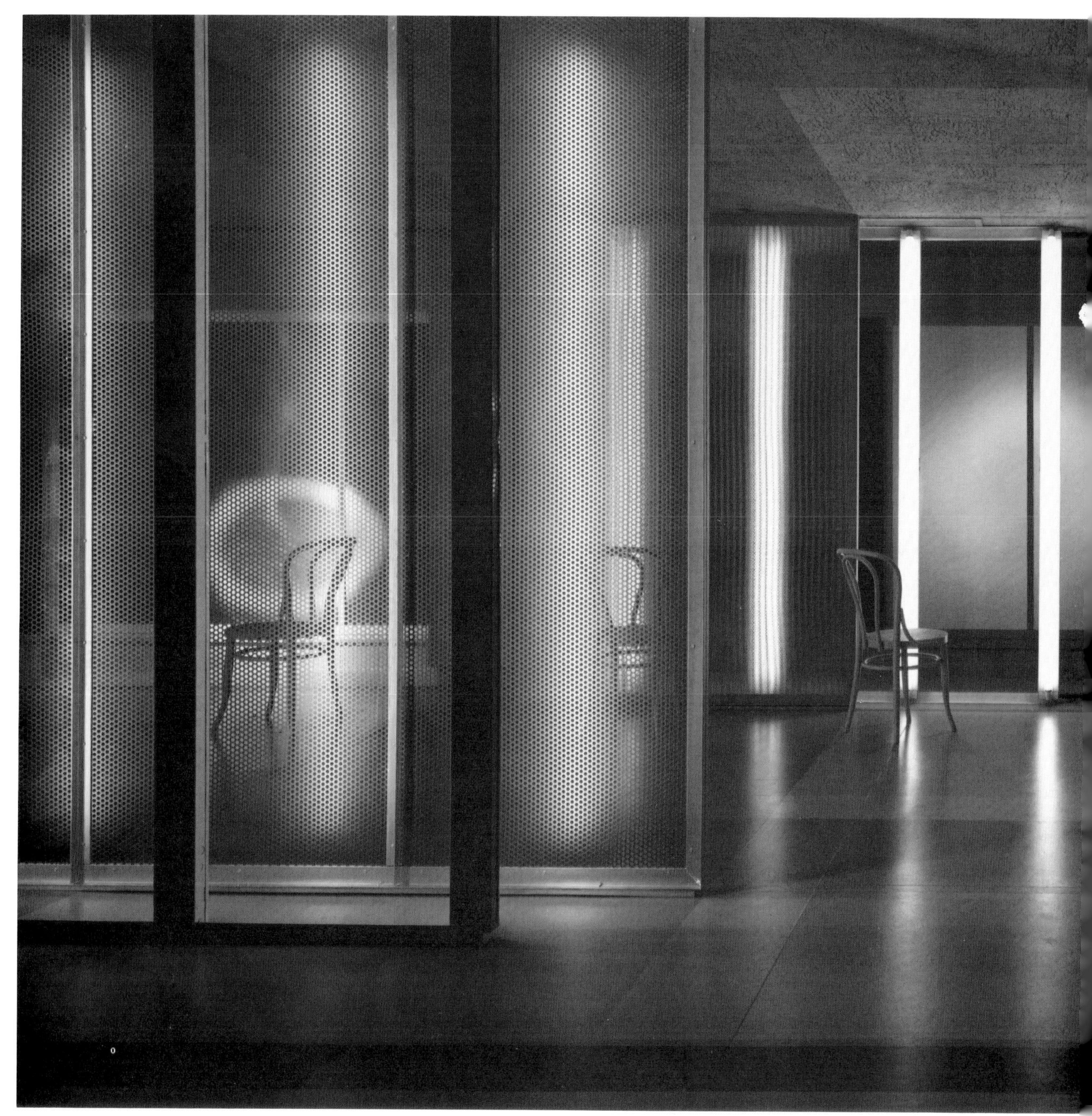

Krueck & Olson.
Thonet Showroom. Chicago, Illinois, 1981
(courtesy of Nick Merrick, Hedrich-Blessing).

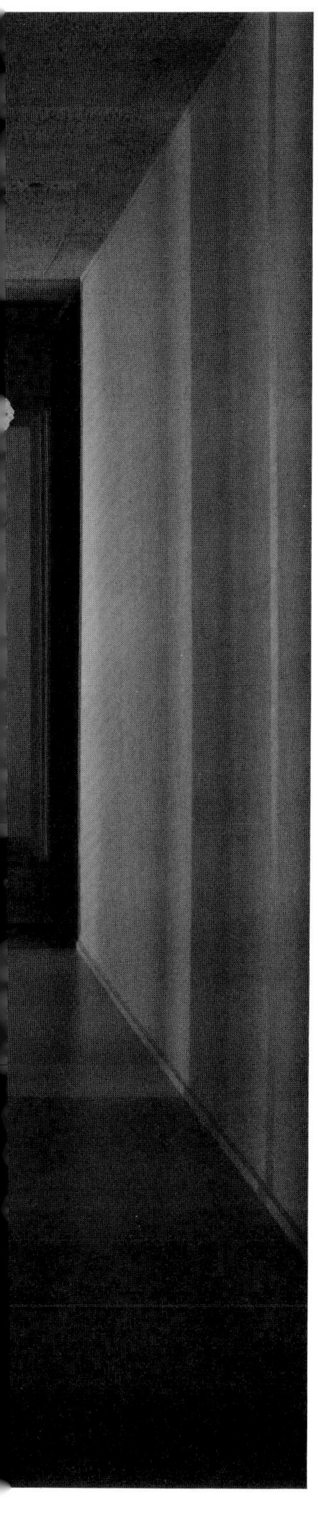

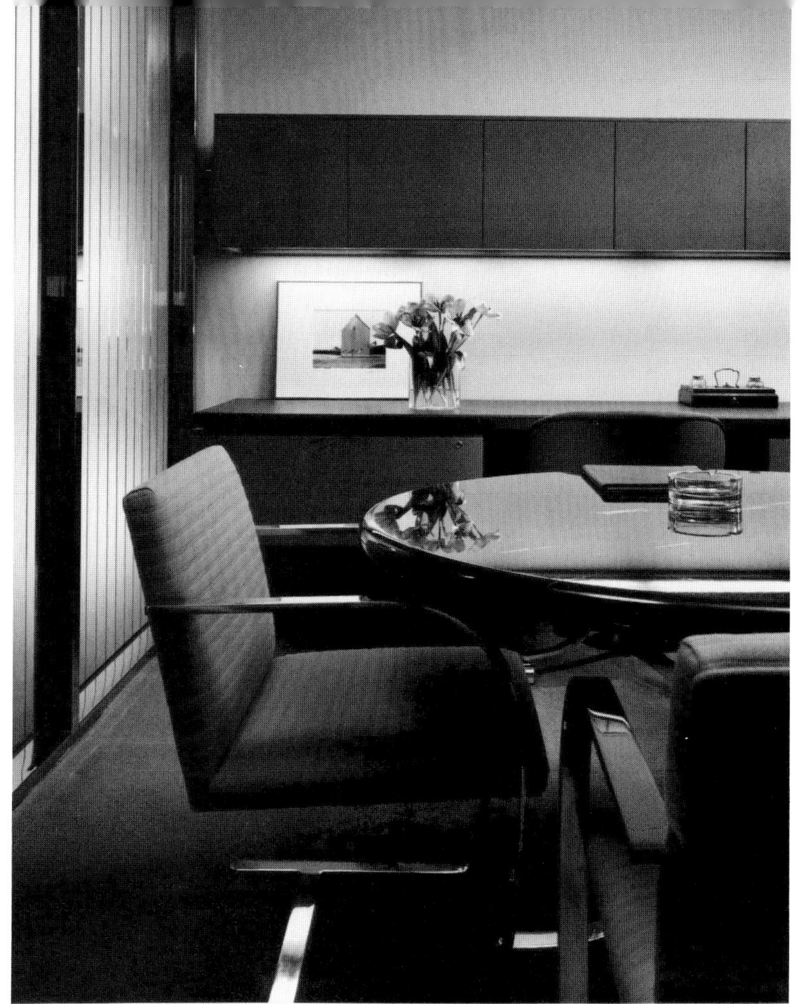

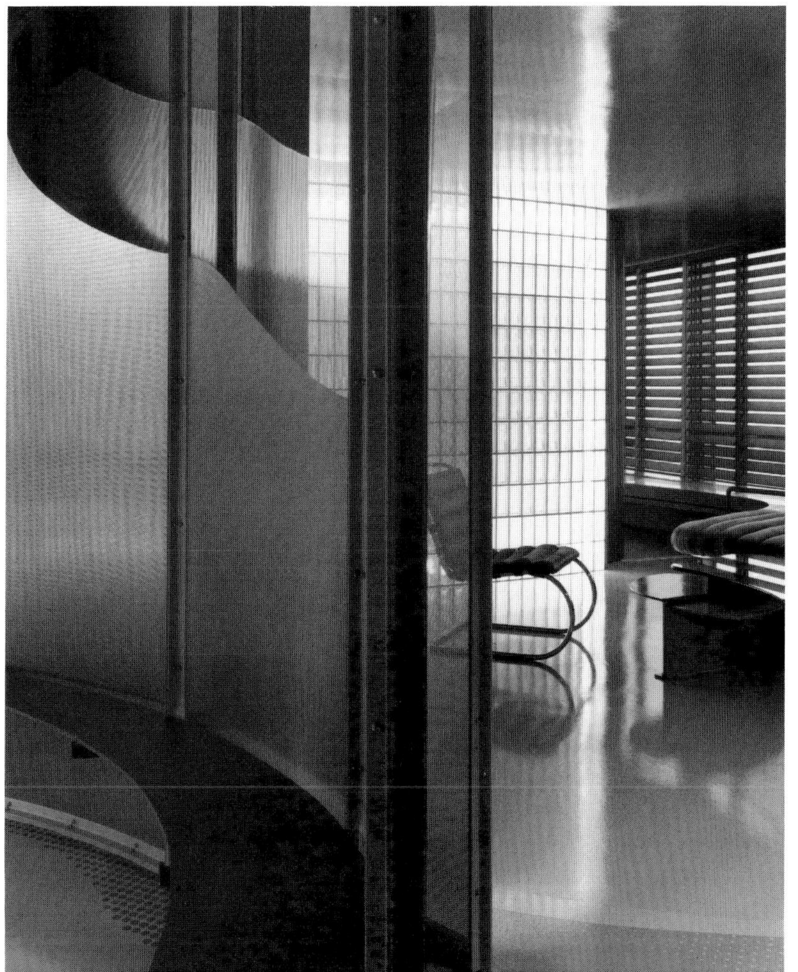

TOP: Skidmore, Owings & Merrill. First Federal Savings & Loan. Little Rock, Arkansas, 1982 (courtesy of Nick Merrick, Hedrich-Blessing).

LEFT: Krueck & Olson. "A Painted Apartment." Chicago, Illinois, 1983 (courtesy of Nick Merrick, Hedrich-Blessing).

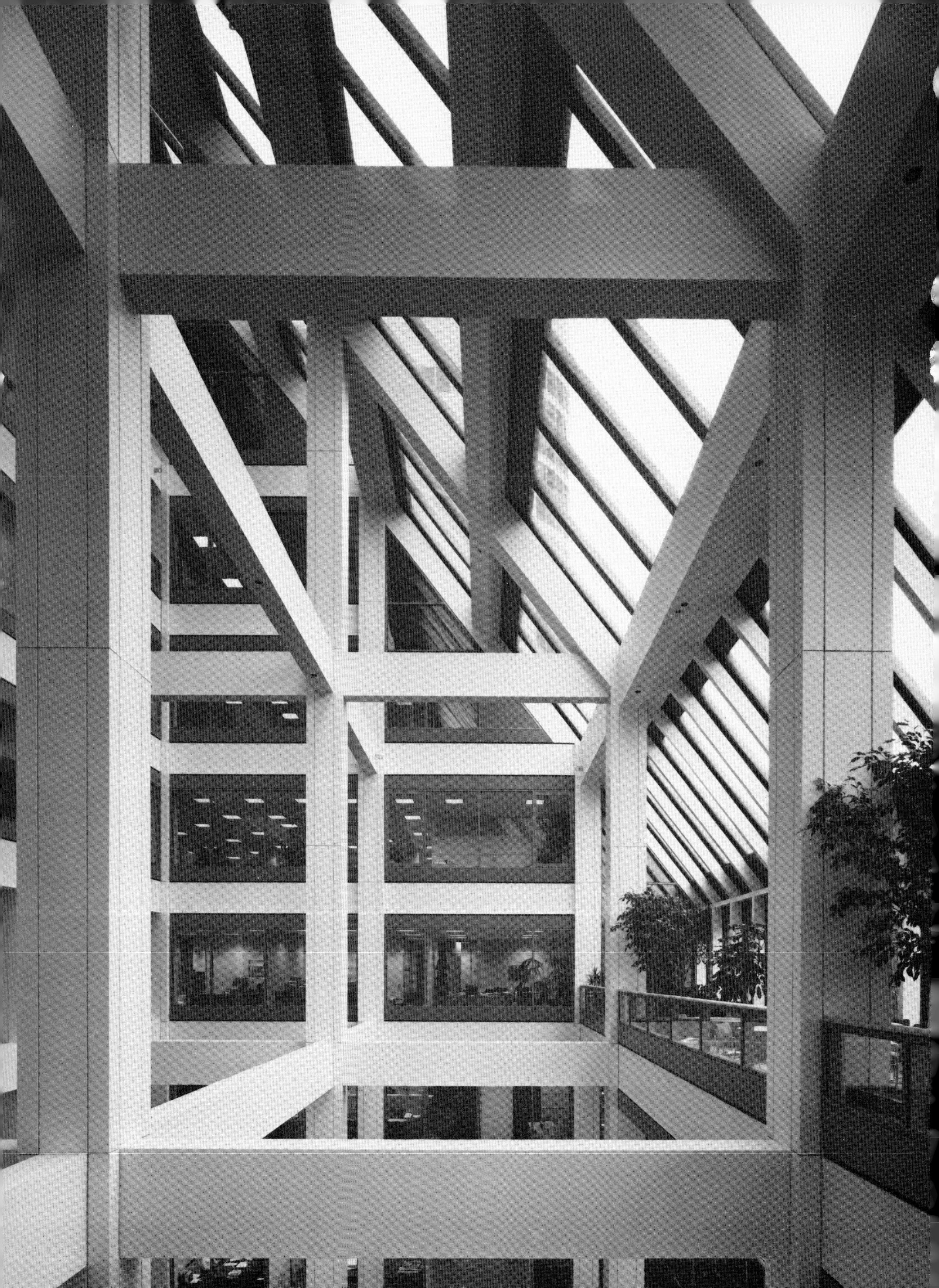

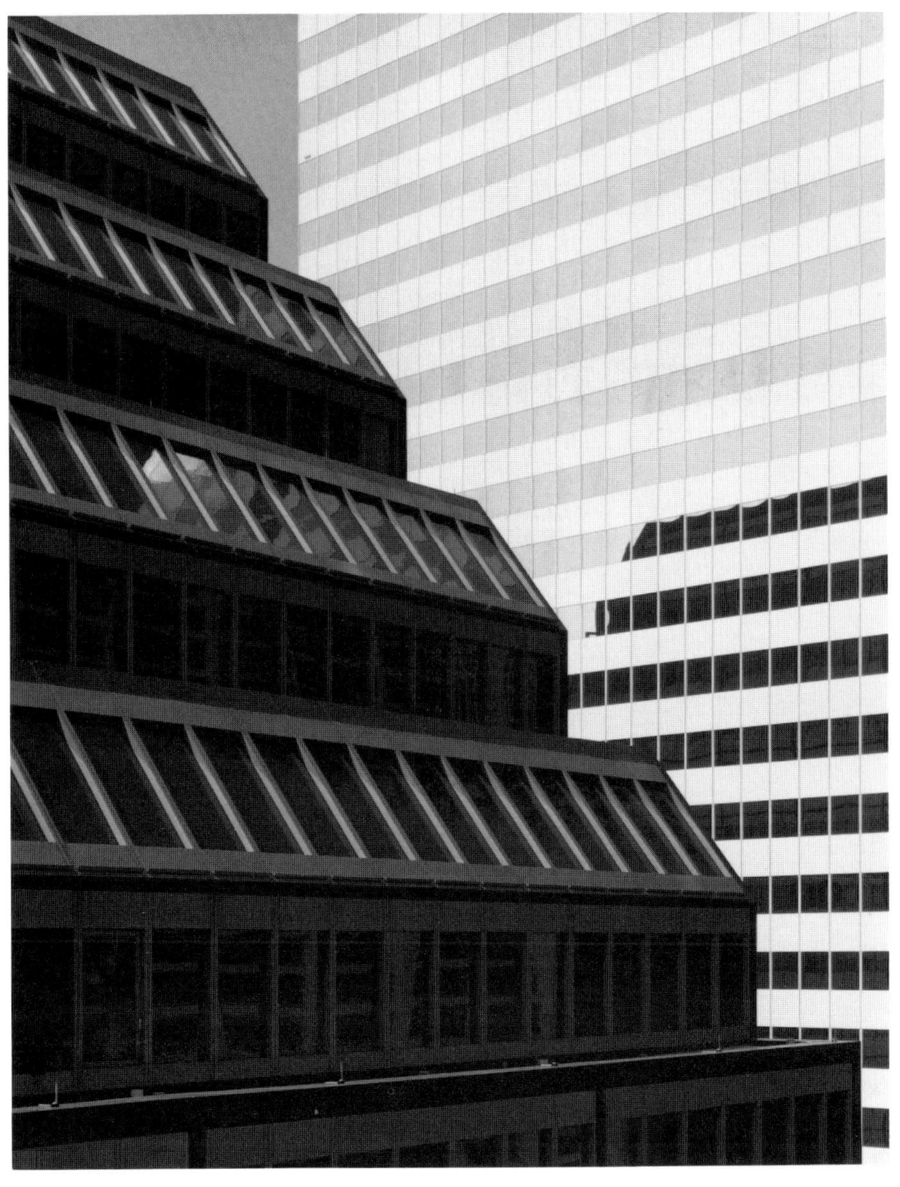

Skidmore, Owings & Merrill.
33 West Monroe Building.
Chicago, Illinois, 1981
(courtesy of Nick Merrick,
Hedrich-Blessing).

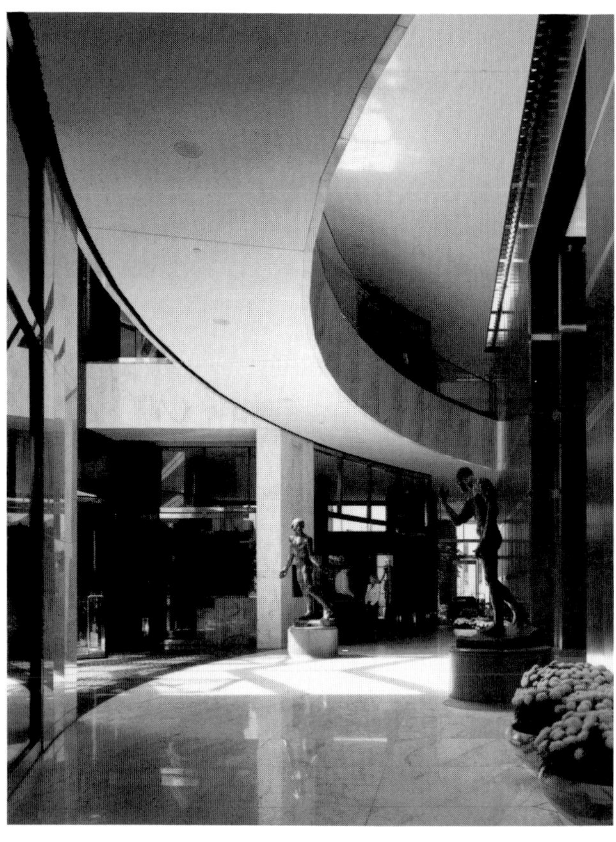

ABOVE: Skidmore, Owings & Merrill. LTV Center. Dallas, Texas, 1985 (courtesy of Nick Merrick, Hedrich-Blessing).

FACING PAGE AND RIGHT: Skidmore, Owings & Merrill. Pillsbury Center. Minneapolis, Minnesota, 1982 (courtesy of Nick Merrick, Hedrich-Blessing).

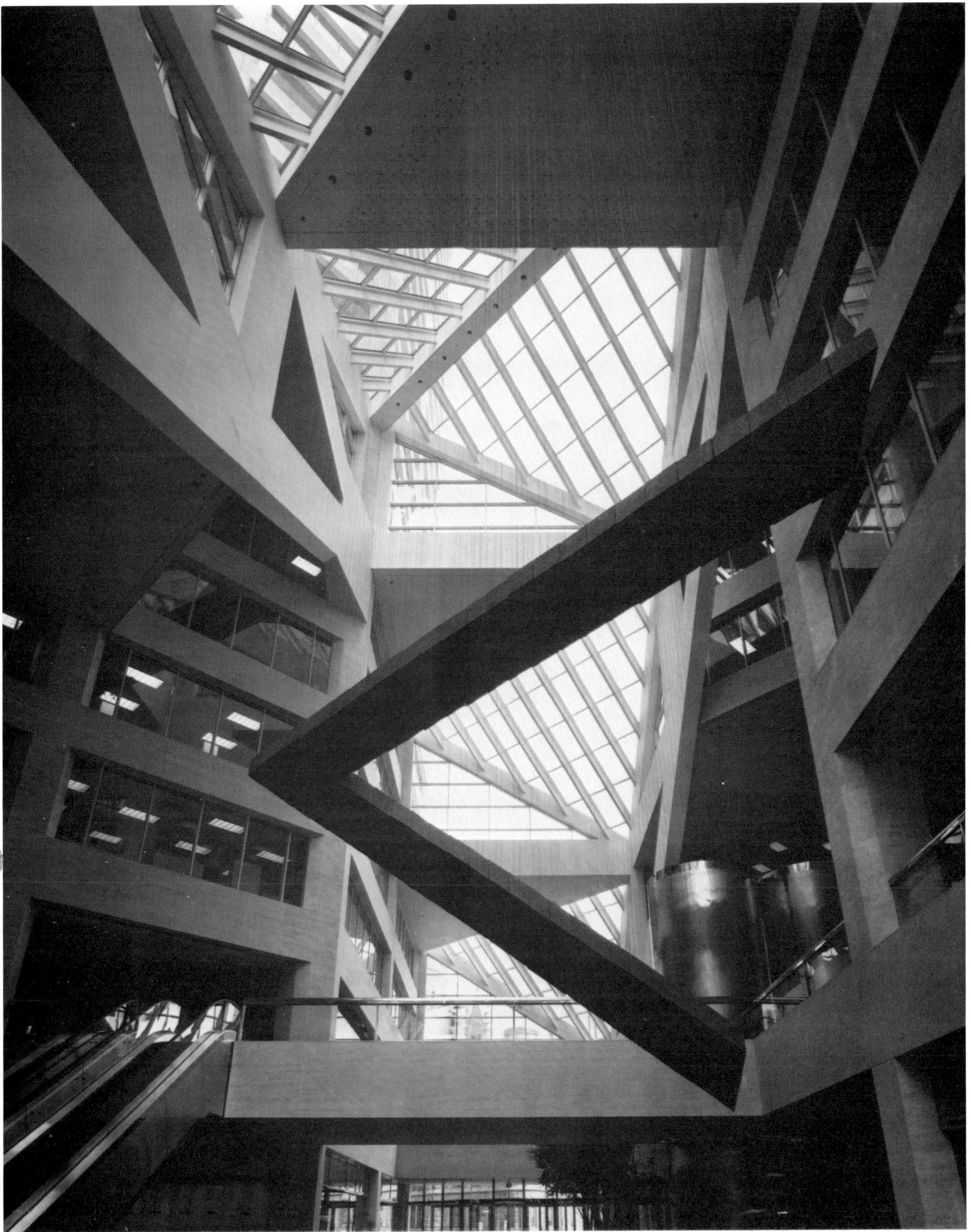

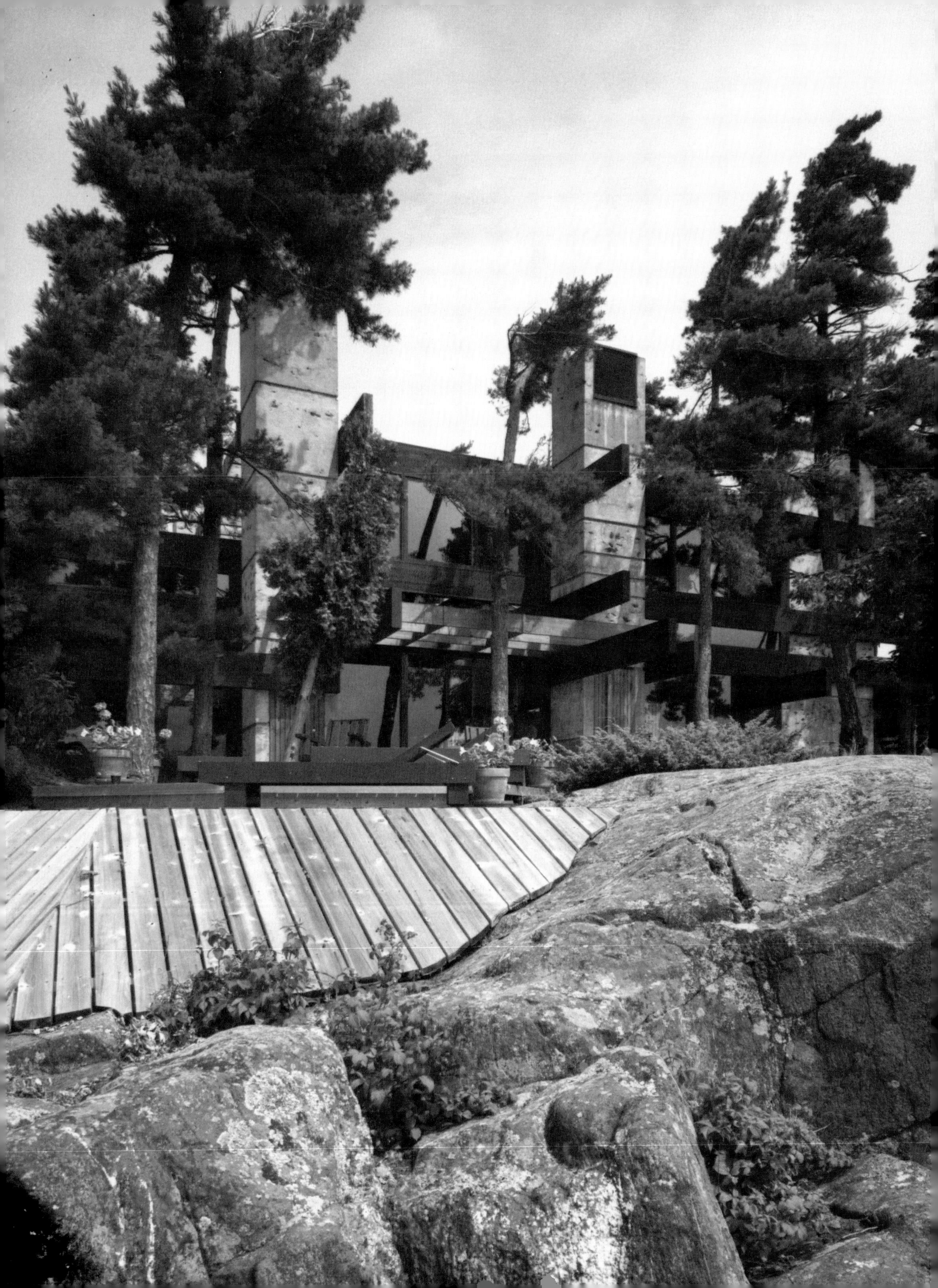

ROBERT PERRON

"The architectural element that interests me most is staircases," says Robert Perron. "Perhaps it's because they're the only structural element in the house really shaped by function. Everything else is just a box, a rectangle you do something in." It is this sense of function that is most clearly conveyed in Perron's photographs. What they give us is a factual account of space, the pertinent data; their purpose is to inform. A window or a skylight in a Perron photograph is not an architectural element alone; rather, it informs the viewer as to how space takes its shape from light.

"I want to feel the space flow around me," says Perron, and his photographs account for this. It is not necessarily, he observes, the account of the architect. Which is to say that in many cases, the composition of a photograph suggested by the architect is one derived from working drawings. Ironically, Perron notes, because the architect's perception of a building often evolves from working drawings, his vision can remain two-dimensional. And this is one of the more perplexing ambiguities confronting the photographer: although his medium is two-dimensional, he is often more inclined than the architect to perceive the building in three dimensions. Because the photographer is setting out to translate spatial perceptions to a flat sheet of paper, he must first fully decipher the three dimensions.

Perron began his now twenty-year career as a graphic design student at the Yale School of Art and Architecture. "But I was solving all the graphics problems photographically," he recalls. "Graphic design was the only way to get to photography in those days." And because the urban renewal programs sweeping through so many American cities in the sixties transformed New Haven's landscape to a comprehensive catalog of contemporary architectural styles, these buildings became a natural subject for Perron.

Perron's background in graphic arts is not inappropriate to trends in contemporary architectural photography. There is an appeal, he points out, for photography that favors graphic detail, for compositions that appear to be almost two-dimensional in their attention to surface texture. But while these photographs may be long on rich, expressive surfaces, they are short on spatial information. "You can get the essence of the finish in these detail shots," he says, "but you don't get the real essence of the space." The two-dimensional photograph, often of an

FACING PAGE: C. Blakeway Miller. Private Residence. Lake Huron, Ontario, 1974.

architectural detail, while increasingly prevalent, says little of spatial progression. "You can have a good time taking shots that don't give any information, and the graphic detail may make for a strong cover shot," he says, "but I've spent twenty years trying to convey information, and a single shot of a gable doesn't tell you much about the architecture."

Like many of his colleagues, Perron works best, initially at least, unaccompanied on the site. While he sometimes uses assistants for technical help, he prefers to determine for himself the terms of the architecture. But unlike many of his colleagues, he prefers to approach the architecture knowing little or nothing about it, finding that preconceptions may diminish the value of first impressions. While many architectural photographers may try to visit the space before photographing it, or learn about it by studying architectural renderings and floor plans, and by discussing it with the architect and its eventual users, Perron relies more heavily on his own first impressions. "Everybody wants to show you their own picture, and that can deflate your own impressions. It can take the edge off things."

Perron depends on direct, immediate contact, a half hour on the site to get his visual bearings. For the remainder of the shoot, he works as a technician, transferring these initial impressions to the photograph. Which is not to say that the photograph is a quick shot. "I can get three to six really good shots in a day," he explains, dispelling any notions that recording these first impressions is as rapid a process as having them in the first place.

To transcribe his impressions visually, Perron usually uses a 35mm Canon, a hand camera that "comes as close to my own eyes as I have found." It is a camera, that is to say, that can frame and record almost as spontaneously as the eye sees, and the camera most able to record the instantaneous observation. For more studied photographs, Perron uses a four-by-five view camera, what he refers to as the "big gun," and one he finds more suited to quiet interior or exterior portraits, spaces that might best be presented as still life compositions. Perron has found, though, that these large-format photographs are more likely to be cropped before their publication, while a 35mm photograph is more apt to retain its original composition. Rarely does he use both cameras on a single shoot, finding it awkward—both physically and visually—to alternate between two pieces of equipment.

Perron also uses the hand camera if the photographs are to include people. While these informal shots may round out a layout, they are rarely the most eloquent or informative architectural photographs. Nevertheless, they can evoke a kinetic, fluid quality that may be intrinsic to the feel of the architecture. A series of photographs of urban playgrounds, for example, would have been incomplete without the documentation of children using the space and its structures.

Yet using people in architectural photographs simply to elicit the human element is less easily justified. Perron recalls a brief period when popular editorial trend dictated that the architectural photograph be inhabited. "We had to start editing people; we had to consider what people looked like as well as what the space looked like." He adds, with only slight remorse, that he lacks the spirit of humanism that such photography begs.

The architecture itself should imply a human presence and a sense of scale, he observes, without relying upon the human figure. Unfortunately, this has not always been the case. "There are instances, especially in some recent monumental architecture," he points out, "where you can take the photograph, and insert on to it cutouts of people in four different sizes; and they all look as though they belonged there, simply because there is nothing in the architecture to suggest scale." Perron has found, nevertheless, that buildings designed by younger architects tend to be more attentive to scale, having to them a more anatomical feeling. Not suprisingly, this is the architecture he is most drawn to.

Another of Perron's practices somewhat atypical of the profession is story initiation. Rather than simply respond to assignments, he frequently generates his own story ideas to the architecture and design press. Perhaps because he sees much of his work as "salvage work," in which the photographer is asked to rescue undistinguished architecture from editorial oblivion, when he finds provocative design that has not yet been documented, Perron often photographs it for his own files and story queries. Underground housing, solar design, and swimming pools are all areas of design that have benefited from his inquiry and documentation.

Perron has noted significant changes in his now twenty-year career, not the least of which is the origin of the photographer's commission. In the past, the design press commissioned a photographer with due regard for his specific skills. But contemporary magazines are more likely to use photographs supplied to them by the architect, who has become far more astute in the business of marketing his goods. The contemporary architect, that is, is likely to hire the photographer himself and will have some degree of influence on the shots that are taken, which are subsequently forwarded to the magazine. "So," Perron concludes, "you end up with material that is presented really less objectively. You're seeing, in fact, what the architect sees." While the benefit to this is that the photograph may reflect the intent of the architect more purely, the disadvantage, clearly, is that the photographer's own observations remain outside the frame. Whether the architect is consistently the most reliable judge of his own work is the recurring question in the profession.

Perron also points out the fact that contemporary magazines are more prone to "style" the photography they publish, to shape the material to conform to an editorial format. While early architectural photography tended to be a matter of more straightforward documentation, it must often now consider the style and approach of the publication in which it is eventually to appear. Hence it has become the practice of many photographers to "overshoot" a job so as to ensure the use of the photographs in more than a single publication.

But if contemporary architectural photography is indeed influenced more by both architect and press, this is not to say that the role of the photographer is necessarily diminished. These are constraints rather than actual limitations, and their effect varies. While the astute photographer may acknowledge the architect's vision or the editor's format, in the end he alone produces the image that brings to life in two dimensions what is three-dimensional.

Perron's work demonstrates how it is done; his photographs give us an account of the space he and his camera inhabit. More particularly, his photographs reveal spatial progressions. Yet for all their nuts-and-bolts utilitarianism, the photographs are often quite expressive. For all their form and structure, they easily lean toward the abstract. The architectural elements that have been so rigorously transcribed become linear, geometric motifs. And for all their observance of the facts of the architecture, they are only a short step from being more painterly, expressive compositions. That there is a tension between the attentive record of the spatial and structural facts of a building and more abstract images is what makes them such compelling visual documents.

FACING PAGE: Boston Government Center Plaza. Boston, Massachusetts, 1974.

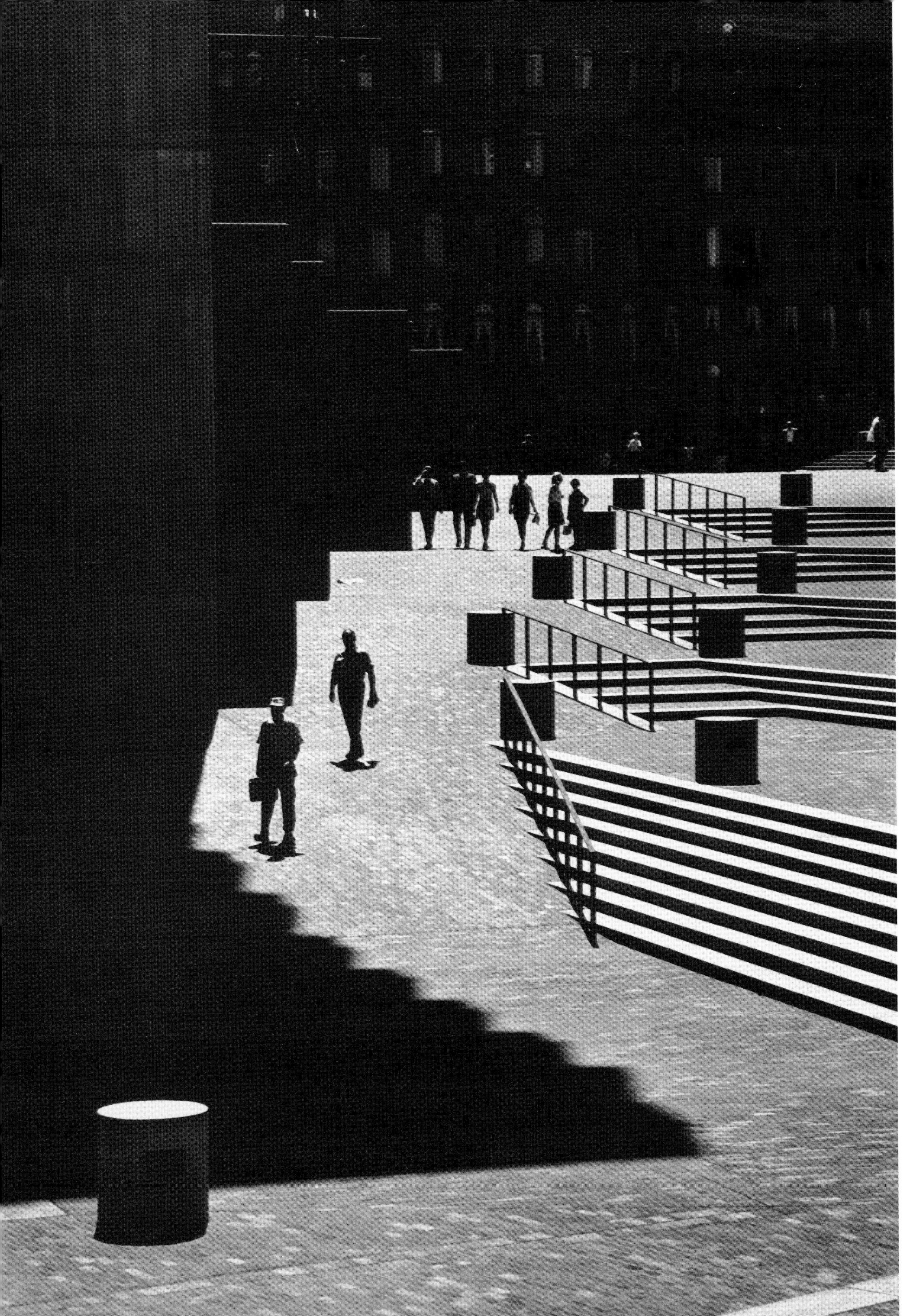

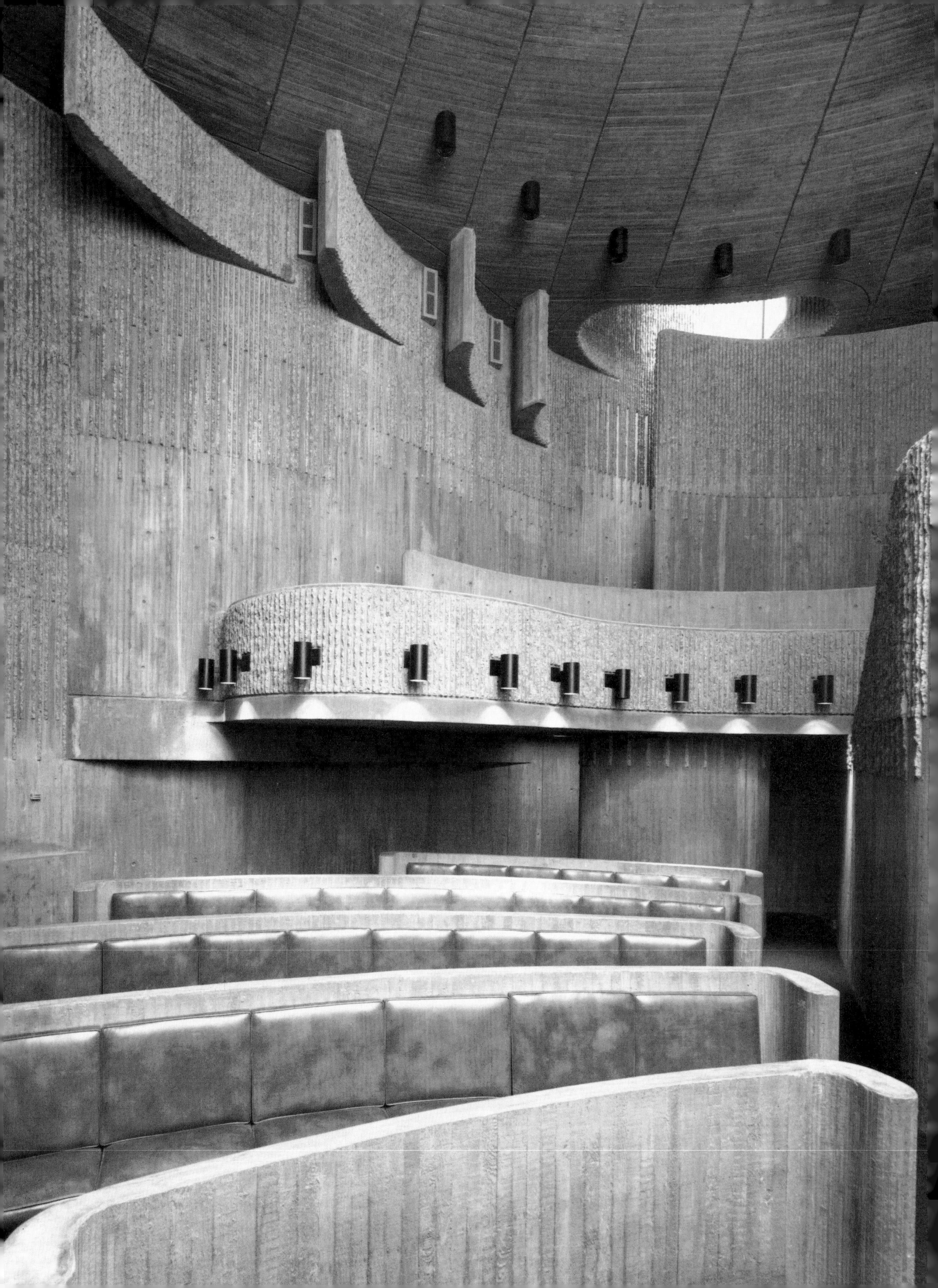

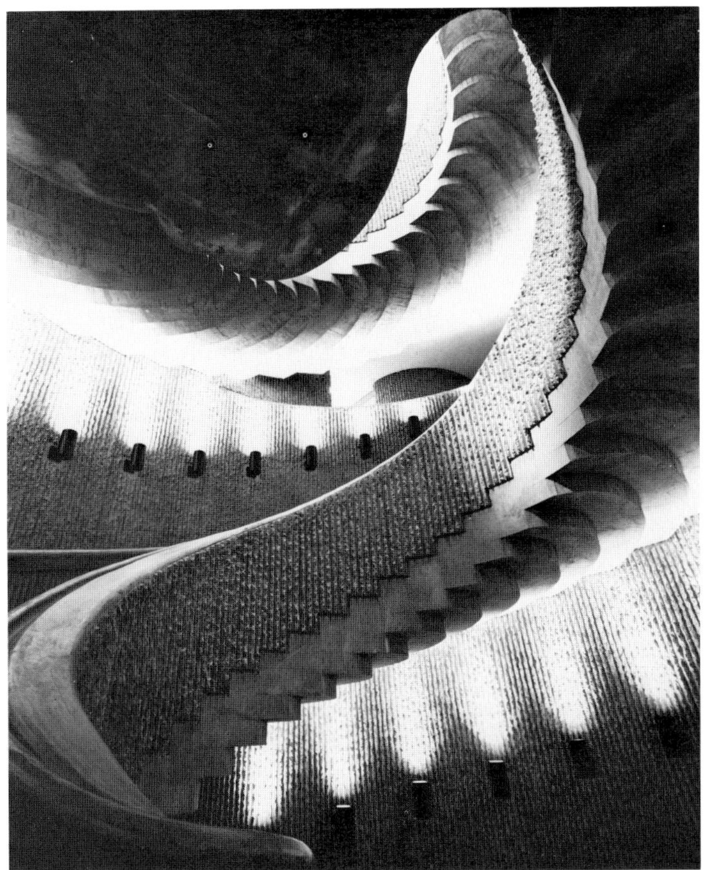

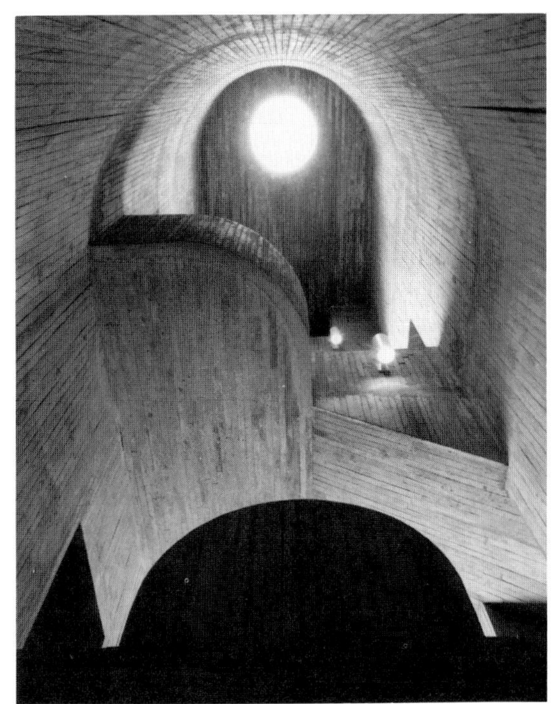

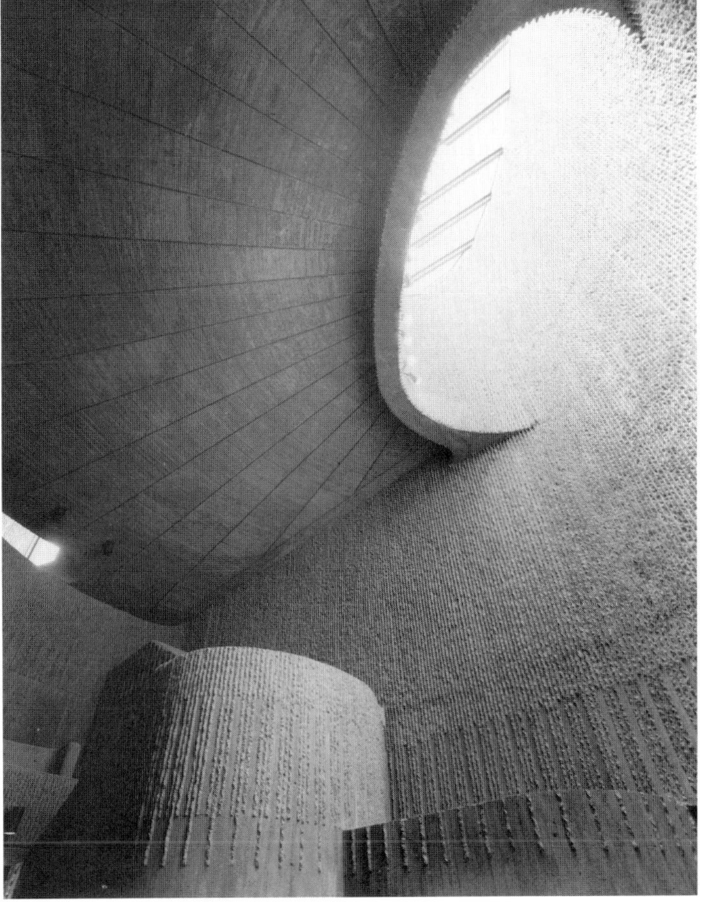

ABOVE: Paul Rudolph. Endo Pharmaceutical Center. Garden City, New York, 1964.

LEFT: Paul Rudolph, coordinating architect. Chapel, Boston Government Center. Boston, Massachusetts, 1973.

FACING PAGE AND TOP (LEFT): Paul Rudolph, architectural design; Desmond & Lord, architects. Massachusetts Mental Health Headquarters, Boston Government Center. Boston, Massachusetts, 1973.

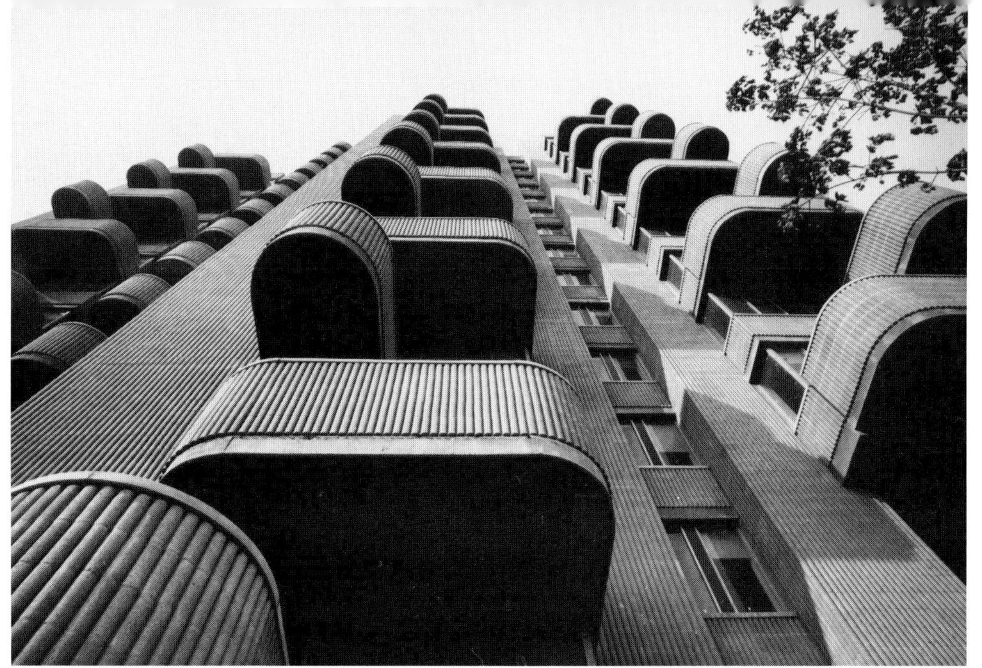

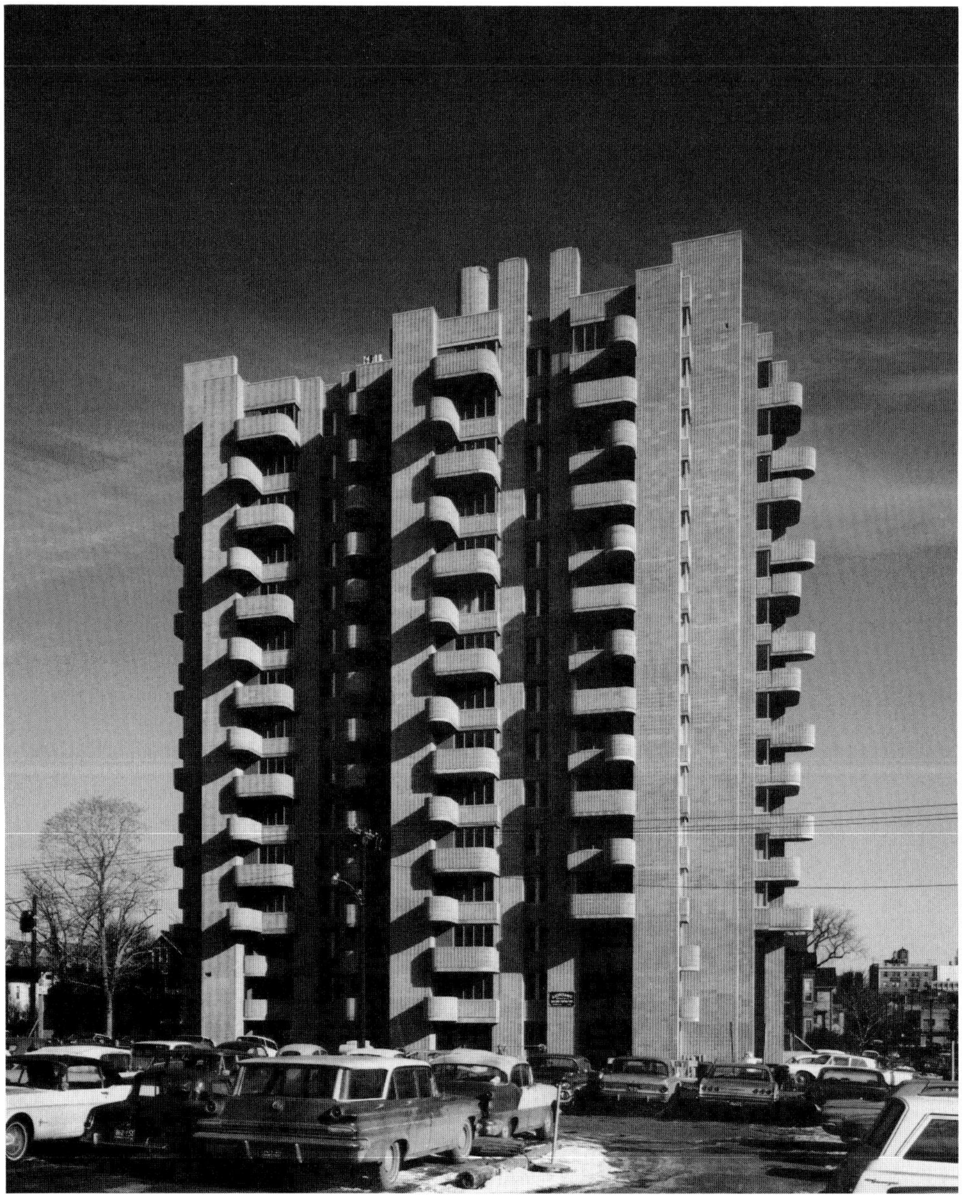

Paul Rudolph. Crawford Manor Public Housing. New Haven, Connecticut, 1966.

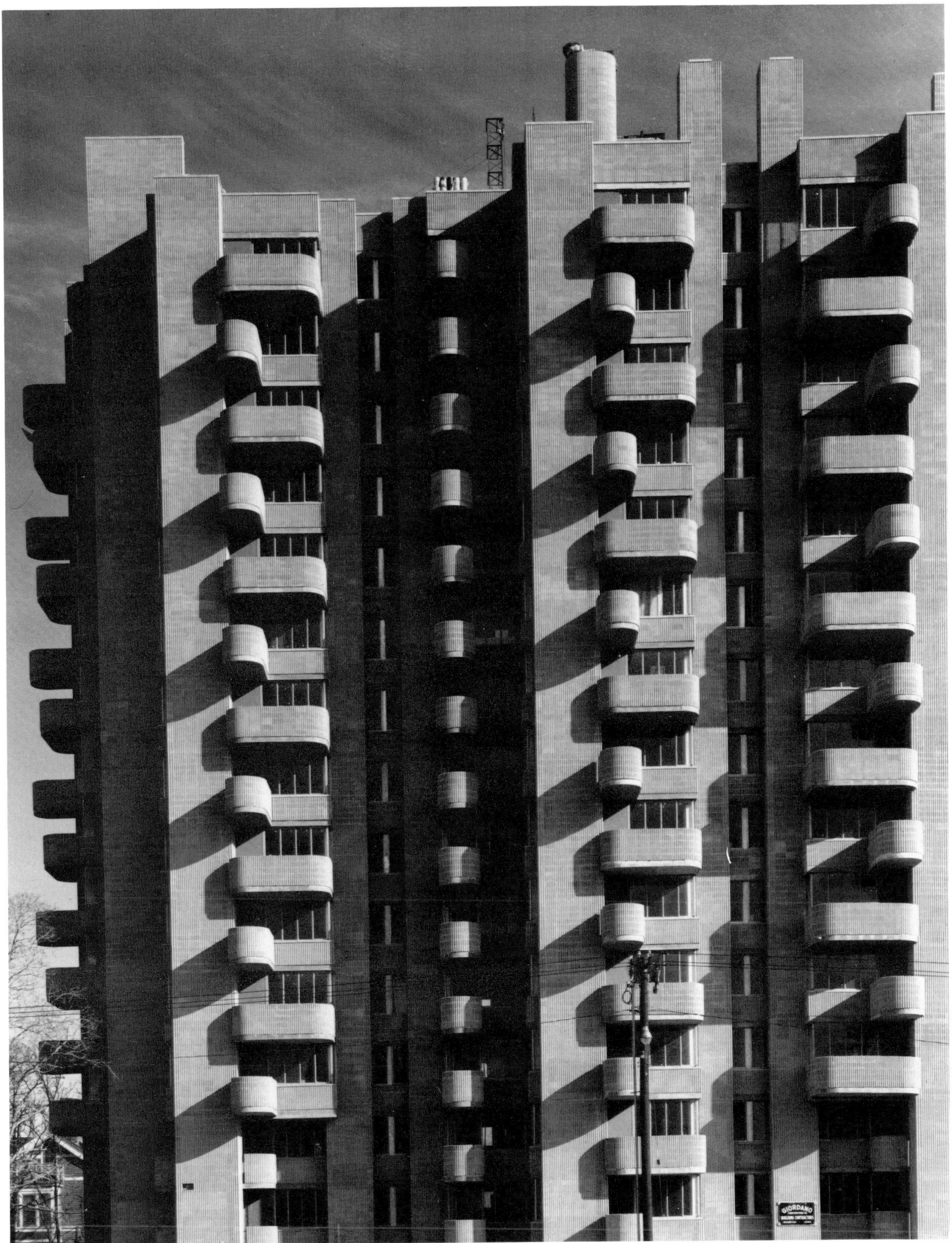
GIORDANO

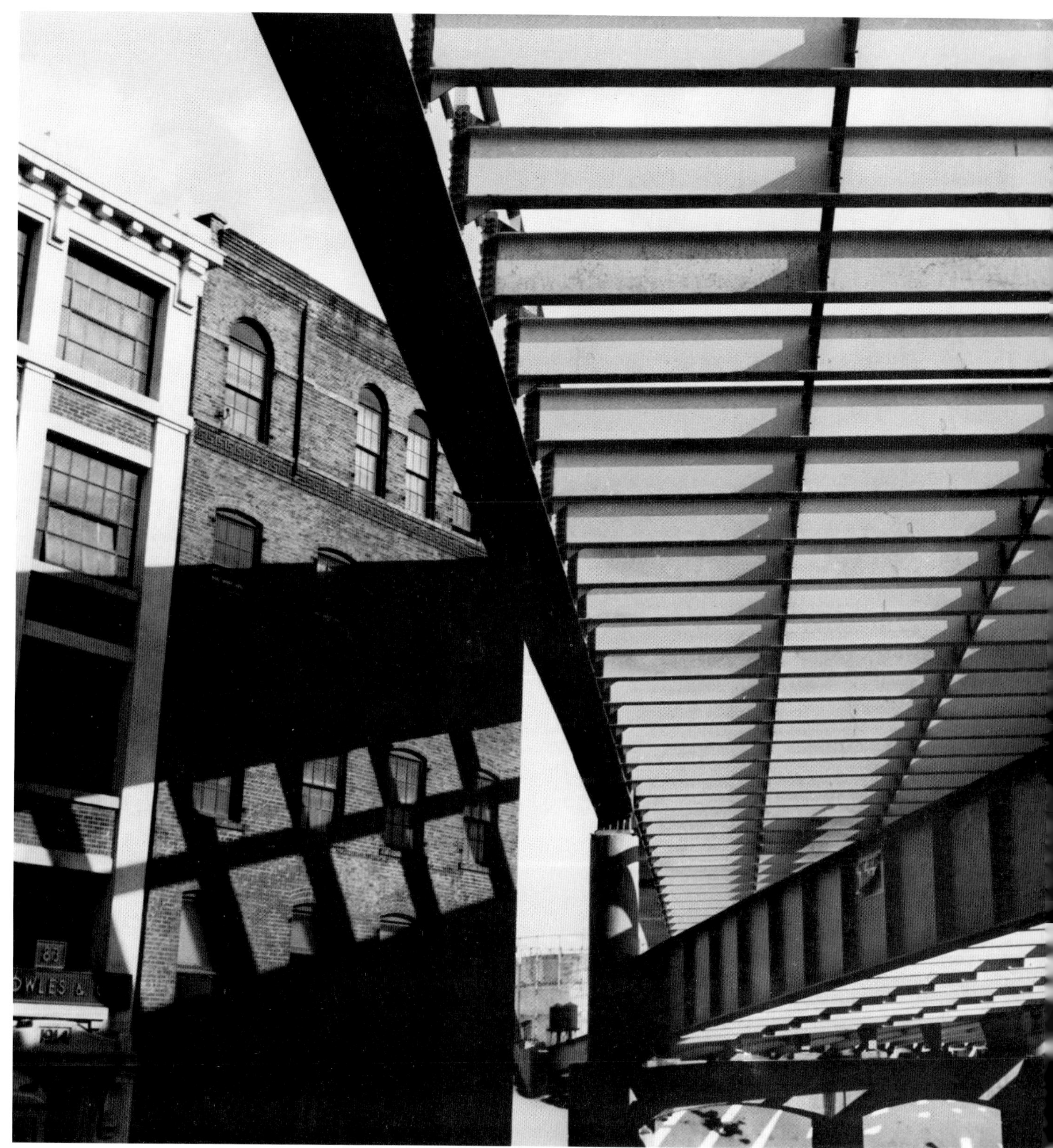

Interstate 95 Interchange
during construction.
New Haven, Connecticut,
1968.

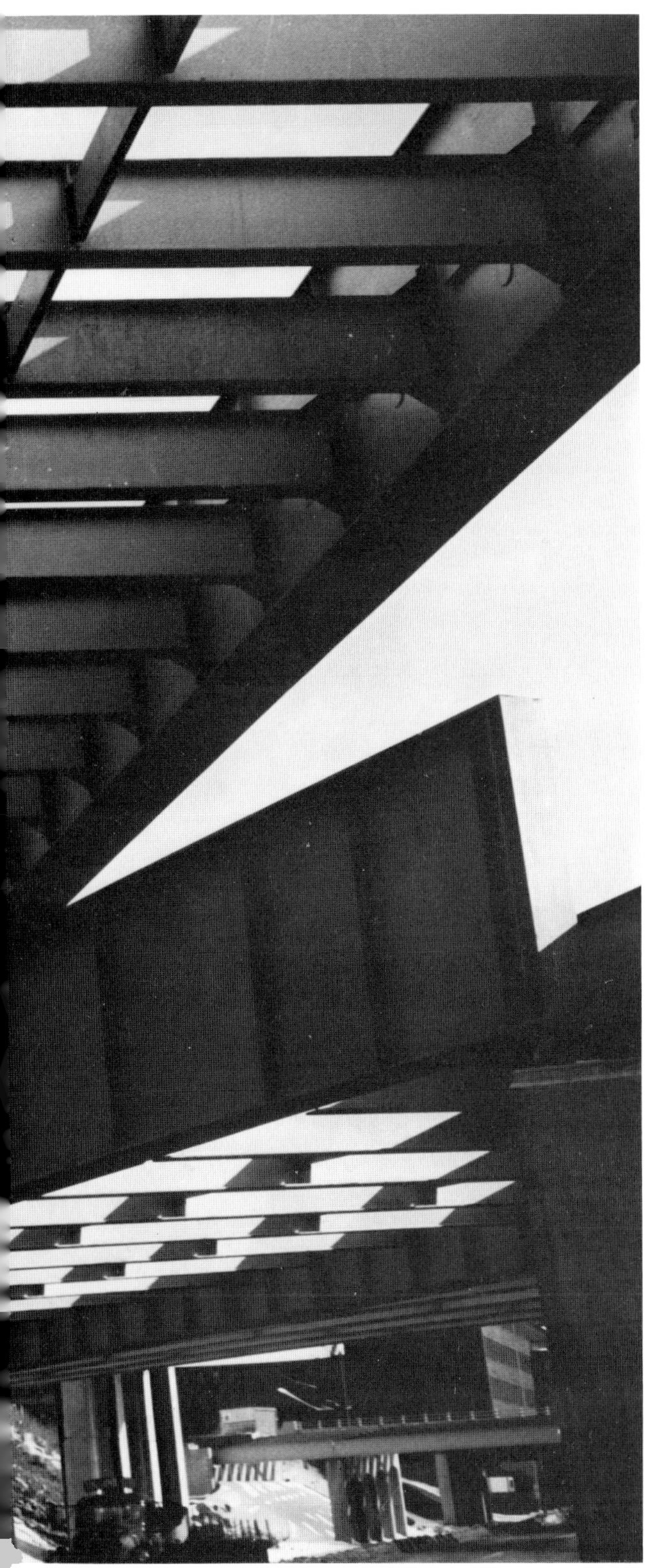

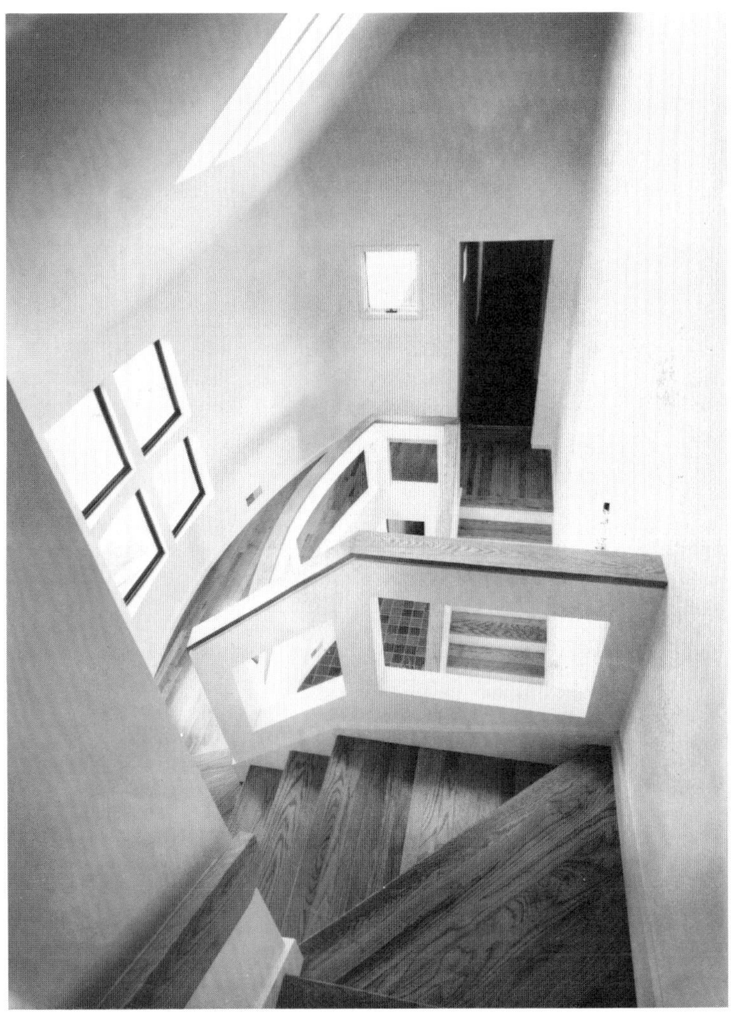

Peter Woerner.
Private Residence.
Guilford, Connecticut,
1984.

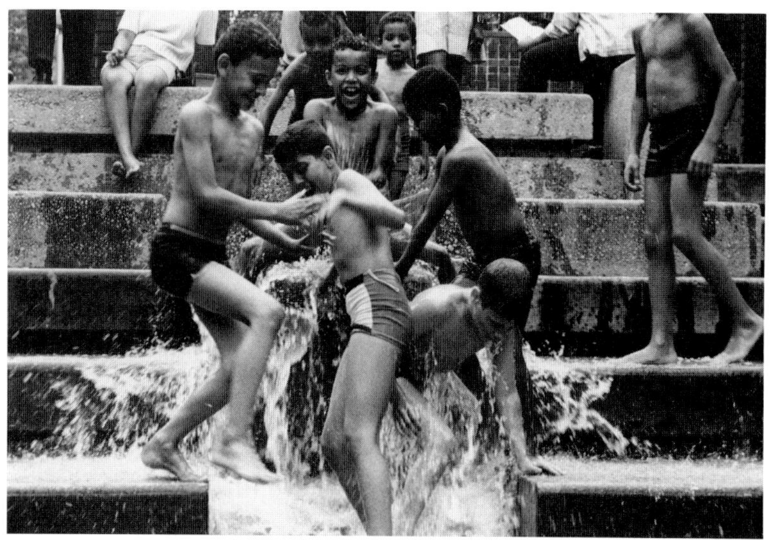

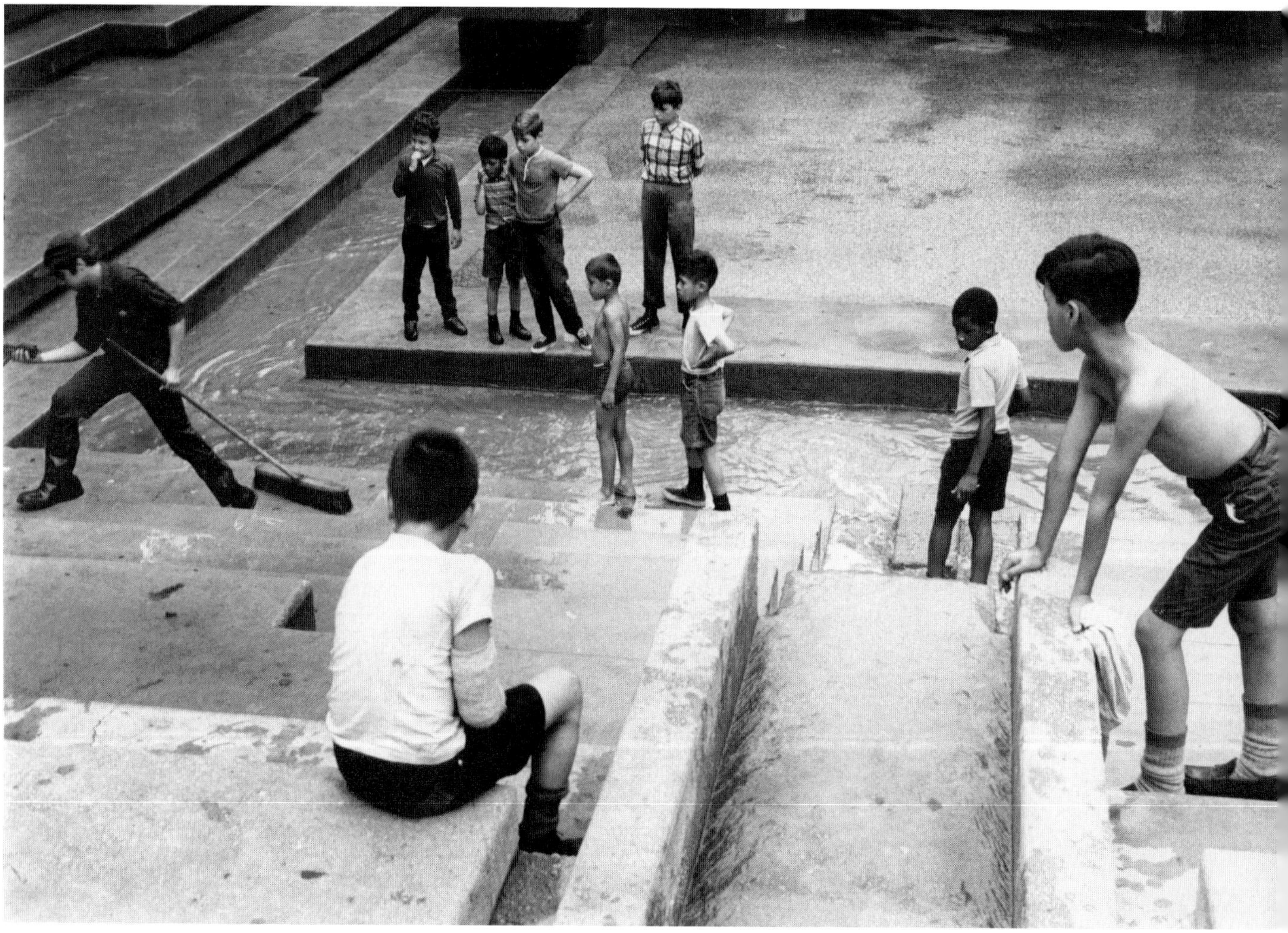

M. Paul Friedberg & Partners. Jacob Riis Playground. New York, New York, 1964.

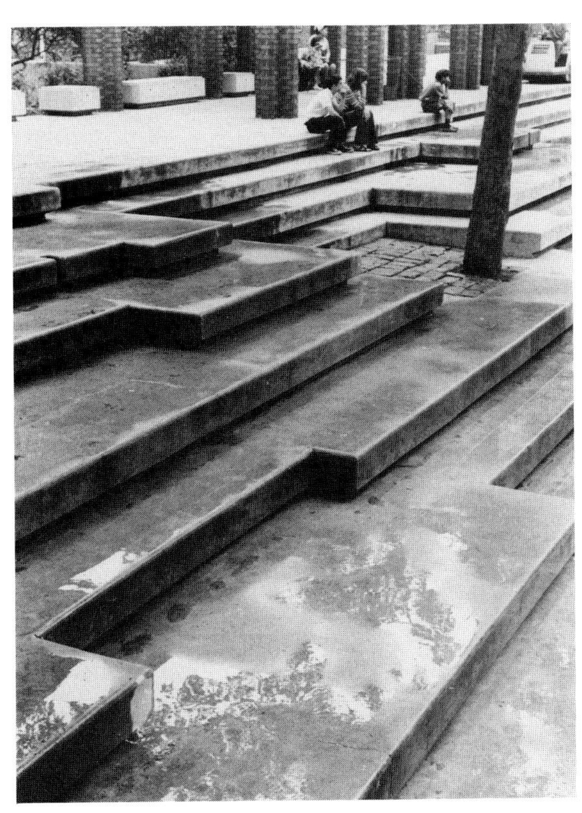

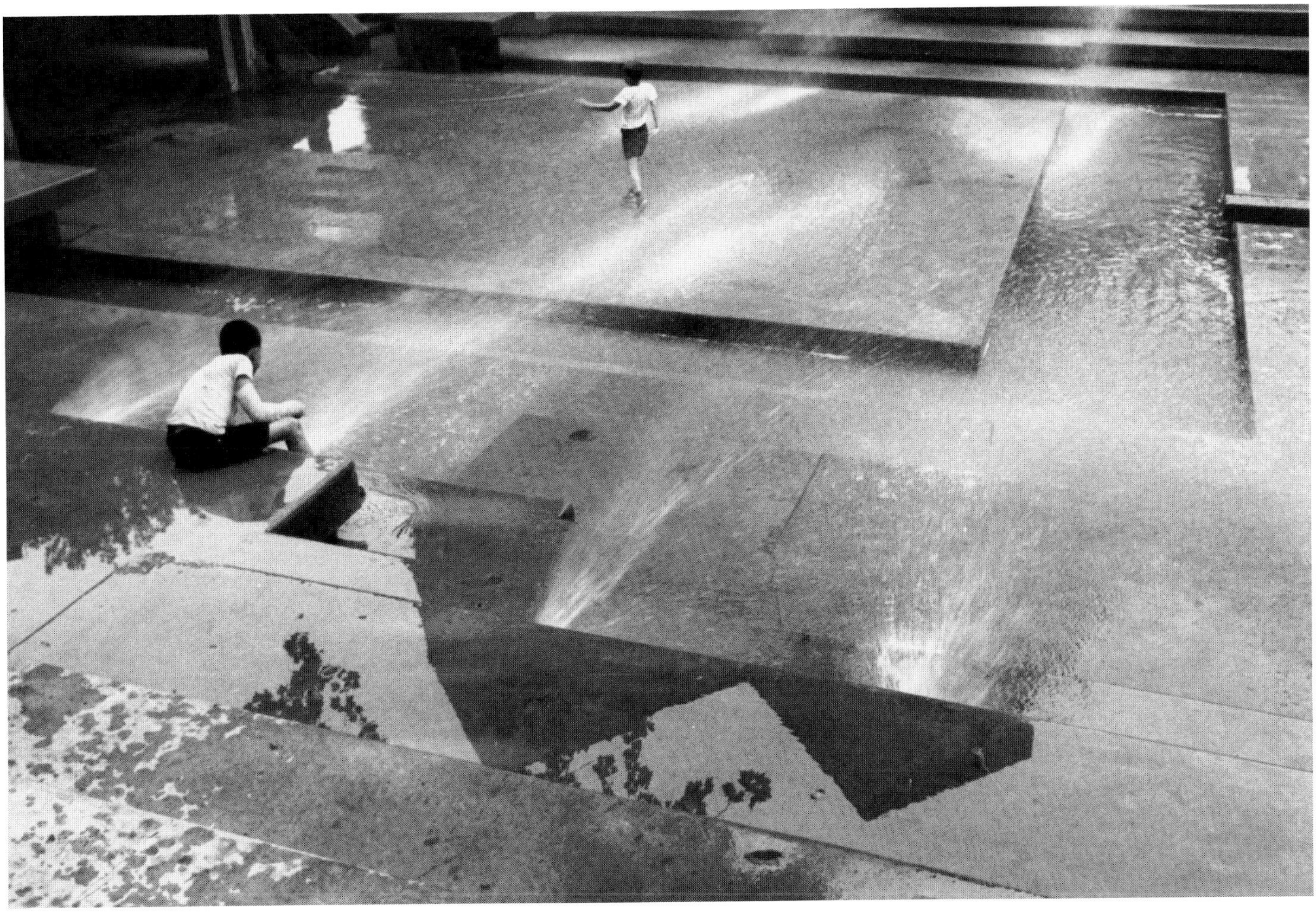

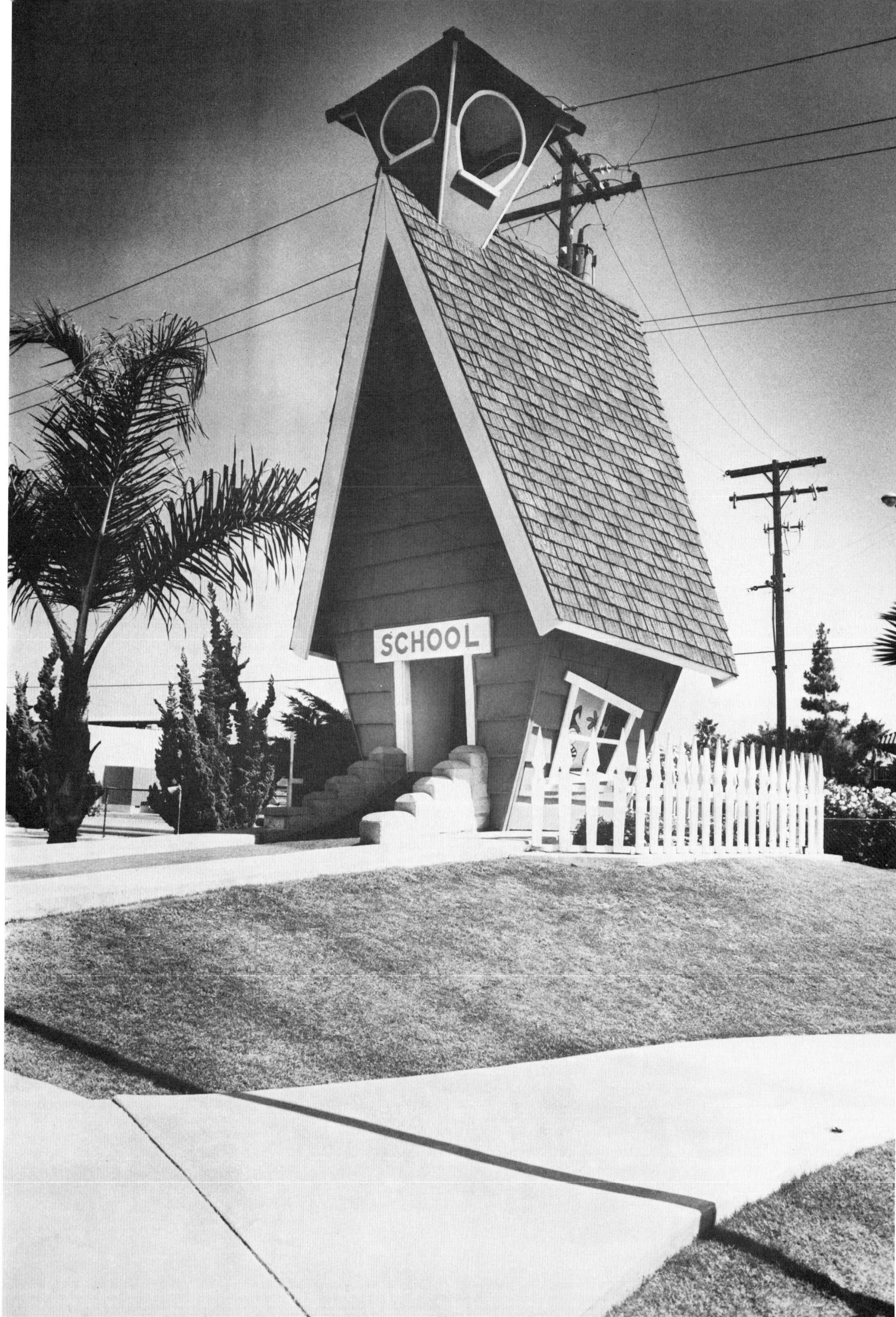
SCHOOL

TIM STREET-PORTER

In many cases, when a photographer has been commissioned to photograph a building, that building stands at a moment in time when its ownership is slightly obscure. In the beginning, of course, the building is possessed by the architect. It is an idea and an image, and he is its sole proprietor. And to varying degrees, he remains that as he guides it through its innumerable stages of design and construction. But in one sense, then, when the building is complete and occupied, its ownership must be relinquished to its tenants—its users as well as the greater public that will continually be exposed to it through its lifetime. As the architect's experience and association with the building may diminish, that of its users and public grow. And it is usually sometime during this period of the building's transition that the photographer arrives at the site.

Often, then, he is faced with the choice of representing the architect's vision of the building and a broader, more inclusive perception of it. He is also faced with the fact that architects, like artists working in any other medium, are not necessarily the most accurate or reliable judges of their own work. Nevertheless, if the photograph ignores or dismisses the esthetic and intellectual credos on which the architect has based his work, it will surely tend to be a looser, more private interpretation than a document clarifying the design of the building. Tim Street-Porter's photographs tend to acknowledge a graceful balance of these two visions; his photographs speak both for the architect and for the building.

Street-Porter describes his approach as photojournalistic: "You're not trying to produce slavishly flattering portraits or glorify the building. Rather, you're trying to let the photograph communicate for the building. I regard my role as that of a journalist, and what the photograph shows about the building is not always its most flattering aspects." His photographs work to articulate whatever intellectual statements or remarks the architect has made. But they acknowledge as well that buildings are used; that they weather and have an everyday quality. "My allegiance," he states, "is to the spirit of reportage."

But as well as having a photojournalistic grit to them, Tim Street-Porter's photographs can often be distinguished by their abstract, graphic composition. While they may yield information about the architecture, they are also often strong geometric compositions in themselves. That they have the capacity to be reportorial and expressive simultaneously is what gives them much of their power.

FACING PAGE: School House, Miniature Golf Course. Los Angeles, California, 1978 (courtesy of Tim Street-Porter).

The realism that distinguishes Street-Porter's work is indeed a departure from the technical perfection found in the photographs of many of his colleagues. He prefers to work in two-and-a-quarter format, rather than the customary four-by-five, finding that the flexibility of the smaller camera enables it to record a more accurate or realistic image. His photographs exploit the accessibility of the smaller format and are more likely to include people in motion, a speeding vehicle, abrupt washes of light and shadow. The truths they evoke are ephemeral; their images convey the sudden and startling gestures of climate and geography that the four-by-five view camera, for all its careful deliberation, cannot. The images recorded by the four-by-five view camera, he finds, can sometimes have "a cold quality—too technically perfect."

The two-and-a-quarter format also dictates an entirely different approach to shooting than the four-by-five. The latter quite often dictates that the photographer spend long hours composing behind the camera. It will also nurture a stamina and patience that come with waiting for ideal lighting conditions and will yield a select few frames that have been arranged and attended to as still lifes. Shooting with a two-and-a-quarter camera, on the other hand, is done more quickly. More rolls are shot with the higher chance of achieving graphically strong images. "An editor can choose," says Street- Porter, "from thirty transparencies of one viewpoint and hope that one would have a girl in a red coat striding across the space in just the right position. Moments like this give a spontaneity and life to a static composition."

It is a spontaneity and graphic style in photography whose master is perhaps Henri Cartier-Bresson. "Composition must be one of our most constant preoccupations," he wrote, "but at the moment of shooting it can stem only from our intuition, for we are out to capture the fugitive moment, and all the interrelationships involved are on the move." [1] It is this fugitive moment that Street-Porter is also after. It is what Cartier-Bresson referred to as well as "the decisive moment," the instant, that is, in which the static elements and the motion within the frame arrange themselves with the greatest intensity and meaning. "Composition," he said, "must have its own inevitability about it." [2]

And it is this same inevitability that Street-Porter's photographs search out; his photographs reveal a similar spontaneity and graphic sensibility. "Cartier-Bresson was a master of light architectural composition, an integral element of which might be a 'blurred cyclist,' " he points out, and his own photographs put a similar value on the kinetics of human movement. "Architecture is intended for people, which means that people should be seen in the building, whatever the formal qualities."

But it is how they are seen in Street-Porter's photographs that is important. His photographs record them in natural activities—sitting, standing, walking—in stances that have not been posed "to resemble waxworks tableaus that consequently reduce the architecture to a stage set." That the human figure is a help rather than hindrance to composition is his departure point. "The exception is where the formal qualities of a building need to predominate, or an architectural mood needs respecting without distraction."

That the pristine architectural image is not his predominant interest is not surprising. Trained in architecture, he is conversant both in its theory and its more material laws, but his subsequent decision to photograph architecture rather than to practice it rests on "preoccupations that were photographic, in two dimensions." An ensuing period of work in fashion photography is reflected in his natural incorporation of people in architectural documentation. Yet his work in fashion photography is reflected elsewhere as well, in an approach that is generally active, animated, mobile. Fashion photography, he points out, demands constant creativity. There are more variables and the photographer is asked for new graphic concepts almost on a daily basis. If fashion is an industry where shock value, the new and the unexpected, is a prized commodity, the photography of fashion must reflect these values. Architecture, relatively speaking, is less preoccupied with novelty. "You have an eye which people recognize as being yours, a visual approach that is recognized as yours, but you don't have to come up with a new concept each time you shoot."

What is nevertheless conspicuous about Tim Street-Porter's visual approach is that it *is* often a record of the unexpected. It is hardly surprising that he finds the work of architect Frank Gehry among the most rewarding to photograph. Gehry's structures celebrate surprise. Rather than investigate the technical challenges explored by much modern architecture, they pursue more intellectual challenges, questioning our preconceived notions of texture and material, space and form. "It's both a radical and a naive way of looking at building," says Street-Porter. And working it out photographically presents obvious problems. That is to say, architectural photographers, out of necessity, often cultivate understatement. Rather than highlight the whole, which will not necessarily fit in the frame, they suggest the whole with a part. Form is implicit rather than explicit. In the architecture of the unexpected, however, the part cannot stand for the whole. Its point is that the part does not represent the whole; if there is a message, it is that form cannot be anticipated. It questions and plays with our expectations and informs us that what we assume is not, after all, to occur.

Gehry's buildings are as much about our perceptions of architecture as they are about architecture. It is a school of design that stresses viewpoint as much as it does view, and this perhaps is what makes it such an appealing subject for Tim Street-Porter. It is architecture with little symmetry; the buildings do not have obvious poses for the camera. Different camera angles reveal its different truths. And Street-Porter's photographs become reliable documents precisely because they recognize and exploit this fact.

Finally, the spontaneity and sense of immediacy evident in Tim Street-Porter's work also reflect a somewhat unusual, far less often acknowledged motive for the photography of architecture and interiors. Street-Porter admits to vicarious, voyeuristic motives in interior photography. "People's homes are private places," he explains, "places we cannot visit and see except in pictures. To see how people live, particularly famous people, is irresistible." Photography as voyeurism, while not exactly a new thought, is one to which its practitioners do not often confess. That these photographs are small windows not only to buildings, but very often to people's lives, gives them a value apart from their architectural reportage. That Tim Street-Porter admits to and cultivates this sense gives his work a human quality that is an unusual ingredient in architectural photography.

And it is this innate humanism, along with the journalistic realism, that sets apart Tim Street-Porter's photographs as contemporary documents. In documenting the work of Louis Sullivan, John Szarkowski observes that "in our own day perhaps the best architectural photographs have been the casual products of the photographer-journalist, where the life that surrounds and nourishes the building is seen or felt." [3] While his predecessors in the field often cultivated a more immaculate, ideal image, Street-Porter indeed acknowledges this life that surrounds and nourishes; and in doing so, he brings a sense of immediacy, a liveliness and worldliness to the photograph. His are active rather than static representations. And by so being, they expand and bring a new vision to the traditions of architectural photography.

---

1. Henri Cartier-Bresson, "The Decisive Moment, 1952," excerpted in *Photography in Print: Writings from 1816 to the Present,* ed. Vicki Goldberg (New York: Simon and Schuster, 1981), p. 385
2. Ibid.
3. John Szarkowski, *The Idea of Louis Sullivan,* (Minneapolis: University of Minnesota Press, 1956), photographer's foreword.

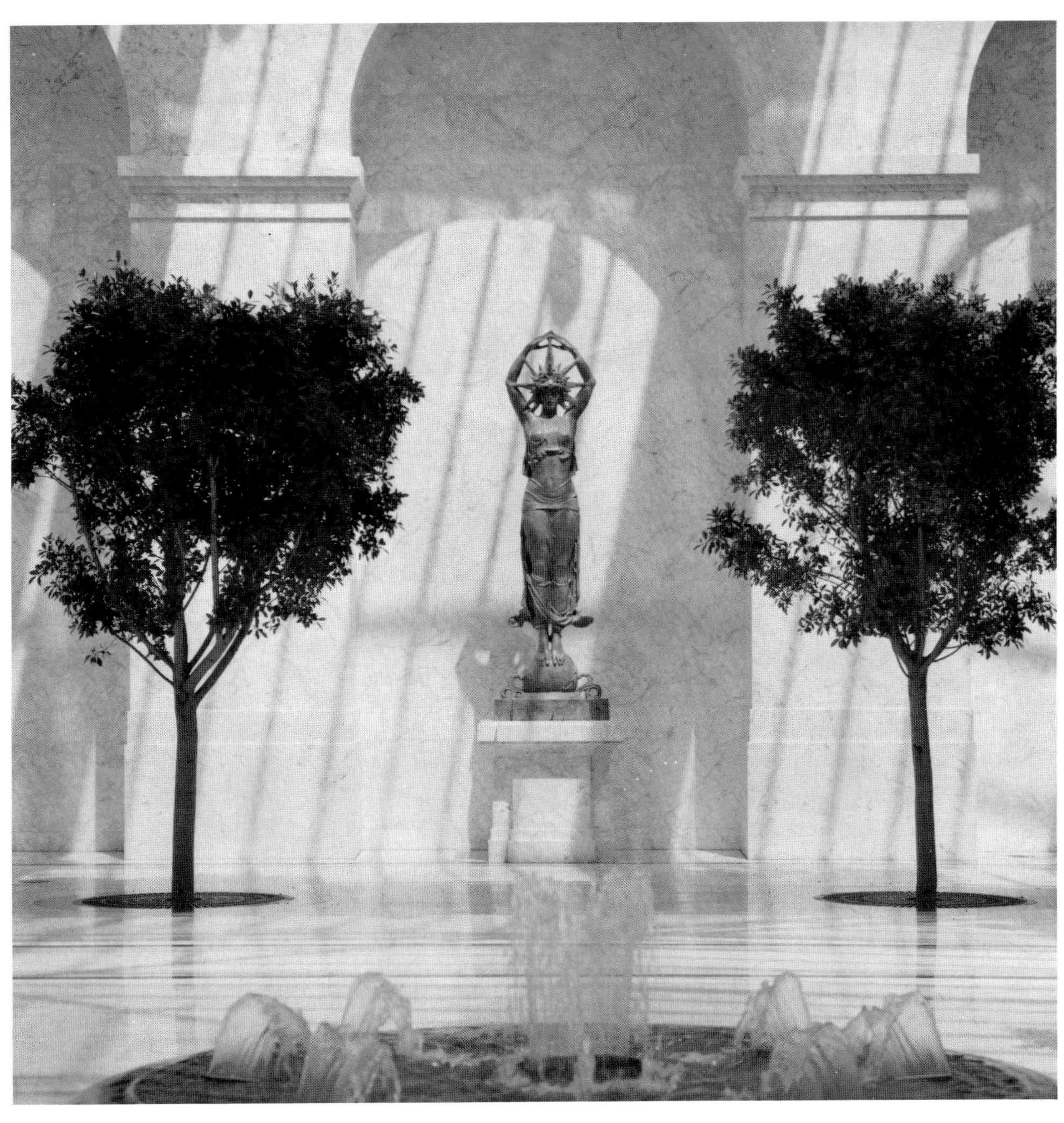

William Pereira & Associates. Citicorp Center, forecourt. San Francisco, California, 1985 (courtesy of Tim Street-Porter).

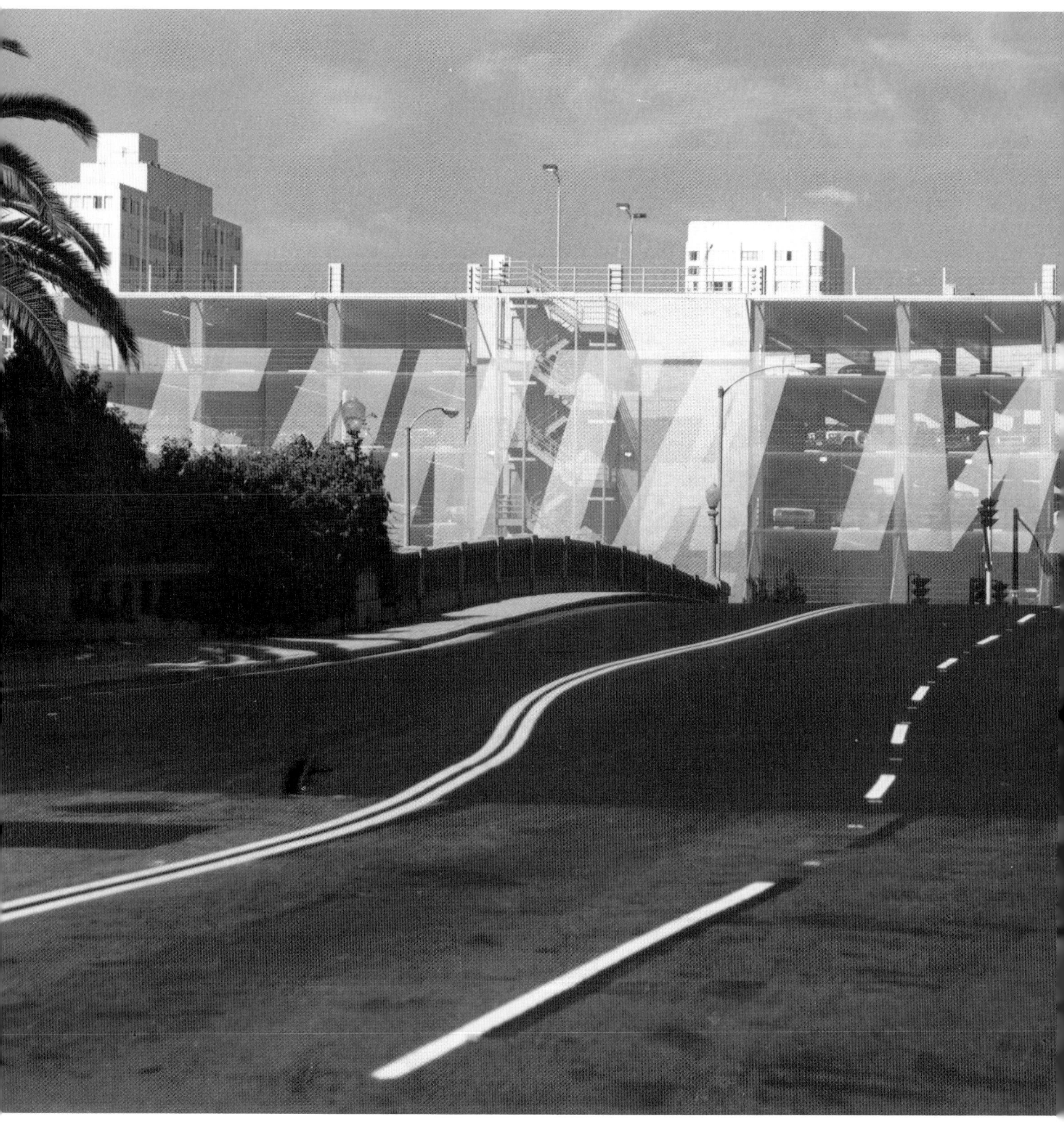

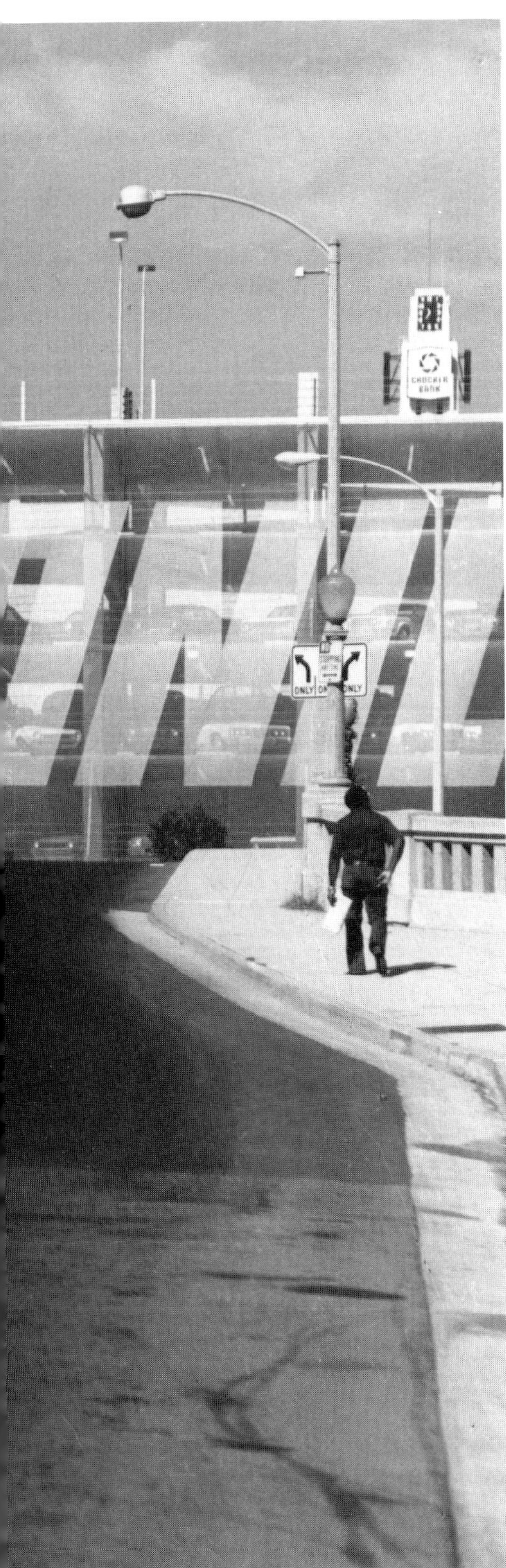

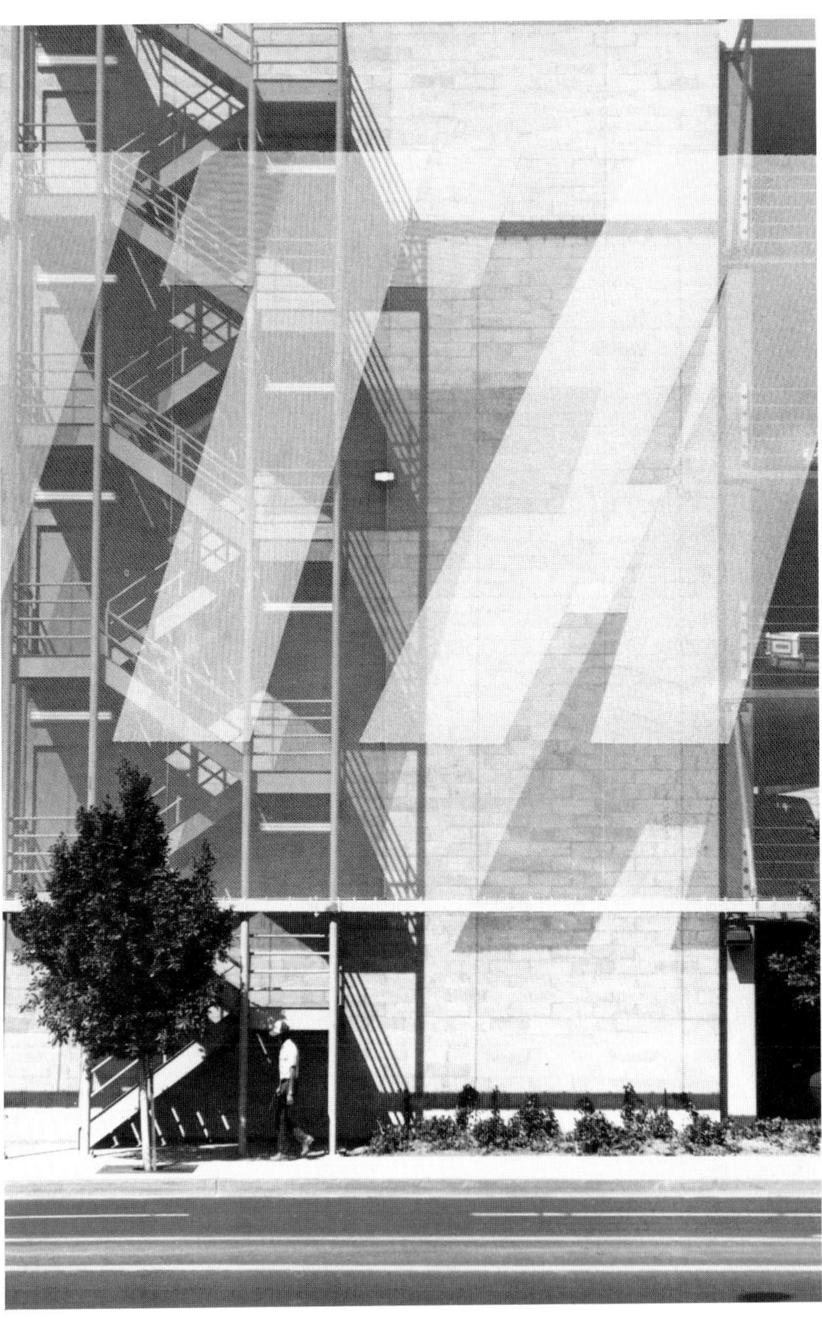

Frank Gehry & Associates. Santa Monica Place Shopping Mall. Santa Monica, California, 1980 (courtesy of Tim Street-Porter).

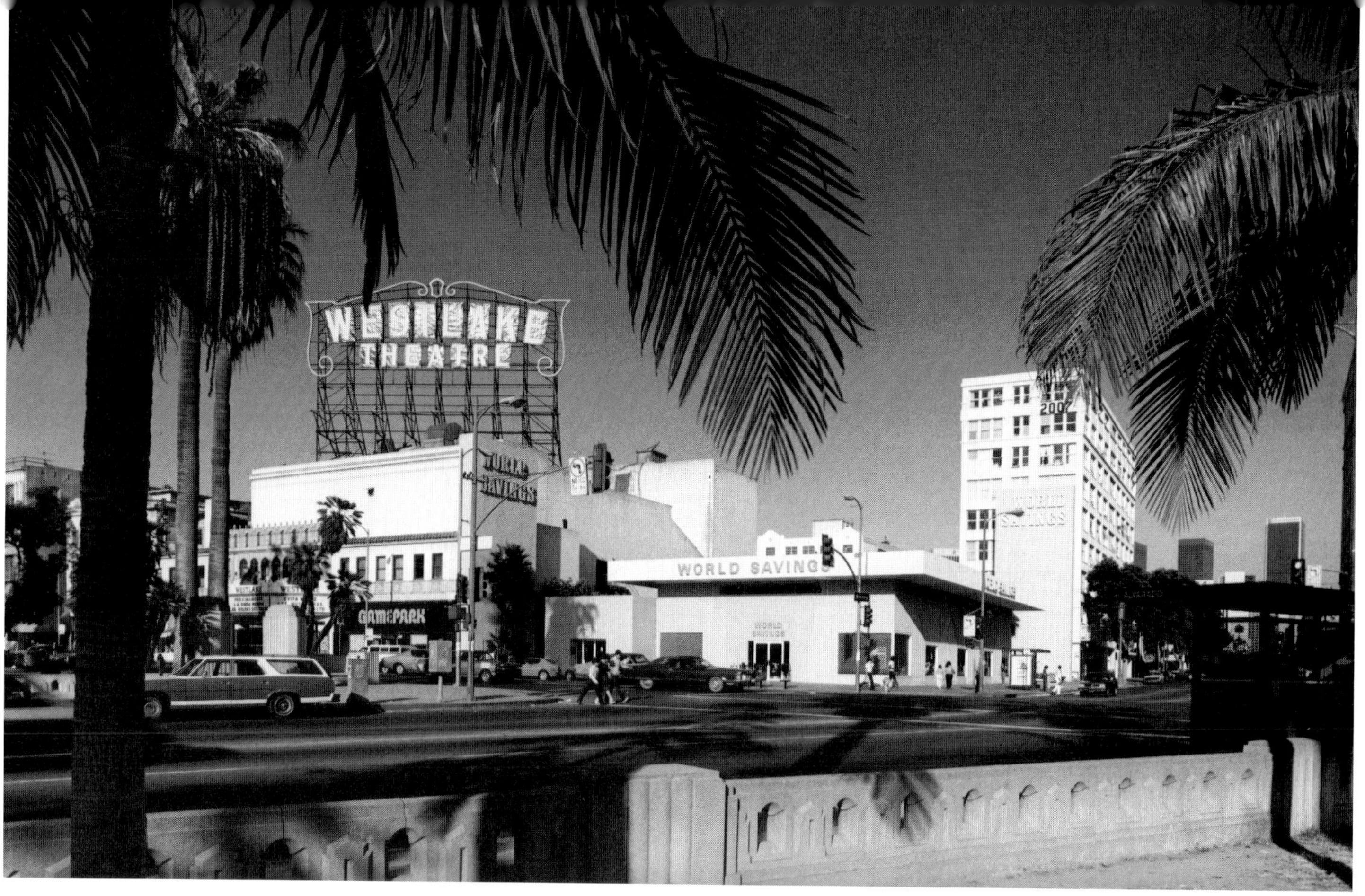

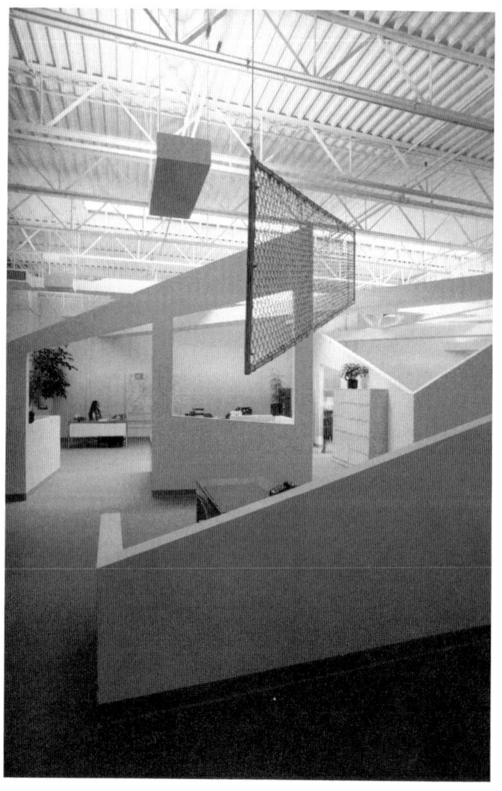

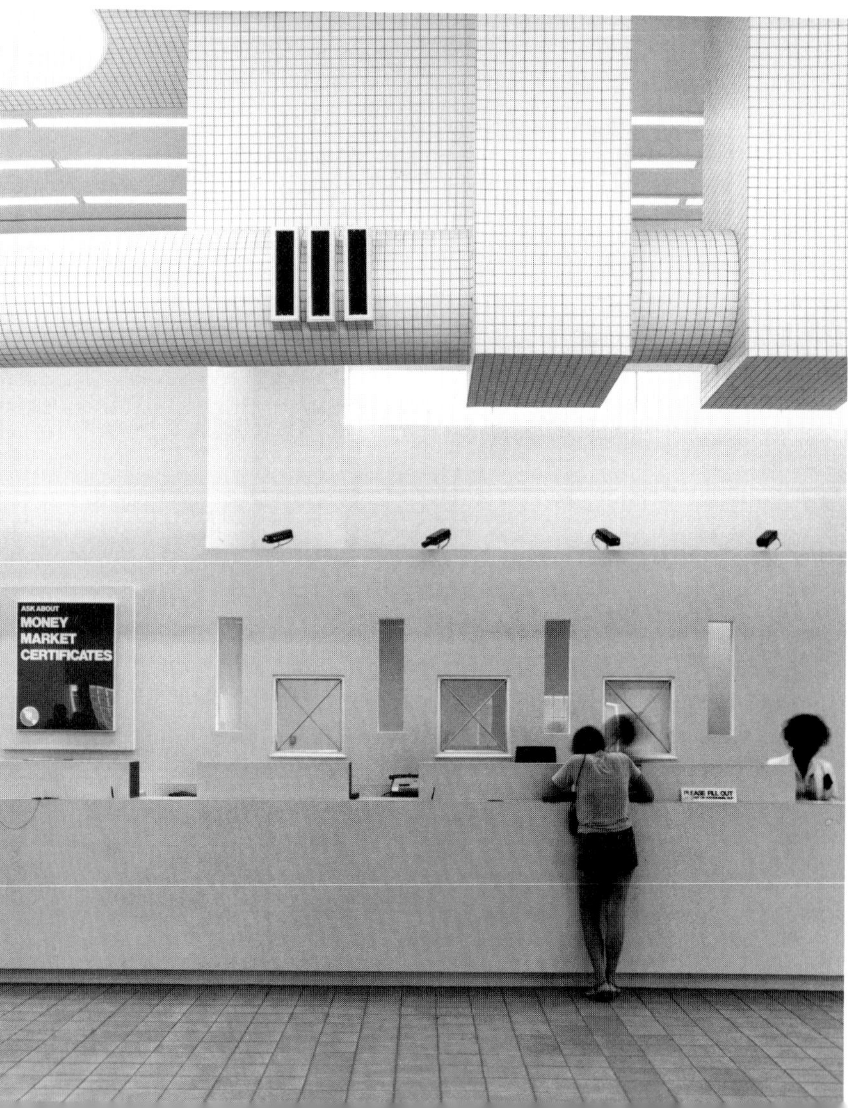
ASK ABOUT
MONEY
MARKET
CERTIFICATES

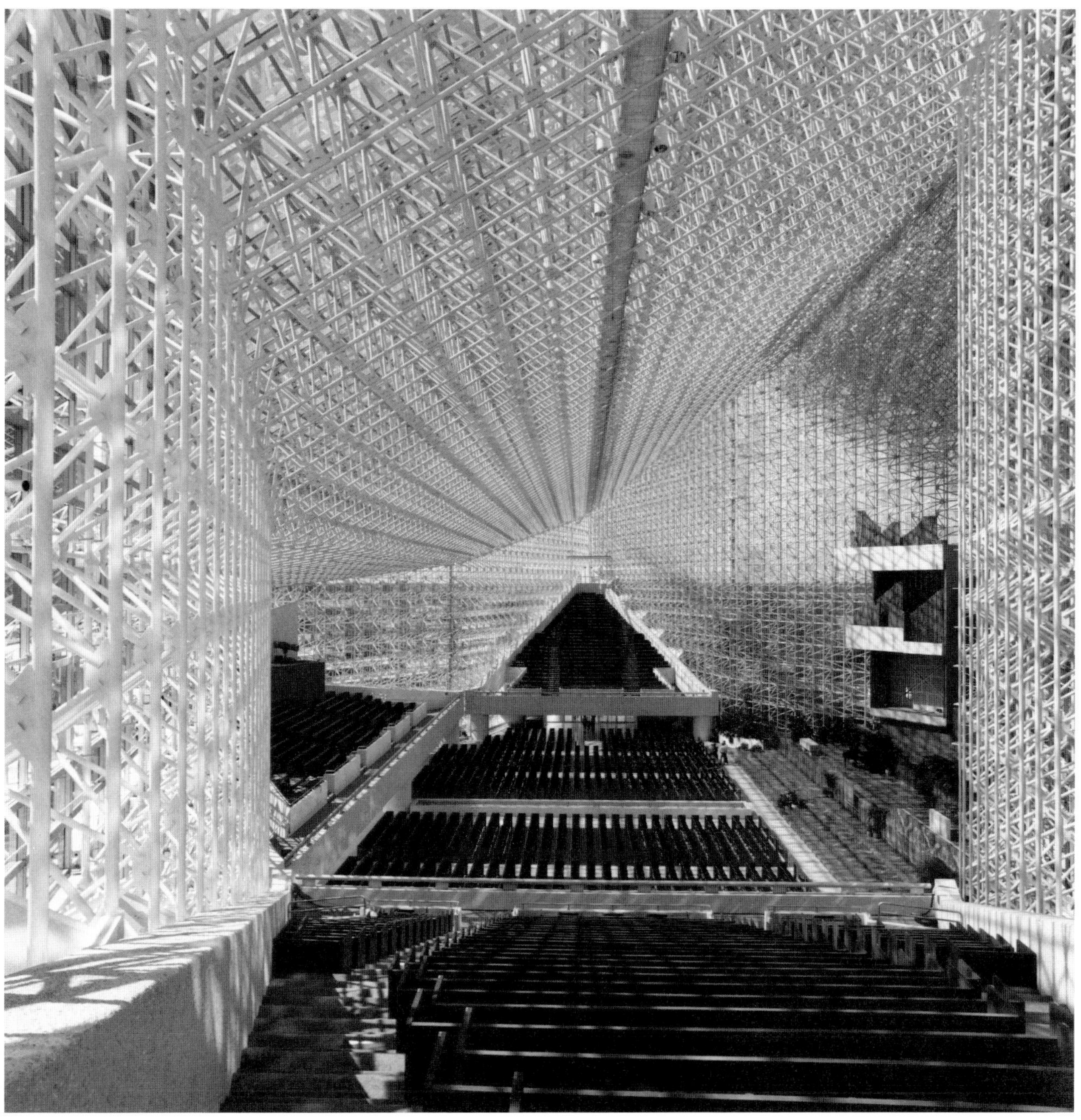

FACING PAGE (BOTTOM-LEFT): Frank Gehry & Associates. Toyota Corporate Headquarters. Baltimore, Maryland, 1979 (courtesy of Tim Street-Porter).

FACING PAGE (TOP AND BOTTOM-RIGHT): Eric Moss. World Savings Bank. Los Angeles, California, 1983 (courtesy of Tim Street-Porter).

ABOVE: Johnson-Burgee Architects. Crystal Cathedral. Garden Grove, California, 1980 (courtesy of Tim Street-Porter).

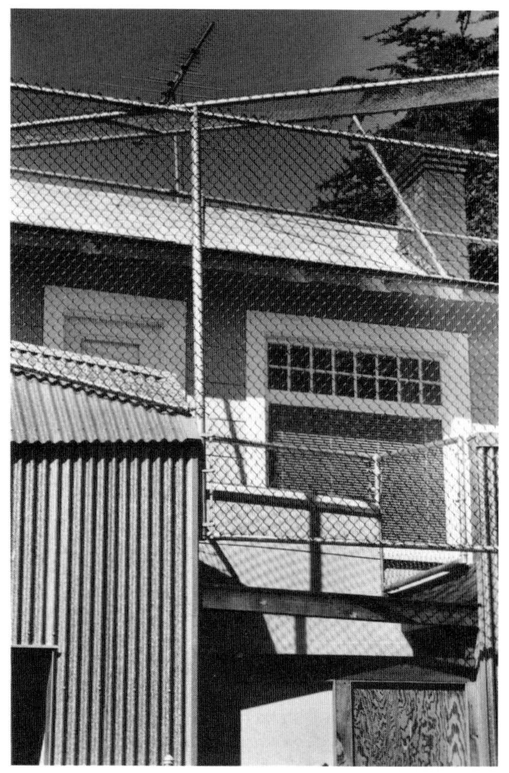

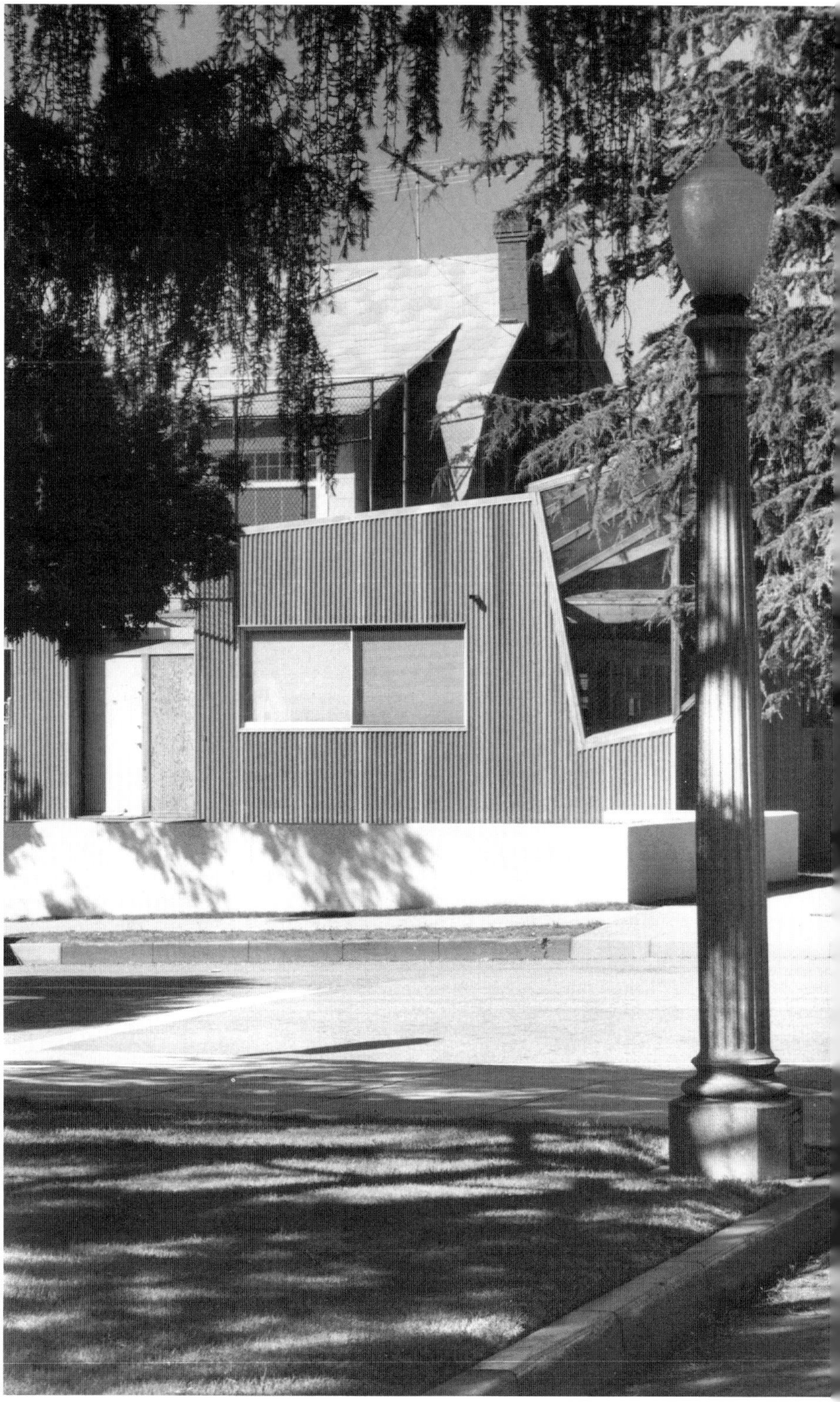

Frank Gehry & Associates. Gehry Residence. Santa Monica, California, 1980 (courtesy of Tim Street-Porter).

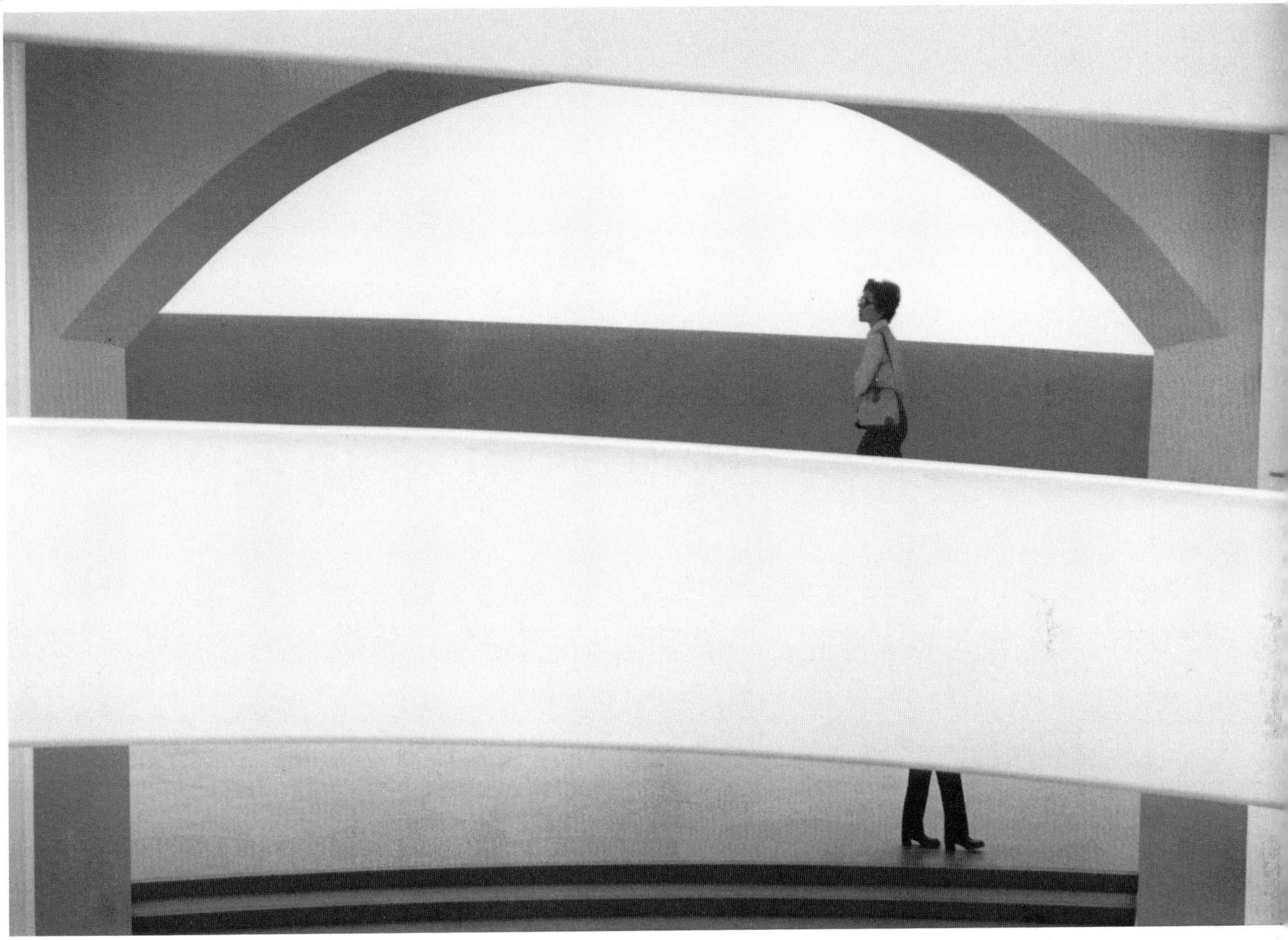

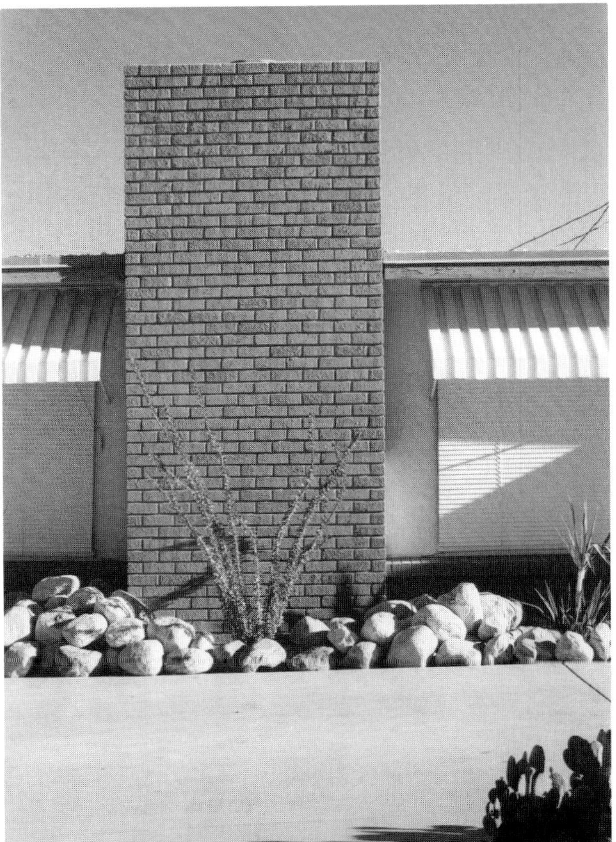

ABOVE: Frank Lloyd Wright. Guggenheim Museum. New York, New York, 1981 (courtesy of Tim Street-Porter).

LEFT: Private Residence. Palm Springs, California, 1979 (courtesy of Tim Street-Porter).

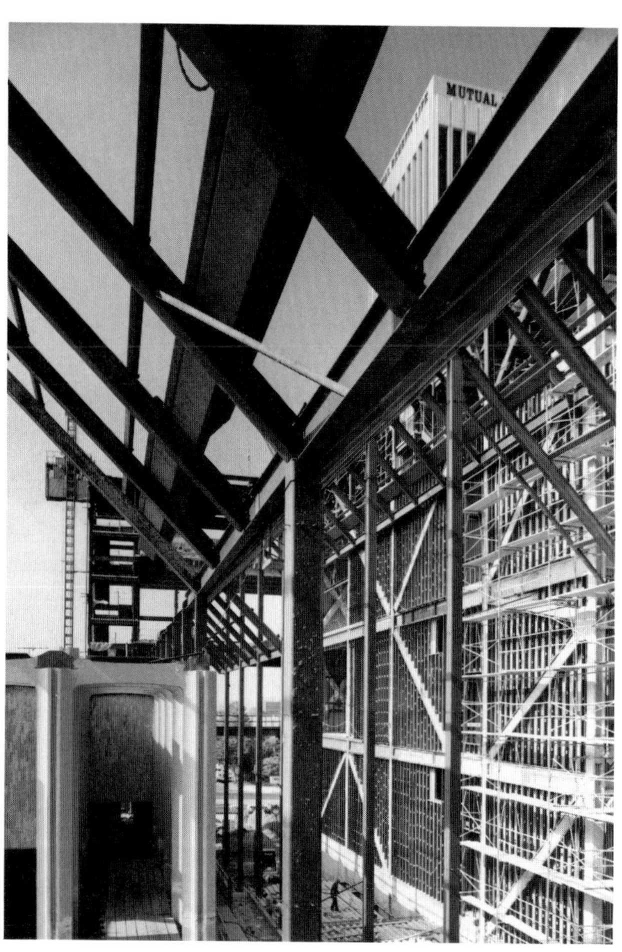

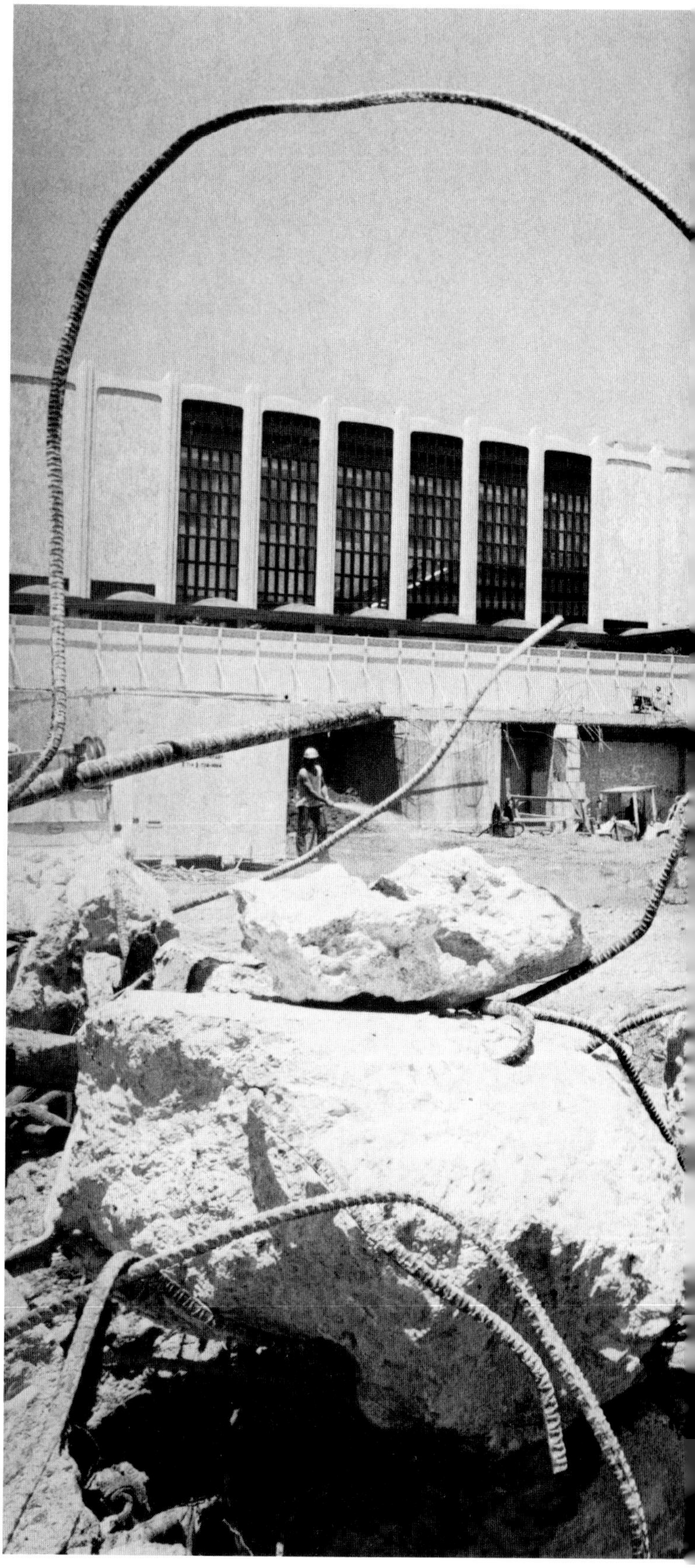

Hardy Holzman Pfeiffer Associates. Construction, Anderson Gallery, The Los Angeles County Museum of Art. Los Angeles, California, 1984–86 (courtesy of Tim Street-Porter).

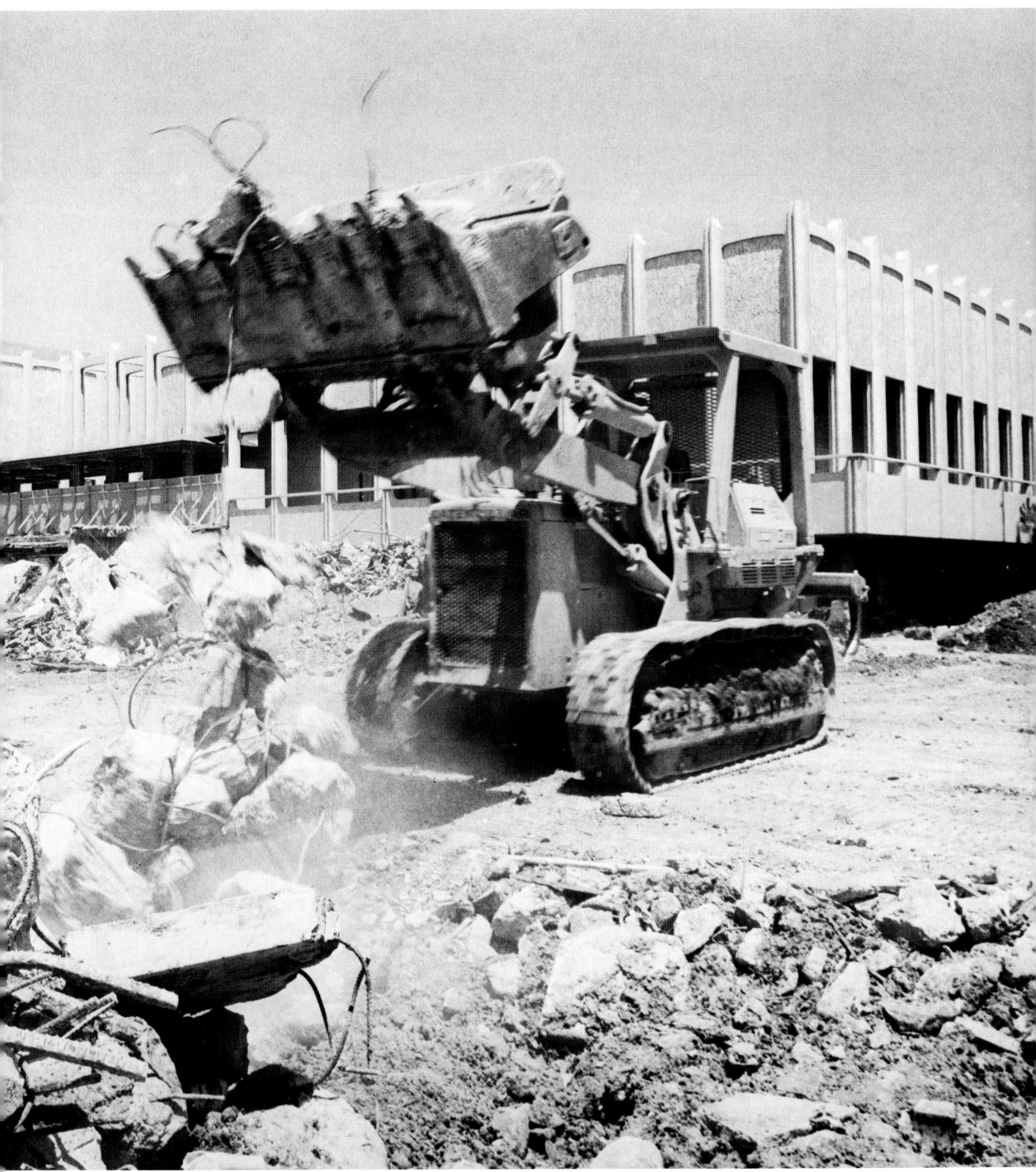

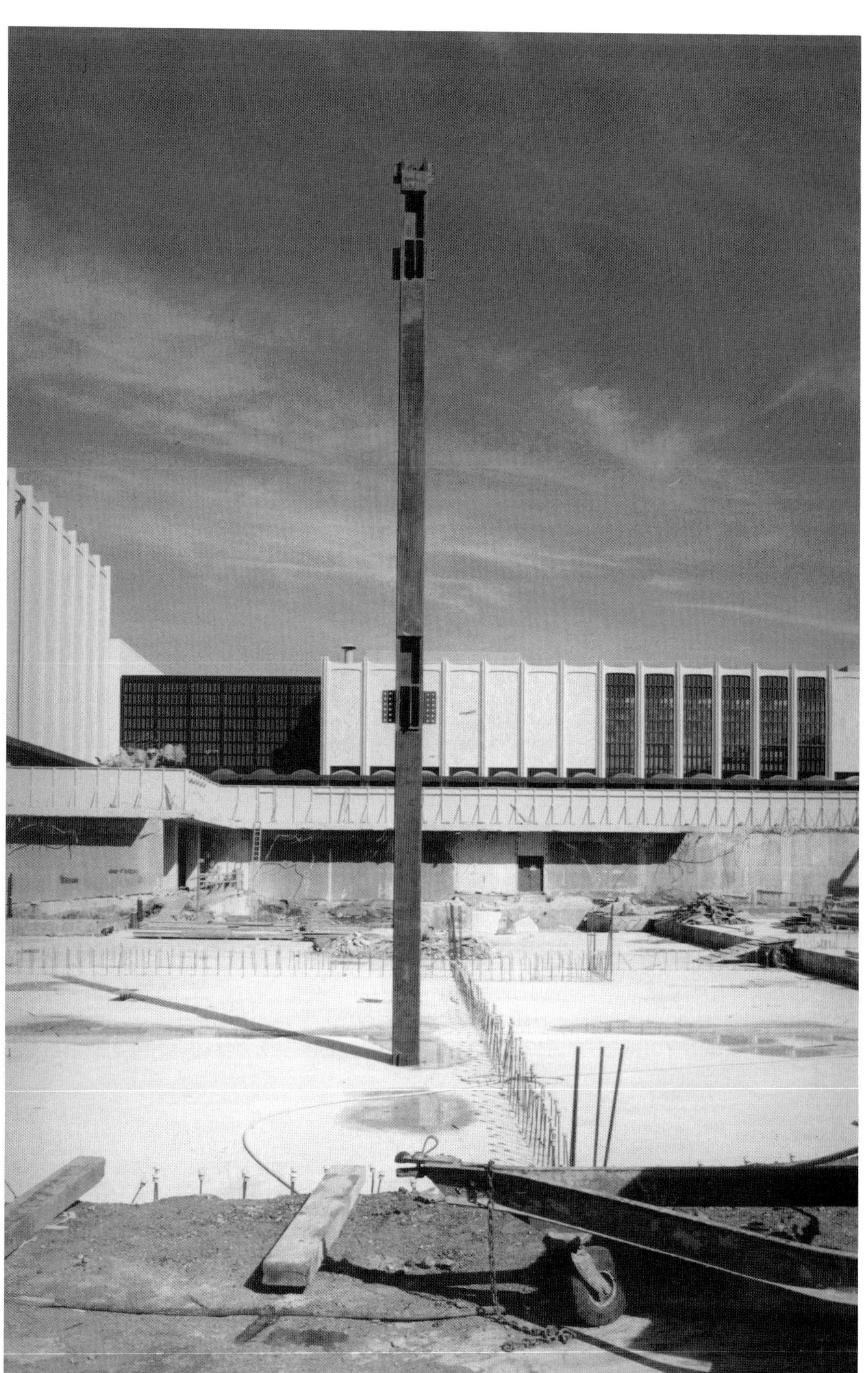

FACING PAGE (TOP) AND RIGHT: Hardy Holzman Pfeiffer Associates. Construction, Anderson Gallery, The Los Angeles County Museum of Art. Los Angeles, California, 1984–86 (courtesy of Tim Street-Porter).

FACING PAGE (BOTTOM): William Pereira Associates. New Construction. Long Beach, California, 1985 (courtesy of Tim Street-Porter).

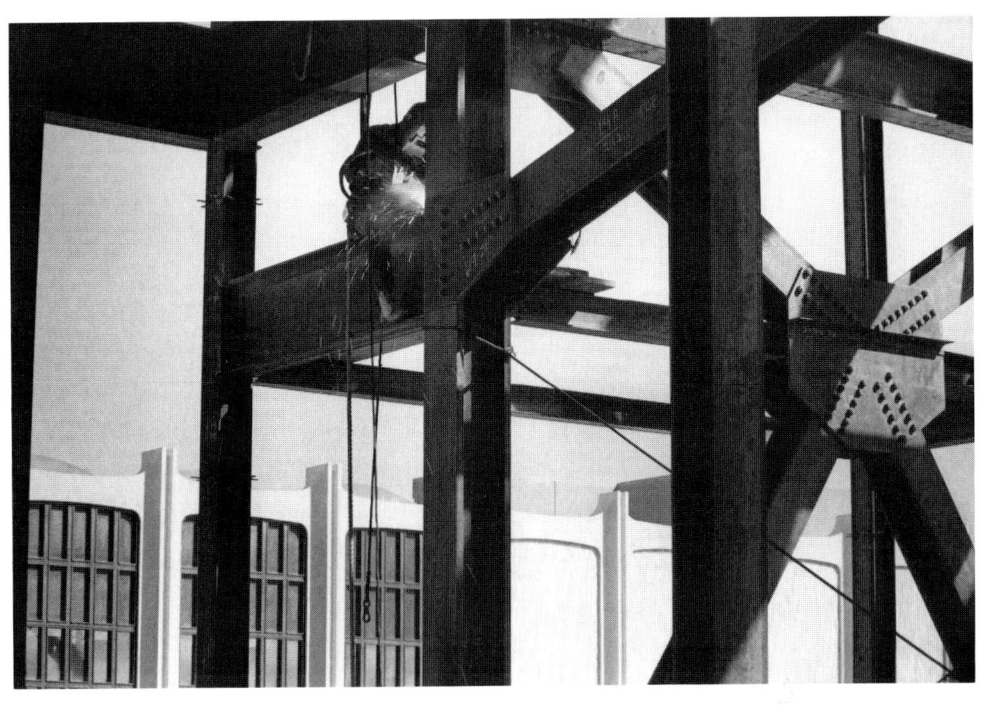

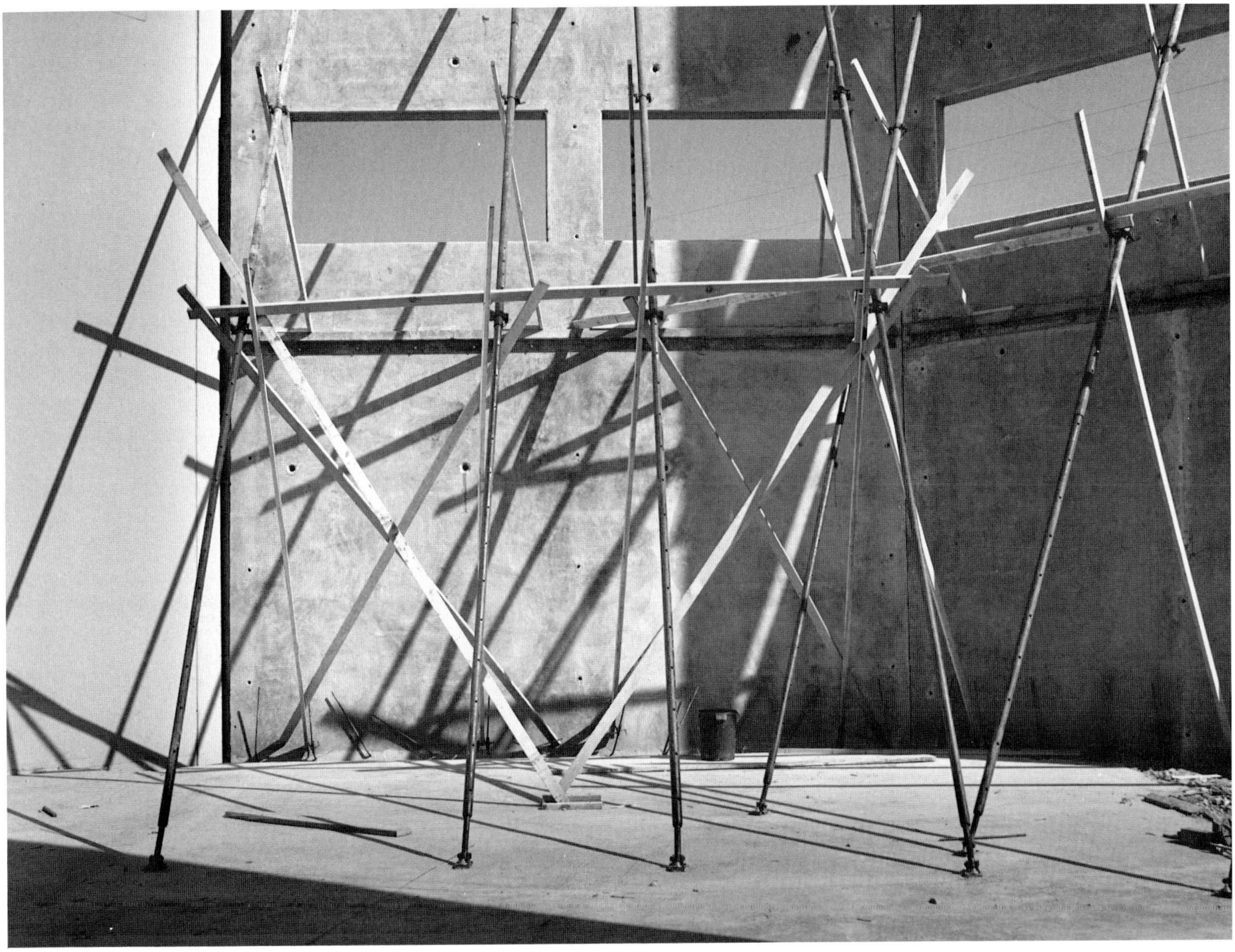

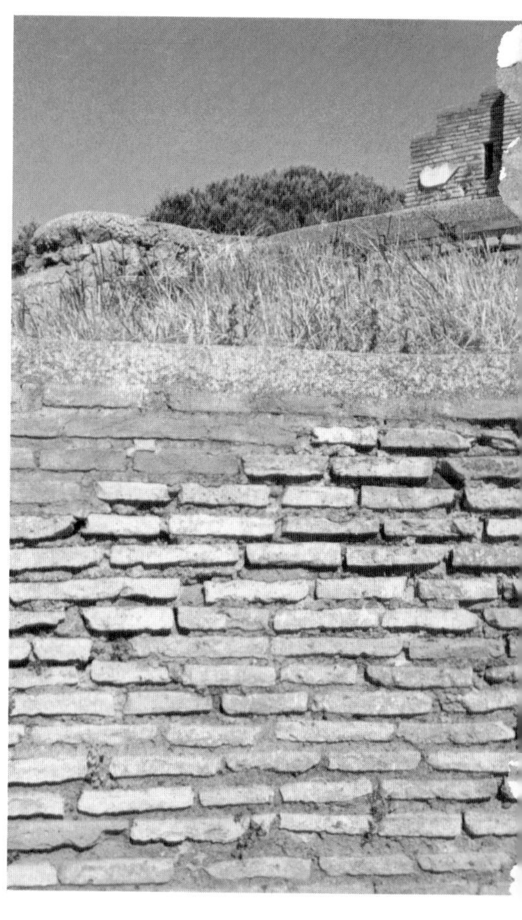

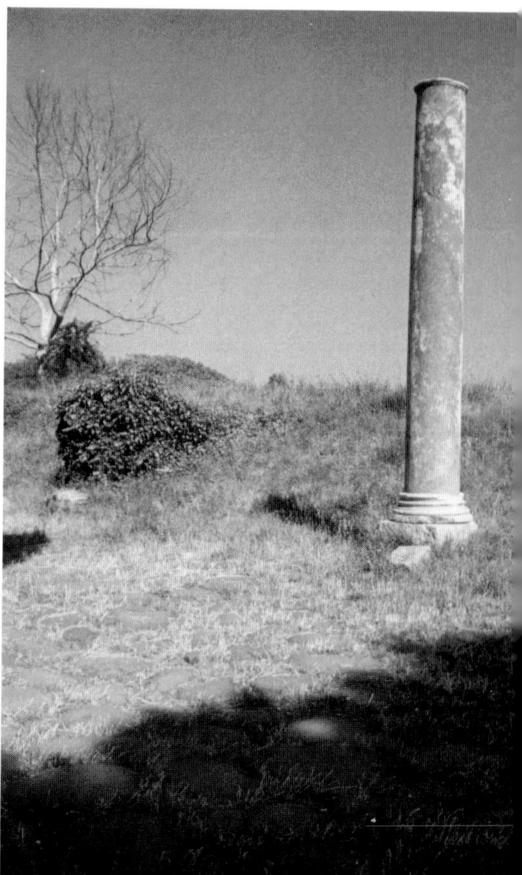

Ostia Antica. Rome, Italy, 1981 (courtesy of Tim Street-Porter).

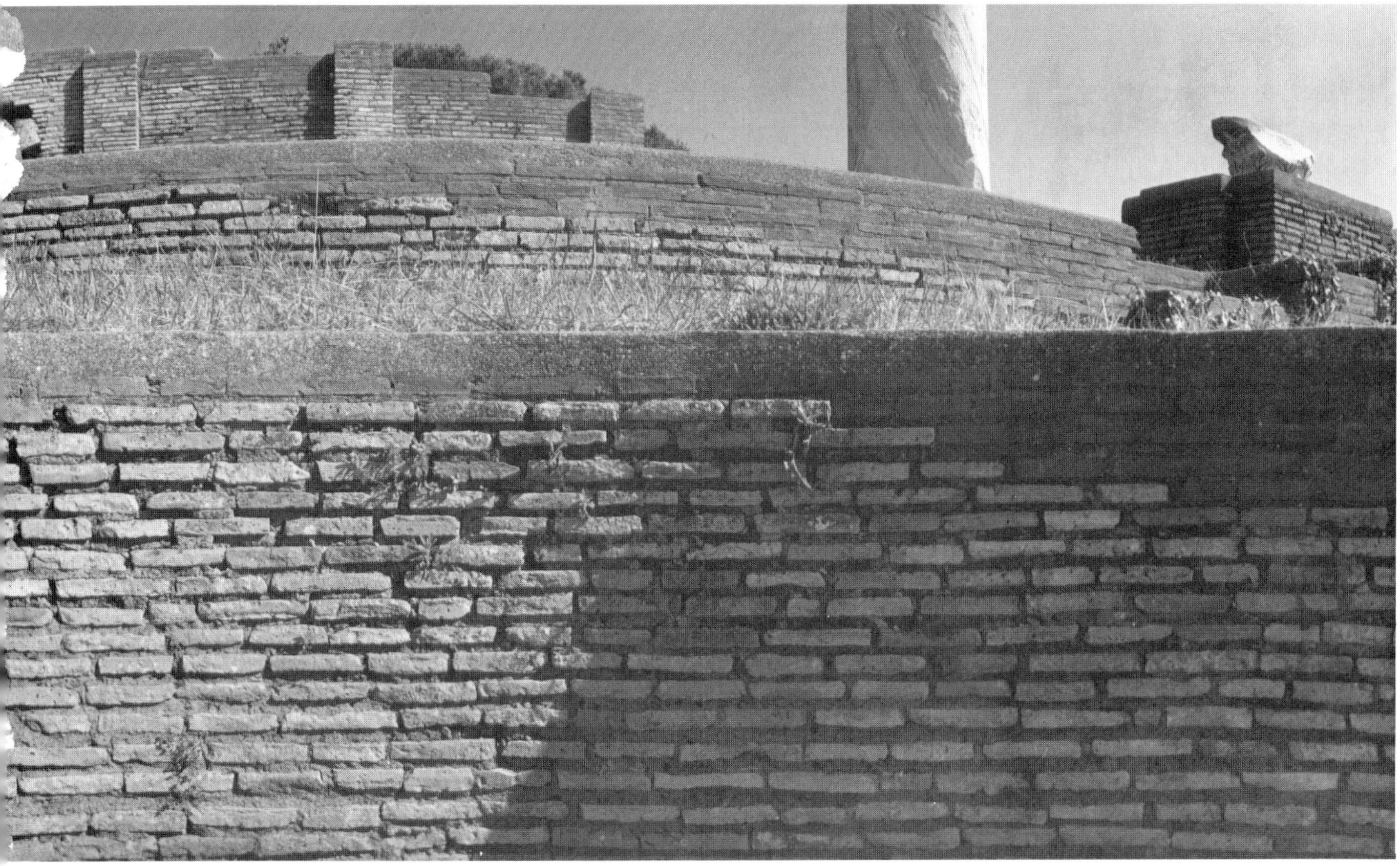

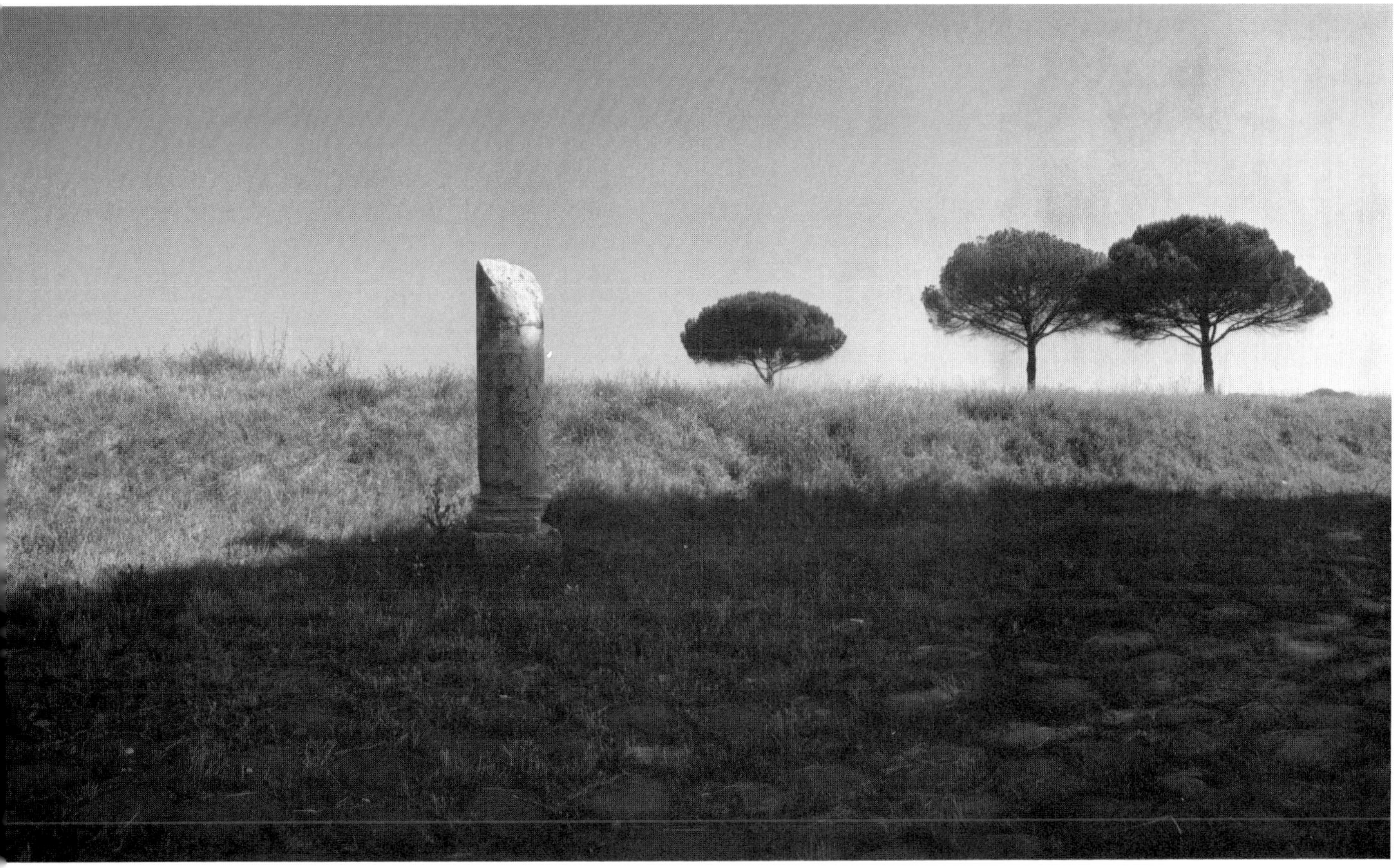

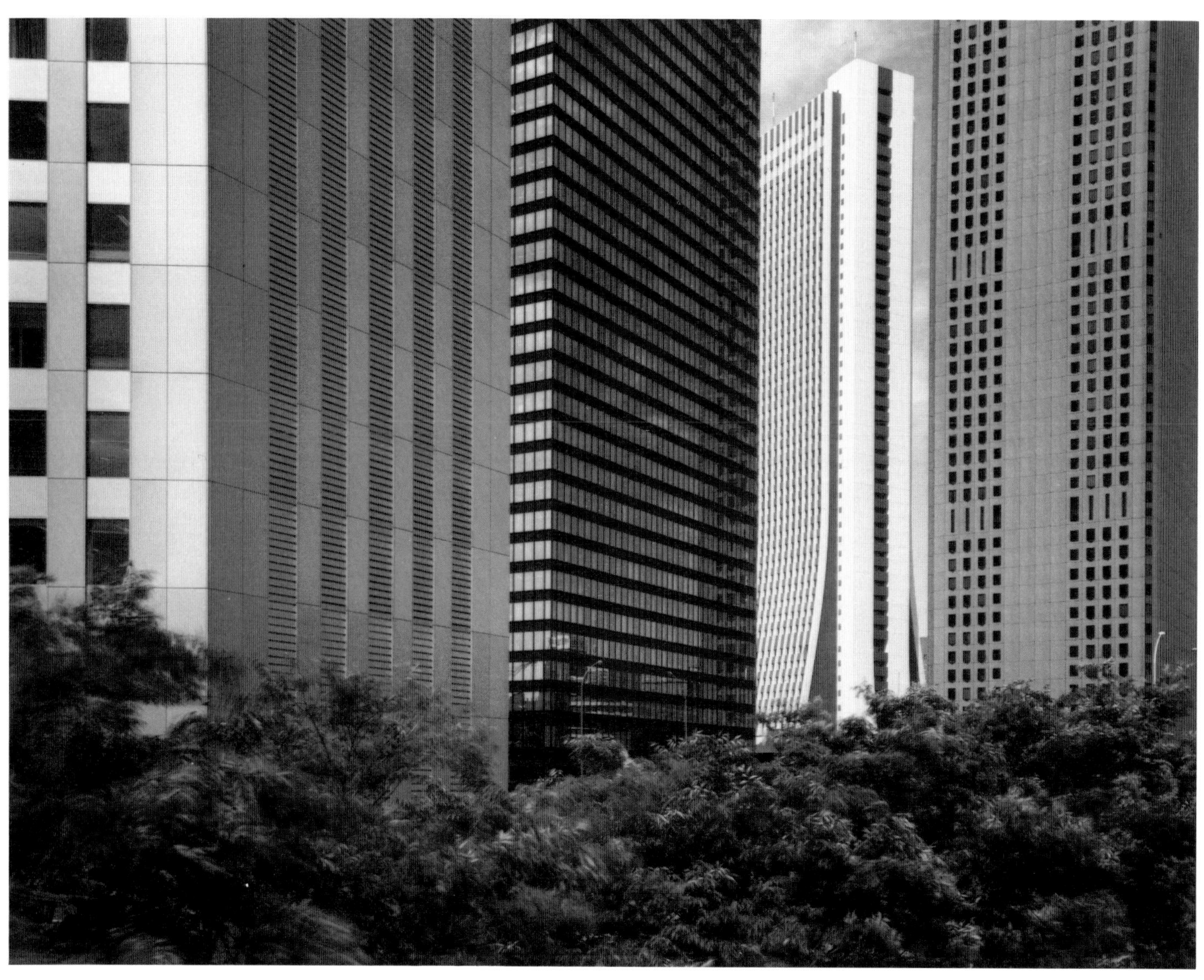

Shinjuku, Tokyo, Japan,
1983.

PAUL WARCHOL

Of all the artistic processes, it is perhaps the process of architecture that is the most oblique, the most difficult to identify and trace. The seeds of thought and often obscure theory that are at the conception of a building grow to be tested by a form that must adhere to more material laws of practical engineering and human interest. Ideology is translated in structure. From conception through construction, the development of a building follows an obscure trail investigating both polemics and pragmatism. While the finished building may remain true to its conceived image, it also has a life of its own. As architect Hugh Hardy points out, "The finished building has a texture all its own, a smell, a sound, a feel to it that radiates. You don't know what it is until it's there. And when it's finished, it is, in part, a discovery to the architect." [1]

Just as the architect "discovers" the finished building, the photographer can contribute to this discovery; rather than simply reflect what the architect already knows about the building, the photographer can observe those facts for himself, acting separately as witness to the new life of a finished building. It is this sense of discovery that Paul Warchol values in the documentation of architecture. "On a three-day shoot," he says, "you might spend the first day getting the obvious pictures. But then you look over your shoulder and start to notice the more subtle shots. And then the whole thing begins to come together. It's a photographic discovery; it's a discovery of how things configure in a four-by-five rectangle."

Not unlike other discoveries, the way these are made involves a certain amount of risk. Says Charles Gandee, senior editor at *Architectural Record,* "While architecture is sometimes photographed as perfect architecture in a perfect world, photographers like Paul Warchol are more willing to take risks. They don't wait hours on end for the light to do something extraordinary, but they take the chance. Warchol exploits chance; he exploits the changes in the sky for example." [2] And the images that emerge from these risks are often the most compelling and memorable images of the architecture.

While Warchol is indeed as much a technician as any, his work makes clear that he also relies upon more imprecise sciences: luck, as well as risk, plays a part in his work. "While I have a respect for the theatrical lighting that is often used in interior photography," he explains, "that's really artificially created drama. There is also a real drama in the landscape or sky, and these too can be captured." And clearly, the dramatic effect of a stormy sky can hardly be anticipated; rather, it is captured at the moment. "The theatricality may look planned, but it's really not. If there's any intent here, it's to be lucky."

Indeed, whether it is a darkening sky or a quiet, sunlit room, Warchol's photographs are graceful exploitations of available light. The light filtering through a window perhaps has more integrity than strobe, he suggests. "There's something about pointing your light at something. It can be entirely appropriate sometimes, but there is something more romantic about window light. There isn't any real value judgement here, but there is something about using available light, that kind of north light, that seems unquestionably valid." Architect Wayne Berg concurs, finding in Warchol's expressive, and often lyric use of light an almost painterly quality: "The way Warchol is able to use available light, and then augment it with filters, reflects his background as a painter. He has a painter's eye for composition and lighting. His perception combines that of artist and technician." [3]

Although the science of available light may be inexact, the equipment with which Warchol investigates it is more precise. Many of these shots are taken by a Hasselblad two-and-a-quarter, a camera that corresponds to "a different kind of noticing, maybe one more ephemeral." Warchol finds that the photographs taken with the Hasselblad are lighter and more lyrical than those produced by the methodical four-by-five view camera. "Maybe the light is going to change in three seconds, and you want to see what it looks like raking across a textured wall. You're not going to be able to capture that on four-by-five, because that takes too long. They also can become too stiff; working in a larger format, you can tend to line things up." Still, he emphasizes the fact that the more ephemeral exposures do not necessarily make for substantive documentation. They are remarks, perhaps, more than they are complete statements. While they may add dimension to the building's portfolio, rarely do they provide information sufficient to complete the visual record of the architecture. Rather, they are evanescent moments that work to supplement the more careful compositions recorded by the view camera.

Warchol's compositions are clearly not lined up. On the contrary, many of his compositions seem to establish a sense of symmetry only quietly to disrupt it. A visual balance is constructed only to be slightly distorted, twisted, disturbed. What throws the viewer off balance is usually something slight—an angle that is only slightly off center, a small human figure bringing motion to the still symmetry of a facade or a chair that has been knocked slightly out of place. A still life is composed and then quietly and gently disrupted. The visual provocation that is implicit in such a composition seems to be saying, again, that this is not perfect architecture in a perfect world, which perhaps is why it is worth examining all the more.

Warchol often uses the human figure in architectural documentation for this visual provocation. And, often, the figure is blurred, slightly out of focus. The use of the figure as such is a graphic device; out of focus, it conveys little of the warmth or sense of occupancy that it may sometimes bring to the photograph. Nor does it intend to. Rather, the wash of color and sense of motion that it does bring are purely graphic properties, sudden gestures and movements that work visually to jolt the immobility of the architecture.

Warchol acknowledges the fact that, among his architectural portraits, some may have a value of their own, separate from the architecture they represent. That some photographs may have an appeal beyond the documentary is something he is aware of, often consciously striving for it. He points out that architects may be appreciative of these works as well. "That their work has caused the photographer to take an interesting picture also reflects on them. It's flattering." Often, Warchol concludes, the complete documentation of a building will depend upon a balance between the more representative photographs and the more lyrical or expressive.

Warchol's photographs are also distinguished by the fine-tuning of their framing. As a one-time student of Ezra Stoller, Warchol speaks of the authority with which Stoller finds and fills the frame. "That's what I'm trying to do," he says. "Develop my own authority, fill a frame and have that be my idea about it, an idea that is worthwhile enough to take a picture." To do so, he constructs and maneuvers ideas of what is too much and what is too little, composing and filling the frame down to the quarter inch. It is a sense of play that frequently brings a provocative detail to the frame's edge—a piece of molding or the glitter of table utensils that catch the eye. Such details serve a double purpose; they define the outside edge of the photograph, while simultaneously suggesting the larger whole that lies outside the frame.

Warchol's scrupulous regard of borders is often apparent as well in the interiors of his photographs. A building may appear in the distance, framed between the branches of a tree. The interior scaffolds and structures found within the photographs—branches, signposts, fences—often provide a natural framework for a small composition within the large.

Yet as tightly framed as many of his photographs are, they also suggest a continuity. "My work has a certain amount of layering to it," says Wayne Berg. "How the spaces connect and relate to each other to form a wholeness is important to me, and it's important to get this in the photograph. Which Warchol does." [4] That this sense of spatial continuity can coexist with its seeming contrast of a tight, full frame is perhaps a mark of the photographer's skill.

"I'd like to say my work is about putting a frame, in a clear and forceful way, around the facts that are the building," Warchol says. "Being able to grasp what those things are intuitively and stating them in the picture, just as you would in a paragraph. Or just the way a well-played piano sonata has clear lines running through it. That kind of clear statement is important to me."

And it is a clear statement that his photographs express. Warchol's painterly compositions poised within their deliberate borders are indeed complete; that they simultaneously convey an impression of what lies outside the frame is, at first, curious. But that his work can accommodate two seemingly contradictory notions says something of its complexity, and in the end, of its clarity as well.

---

1. Conversation with author, April 1985.
2. Conversation with author, April 1985.
3. Conversation with author, April 1985.
4. Ibid.

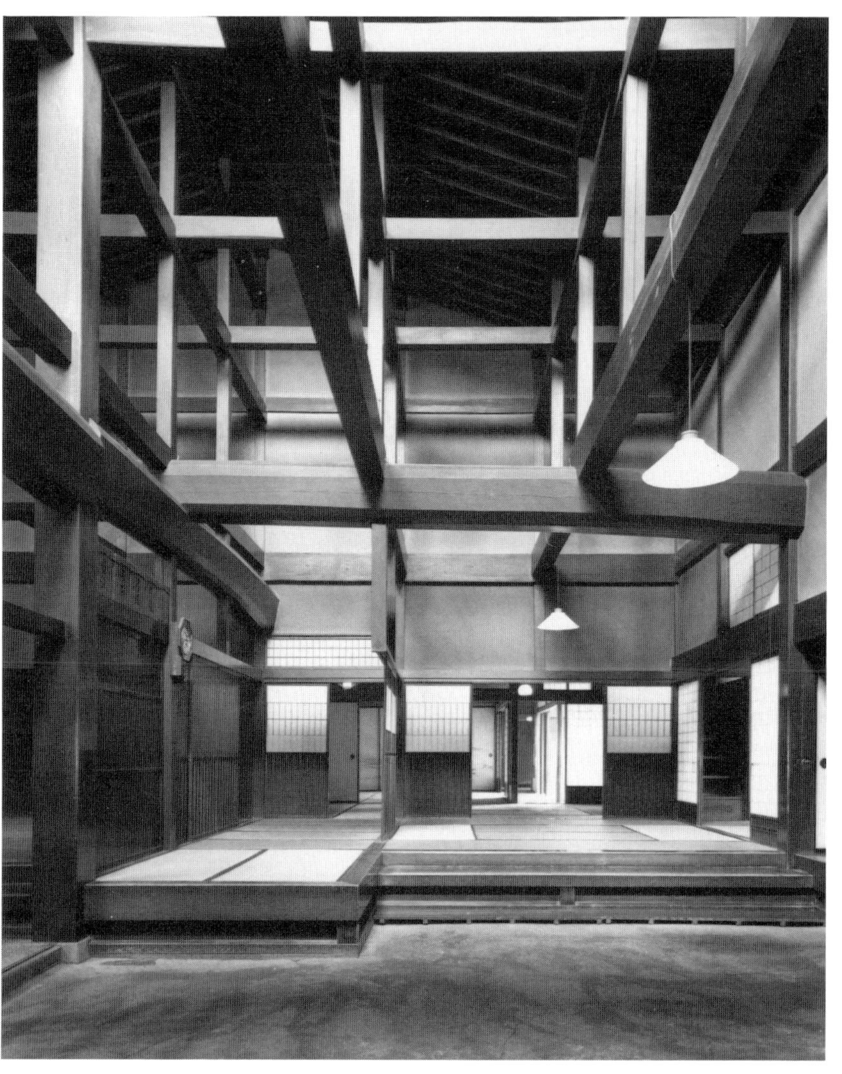

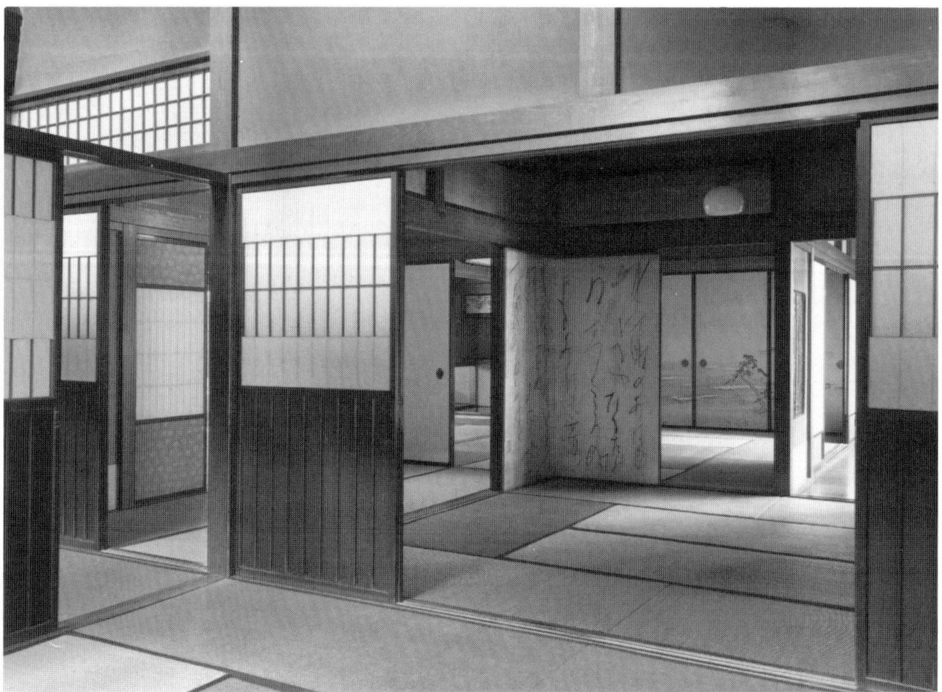

Yoshijima House.
Takayama,
Japan, 1983.

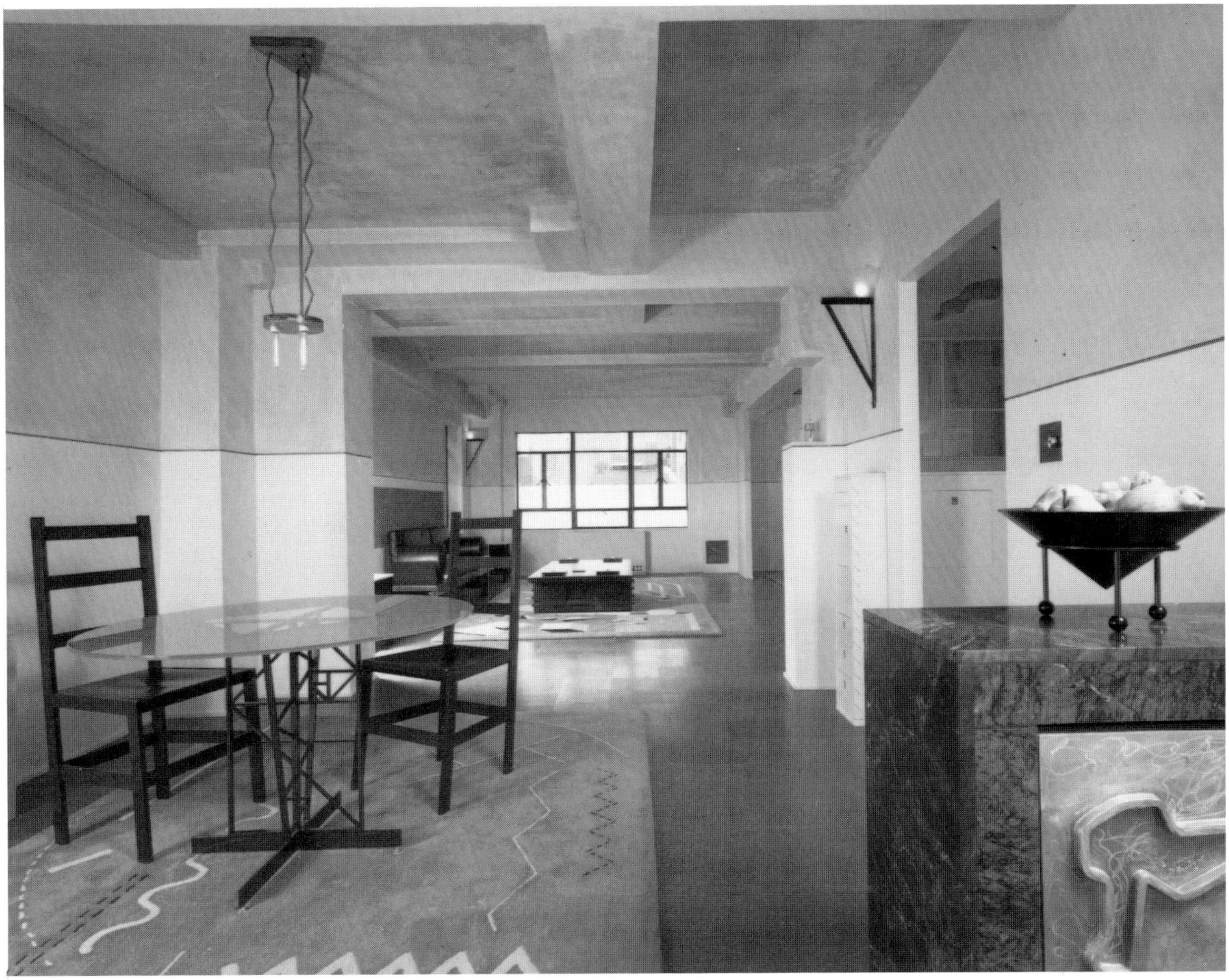

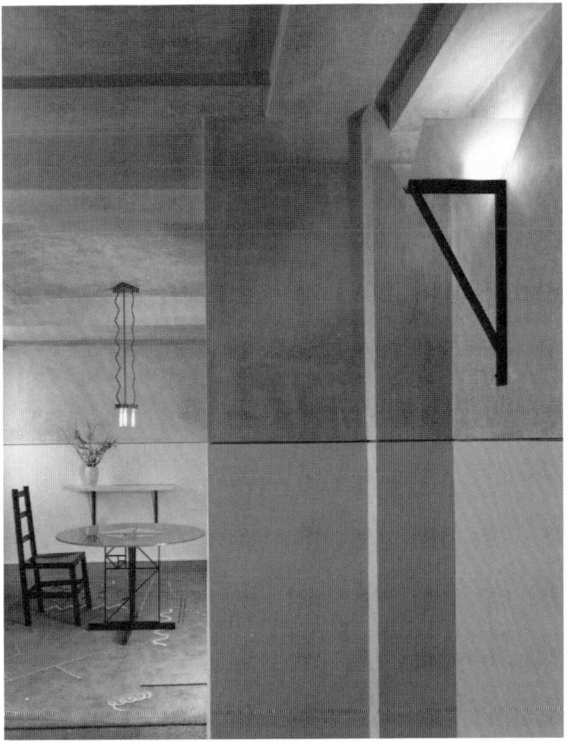

Steven Holl. Cohen Residence. New York, New York, 1984.

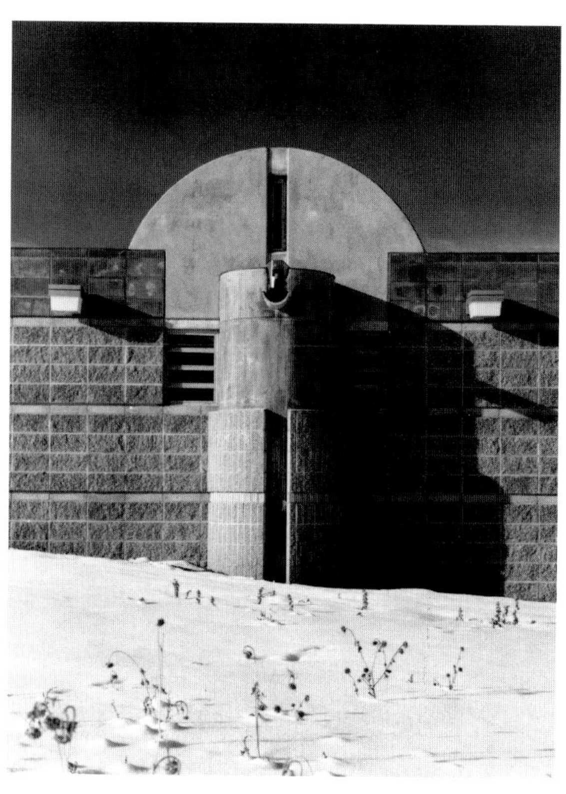

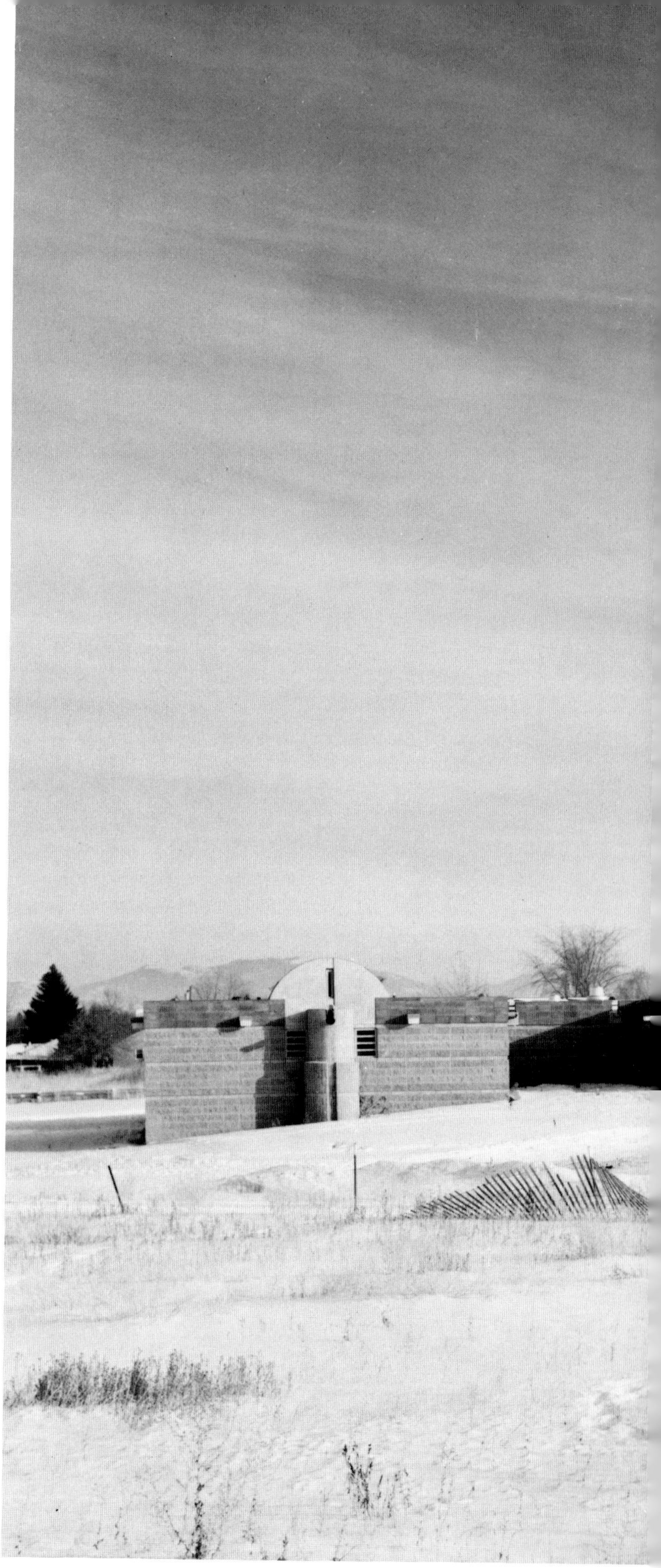

BGS Architects with Wayne Berg. Gallatin County Detention Center. Bozeman, Montana, 1982.

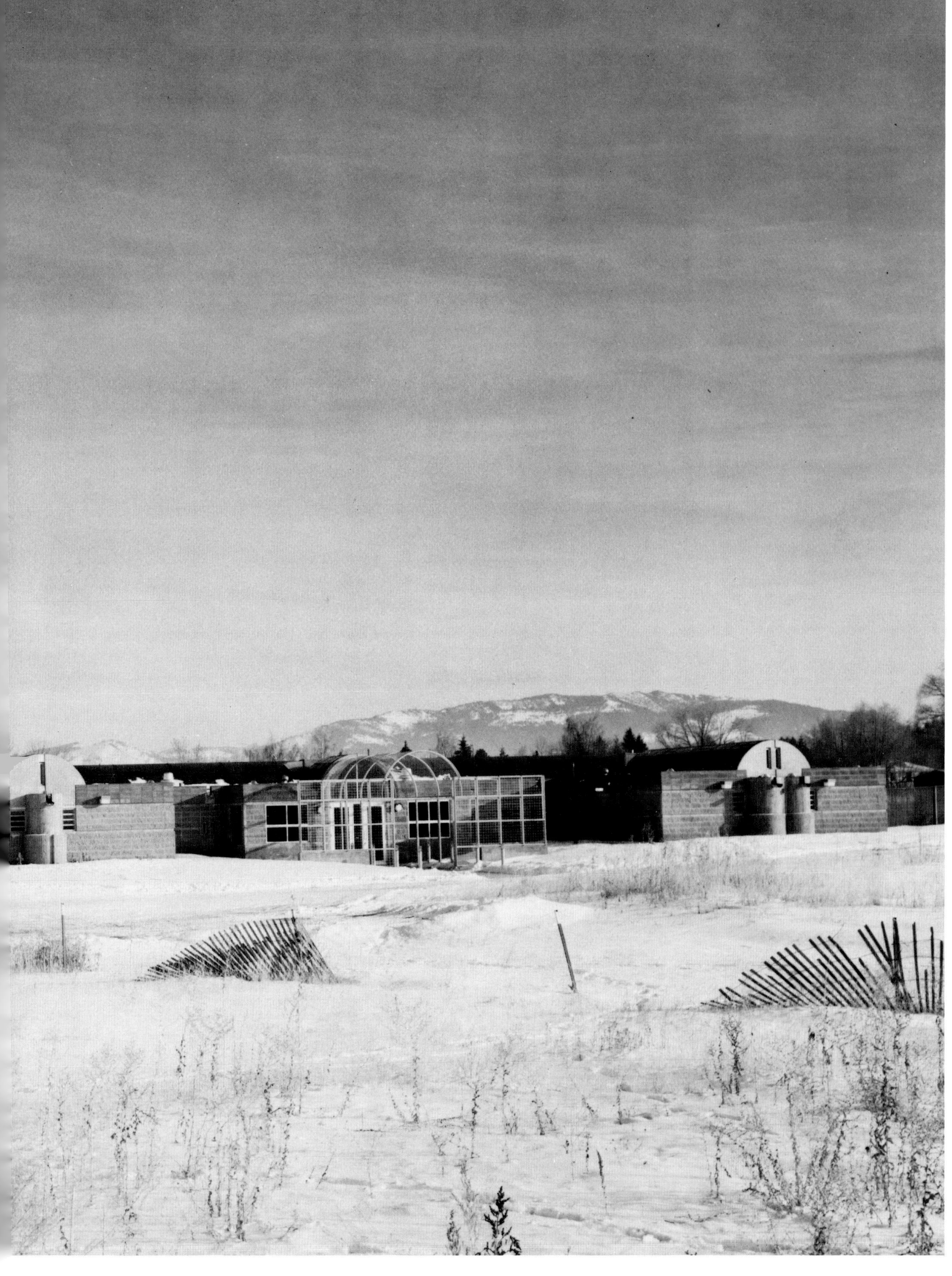

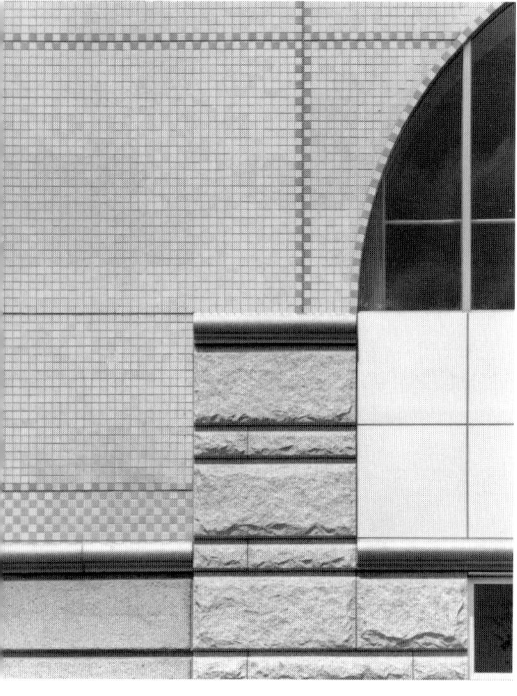

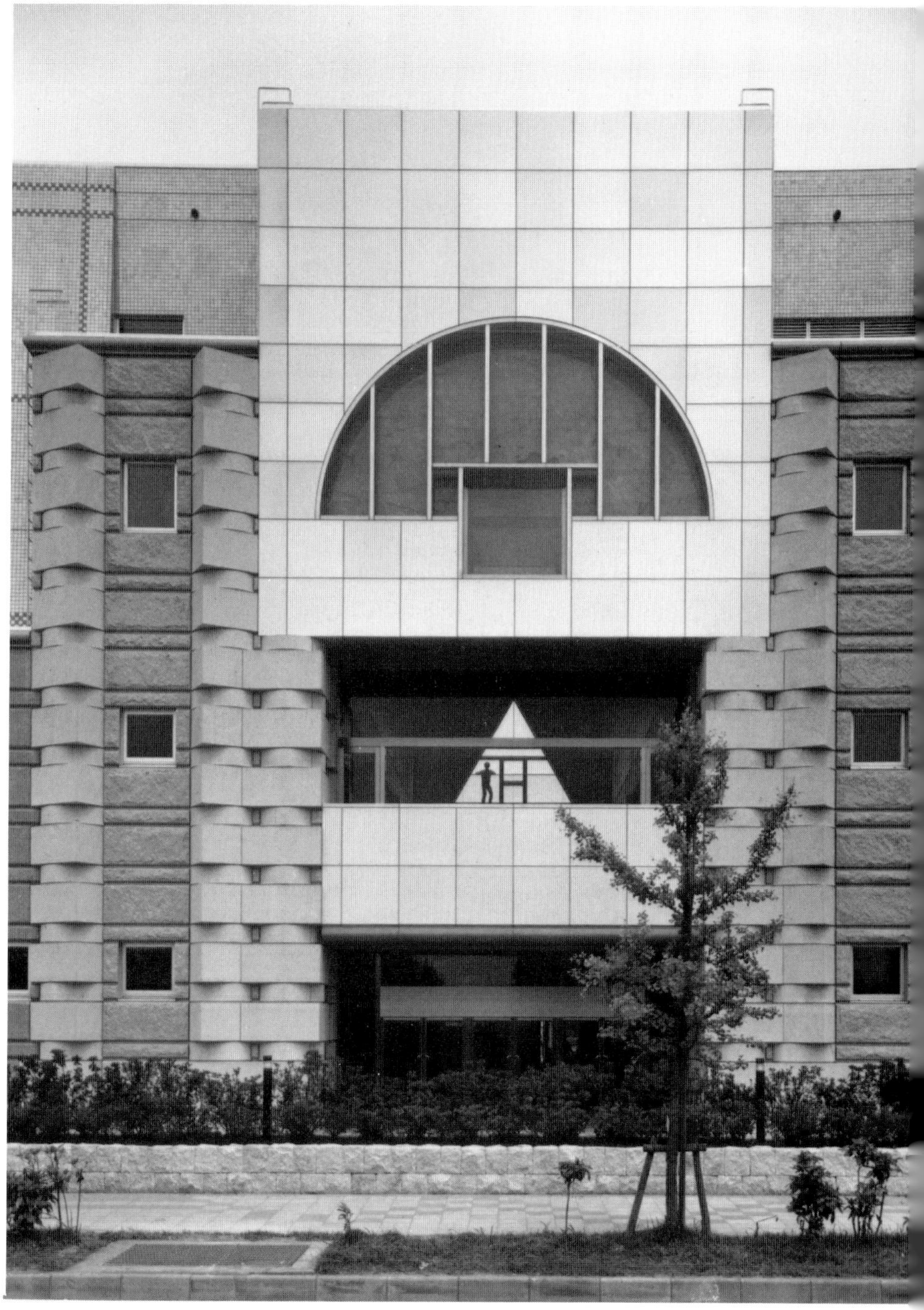

Arata Isozaki.
Tsukuba Center Building.
Tsukuba, Japan, 1983.

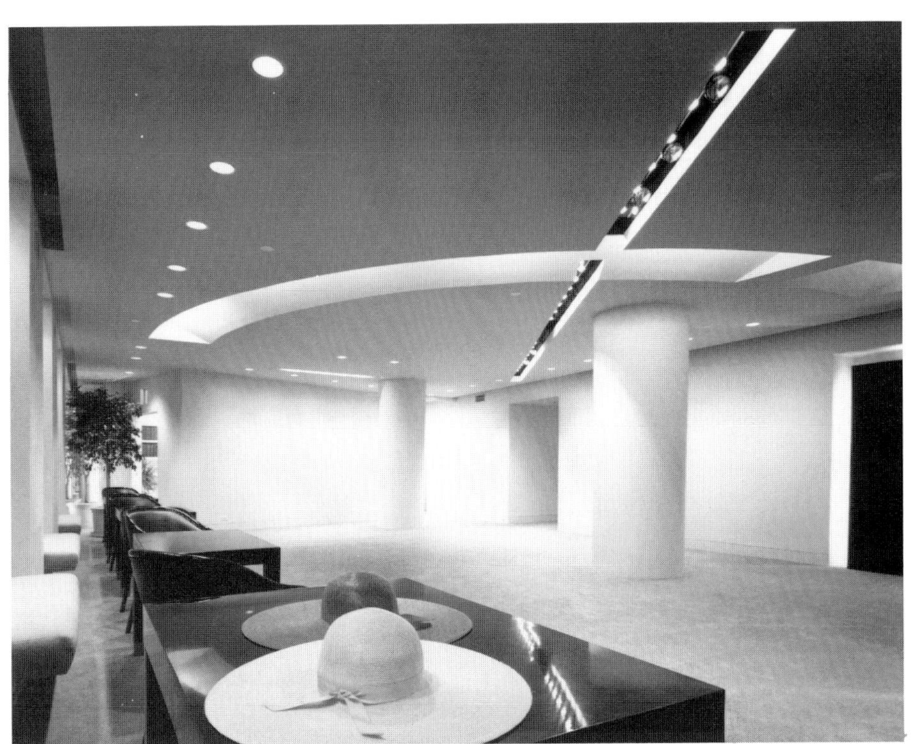

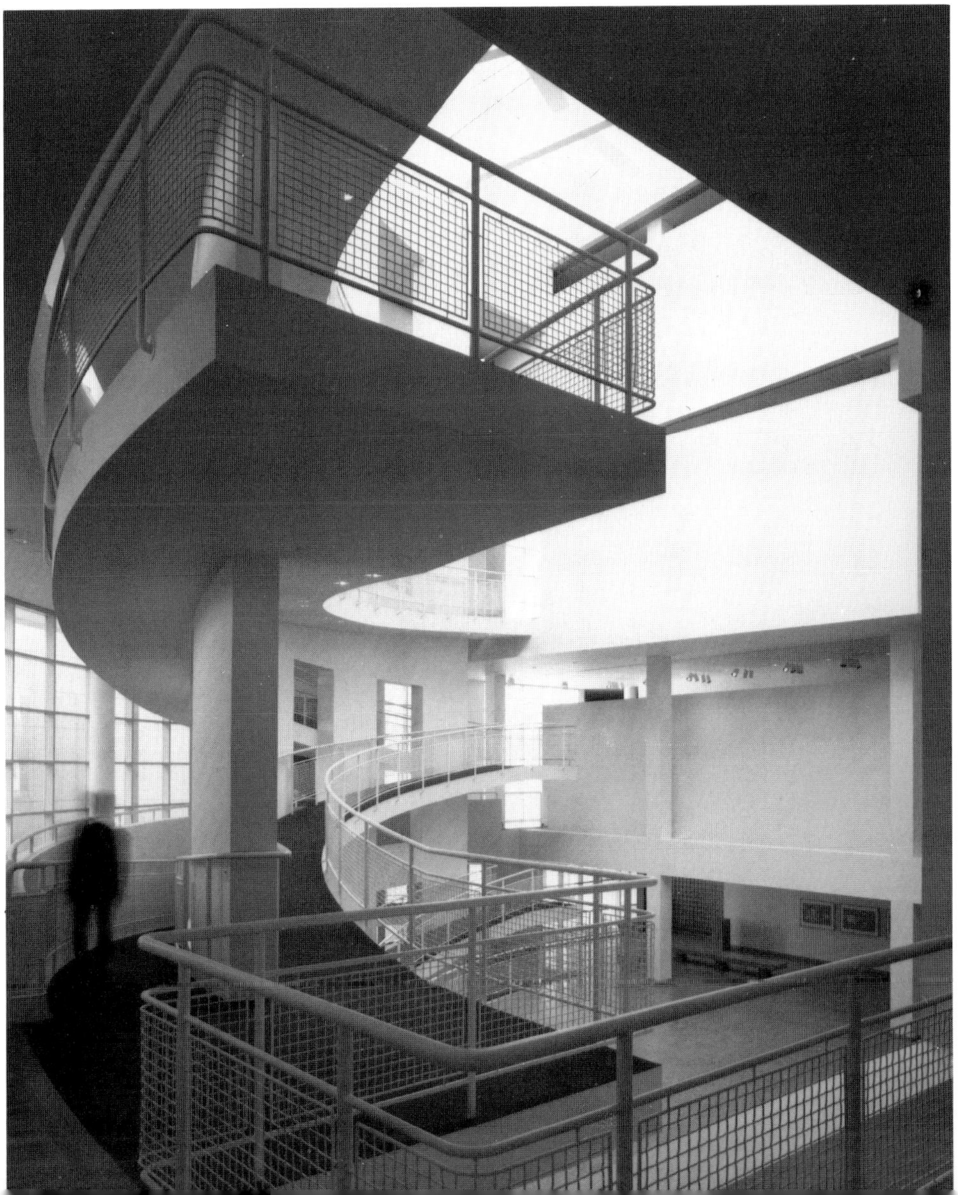

ABOVE: Wayne Berg.
Bill Blass Showroom.
New York, New York,
1982.

LEFT: Richard Meier.
The High Museum. Atlanta,
Georgia, 1983.

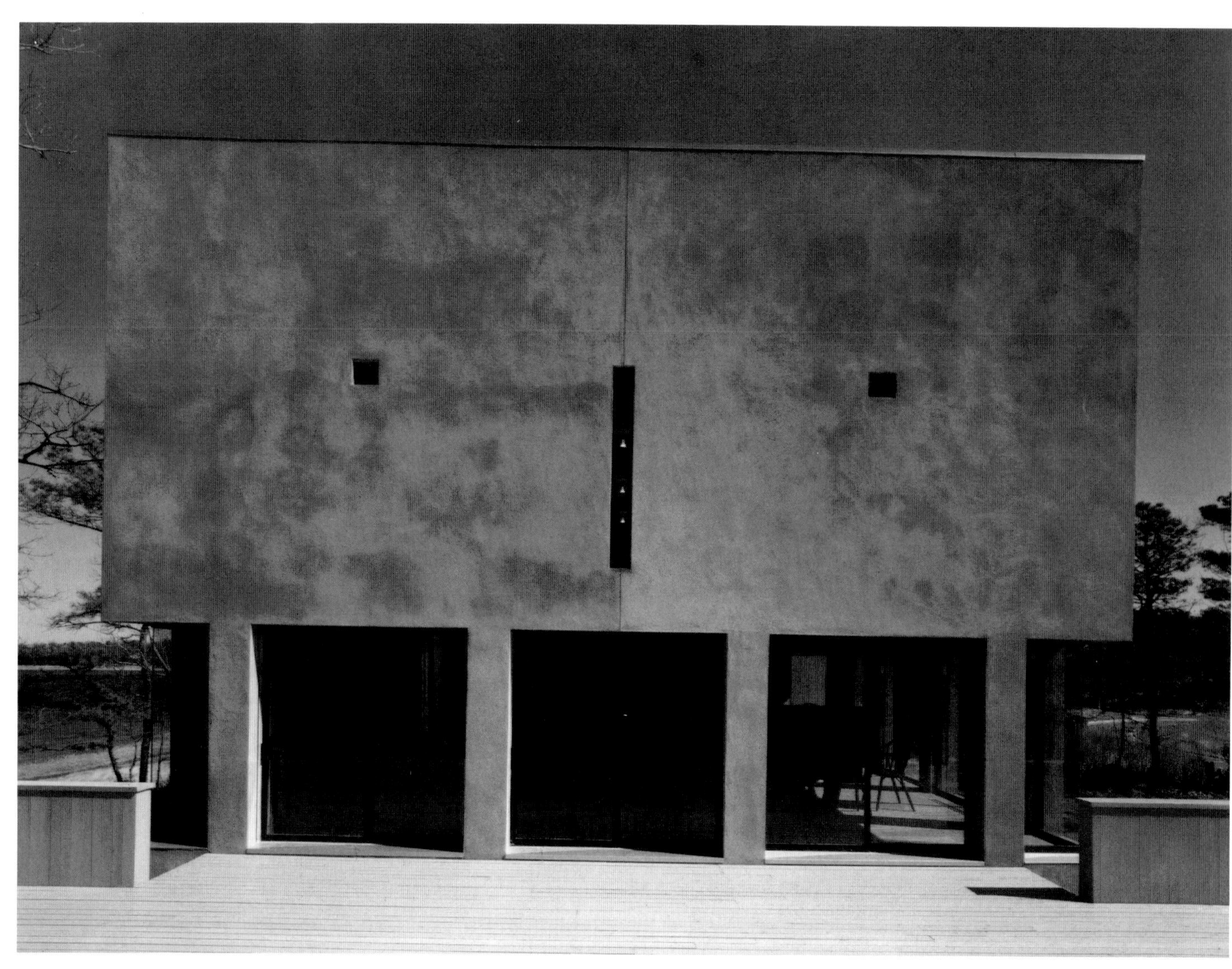

Robert McAnulty and Tod Williams; Tod Williams and Associates. Private Residence. Southport, New York, 1985.

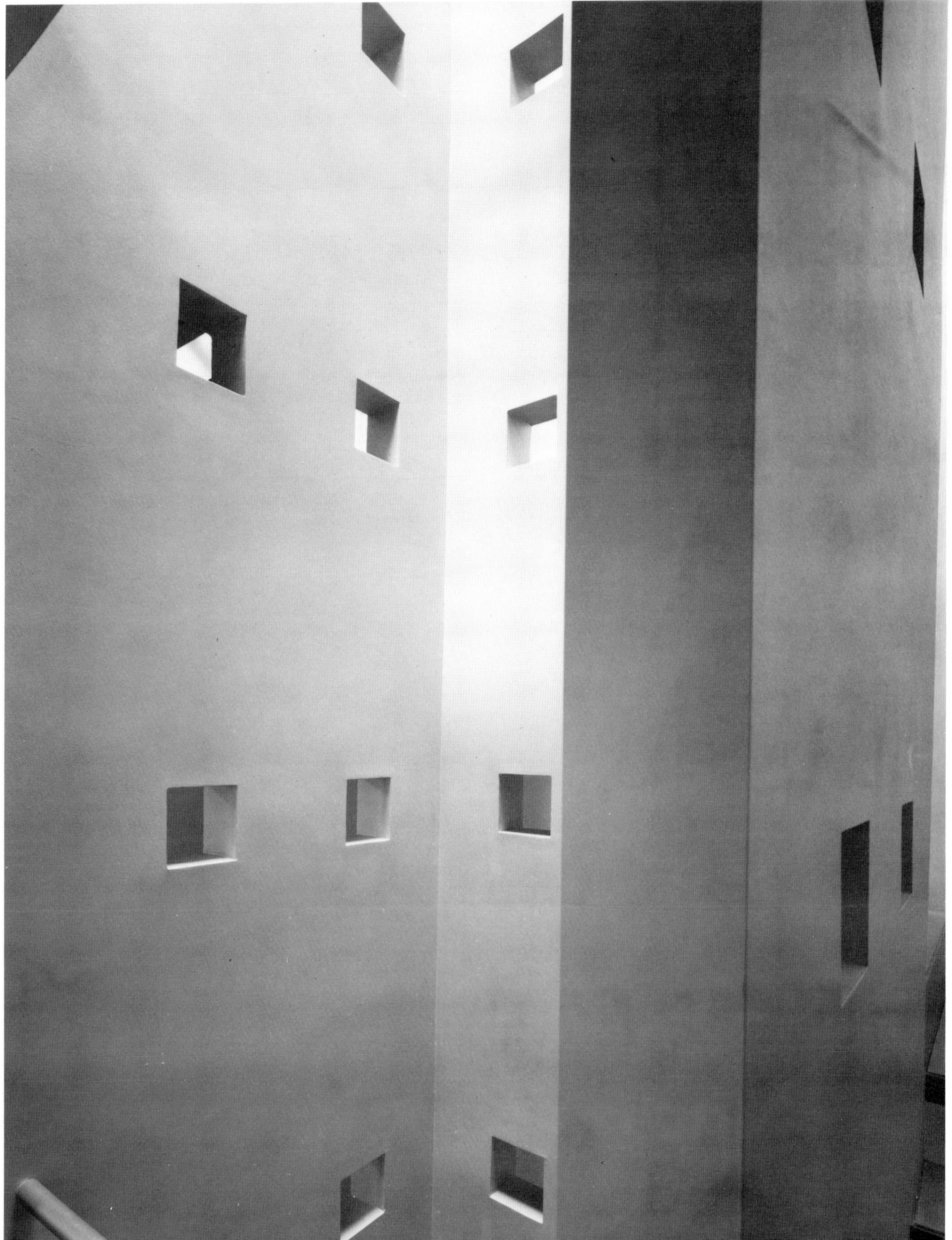

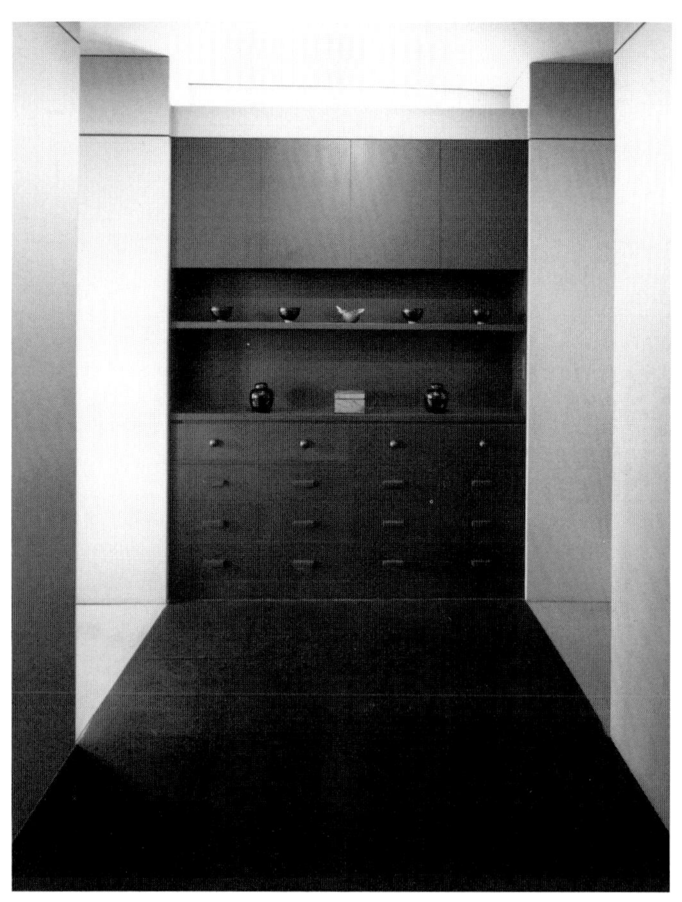

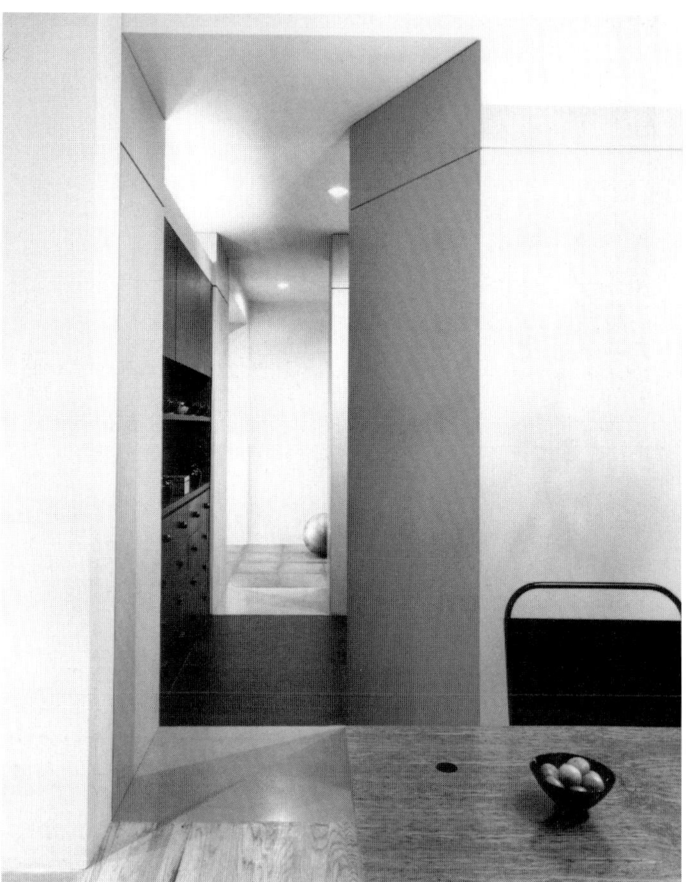

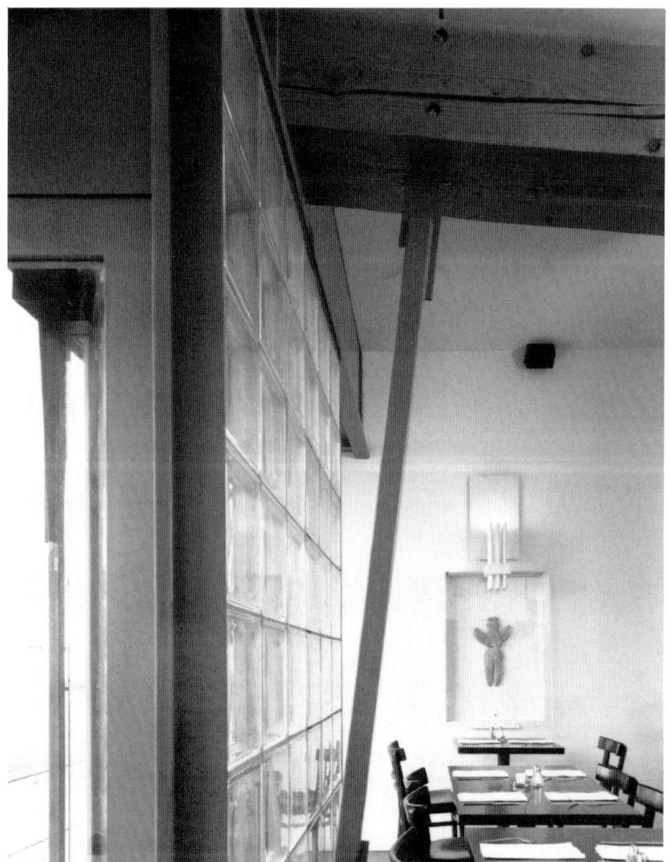

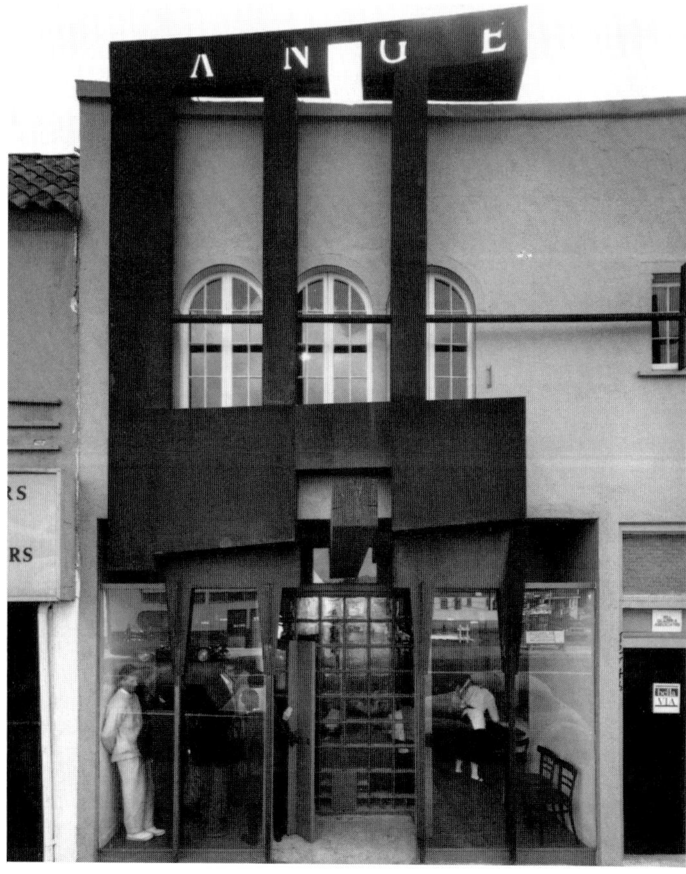

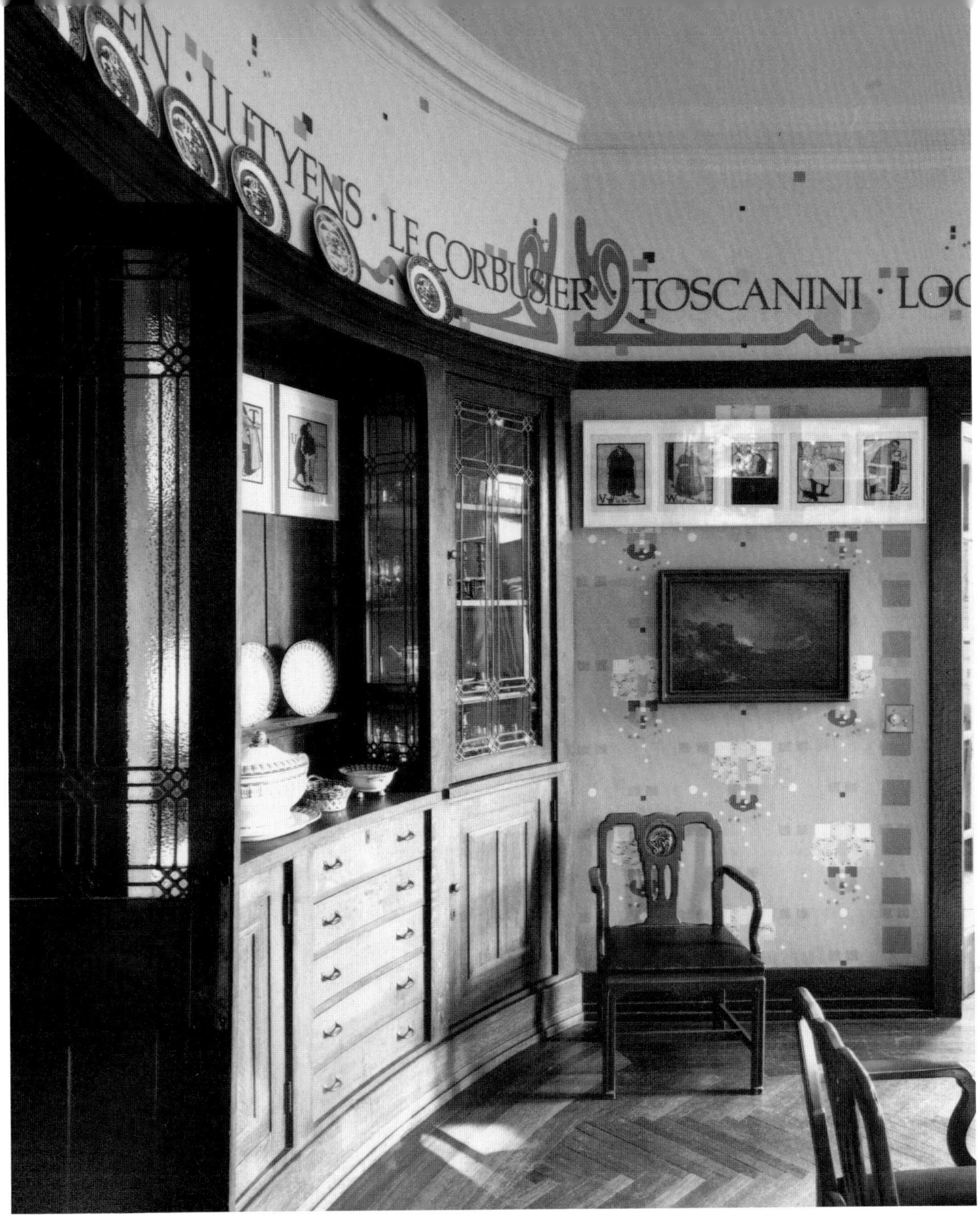

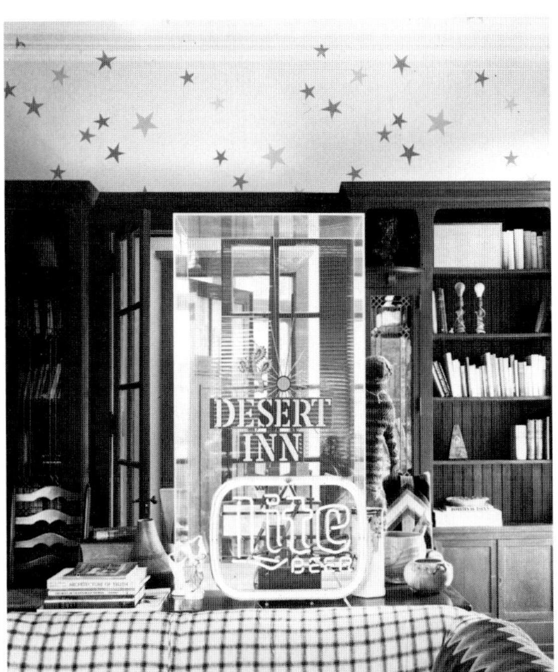

TOP AND LEFT: Robert Venturi. Robert Venturi and Denise Scott-Brown Residence. Philadelphia, Pennsylvania, 1983.

FACING PAGE (TOP): Calvin Tsao. Calvin Tsao Residence. New York, New York, 1983.

FACING PAGE (BOTTOM): Mayne-Rotondi/Morphosis. Angeli. Los Angeles, California, 1985.

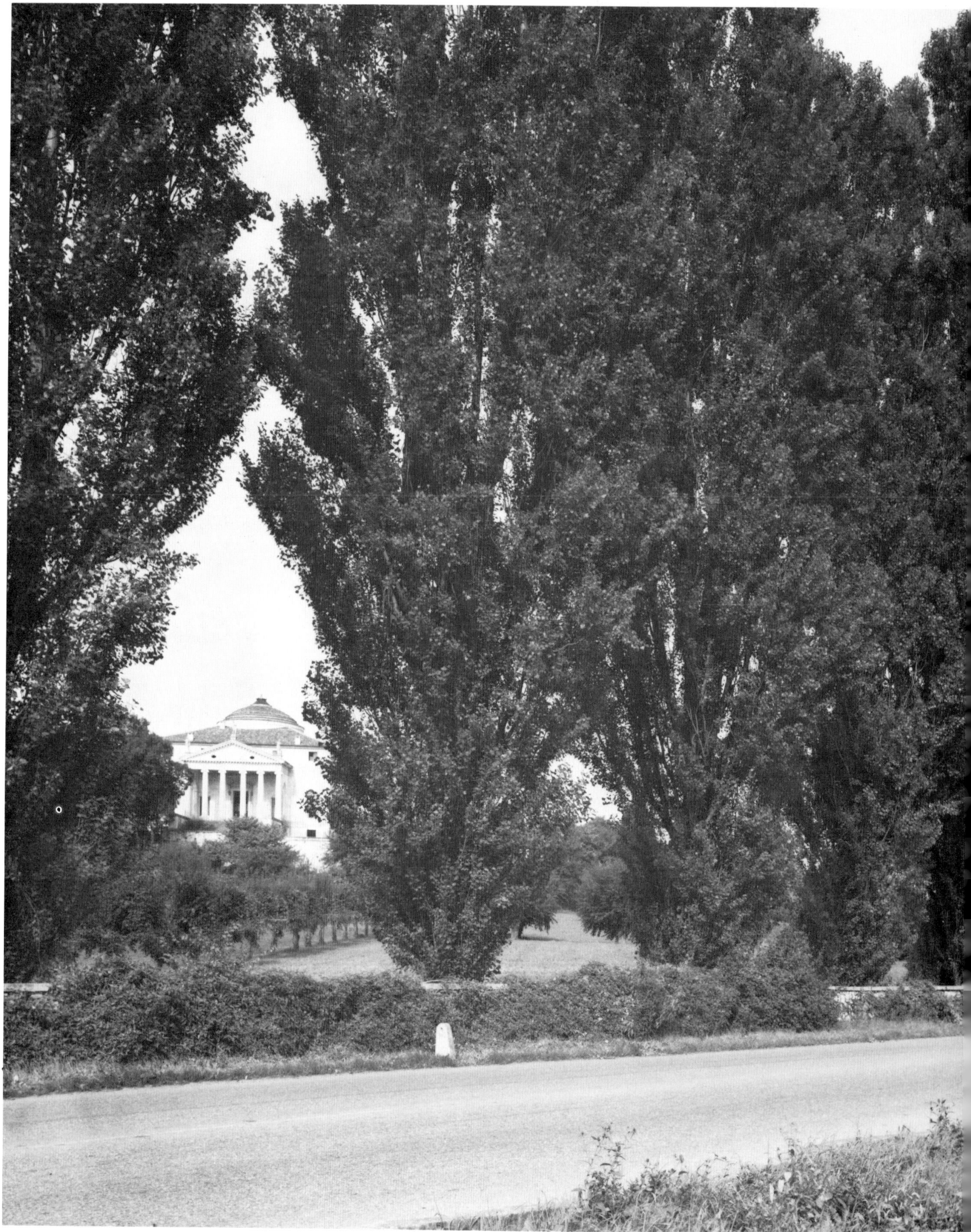

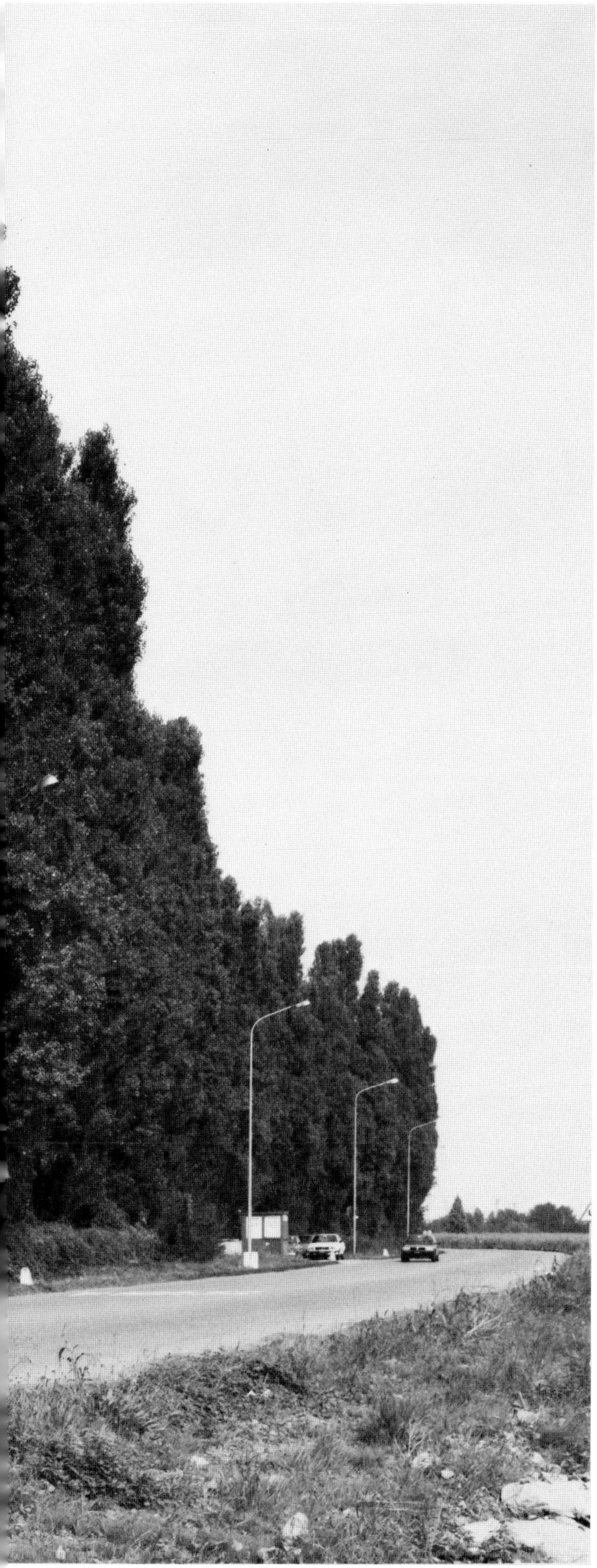

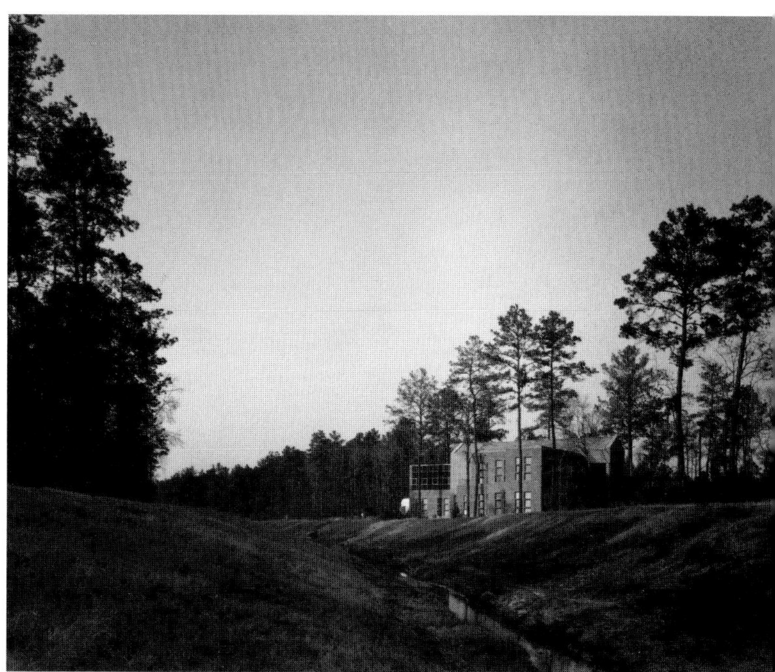

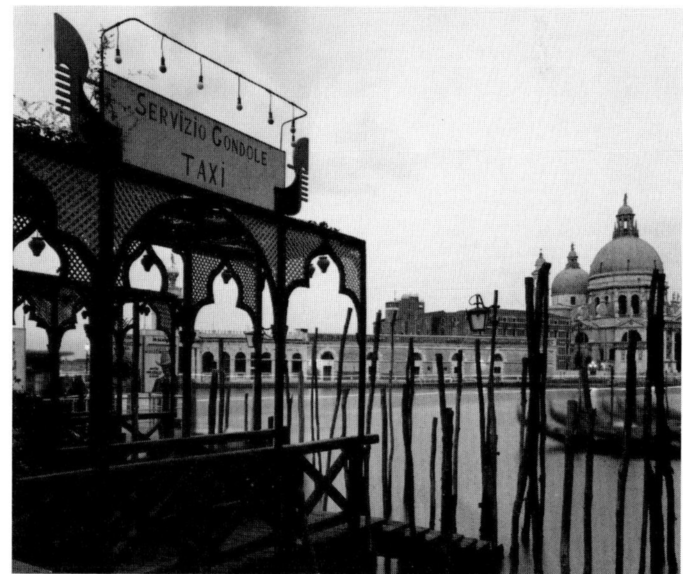

TOP: Taft Architects/John J. Casbarian, Danny Samuels, Robert H. Timme. Water Resources Office Building. The Woodland, Texas, 1985.

BOTTOM: Venice, 1984

FACING PAGE: Andrea Palladio. Villa La Rotonda. Vicenza, Italy, 1984.

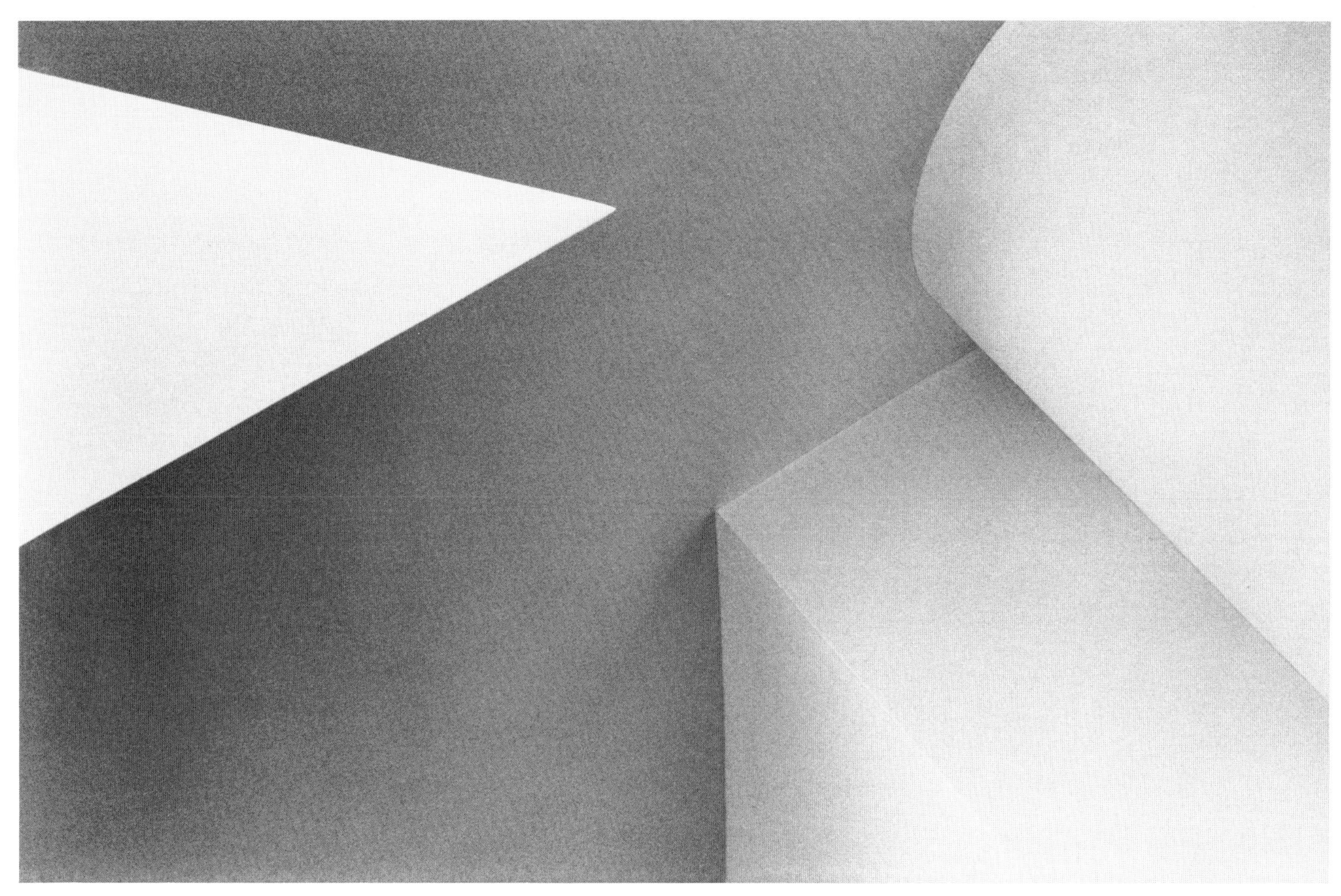

Davis, Brody and Associates. Philip Morris U.S.A. Operations Center. Richmond, Virginia, 1982.

JUDITH TURNER

"I do not believe that at first any architect has a total image of an entire architecture simultaneously—to my experience or knowledge it doesn't work that way. There may be a series of images one after the other over a period of time, but that period of time, no matter how small, is a necessary ingredient for the evolution toward a totality. It must be understood that so-called total architecture is ultimately made up of parts and fragments and fabrications." [1]

In this introduction to *Judith Turner Photographs Five Architects,* John Hejduk suggests that the architect's image of a building is, in fact, a series of images; while these fragments may compose themselves into a whole in the building, they remain, in the mind's eye, fragments. These fragments, then, are the subject of Judith Turner's work. She observes that "if an architect designs a building with a series of images in mind, then it follows that one photograph of one fragment can capture the idea of the architecture."

Turner's architectural still lifes indeed record these fragments. As architect Michael Graves points out, they are not details, and this fact "is what gives them their great interest." [2] The difference is crucial to Turner's work. Architectural details are complete items in themselves—a cornice or the capital of a column, a porch or a gable. A fragment is a piece of the whole; it is not complete, but rather a part or portion that may be suggestive of the whole.

But it is not only these pieces of the built world that interest Turner, but the less material components of architecture. "Architecture is the perfect subject matter for the things I'm interested in," she explains. "Ambiguity, form, light, and geometry. I can explore these through architecture; architecture is a point of departure."

What separates Turner's work from the work of so many other photographers who use architecture simply as a point of departure is that her work also reveals the architecture. Many photographers have chosen architecture as their subject matter without becoming architectural photographers. It is a profession that is constituted, perhaps, by the ability and willingness to give equal recognition to architecture and photograph, to the building and its representation. It is a medium that reveals and, at its best, illuminates the intent of the architect, and its value is in how clearly it represents the building rather than how deftly it reconstructs the image to make its own point.

What distinguishes Judith Turner's work is that while her photographs clearly use architecture as a departure point, they *also* clarify it. Her visual renderings of space, light, and form set out to capture fragments and essences of architecture, and the distinguished roster of architects who value her work suggests that the photographs have succeeded. While her work is clearly interpretive, the interpretations coincide gracefully with the intentions of the architects she works with. Says one, "Her work doesn't refer very strongly to any large-scale composition, but it does deal with the spirit of architecture. Judith Turner captures details, textures, patterns, the quality of light rather than the overall images; it's the spirit of the building rather than its more practical side." [3] Turner's clients are not the architectural press, nor advertisers, nor public relations firms, but architects themselves who find in her abstract compositions illuminating portraits of their work.

Turner's photographs reveal architecture in a manner very different from more conventional architectural photography. In introducing the photographs of Eugene Atget, John Szarkowski, director of the department of photography at the Museum of Modern Art says, "From the hundreds of photographs that he made at Versailles, one could not reconstruct an approximate diagram of the park's form or extent, for he photographed not the topography of the place, but what he understood to be its essence." [4] The same might be said for the manner in which Turner records buildings; her photographs are interested neither in an approximate nor inapproximate diagram of the place. It is spirit rather than substance she locates through them.

To do so, Turner has reduced architecture to its most elementary components. Two-dimensional shapes, used sparingly and concisely, make up a fundamental vocabulary that reflects a longstanding interest in graphic design and painting. Architecture, in Turner's eye, is made up of flat planes; walls, ceilings, floors, and columns connect to compose three-dimensional forms. Even the skies in Turner's photographs are cloudless. "I want the sky to read as a flat plane," she explains. "That's part of my interest in form. If there's a cloud, then the surface becomes a sky rather than a flat plane."

To reduce the visual world to its most elementary components, Turner uses a simple vocabulary of light and form. It is no surprise, then, that the architecture of or influenced by the modern movement is her most frequent subject matter. "God is in the details," wrote Mies van der Rohe, and indeed, in much of International Style architecture, how an arch rests against an exterior wall or a railing leads to a window may suggest the movement and form of the entire space. The preoccupation of postmodern architecture with surface detail is less compelling. Perhaps because its ornamentation, color, and surface detail tend to be small, separate statements in themselves, they remain provocative interjections that are not necessarily integrated into or reflective of any larger whole.

That photography and architecture have found such a graceful fusion in Turner's work is perhaps because her terms—form, geometry, light, and ambiguity—are also the terms used by architects. Turner's photographs are indeed deliberate notations on the rhythm and repetition of form. Progressions of form, intersections and connections, frontal and oblique views are evident in her work. Likewise, geometric studies of form and space inform her work. Her line of vision follows straight, curved, and broken lines; squares, circles, triangles and horizontal, vertical, and diagonal planes are all noted.

Turner studies as well how architecture is informed, and transformed, by light. But she examines not only how the built world takes its shape from light, but how we perceive it, how our perceptions are shaped and directed by the quality of light, and how illusions are created, revealed, and accepted often as stand-ins for the real thing. Which brings us perhaps to the quality that gives Turner's work its most enduring value—the fact that these photographs not only record buildings, but record the way buildings are perceived.

And in this sense, Turner's work is a register of ambiguity in our perceptions of the built world. It traces positive becoming negative and negative becoming positive. It suggests the ease with which a solid becomes a void. While the fact that things are not always what they seem to be has certainly been suggested before, it has not always been with such visual eloquence. A shaft of light appears to have the strength of a marble column; the curve of a stone arch conveys a lightness that disputes its physical mass.

But there is more to the ambiguity than this. On the one hand, her work gives us an accurate transcription of material—the textures of the glass and granite, the feel of plaster and steel. Yet simultaneously, the images are abstract compositions with a value of their own, maintaining a sure distance from the material world of architecture. Removed from the context of architecture, they remain evocative visual statements with a broader universal appeal. That they are able to achieve both again emphasizes their innate ambiguity.

In his introduction Hejduk also points out Turner's recognition of "the precarious balance between the representation of the subject and its realities." [5] What her work observes as clearly is the difference between the perceptions of the subject and its realities. These photographs are as much about seeing architecture as they are about architecture. Turner's photographs record buildings and a way of looking at them. "For me, space is ambiguous," she says. "It's difficult for me to think of it as anything straightforward or well defined. I understand forms as connecting and juxtaposing, both intersecting and penetrating, and space as something formed in and around and through them."

And this, perhaps, is what transforms her fragments into powerful visual images. Space is best defined by what surrounds it—the walls and ceilings that shape it, the arches, doors, and windows that extend it. And like anything else that can be defined only in such indirect terms—in terms, only, of what it is not—it remains ambiguous. Architectural space is itself ambiguous, and it is as records of this ambiguity, perhaps, that these photographs have their most enduring appeal. By being fragments that suggest and evoke, rather than delineate precisely, Turner's vocabulary is indeed one that suits her subject.

---

1. Judith Turner, *Judith Turner Photographs Five Architects* (New York: Rizzoli International Publications, 1980), p. 10.
2. Michael Graves, "International Style Architecture: From Europe to Israel and the United States" (Lecture given at the Jewish Museum, New York, N.Y., 23 October 1984).
3. Arthur May, partner, Kohn Pederson Fox Associates, New York, N.Y. (Telephone conversation with the author, 15 March 1985).
4. John Szarkowski, *The Work of Atget: The Ancien Regime* (Notes for an exhibition at the Museum of Modern Art, New York, N.Y., 14 March–14 May, 1985).
5. Turner, *Photographs Five Architects,* p. 11.

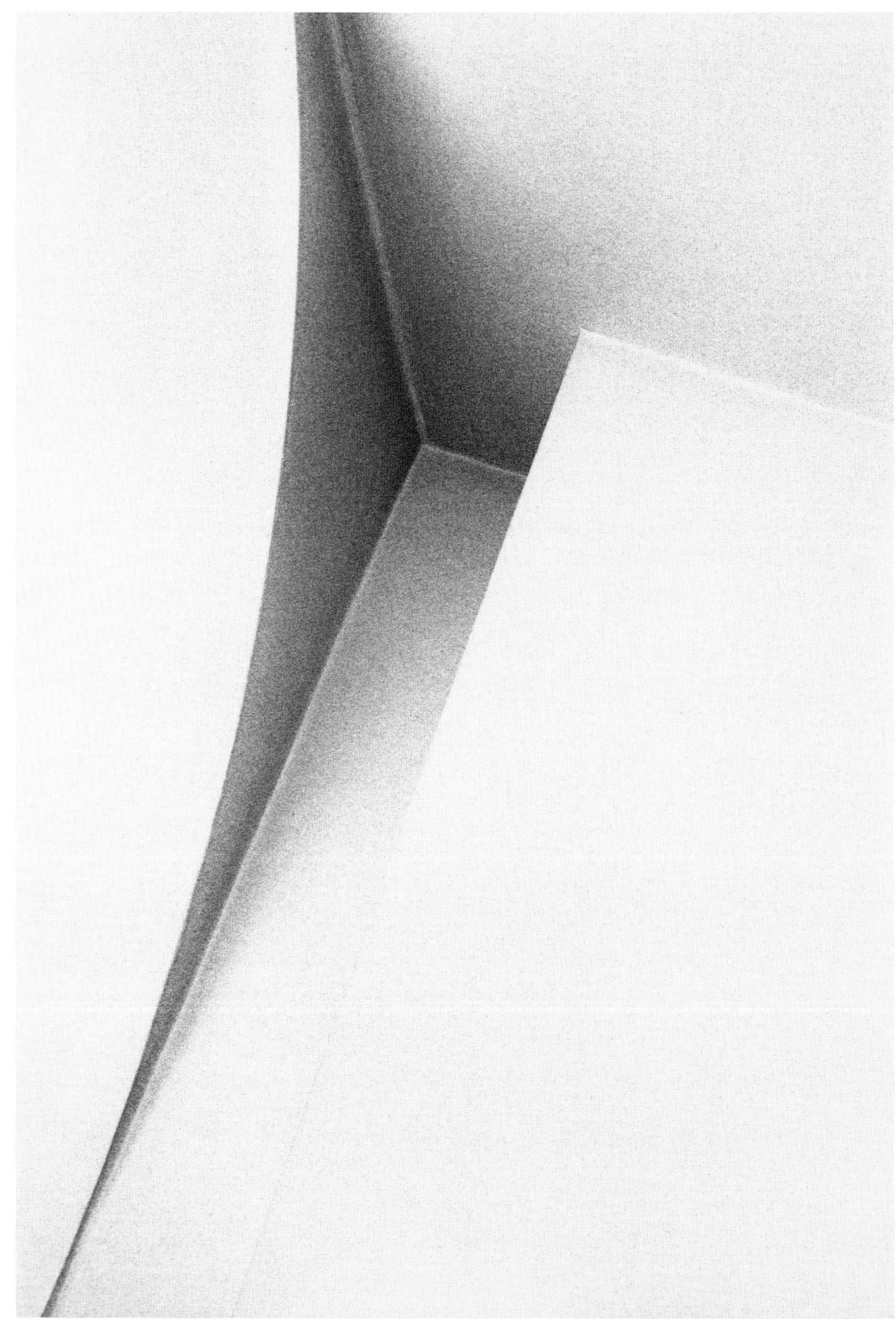

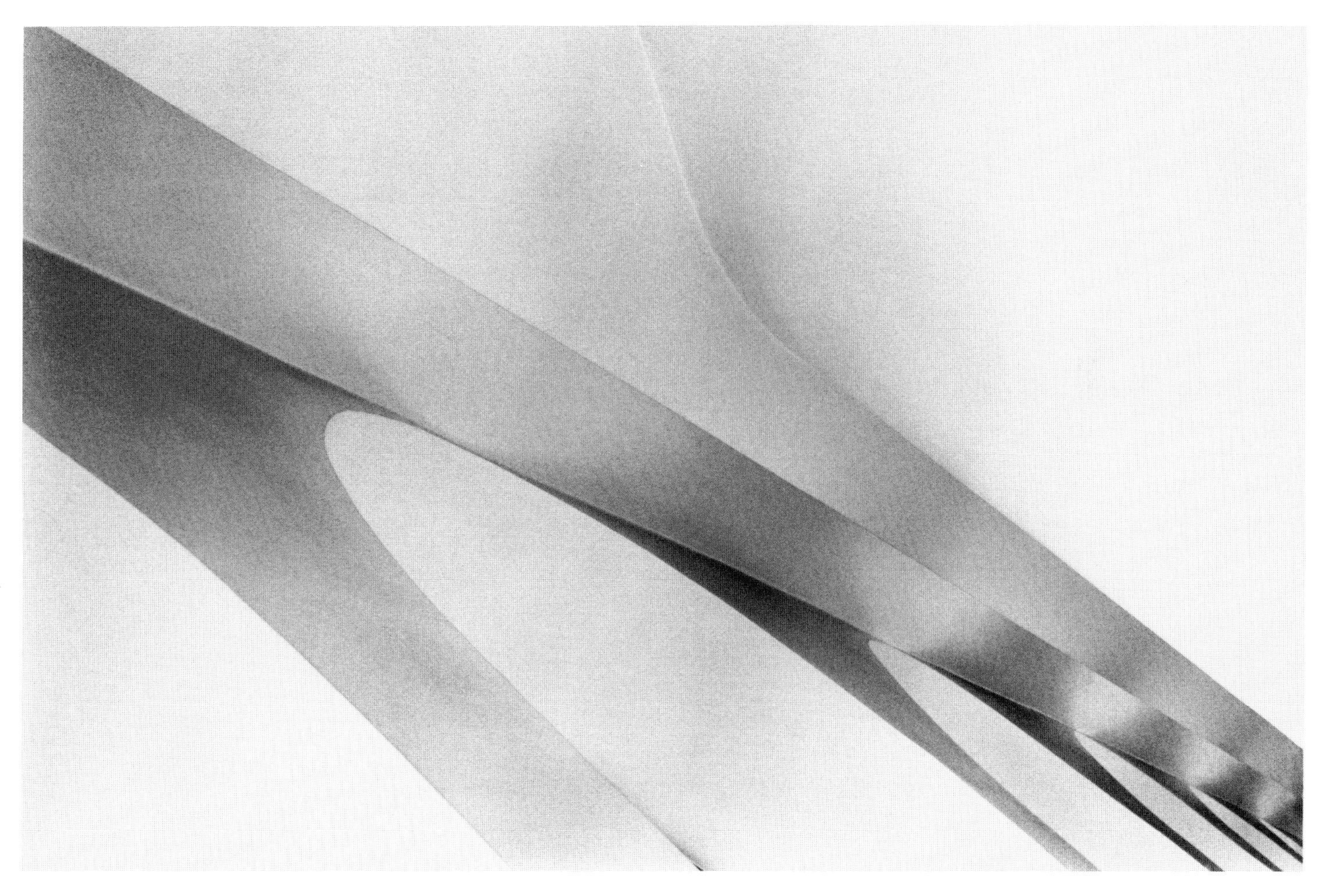

John Hejduk. Cooper Union Renovation. New York, New York, 1979.

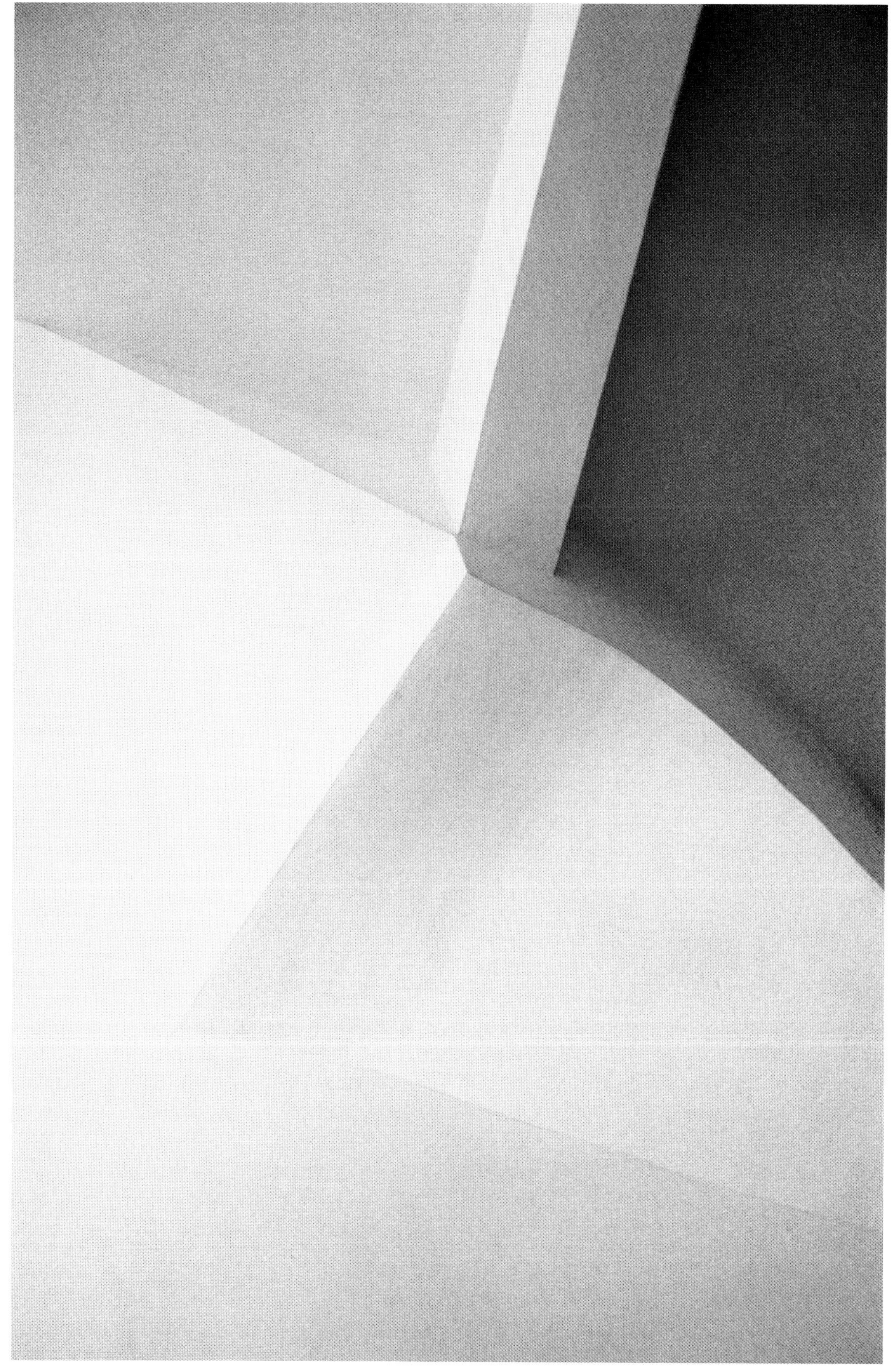

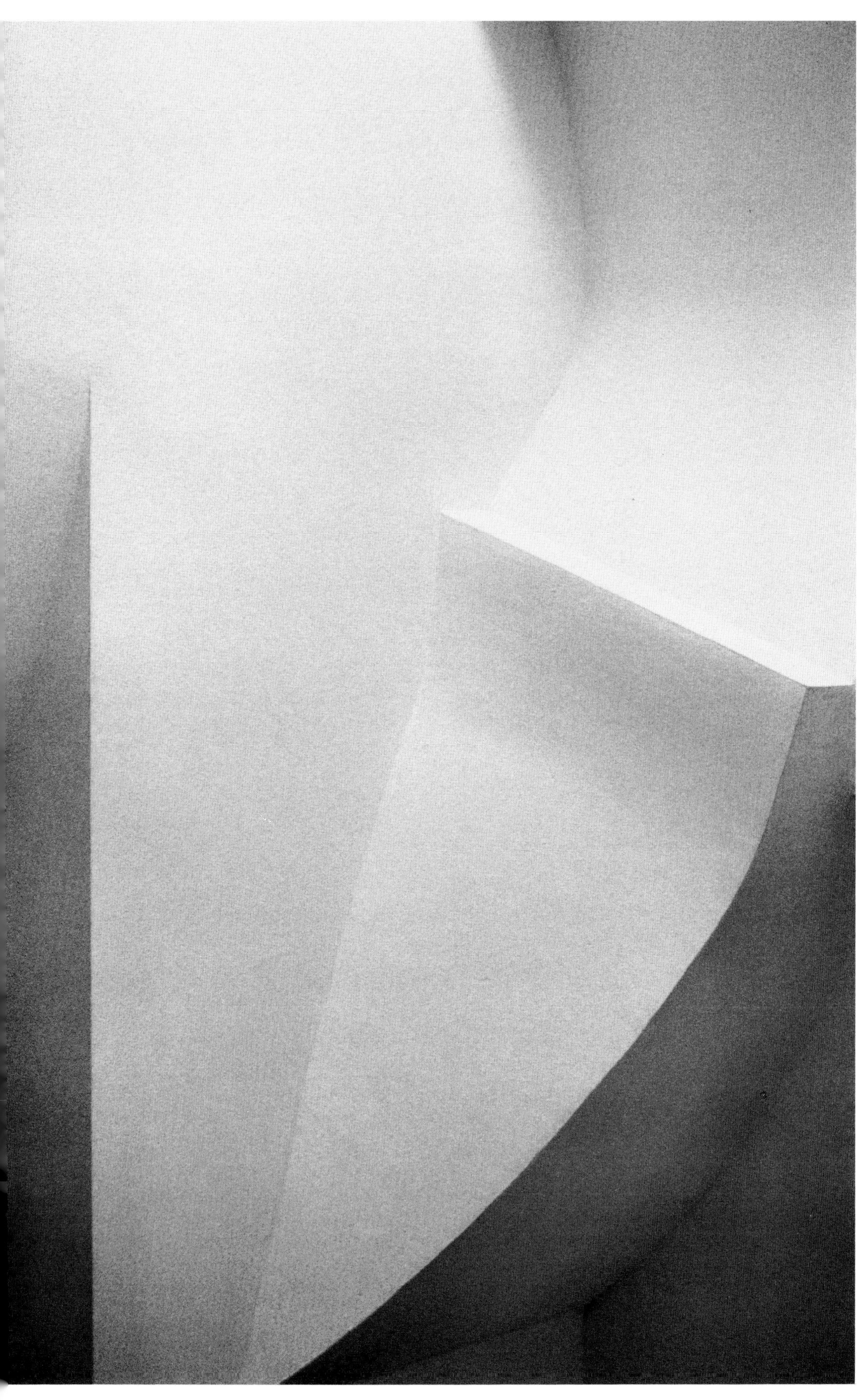

Mallet Stevens.
Private Residence. Paris,
France, 1979.

RIGHT: Coliseum Book Store. New York, New York, 1979.

FACING PAGE: Barnard College, Columbia University. New York, New York, 1979.

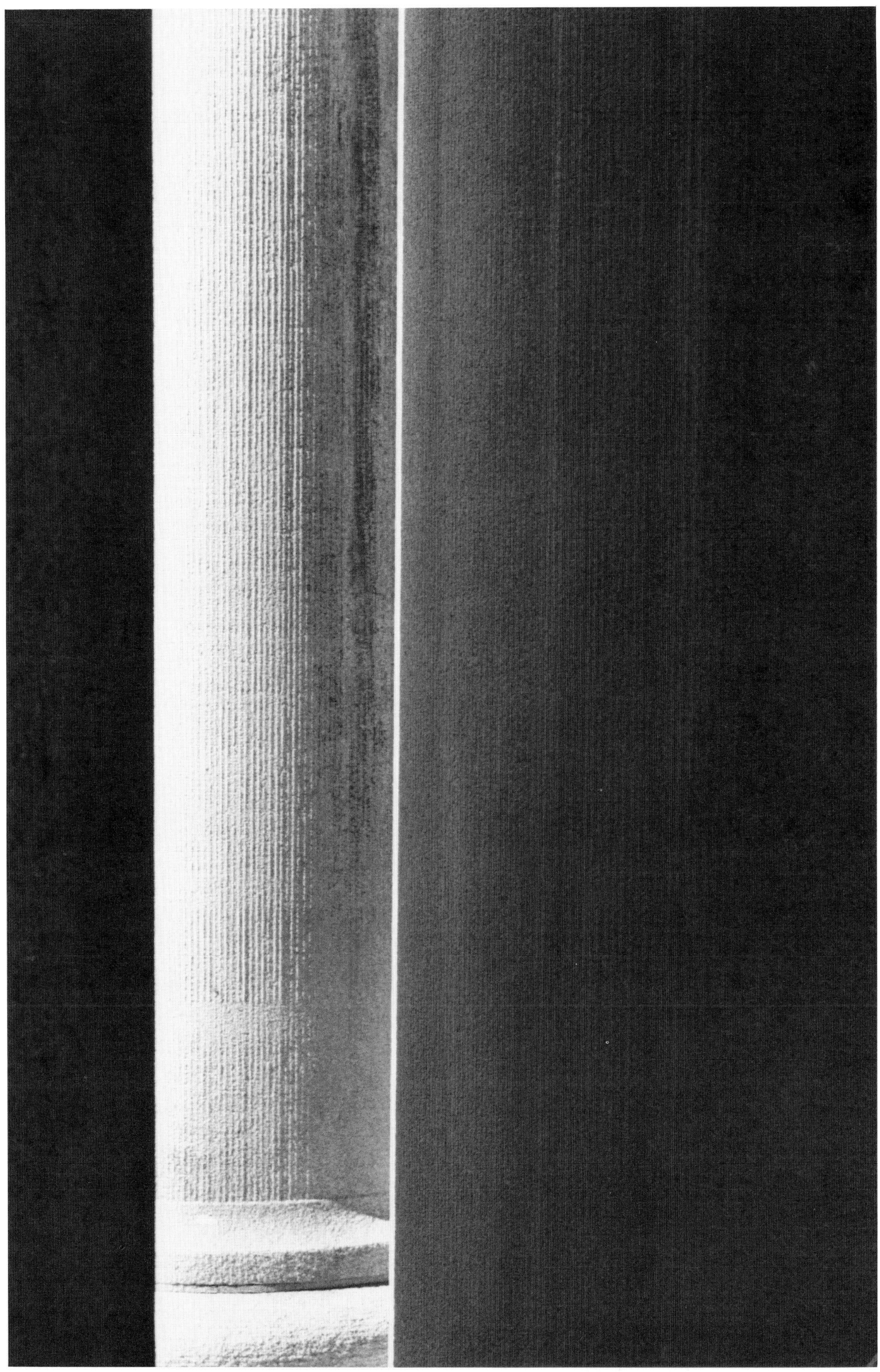

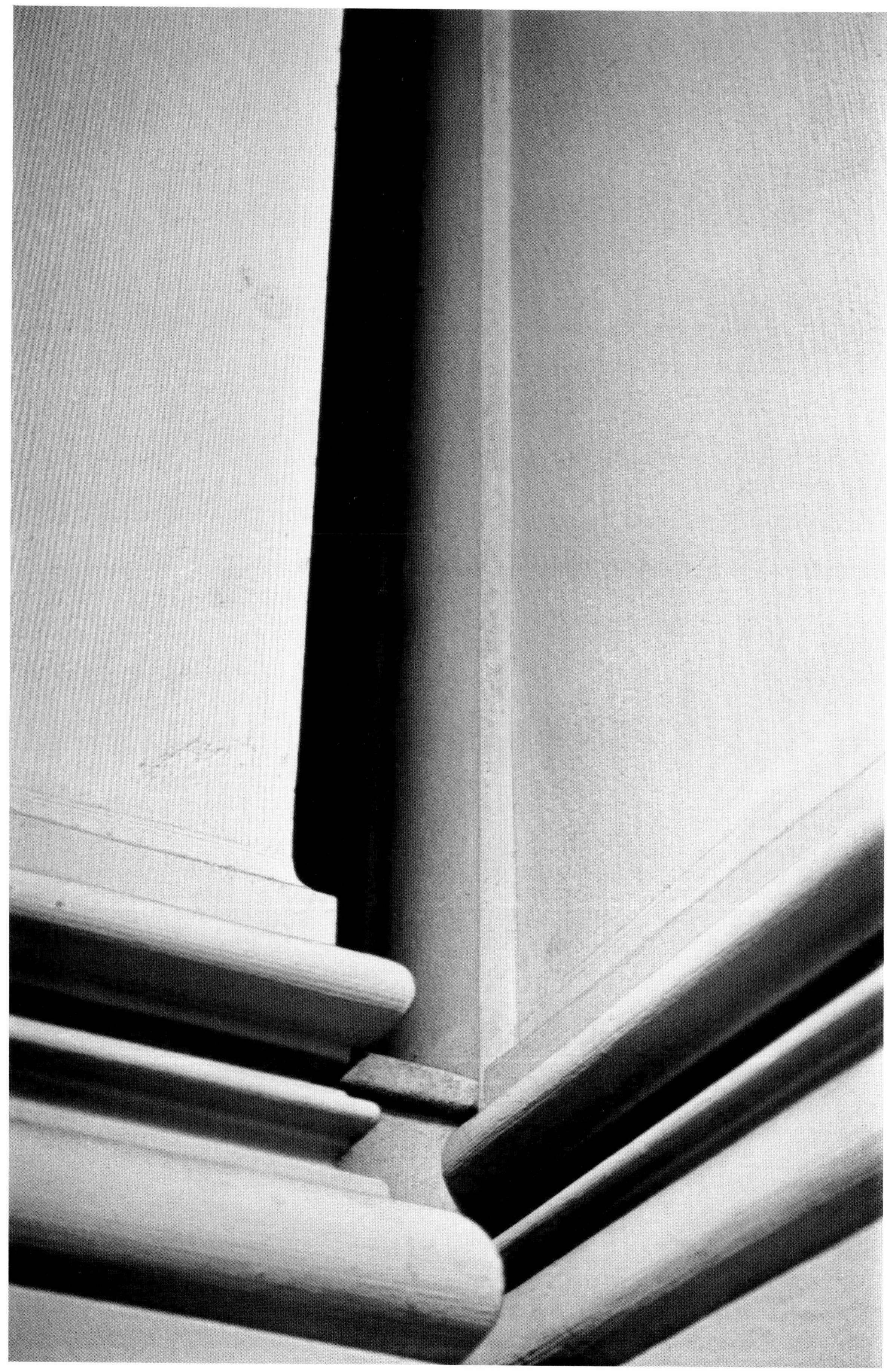

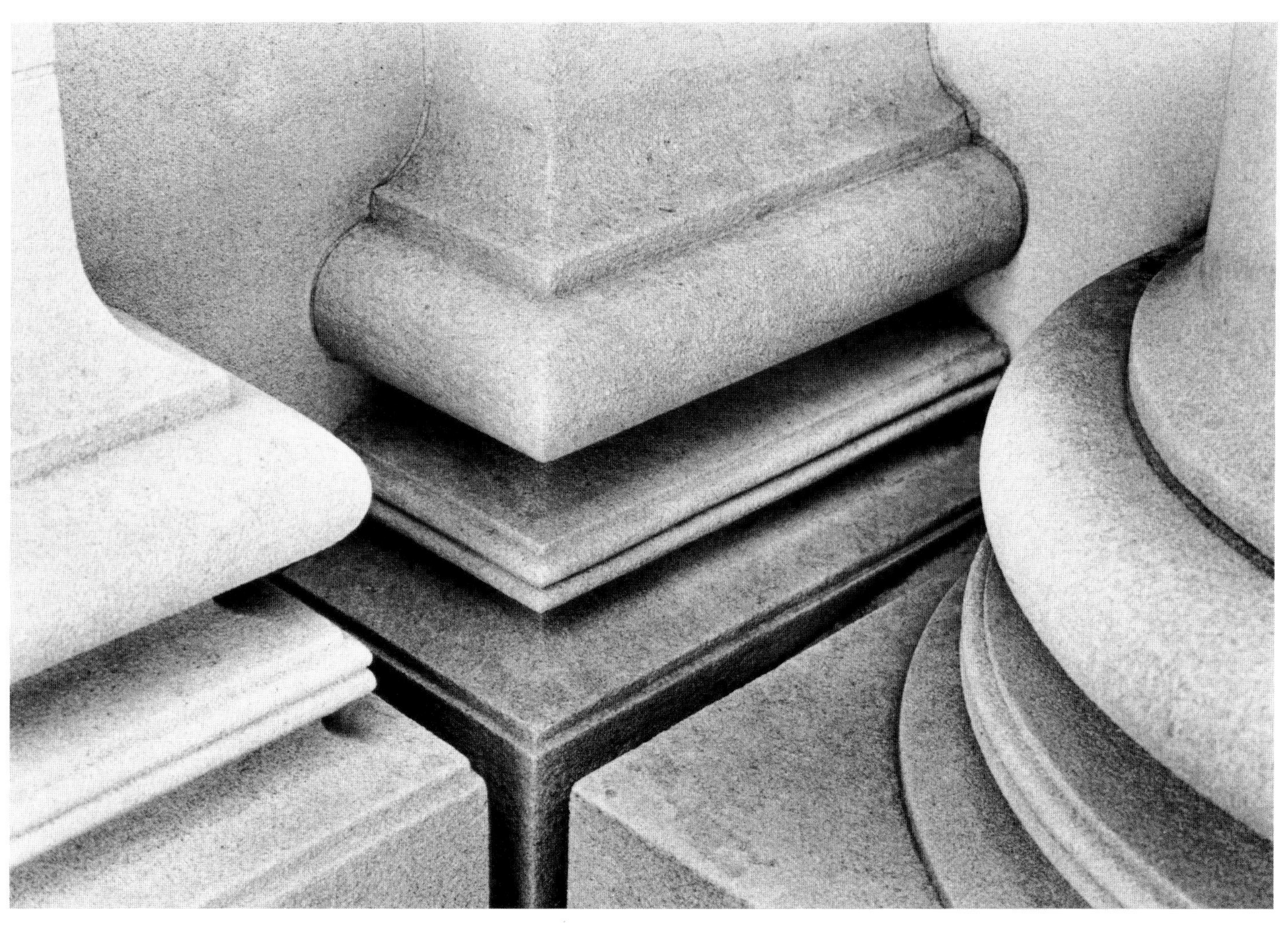

Columns. New York,
New York, 1979

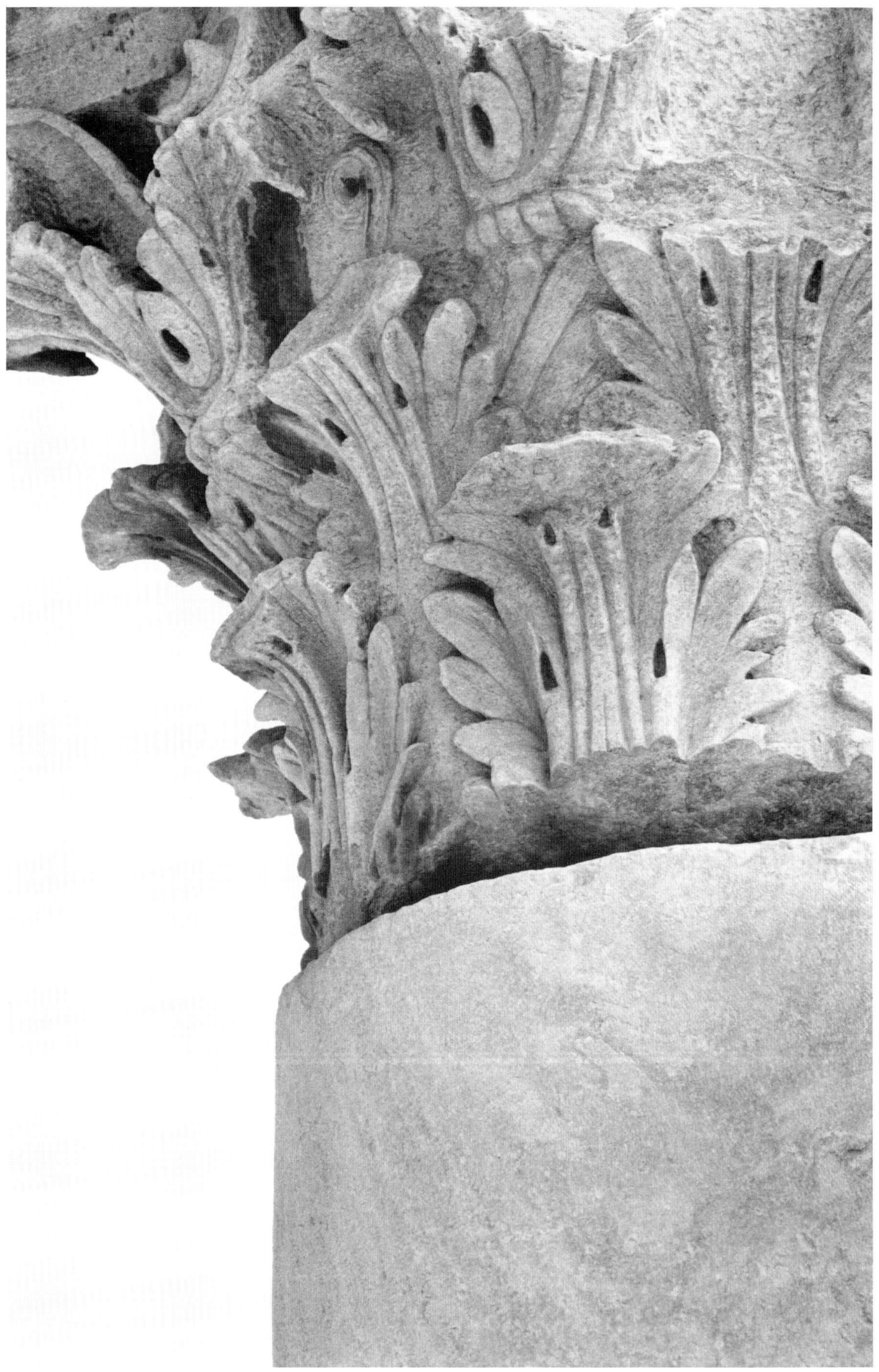

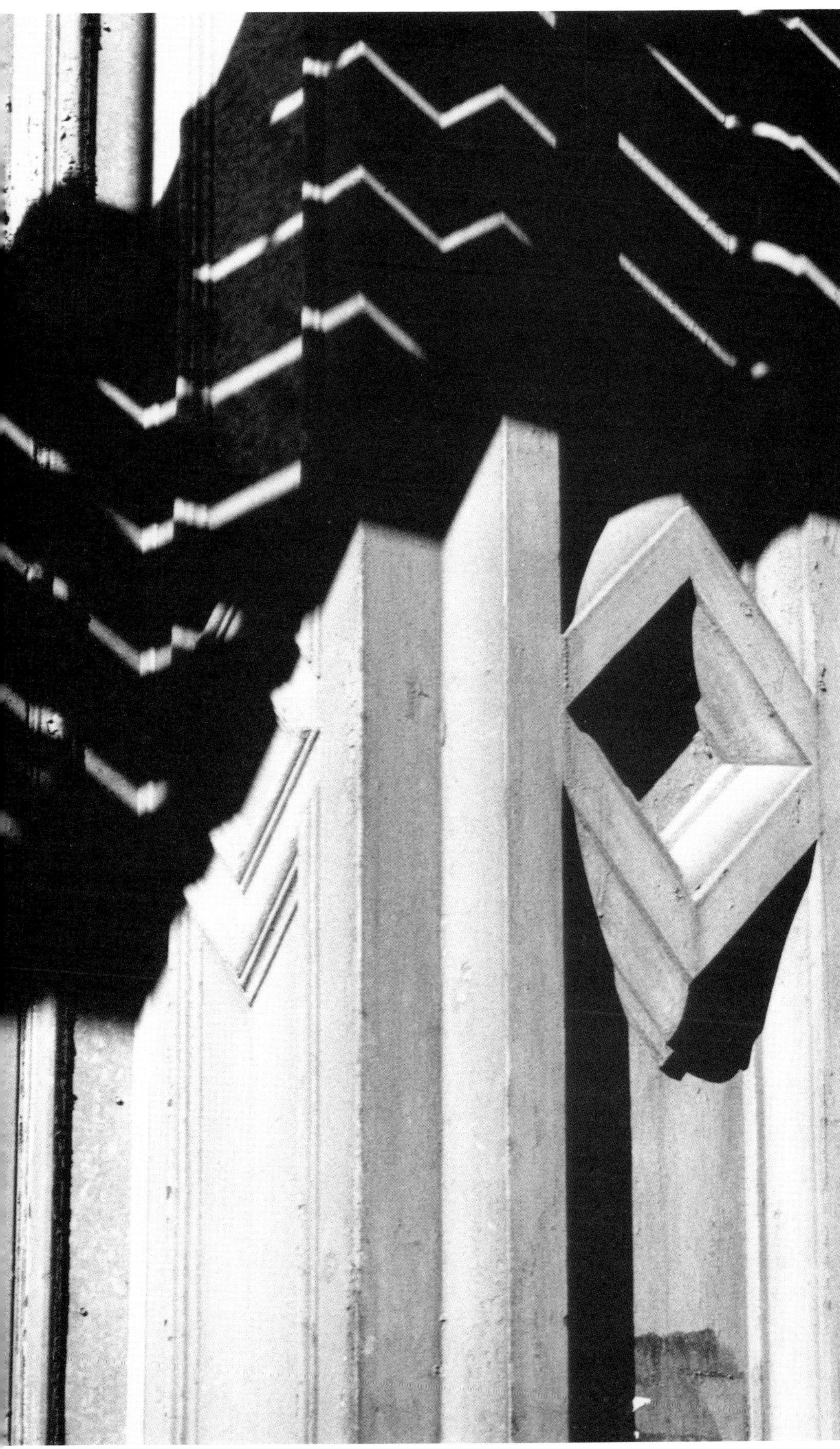

LEFT: Columns. New York, New York, 1979.

FACING PAGE: Corinthian Capital. Corinth, Greece, 1980.

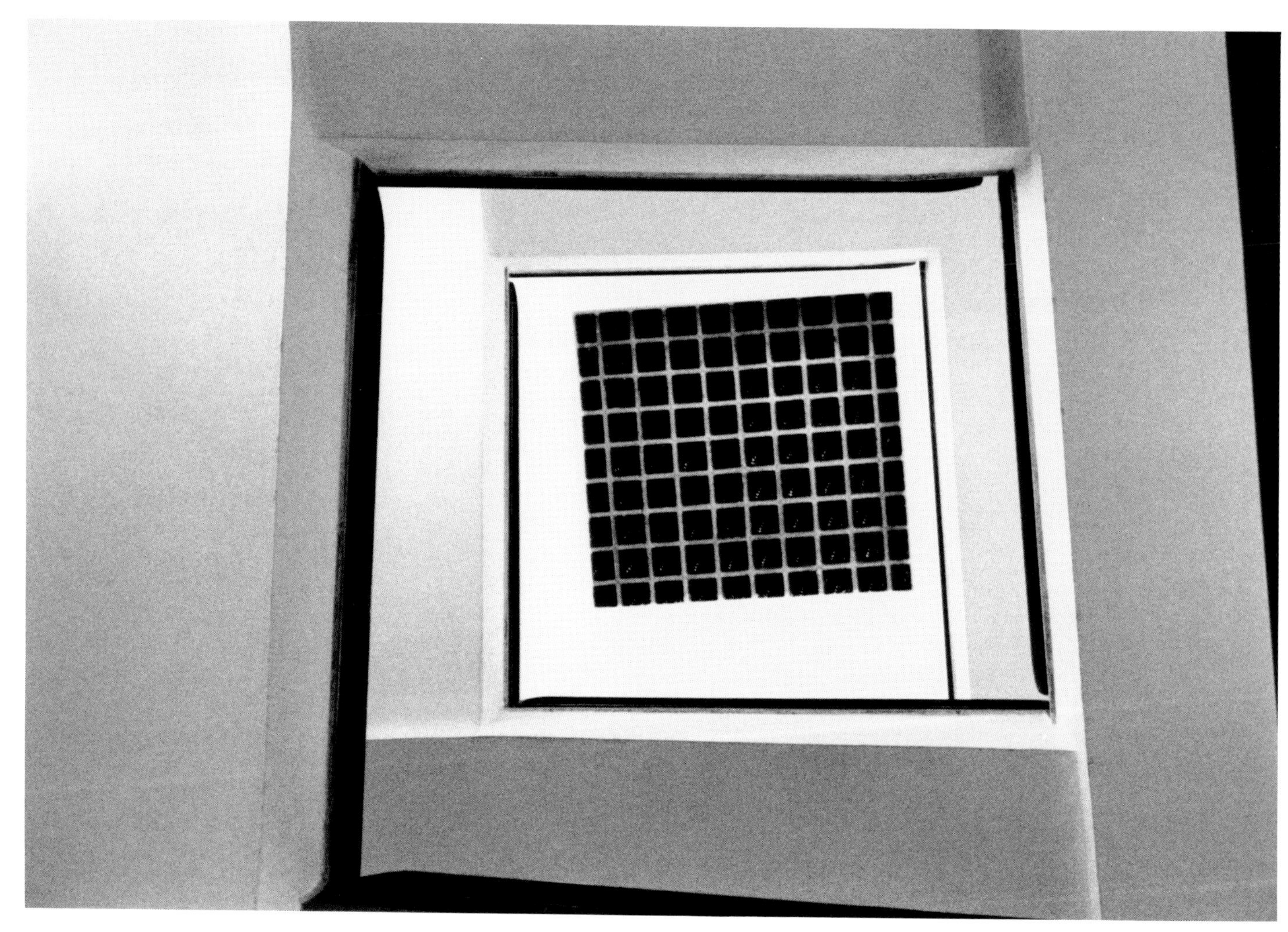

P. Hutt. Apartment
House. Tel Aviv, Israel,
1983.

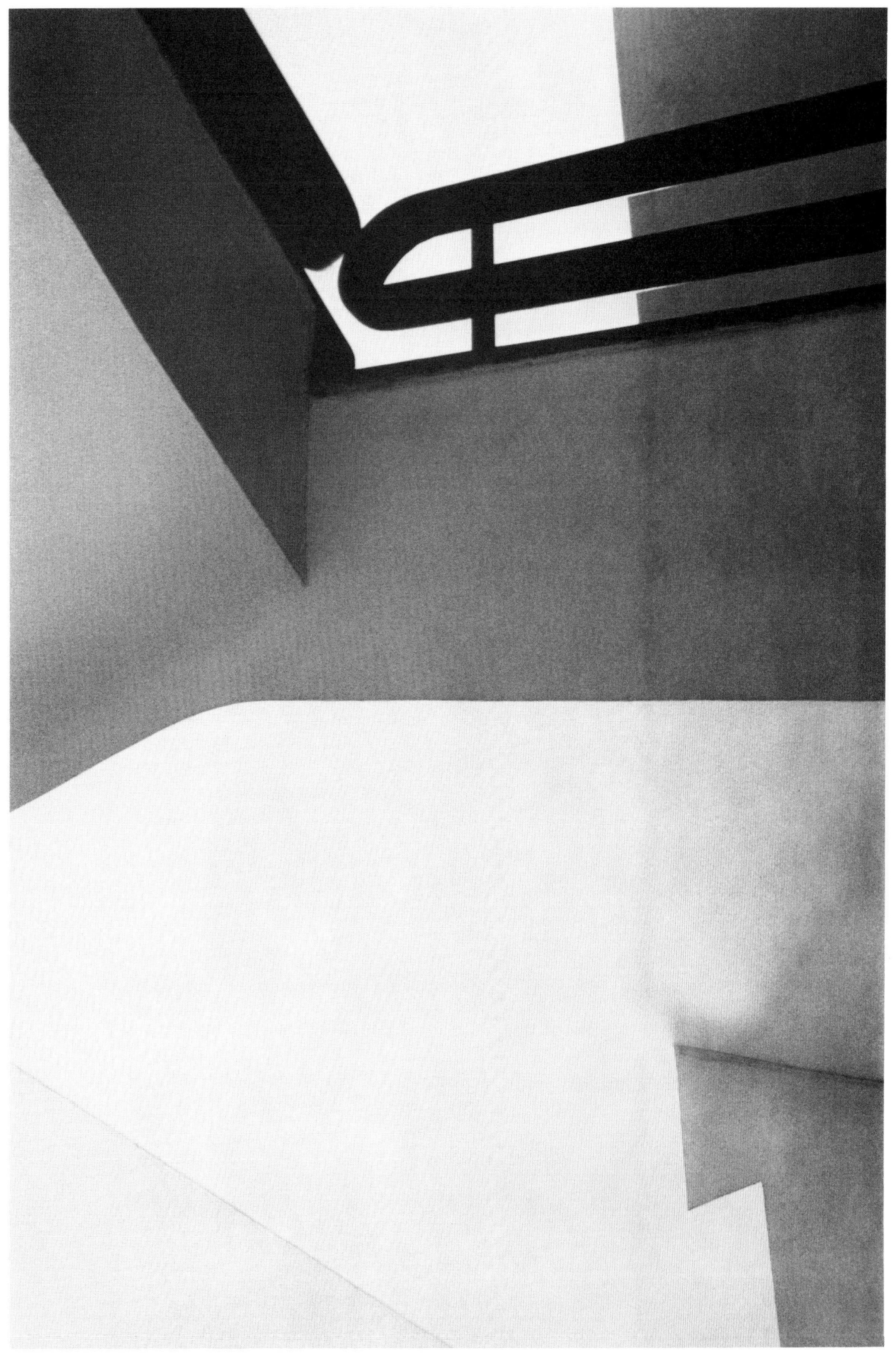

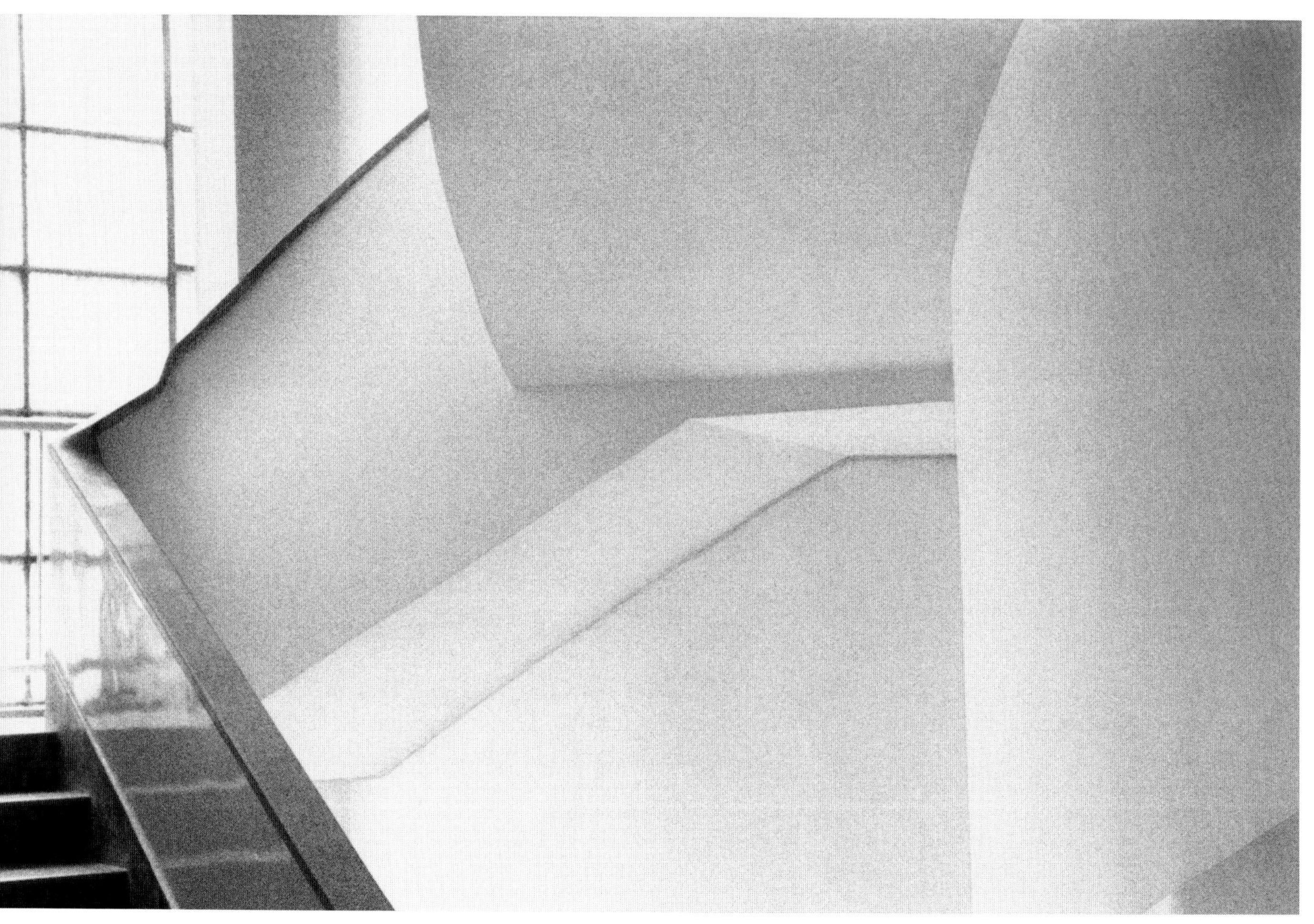

A. Friedman. Apartment House. Jerusalem, Israel, 1982.

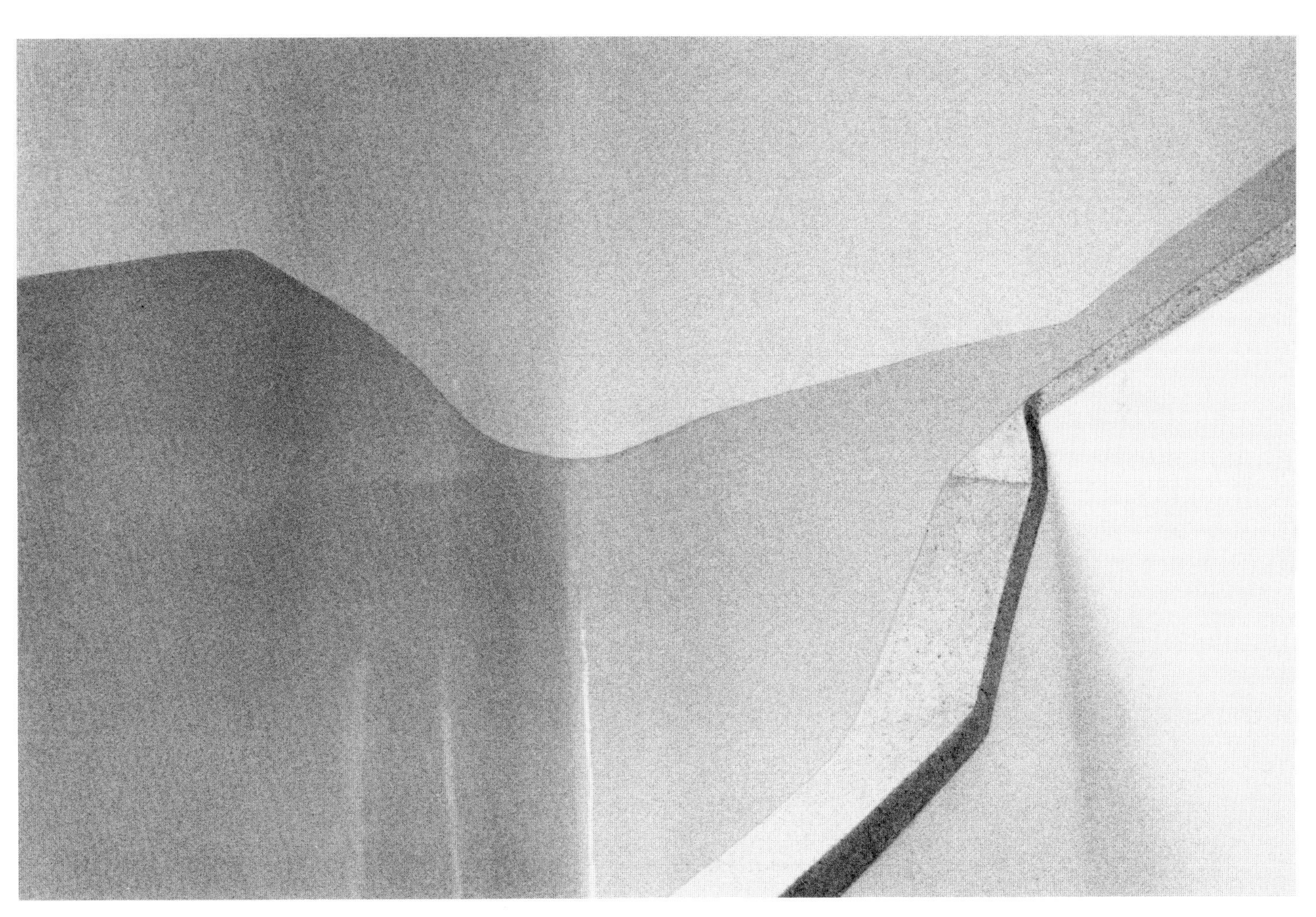

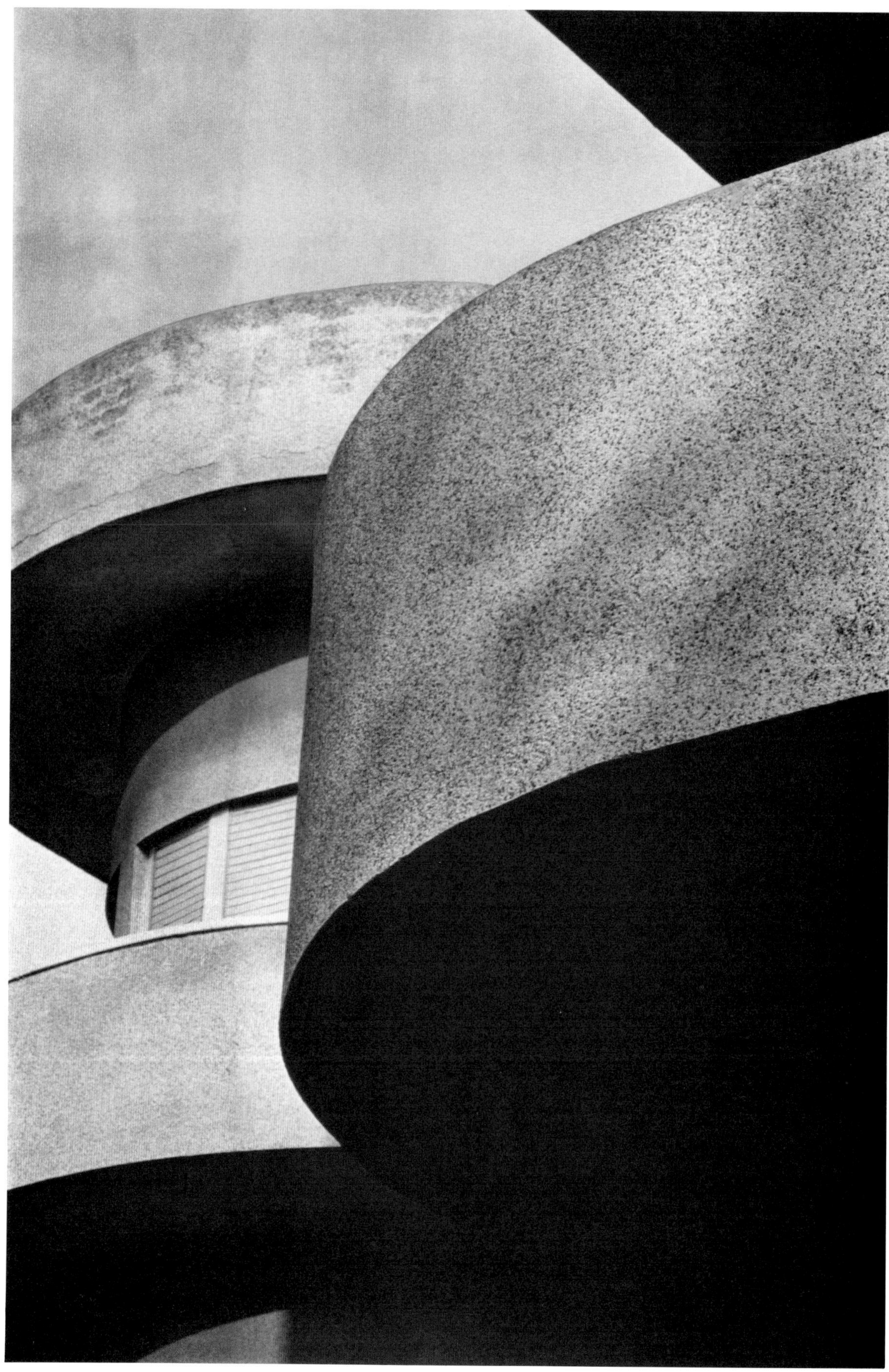

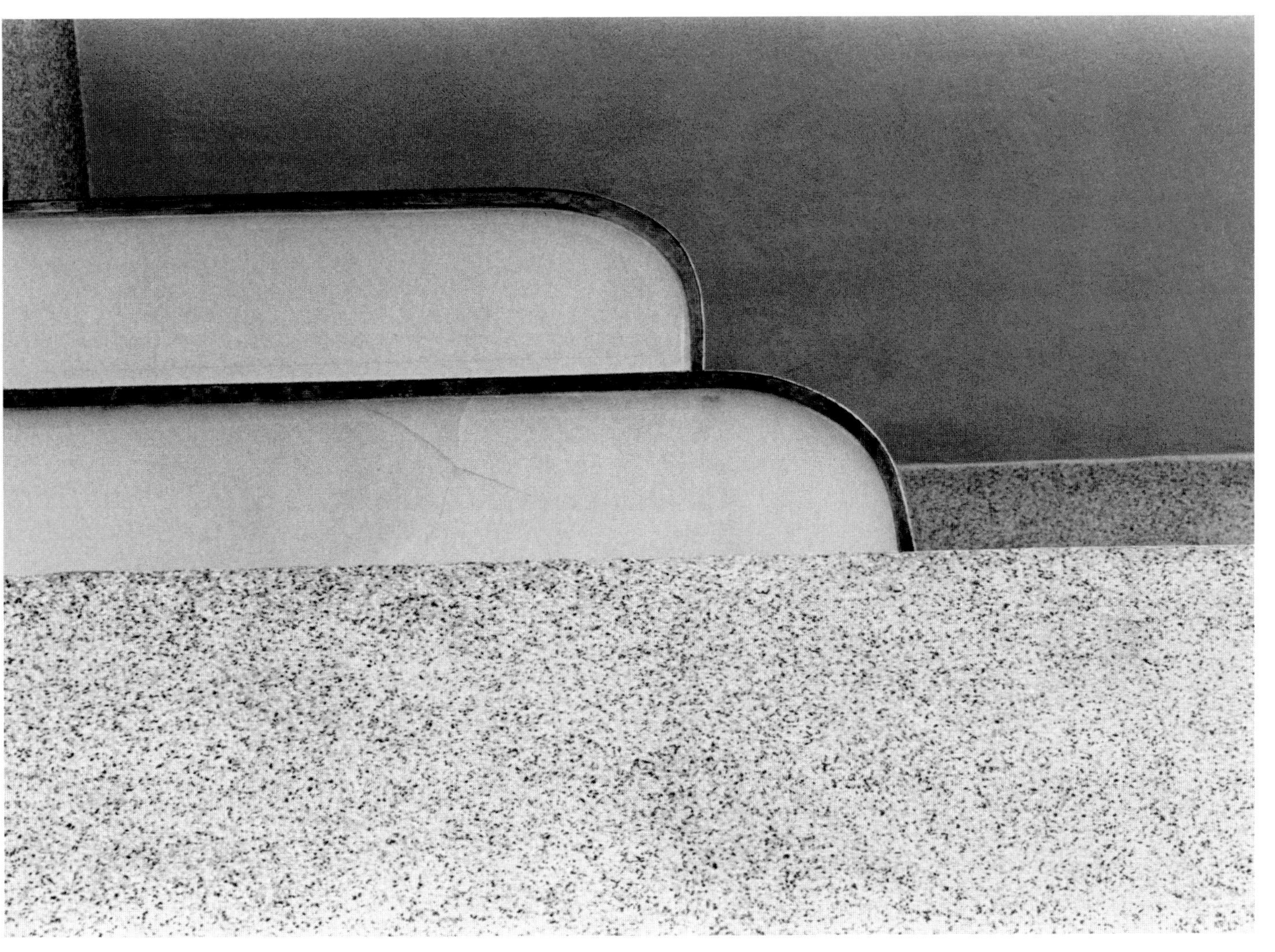

Friedman Brothers.
Apartment House. Tel Aviv,
Israel, 1983.

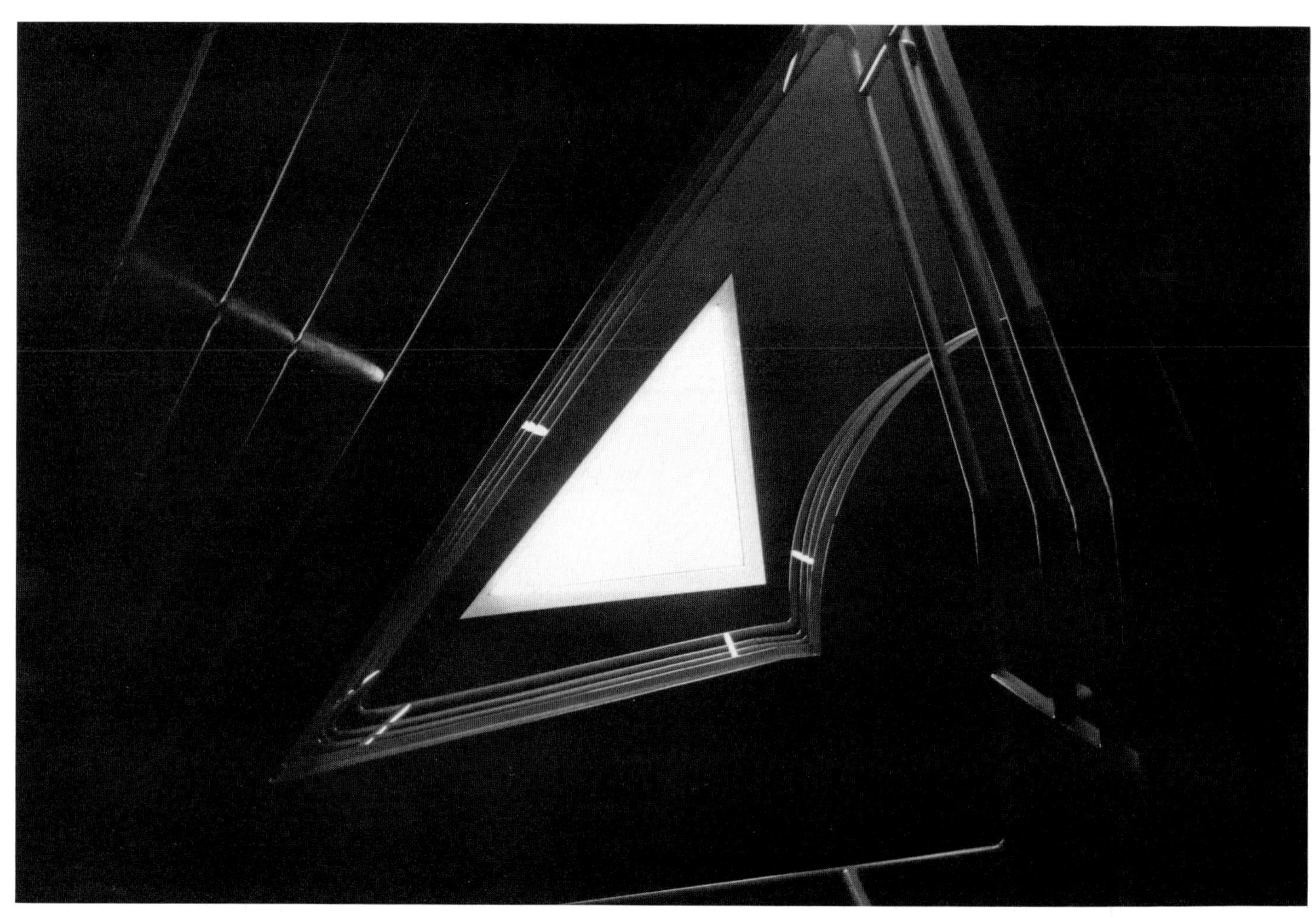

Davis, Brody and Associates. Philip Morris U.S.A. Operations Center. Richmond, Virginia, 1982.

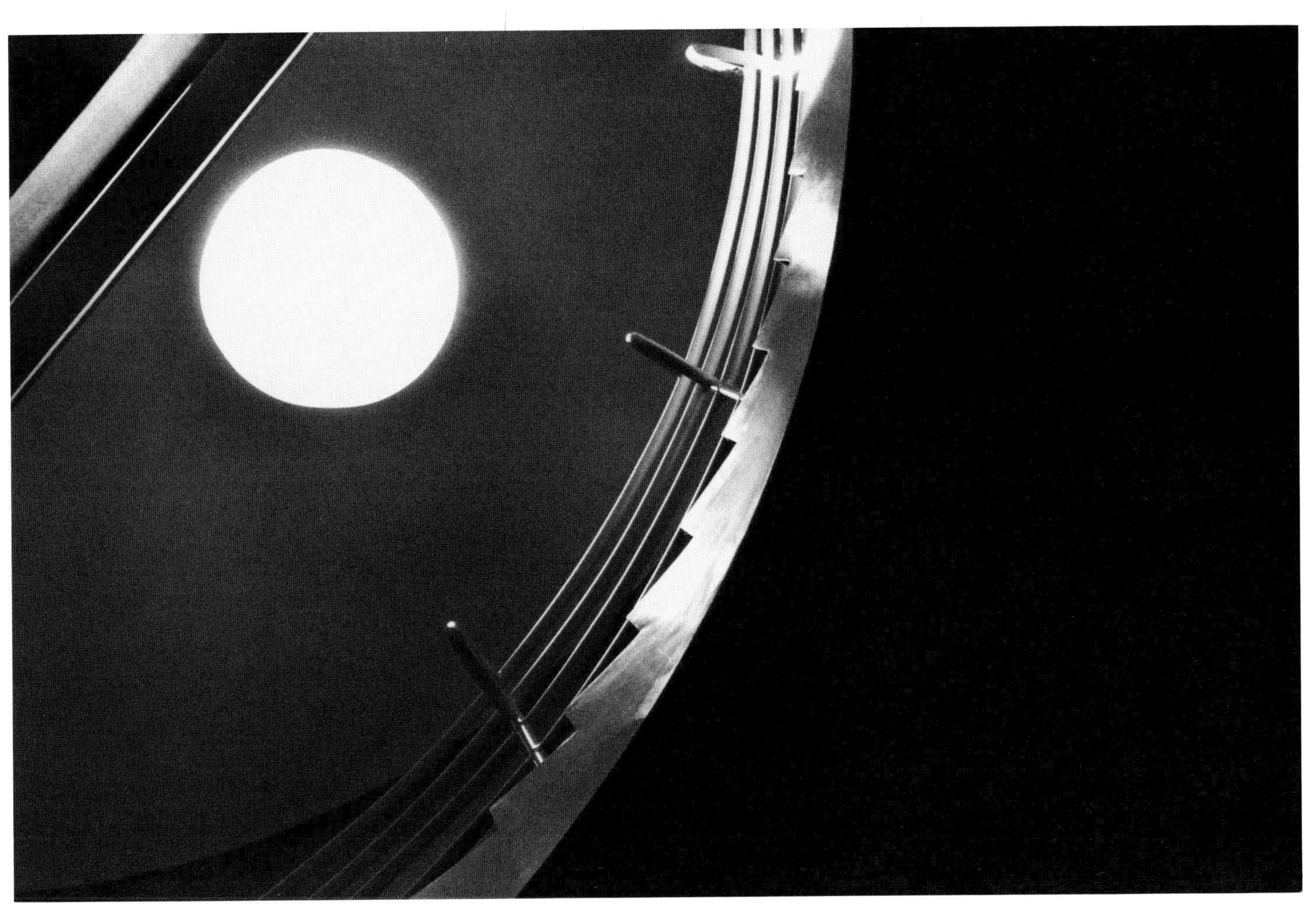

BIBLIOGRAPHY

Archetype 2, (Spring 1981).

Berman, Avis. "The Unflinching Eye of Berenice Abbott." *ARTnews,* January 1981, pp. 86–93.

Fabian, Rainer, and Adam, Hans-Christian. *Masters of Early Travel Photography.* New York: The Vendome Press, 1983.

Goldberg, Vicki, ed. *Photography in Print: Writings from 1816 to the Present.* New York: Simon and Schuster, 1981.

Hales, Peter Bacon. *The Photography of American Urbanization, 1839–1915.* Philadelphia: Temple University Press, 1984.

Lancaster, Clay, ed. *Joseph Byron, Photographs of New York Interiors at the Turn of the Century.* New York: Dover Publications, 1976.

Muschamp, Herbert. "The Portable Room." *Art & Antiques,* June 1984, pp. 76–88.

Pare, Richard. *Photography and Architecture 1839–1939.* Montreal: Canadian Centre for Architecture, with Callaway Editions, 1982.

Shulman, Julius. *The Photography of Architecture and Design.* New York: Whitney Library of Design, 1977.

Sobieszek, Robert A., ed. *The Architectural Photography of Hedrich-Blessing.* New York: Holt, Rinehart and Winston, 1984.

Szarkowski, John. *The Idea of Louis Sullivan.* Minneapolis: University of Minnesota Press, 1956.

Szarkowski, John. *Looking at Photographs: 100 Pictures from the Collection of the Museum of Modern Art.* New York: The Museum of Modern Art, 1973.

Traeger, Philip. *Photographs of Architecture.* Middletown, Connecticut: Wesleyan University Press, 1977.

Turner, Judith. *Judith Turner Photographs Five Architects.* New York: Rizzoli International Publications, 1980.

———. *White City, International Style Architecture in Israel.* Tel Aviv: Tel Aviv Museum, 1984.

ACKNOWLEDGMENTS

Of the many I am grateful to for this book, I must first thank the twelve photographers whose work has been shown here. They gave generously of their time in discussing their work with me and were unstinting in craftsmanship in preparing the photographs that have been used here. Their willingness to participate, their availability despite demanding schedules, and their continued contributions, suggestions, and overall attentiveness from start to finish have all made working on this book a pleasure.

I am also grateful to Erica Stoller of ESTO, whose patience, generosity, and efficiency were constant encouragement; and I am indebted as well to Hugh Hardy, Ed Mills, Jack Hedrich, Bill Tompkins, Lee Ryder, and Paul Goldberger for sharing their thoughts with me.

In addition, I must thank Dorothy Spencer who guided the book from conception through completion. Lastly, my thanks to Brian, for all the help along the way.

INDEX

Page numbers in *italic* indicate illustrations.